The Birds of Radnorshire

by Peter Jennings

illustrated by Alan Harris

Published 2014 by Ficedula Books, Park View, Staunton-on-Arrow,
Leominster, HR69HT.
radnorshirebirds@hotmail.com

ISBN 978-0-9513070-1-4

Printed in Aberystwyth by Cambrian Printers.
Design: jenksdesign@yahoo.co.uk • 07506 471162

Contents

Preface and Acknowledgements

Regional avifaunas, such as *The Birds of Radnorshire*, have been produced for many counties in England, Wales and Scotland, as well as the Isle of Man, over recent decades. It is no wonder that these often take many years to put together as records of birds are to be found in a wide variety of places; in museums, private collections and archives, the files, publications and databases of national and local bird and wildlife organisations, the old notebooks of individual birdwatchers and in many publications which, from time to time, include interesting and sometimes significant contributions to local ornithological knowledge. It often becomes obvious early on in the compilation process that there are very considerable gaps in the existing knowledge of a particular species, habitat type or site and that these require some effort at filling with a programme of fieldwork to provide a fuller picture.

Most counties have many keen birdwatchers between whom may be shared the task of producing an avifauna. Radnorshire is not one of those counties. With a population of under 26,000 spread over 470 square miles it has the lowest population density of any county in England and Wales. The few enthusiastic birdwatchers that live in the county could quite easily fit into a Mini (probably just on the back seat) but fortunately there are many more who live over the borders various and regularly visit Radnorshire for its wildness, large areas of open country and comparitively unspoilt and bird-rich habitats.

Little has changed in many ways over the last 150 years – e.g. the 1851 population was 24,716. Nineteenth-century bird records for Radnorshire were largely those which occasionally appeared in *The Field, Zoologist* or the *Transactions* of the Woolhope Naturalists' Field Club whose intrepid members regularly set off from Hereford on long days afield, perhaps once a year into Radnorshire. Several of the larger estates kept detailed shooting records, especially in the 19th and 20th centuries, and their gamekeepers would occasionally shoot any strange bird they came across whilst on their rounds and this was sometimes mounted for a show-case or shown to someone learned.

Some more serious ornithologists, often egg-collectors, visited Radnorshire in Edwardian times and between the World Wars. John Walpole-Bond produced '*Bird Life in Wild Wales*' in 1904, having lived in Builth Wells for some years before, and Professor J.H. Salter (Prof. of Botany at the University College of Wales, Aberystwyth) sometimes ventured east into Radnorshire. E.P.Chance and Captain H.A.Gilbert were also active in the county prior to WWII and many significant records and notes contributed by generations of birdwatchers have appeared in *British Birds* magazine over the last hundred years.

Geoffrey Ingram and H.Morrey Salmon were both members of the Cardiff Naturalists' Society and they produced seven avifaunas for Welsh counties beginning in 1936 and including '*A Hand List of the Birds of Radnorshire*' printed in 1955, a 40-page booklet covering a total of 176 species. Most bird recording in Radnorshire continued to be carried out by enthusiasts from over the borders and as a result sightings were largely published in the reports of the Herefordshire Ornithological Club from the early 1950s until the 1980s when Radnorshire began to find its own voice with, for the first time, its very own county bird recorder closely followed by the formation of the Radnorshire Wildlife Trust.

The idea for a more comprehensive avifauna for Radnorshire was hatched in the early 1990s and development progressed in fits and starts until all work was completed and everything safely gathered in for this publication some twenty years later.

Thanks are due to all those birdwatchers who have sent in their reports to the county bird recorder over the years and so contributed to the county record as well as the ornithological knowledge and conservation of Radnorshire's birds and their habitats.

I am also grateful to everyone who has responded to my requests for help and information over the years: Julian and M-T. Gibson-Watt (owners of the Doldowlodd Estate), Walter de Winton (owner of the Maesllwch Estate), Peter Howlett (The National Museum of Wales, Cardiff), Hein Van Grouw (Natural History Museum at Tring), Will Adams (The Radnorshire Museum, Llandrindod Wells), the B.T.O. Ringing Office, Anna Georgiou and Janet Imlach (Biodiversity Information Service for Powys and the Brecon Beacons National Park), Steve Coney (Herefordshire Bird Recorder) and Andrew King (Breconshire Bird Recorder). Dai Jones of Cambrian Printers and Malcolm Jenkins of JenksDesign for their help and encouragement, and of course Alan Harris for his superb illustrations.

An Introduction to Radnorshire

The county of Radnorshire was formed in 1536 by Henry VIII's Act of Union via the Laws in Wales Acts of 1535-1542 and is one of the thirteen historic counties of Wales. It corresponded very closely to the area previously known as Rhwng Gwy a Hafren (Between Wye and Severn) which came under the control of the Marcher Lords at the end of the 11th century. Being on the border with England there were many bloody battles to and fro during the Mediaeval period.

The name 'Radnor' derives from the Anglo-Saxon 'rade', a road, and 'nore' meaning narrow. The whole meaning 'the land of mountain tracks'. Radnorshire is often referred to today by tourism promoters as 'The Heart of Wales' not only because it lies in the middle of the Principality but also because it is roughly heart-shaped. Its shape is also very similar to that of Africa. To the east it is bordered by Shropshire and Herefordshire, with Breconshire to the south, Montgomeryshire to the north and Ceredigion to the west.

The well-travelled writer Arthur Granville Bradley (1850-1943) said that Radnorshire was 'more uniformly beautiful than Devonshire' whilst the poet Percy Bysshe Shelley described it as 'most divine' with 'highly romantic' scenery; going on to, 'Nature is here marked with the most impressive characters of loveliness and grandeur'. Even Shakespeare went so far as to describe Fferllys (most of Radnorshire) in King Lear as, 'With shadowy forests and with champions rich'd/With plenteous rivers and wide-skirted meads'.

Population

Radnorshire is a very rural county with a population that has changed comparitively little over the last 200 years. In 1801 the census figure was 19,135 rising to 24,651 in 1831 but then dropping to 21,791 in 1891. The 1911 count was 22,589 but by 1971 there were just 18,271 residents. This rose to 24,805 by 2001 and 25,821 in the most recent, 2011, census.

The largest towns are Llandrindod Wells (population 5,309 in 2011), Knighton (3,007), Presteigne (2,710) and Rhayader (2,075). Radnorshire has by far the lowest population density of any county in England and Wales averaging just 55 Radnorians per square mile or 21 per square km.

Topography, Climate and Geology.

The total boundary of Radnorshire, with all its neighbours, is some 98 miles (160km) and its other vital statistics are 26 miles (42km) north to south and 29 miles (46km) east to west. The area of the county is about 471 square miles (1,219 sq.km, 301,165 acres or 121,929 hectares).

Radnorshire was often referred to as 'rugged Radnor' and more than 55% of the county is over 1,000 feet above sea-level with the highest points being in the centre of the county on the plateau of Radnor

Forest. Rhos Fawr (Great Rhos) reaches 2,165 feet (660 metres) whilst about a mile to the northeast, on the other side of Harley Dingle, is Black Mixen at 2,133 feet a.s.l.(650metres). In all there are over a hundred hilltops in the county between 1,500 and 2,000 feet. The only land below 500 feet in the county is in the Wye Valley from Newbridge downstream and in parts of the the extreme east. The lowest point in the county is 246 feet a.s.l. (75 metres) where the River Wye flows into Herefordshire in the far southeast at Cabalva.

The hilliest area is in the northwest, an area commonly known as the Elan Uplands or the Elenydd. Nearly all the 60 square miles or so (c.155 square kms) is between 400m and 500m (1,300 and 1,650 feet a.s.l.) with high points of 549 m (1,800 feet) in the furthest reaches of the Claerwen catchment. Here there is measurable rain on an average of 230 days each year, and on over 300 in some, producing annual totals of over 2,000 mm (80 inches). Rainfall levels rapidly decrease at stations in the county to the east with just 800-900 mm (30 to 35 inches) around Presteigne, Clyro and Michaelchurch. Snow lies on average for thirty days each year on the upland areas and *The Climatalogical Atlas of The British Isles* (HMSO 1952) described central Radnorshire overall as the coldest part of England and Wales!

The geology of Radnorshire can be divided simplistically into four parts. In the southeast there is an area of late Silurian (Pridoli formation, 423-419 million years ago) Old Red Sandstone north of the Wye Valley whilst the main central part of the county comprises rocks of the Silurian period, mainly flagstones and gritstones, of the Ludlow formation (427-423 m.y.a.). Immediately west of these is an area of Pre-Caradoc/Llandeilo (c.450 m.y.a.) Ordovician rocks, including some volcanic areas, and a band of Wenlock Group (433-427 m.y.a.) Silurian rocks comprising mostly of shales, but some limestone, and running roughly south to north. Further to the west, including the Elan Uplands, most of the rocks are slates, grits and shales of the Llandovery formation (443-433 m.y.a.) of the Silurian period. However, by far the oldest rocks visible in the county are in parts of the Old Radnor to Stanner area where the Pre-Cambrian igneous intrusions date from about 700 million years ago.

Bird Habitats

Woodlands

The woodlands of Radnorshire can roughly be categorised as the classic Sessile Oak woodlands, especially found in the west of the county, the mixed deciduous riparian woodlands of the river valleys and the coniferous plantations. The few remaining Sessile Oak dominated woodlands are only species-rich for birds where livestock are excluded. Here as well as the classic species such as Pied Flycatcher, Wood Warbler and Redstart there are also good populations of tits (although the 'brown' species are rare) especially Great Tits, most other typical woodland bird species and, in more open areas and along the woodland edge, Tree Pipits.

A quiet and fine early morning in late May or early June in an ungrazed Radnorshire Sessile Oak woodland with a good Bilberry or heather ground layer and a healthy, well-developed, understorey is probably the county's best birding experience.

However, some of the mixed deciduous, ungrazed, woodlands of the river valleys hold the greatest variety and density of breeding birds, not only in Radnorshire but also probably anywhere in the British Isles. Wet woodlands composed almost solely of Alder or willows are unfortunately much scarcer than previously with many having been over-grazed, felled and/or drained in recent decades.

The main threat to the county's native woodlands is the lack of natural regeneration due to grazing. There have been various government grants available to farmers and landowners to exclude livestock from broadleaved woodlands e.g. under the Radnorshire and Cambrian Mountains Environmentally Sensitive Areas, Tir Gofal, Glastir and the Better Woodands for Wales schemes. But as these agreements come to an end there have been many instances throughout the county, especialy in recent years, of all the good work being quickly undone with sheep and sometimes cattle and ponies being let in again and grazing out any restored habitat.

All these broadleaved woodlands are mostly semi-natural ancient woodlands which at one time covered almost all the county. The remains of birch trees have been found preserved in peat on the very highest ground and carbon-dated at c.8,500 years before present.

Clearances of woodland for grazing animals began several thousand years ago and further large areas of mainly oak woodland were cleared in early mediaeval times and up to the early 19th century for ship building. In more recent times, over the last 150 years or so, the county's natural woodlands have halved again leaving about 7,400 acres (3,000 hectares) today. Well over half of these latest losses have happened since 1947 due to clearances for new conifer plantations and government grants to clear land for grazing. By far the largest areas of coniferous woodlands today are in the north of the county at Radnor Forest, around Abbeycwmhir and north of Bwlch y Sarnau. These were mostly planted in the 15-

20 year periods either side of WWII but continued in places until the end of the 1980s, including on heather moorland.

Although generally species-poor for birds, the management and development of many of these larger conifer blocks has changed greatly since the 1990s, and especially since the turn of the millenium. These changes have been much more focussed on amenity use, broadleaved tree planting and more diversity in age structure. All these ongoing changes have been of benefit to the birdlife of these large, non-native, conifer-dominated areas and together they are by far the most significant developments affecting the county's woodland birds in recent decades. Areas a few years after clear-felling are often attractive to breeding Grasshopper Warbler and Whitethroat, provide good feeding areas for Nightjars and even occasional nesting places for Hen Harrier and Short-eared Owl as well as sometimes holding a wintering Great Grey Shrike. The mature areas of Sitka Spruce and larch often support large numbers of Crossbills and Siskins and provide safe nesting sites for birds of prey and habitat for Long-eared Owls. The total area of conifer-dominated plantations in Radnorshire today is some 4,450 hectares (c.11,000 acres).

Rivers

The major river of Radnorshire is the Wye which forms most of its boundary in the south and west. In total 44 miles of the county's 98 mile boundary is formed by the river with 34 miles shared with Breconshire and 10 with Herefordshire, plus a further ten miles wholly within the county north to the Montgomeryshire border. The River Ithon joins the Wye below Newbridge, its tributaries having begun their journey some 30 miles to the north on Red Lion Hill, Beacon Hill and in Montgomeryshire to the west of Kerry Hill. The Elan joins the Wye from the west below Rhayader and the Marteg ('the handsome river') comes in from the northeast north of the town. The Edw and the Bach Howey are the main tributaries feeding into the Wye in the south of the county below Builth Wells.

The River Teme forms the county boundary east and northwest of Knighton and this, together with the Arrow, Lugg, Gladestry Brook and Summergil Brook all flow east into the Severn.

The classic birds of these, mostly fast-flowing, rivers and streams are Dipper, Kingfisher, Grey Wagtail and Common Sandpiper. Tighter control on sheep dips has undoubtedly increased Dipper numbers in places in recent years but many rivers and streams also have to deal with a range of other pollutants and run-off problems especially in the more intensively farmed east and southeast of the county and below conifer plantations.

Newcomers to the rivers are Goosanders, since the mid 1970s, and Mandarins, since the mid 1980s, otherwise the rivers are generally poor for wildfowl. Sand Martins breed wherever there are suitable banks. Oxbow lakes in the lower Wye Valley support some wildfowl, especially in winter, as well as occasional passage and wintering waders, whilst the extensive shingle deposits sometimes have breeding Little Ringed Plover and Oystercatcher.

A great deal of good work has been carried out by the Wye and Usk Foundation in recent years by way of the fencing-off of many sections of the banks of the smaller rivers to exclude livestock and so benefit trout and Salmon populations. This has locally greatly benefitted many riparian birds by providing safe nesting places.

Lakes and Reservoirs

The reservoir system in the Elan and Claerwen Valleys was created in two phases; the first series was constructed between 1893 and 1904 and the Claerwen between 1946 and 1952. All are water supply reservoirs, mostly steep sided and so generally poor for birds. Dol y Mynach Reservoir is an unfinished reservoir, shallow and with more aquatic vegetation and so generally more attractive to wildfowl.

Goosanders and Mallard both breed and are commonly seen in small numbers, as is a recent arrival, the Canada Goose. Teal are increasingly scarce at all seasons and now and then groups of Common

Scoter drop in, usually during wet and foggy weather. During low water levels extensive areas of mud are exposed. However, this is mostly nutrient poor and consists mainly of clay or peat and so supports few invertebrates which might hold passage waders although the reservoirs have attracted the occasional interesting gull, tern, wader and diver over the years and Osprey are recorded on passage most years.

Llyn Heilyn may be an artificial lake but it is the only one in Radnorshire to regularly have much of interest bird-wise during the migration periods being positioned high up on routes from the east into the Wye catchment and from the west rising over the headwaters of the Edw. Unlike other lakes in the county it is not surrounded by trees. However, it is quite often disturbed and generally does not hold waders for long as there is rarely much mud exposed except after the driest of summers. Having said that it has had Wilson's and Red-necked Phalarope over the years. Wildfowl can be interesting but very sadly shooting has been allowed there in the last year or two.

Llanbwchllyn is mostly surrounded by willows and reeds and supports some wildfowl although breeding success is very low due to predation by large Pike which have been present since at least the mid 16th century. Great Crested Grebes breed in most years, there is usually a flock of Tufted Duck and it has attracted a few unusual species in the past including Whiskered Tern, Bittern, Smew and Great Northern Diver. A few Reed Warblers breed and Water Rails are regular, especially in winter.

Llandrindod Lake by way of its position near the centre of the town is probably the only site in Radnorshire which could be described as well-watched for birds. It has had its ups and downs over the years being quite attractive in its late Victorian and Edwardian days when it was relatively clean and clear with water lilies and Mute Swans and spa-goers gently boating. Until recently it had for many years been a rather sad, murky, water body with bare banks. The waters were permanently churned up by large carp and frequented by Brown Rats at night and increasing numbers of Canada Geese and Mute Swans by day - all sustained by large amounts of white bread thrown out daily for the wildfowl by the general public.

Recently there has been a large amount of public money spent on planting lakeside vegetation including small areas of *Phragmites* which have successfuly brought in breeding Reed and Sedge Warblers and Reed Buntings. More aquatic vegetation has been allowed to grow and now it is a more healthy place for people and birds and the variety of breeding wildfowl with increases in Coot, Moorhen and Tufted Duck and regular attempts by Great Crested Grebe, visits by Wigeon and other duck species. Also the number of Canada Geese has dropped considerably from highs of around the hundred mark which is also good for other birds and public health.

The lake and the surrounding excellent, ungrazed, broadleaved woodlands have recently (after more than twenty years of effort) been designated as the county's first Local Nature Reserve which hopefully should lead to the enhancement of its attractiveness to birds and other wildlife.

Other areas of open water which are good for birds in the county are at Pentrosfa Mire,Glan Llyn (northwest of Rhayader), Knill Pool and Pencerrig Lake as well as many of the farm and private ponds, big and small, which have been created in recent decades under various grant schemes.

There are several other lakes in the county which were once good for birds but which are now not so good having either been drained totally or improved for livestock/angling or surrounded with conifers – or all three. In these categories may be included Penyclawdd and St Michael's Pools and, to some extent, Llyn Gwyn which Benjamin Malkin described at the end of the 18th century as 'the only picturesque lake of Radnor' but which is now an all-year round fishery, although still retaining some birdlife.

Moorland

Lewis Davis writing in 1912 said in his book on Radnorshire 'Heather is everywhere plentiful in the uplands, and as a consequence grouse abound'. By 1955 Ingram and Salmon were saying 'There are extensive areas of heather-covered moors which carry a small stock of Red Grouse, but the greater part is rough grass-land'.

Further huge areas of heather moorland were turned into upland improved grassland in the 1960s and 1970s and losses even continued into the 1990s. Most of the Elan uplands were heather covered well into the 19th century but burning and increased grazing has resulted in about 5% remaining as well as huge areas of Purple Moor-grass *Molinia caerulea*. However, the rank heather moorland that is left is the best for birds in Radnorshire and supports 10-15 Red Grouse territories. This deep heather together with the extensive areas of dense *Molinia* also provides safe nesting sites for Hen Harrier, Short-eared Owl, Curlew and Snipe.

For a time from the 1960s to the early 1980s so extensive was the over-grazing and burning that the resulting tundra-like landscape attracted many breeding Golden Plover. The only breeding Golden Plovers (and Dunlin, the 'Plover's Page') left today are on the naturally dwarf wet moorland and mire areas, mainly on and around the Claerwen National Nature Reserve.

Many of the county's moorland areas have ponds called mawn pools, some of which dry up in summer. Large colonies of Black-headed Gulls bred at some of these in the past but there are few today. Similarly only a few of the quieter pools with lots of marginal vegetation still have nesting Teal.

Some of the remaining heather moorlands in the centre of the county are managed for Red Grouse shooting and whilst these provide good habitat for those species which like a lot of very short heather, such as Skylark and Meadow Pipit, they are not so good for those which prefer deep heather.

On the edge of some of the moorland areas are cliffs and crags, the haunts of Peregrine, Raven and here and there a few pairs of Kestrel and Ring Ousel.

Commons

Radnorshire has more commonland than any other county in Wales. In total there are 69 commons ranging in size from 1 acre (0.4 ha) to nearly 7,000 acres (2,800 ha). Some are owned by the larger estates and others by the Crown Estate and various individuals. They are very variable in their grazing levels and management and so their habitats and birdlife. Generally their attractiveness for birds has greatly declined in recent decades due to burning and overgrazing; overall they have some 35% bracken cover and 20% gorse and heather but some are now just improved grassland and heavily grazed.

The Begwyns is owned by the National Trust and still has a good variety of breeding birds as well as wintering Golden Plover, which have been seen there for at least 150 years. It has an interesting mix of Bracken, gorse, semi-natural grassland, Hawthorn and birch scrub. However, it has lost a great deal of its gorse in recent years due to cold winters and mowing and so there are many fewer Linnets, Stonechats and Yellowhammers. As elsewhere, it has many fewer breeding Lapwing and Curlew than in the past.

Maelinydd is now a shadow of it what it was up until the 1980s. It formerly had many breeding waders including Lapwing, Curlew, Snipe and Redshank but few remain today and Redshank have not been seen for many years. Despite the area being a Site of Special Scientific Interest, illegal burning takes place most years and the extent of gorse and other habitats for birds is fast disappearing. Similarly Penybont Common is now in very poor condition for birds and many of the smaller commons, such as Hundred House and Perthi, have lost most of their bird interest due to encroachment, mowing and/or overgrazing.

However, some of the larger commons still have extensive areas of Bracken, gorse and dense rough-grassland with scattered birch, Hawthorn and Rowan. And these habitats support many Whinchat, Stonechat, Skylark, Meadow Pipit, Tree Pipit, Linnet and Yellowhammer with sometimes Snipe in the wetter areas and Wheatear around any rocky outcrops and dry-stone walls.

Ffridd

Between the upland areas and the lower pastures there is often a hillside habitat called ffridd which usually consists of extensive areas of Bracken and or heather with scattered trees, especially Rowan or Hawthorn, and sometimes areas of gorse. This is still a very common habitat in Radnorshire although much less so than in the past.

It is an important habitat for many species of breeding bird including Whinchat, Tree Pipit and Cuckoo and, where there are good numbers of trees, there may also be Redstart and Willow Warbler, and where gorse is present, Yellowhammer, Stonechat and Linnet.

In the early autumn the areas dominated by tall Bracken often hold numerous tits, warblers and Redstart feeding on the often abundant caterpillars of the Brown Silver-line moth (*Petrophora chlorosata*) and, together with many thrushes, finding safe shelter and roosting places whilst moulting. Later in the autumn and early winter the berries of the Rowan and Hawthorn attract thousands of Fieldfare and Redwing as well as many Mistle Thrushes, Blackbirds and sometimes a few Ring Ousels.

Farmland

Although many of the habitats already mentioned are farmed land i.e. grazed by livestock it is mainly in the lowlands where the most productive pastures are and where most arable land is found. Grass, for grazing, hay and silage making, is by far the major 'crop' and most is used for feeding sheep and cattle. In recent decades by way of agricultural incentives there has been a huge increase in the acreage of improved pastures and grassland cut for silage and most damp and rushy fields have long been drained. The most noticeable result has been the almost total disappearance of Lapwing from the Radnorshire countryside and the huge decline in Curlew numbers as both species no longer have safe places to nest.

Since 1937 numbers of sheep have risen from 350,000 to well over a million today and the average hill ewe is today twice the weight of its Welsh Mountain predecessor. Cattle numbers in the same period have dropped from 170,000 to c.50,000. More than 10,000 hectares (c.25,000 acres) of cereals were grown in the county in 1870 but less than half this in 1937 (mainly oats) and just a quarter (mainly barley) by 1988. Since 2006 there has been a very noticeable increase in the acreage of wheat and barley, and in some places oats; also fields of oil-seed rape are now often part of the rotation on farms in the south and east.

This increase in cereal acreages has locally greatly increased numbers of Yellowhammer, Yellow Wagtail, Tree Sparrow, Stock Dove and House Sparrow in recent years and oil-seed rape has also benefitted these species as well as Linnet. Quail have also become more regular in cereals in recent years and several species have taken to nesting in rape crops.

Hedgerows are also a very valuable farm habitat for nesting birds and tall, thick, hedgerows safeguarded from grazing are hugely important to many bird populations in the county. Unfortunately the relatively new 'Hedgerow Regulations' are fundamentally flawed and, despite the need for planning permission, causing the loss of many fine hedgerows in Radnorshire.

Radnorshire – the vice-county.

In the mid-19th century the botanist Hewett Cottrell Watson came up with the boundaries of the 112 vice-counties which have been used ever since for formal wildlife recording in England, Scotland, Wales, the Isle of Man and the Channel Islands. Cornwall is vice-county 1 and Shetland is number 112; Radnorshire is vice-county 43. Ireland also has its vice-counties, numbered from 1-40, thus providing complete coverage for the whole of the geographical unit defined as the British Isles

The Watsonian vice-county system has provided stable county boundaries by remaining unaffected by any political and administrative changes which have been the whim of local and national government from time to time to suit electoral, planning, development and management purposes. The boundaries of all the vice-counties can be obtained from the National Biodiversity Network (www.nbn.org.uk) or, for just the unitary authority of Powys, from the local biodiversity information service (www.b-i-s.org).

Most vice-county boundaries are obvious and well-known and for the most part so are those of Radnorshire. However, one less obvious area is where the boundary leaves the line of the River Wye around Glasbury and so for clarity a map of this area showing the boundary between Radnorshire (VC43) and Breconshire (VC42) is included below.

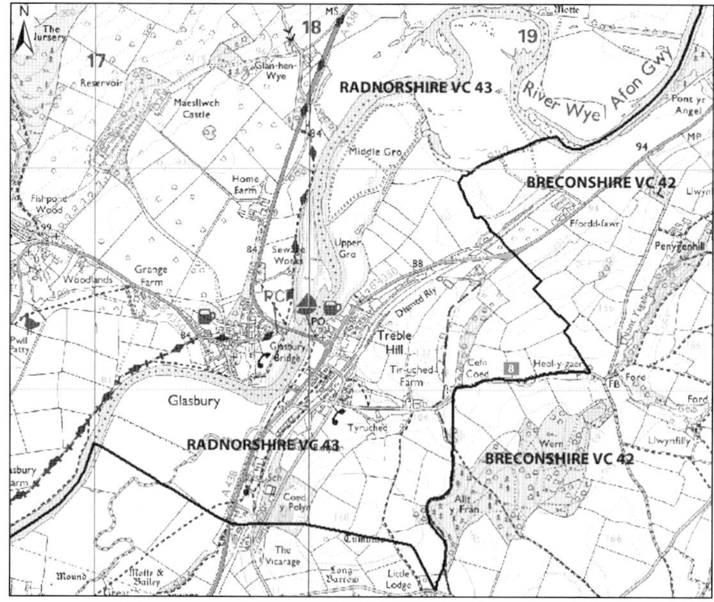

Radnorshire: Major Rivers and Woodlands

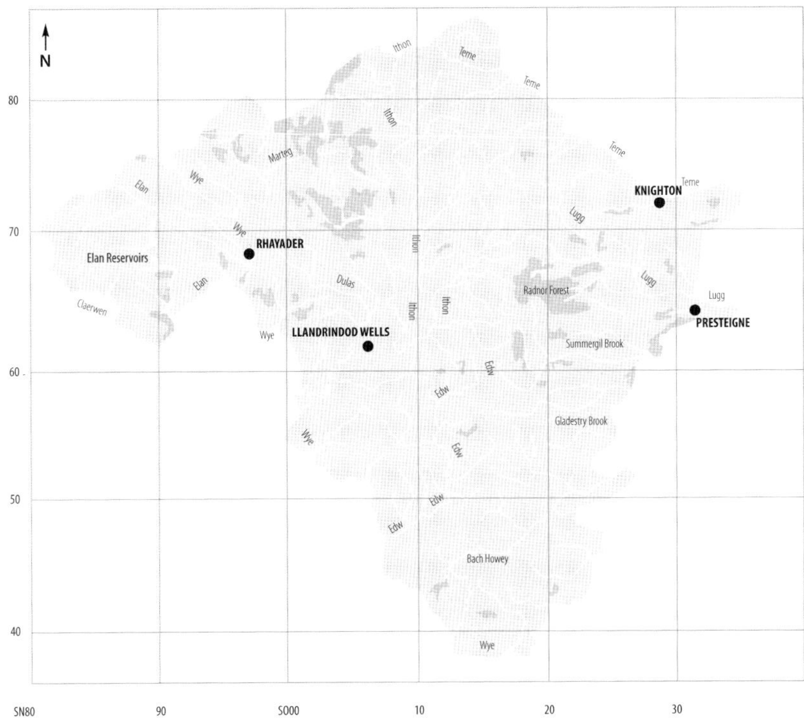

Radnorshire: Roads, Towns and Villages

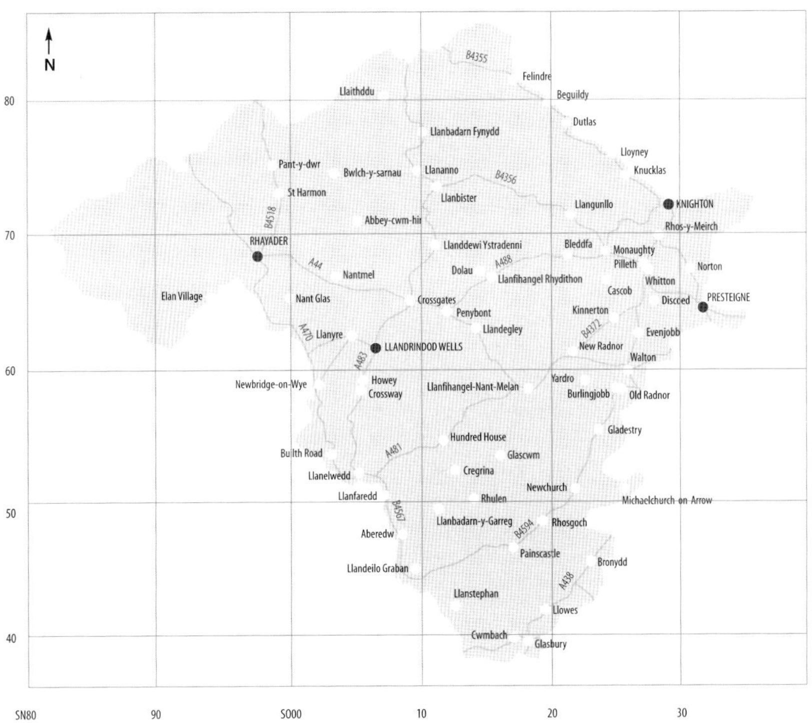

10km Grid for Radnorshire

N

SN88	SN98	SO08	SO18	SO28	SO38
SN87	SN97	SO07	SO17	SO27	SO37
SN86	SN96	SO06	SO16	SO26	SO36
SN85	SN95	SO05	SO15	SO25	SO35
SN84	SN94	SO04	SO14	SO24	SO34
SN83	SN93	SO03	SO13	SO23	SO33

These maps have been reproduced using data kindly provided by the Ordnance Survey and the Countryside Council for Wales:

The Systematic List

The Systematic List gives a synopsis of records for all 254 species of wild bird reliably recorded in the vice-county of Radnorshire (VC43) up to 31st December 2013.

Wild birds are those species included in Categories A-C as defined by the British Ornithologist's Union and included in their *British List* (8th Edition, June 2013). www.bou.org.uk/british-list

B.O.U. Status Categories

A Species recorded in an apparently natural state at least once since 1st January 1950.

B Species recorded in an apparently natural state at least once between 1st January 1800 and 31st December 1949, but have not been recorded subsequently.

C Species that, although introduced, now derive from the resulting self-sustaining populations.

C1 Naturalized introduced species – species that have occurred only as a result of introduction, e.g. Egyptian Goose *Alopechen aegyptiacus*.

C2 Naturalized established species – species with established populations resulting from introduction by Man, but which also occur in an apparently natural state, e.g. Greylag Goose *Anser anser*.

C3 Naturalized re-established species – species with populations successfully re-established by Man in areas of former occurrence, e.g. Red Kite *Milvus milvus*.

C4 Naturalized feral species – domesticated species with populations establshed in the wild, e.g. Rock Dove/Feral Pigeon *Columba livia*.

C5 Vagrant naturalized species – species from established naturalized populations abroad, e.g. possibly some Ruddy Shelducks *Tadorna ferruginea*. There are currently no species in Category C5.

C6 Former naturalized species – species formerly placed in C1 whose naturalized populations are either no longer self-sustaining or are considered extinct, e.g. Lady Amherst's Pheasant *Chrysolophus amherstia*.

There are three other Categories of species which do not form part of the *British List.*

D Species that would otherwise appear in Category A except that there is reasonable doubt that they have ever occurred in a natural state. Species placed in Category D only form no part of the *British List.*

E Species recorded as introductions, human-assisted transportees or escapees from captivity, and whose breeding populations (if any) are thought not to be self-sustaining. Species in Category E that have bred in the wild in Britain are designated as E*. Category E species form no part of the *British List* (unless already included within Categories A,B or C).

F Records of bird species recorded before 1800.

The Species Accounts

Each of the species accounts begins with the name of the bird in English, as in common use, followed by its scientific name as per the *British List,* to subspecies level if appropriate. The B.O.U. Category is given together with a summary of the status of the species in Radnorshire and one of its distribution world-wide.

Mute Swan *Cygnus olor*

AC2

Resident breeding bird and winter visitor.

Breeds discontinuously across central Europe and Asia, north to southern Sweden and Finland, east to northern China and south to Turkey. Mostly resident in western Europe; other populations winter south and west to within the breeding range and to northern Iran. Introduced to South Africa, North America, Australia and New Zealand.

Numbers have increased greatly in Radnorshire over the last 50 years. In the 1950s and 1960s the only regular breeding site was at Hindwell Pool with nesting occasionally recorded also along the lower River Wye. The flock there numbered 12-13 birds in1964/65.

In the early 1980s a few pairs bred on the Wye from Boughrood down river to Rhydspence and the occasional attempt was made further up river as far as Builth Wells and Newbridge. Although 80-100 birds were seen between Glasbury and Rhydspence on 4th November 1975, winter counts in that area were usually around 30 in the late 1970s rising to highs of 64 in 1983 and 78 in 1989.

In 1987 five pairs bred on the lower Wye and its associated oxbow lakes below Boughrood as well as pairs on the still waters at Evenjobb and Hindwell Pool. The national survey in 1990 found 11 breeding pairs and 75 non-breeding birds in Radnorshire. Counts of over 100 birds down river from Glasbury became regular from early 1993 and nine arrived at Llandrindod Lake in December 1994, the species having been a rare visitor there previously. A pair bred at Llandrindod Lake for the first time in 1995 but all five young died in quick succession from lead poisoning and one had a fishing hook found embedded in its gizzard on autopsy.

The lower Wye flock totalled 129 in January 1998 and 155 in December 1999. Since then the mid-winter peak counts have usually been between 100 and 150 birds with 158 counted on 19th January 2004, 161 on 10th March 2010 and 186 on 5th December 2005. The birds feed mainly in autumn sown crops of oilseed rape and cereals alongside the river at Glasbury, Llowes, Clyro and Bronydd. For many years the flock was the largest in Wales comprising some 10%-15% of the total population in the Principality.

Breeding numbers have continued to increase in recent years with 15 pairs found in 2004, 18 in 2009 and 24 in 2012. Away from the River Wye pairs breed regularly at Pencerrig Lake (since 1992), at Llyn Heilyn (1,214 feet a.s.l., since 1998), Llandrindod Lake and the nearby new pond outside County Hall, Llanbwchllyn (since 1999), Evenjobb, Hindwell, Womaston, Knill and Llyn Heilyn.

At Llandrindod Lake numbers have also increased with counts of 27 on 25th December 1997, 37 on 9th January 2003 and 44 on 16th August 2011. Dredging of the lake seems to have removed the threat of lead poisoning from ingested fishing weights and young are raised most years with a brood of eight successfully reared in 1998.

Maximum, county-wide, mid-winter counts have been 231 in 2005/6, 173 in 2006/7, 193 in 2011/12 and 216 in 2012/13.

The usual brood size recorded in Radnorshire is three to five with seven at Llyn Heilyn in 2003 and 2005, Llandrindod in 2002 and 2012 and at Llyn Heilyn in 2005. Broods of eight were recorded at Glasbury in 1979, Llandrindod Lake in 1998, Howey in 1999, Hindwell in 2006 and 2011 and at Llyn Heilyn in 2009. A brood of nine was hatched at Llyn Heilyn in 2013 (eight fledged) and one of 10 at Hindwell in 1966.

Most young hatched at Llanbwchllyn are taken by large Pike whilst Mink and Otter are the major predators of young cygnets along the Wye and Fox often takes the eggs or small young at Llyn Heilyn.

Away from the regular wintering and breeding sites records are rare, e.g. there were just seven records on the Elan Valley reservoirs between 1987 and 2012 whilst at The Begwyns Pool there were 11 on 11th April 1999 and a pair for much of 2012 and 2013.

The lower Wye flock has included birds ringed as cygnets or full-grown from Herefordshire, Worcestershire, Cheshire, Gloucestershire, Gwynedd, Staffordshire, Welshpool (Powys) and Ynyslas (Ceredigion). A second-year female ringed at Caernarfon (Gwynedd), on 30th July 1994 was at Glasbury on 20th April 1996 (142 km SSE). Many birds colour-ringed at Llandrindod Lake, and others from Nantglas and Pencerrig Lake, have been seen subsequently at Llangorse Lake, near Brecon, including a cygnet from Llandrindod which bred at Llangorse from at least 2008-10. A cygnet ringed at Hemlington Lake, Cleveland, on 25th July 2002 was at Llandrindod Lake on 7th January 2004 (291 km SSW) and a cygnet ringed on the Wye at Builth on 17th September 2001 was found dead at Strathclyde, Scotland, on 9th February 2005 (406 km N).

In total there have been 65 Mute Swans ringed elsewhere and recovered in Powys. Birds have come from: Cheshire (12), Gwynedd (10), elsewhere in Wales (8), Shropshire (15), Cleveland, Dublin, Hereford & Worcester (7), Staffordshire (6), Warwickshire (2) and West Midlands (3). Also 96 birds ringed in Powys have been recovered elsewhere going to: Cheshire (9), Clwyd (17), Dyfed (9), Greater Manchester (4), Glamorgan, Gwent, Anglesey, Derbyshire, Gwynedd (16), Hereford & Worcester (9), Lancashire (2), Merseyside (2), Shropshire (19), Staffordshire (4) and Strathclyde.

Bewick's Swan *Cygnus columbianus bewickii* A

Rare winter visitor and passage migrant.

Breeds on tundra across northern Europe and Asia. Winters in southern and south-western Europe, China and Japan.

The first records were in early 1962 when 17 were at Pwll Patti on 15th February and 20 at Glasbury (Maesllwch) on 18th. At Cabalva 18 were present on 24th March and 25 were on the Claerwen Reservoir the same day. In 1963 there were five at Glasbury on 17th March and two adults at Hindwell Pool from 12th-19th December.

Birds were seen in the Glasbury/Clyro/Bronydd area for at least part of each winter thereafter until 1998/9. Peak counts were : 1963/4 -7, 64/5 –13, 65/6 –20, 66/7-11, 67/8-7, 68/9 -27, 69/70-26, 70/71-15, 71/72-2, 72/3-15, 73/74-14, 77/78-10, 78/79-15, 79/80-15, 80/81-14, 81/82-20, 83/84-5, 84/85-38, 85/86-26, 86/87-26, 87/88-10, 88/89-20, 89/90-22, 90/91-30, 91/92-44(12:1:92), 92/93-18, 93/94-9, 95/96-20, 96/97-21, 97/98-1, 98/99-2. There were then no records in the lower Wye Valley until four were seen at Bronydd from 29th December 2010 to 3rd January 2011 rising to 14 from 4th and this flock being seen on and off thereafter until 12th February.

Apart from the records at Hindwell Pool and Claerwen Reservoir above, the only records away from the lower Wye Valley have been 20 at Llanbwchllyn on 27th February 1965, one on Caban Coch Reservoir on 5th February 1967, 17 flying north over Fowler's Armchair on 13th November 1969, five on Caban Coch Reservoir on 4th January 1970 and c. 25 there in late February 1987, one at Glan Llyn on 24th November 1992, three in the Elan Valley on 27th February 1993, 20 on Caban Coch Reservoir on 4th March 1996, eight on Claerwen Reservoir on 23rd December 1997 and 12 on Caban Coch Reservoir on 24th March 2009.

There were no records in the county for the years 2000-2008. The earliest record was on 30th October 1993 and the latest were those on 24th March in 1962 and 2009.

Three birds wearing individually lettered plastic leg-rings have been recorded. YAU 'Ballet' was ringed as a first-winter male at Slimbridge, Gloucestershire, on 5th December 1980. Having been also present at Slimbridge between 18th November 1982 and 26th February 1983, he arrived with a mate at Slimbridge on 16th November 1983 when the female was ringed and named SSY 'Ballerina'. The pair left Slimbridge on 15th December 1983 and arrived at Pwll Patti about the 23rd staying until at least 4th February 1984. The pair were seen at Pwll Patti in December of 1984, 1985 and 1986 and in January 1987 as well as at Slimbridge in October 1984 and November 1986.

'Ballerina' was seen in Holland from 6th to 22nd November 1987 and she returned to Pwll Patti between 24th January and 21st February 1988, but without her mate.

A cygnet ringed 'BCB' at Welney, Cambridgeshire, on 28th October 1984 left there on 20th March 1985. It returned to Welney for much of the 85/86 winter and was in northern Denmark for 28th to 30th March 1986 then in Holland from 20th January to 11th March 1987. It was at Martin Mere, Lancashire, from 9th December 1987 to 20th January 1988 and then near Glasbury from 7th to 21st February 1988. After that there were further sightings at Welney, Martin Mere and Holland until February 1992.

A bird fitted with a blue neck-collar on Kashin Island at the mouth of the Pechora River, Russia, on 10th August 1992 was seen in Estonia from 30th September to 29th October 1993 then in Sweden on 13th November and at Walmore Common, Gloucestershire, on 28th December. It was in Radnorshire between Glasbury and Bronydd on 1st January 1994, by the Leominster by-pass in Herefordshire on 9th January, at Kings Caple, Herefordshire, on 28th February, Welney on 6th March 1994 and at Slimbridge on 21st November 1994.

Whooper Swan *Cygnus cygnus*

A

Rare winter visitor and passage migrant.

Breeds in northern Europe, including Iceland, and in northern and central Asia east to Kamchatka. Winters south to the Mediterranean, Caspian Sea, China, Japan, Korea and India.

The first record was of five birds near Glasbury on 15th February 1962. In the same year a pair and their two young of the year were on Caban Coch and Dol y Mynach Reservoirs from 11th to 18th November.

Up to 12 were seen in the lower Wye Valley in January 1963 and two were there in early 1964. Three were at Pwll Patti on 3rd February 1968 and two in the Glasbury area from November 1977 to January 1978. Since 1980/81 birds have been recorded in the lower Wye floodplain between Pwll Patti and Cabalva in every winter except for three. From 1980/81 to 1988/89 the maximum counts were between seven and 16, apart from 30 present on 5th March 1989 and none at all in 1983/84. Since 1989/90 there have been records for at least a time every winter except 1994/95, 2003/04, 2007/08 and 2009/10. The trend is for fewer birds staying for shorter periods with the only double figure maximum counts being 18 in January 1982, 15 in November 1996 and 13 in January 2000. Just one to four birds are now usually seen most winters with five in November 2008, up to seven from 24th November 2010 to 5th February 2011, six from at least 15th January to 20th March 2012 and up to eight on several dates from November 2012 to the last on 17th March 2013.

Since 1963 records away from the lower Wye Valley have been: one on Dol y Mynach Reservoir on 15th January 1967; two flying over Old Radnor on 27th October 1970; two to five each winter from 1972/73 to 1977/78 on Dol y Mynach Reservoir were also seen occasionally nearby on the Claerwen and Caban Coch Reservoirs and at Glan Llyn; six at Llanbwchllyn on 21st November 1981; two flying south over Llandrindod Wells on 26th November 1981; three on Llyn Gwyn on 13th January 1984; eight on Glan Llyn on 8th April 1984; a pair at the top of Claerwen Reservoir from 31st October 1987 to 7th March 1988 were joined by another six for a time in December; a pair at the top of Claerwen Reservoir from 18th to 22nd January 1990 and three on Caban Coch Reservoir on 9th November; one on Glan Llyn on 13th December 1992; eight on Craig Goch Reservoir on 6th January 2002 and six there on 20th October; three flew over Caban Coch Reservoir on 6th February 2005 and two flew south down the Wye below Rhayader on 26th February; two on Craig Goch Reservoir on 29th October 2006; four arrived from the north to the Claerwen Reservoir on 17th October 2008; one flew down the Wye below Rhayader on 17th October 2010 and four were in the Elan Valley on 29th October.

The earliest record was of a family party of four flying north near Cwmbach Llechryd on 14th October 2012 and the latest at Glasbury on 11th April 1997.

A bird with a yellow plastic leg-ring lettered 'CPF' ringed as an adult male at Sandvatn, Iceland, on 16th August 1992 was seen at Bronydd on 6th February 1993. It was retrapped when moulting at Sandvatn on 4th August 1993 and subsequently seen at Bronydd and Glasbury from 26th December 1994 to 12th February 1995. It was found dead in Iceland on 10th June 1995.

Bean Goose *Anser fabalis* A

Very rare winter visitor.

Breeds from northern Fennoscandia east across Russia to the Bering Sea. Winters in south-west Europe, Kazakhstan, China, Korea and Japan.

The only record is of one shot at Dolyhir on 23rd December 1903.

Pink-footed Goose *Anser brachyrhynchus*

A

Very rare winter visitor.

Breeds Svalbard, Iceland and eastern Greenland. Winters in north-west Europe.

1909:	One was shot at Llanelwedd in January.
1977:	Twenty were in a field beside the Wye below Glasbury on 9th February.
1995:	Five were in a field beside the Wye near Cwmbach Llechryd on 29th December.
1998:	One at Pwll Patti from 12th to 31st December.
1999:	Two at Pwll Patti on 19th January.
2008-10:	One, probably of feral origin, was seen with Canada Geese on many dates in the Glasbury, Clyro and Llowes area between 25th March 2008 and 11th January 2010.

There have been several recoveries in Wales, as far south as Ceredigion, of birds ringed in Iceland.

White-fronted Goose *Anser albifrons*

A

Very rare winter visitor.

Breeds from Arctic Russia east across Siberia, Alaska, northern Canada and western Greenland. Winters in south-west Europe, Iran, northern India, China, Korea, Japan, south-west USA and Mexico.

An immature female was shot on the Wye at Glasbury about 1926. The skin was kept in Hereford Museum and later transferred to the Brecon Museum.
There have been eight definite records since:

1969:	Seven seen flying westwards at Llowes on 19th January 'were possibly of the Greenland race'.
1973:	Four were at Llandrindod Wells on 24th February.
1982:	Two beside the Wye below Glasbury on 1st February.
1986:	One was seen at Cabalva on 26th February and 2nd March.
1997:	Two were between Bronydd and Cabalva from 8th to 11th March.
1999:	Two at Pwll Patti on 19th January.
2000:	Two at Pwll Patti on 11th and 16th November.
2006:	Three of the Greenland race *flavirostris* on Craig Goch Reservoir on 29th April flew off westwards.

The three records for 1997 to 2000 were probably repeat visits by the same pair.

There are also five records reported as 'probably' of this species:

1904:	'Several' at Llanbwchllyn on 26th April.
1954:	A flock of about 70 flew over Gladestry on 11th April.
1954:	Seven flew over Burl Hill on 18th April.
1969:	Four at Llowes on 21st December.
1969:	Twenty-eight flew east over Stanner Rocks on 26th December.

Greylag Goose *Anser anser* AC2C4

Rare visitor which has bred.

Breeds from Iceland east across western and central Europe and central Asia to the Pacific coast. Southern and western populations are mostly resident, others migrate to the Mediterranean and southern Asia in winter.

The first record was of one by the Wye below Glasbury on 31st May 1977. Over the following 15 years the only records were:

1991:	One at Pencerrig Lake in April paired with a Canada Goose.
1993:	Two at Glan Llyn on 14th March.
1995:	Three at Glasbury on 22nd March.
1996:	Three at Glasbury on 28th April.
1997-98:	One to two seen on many dates between 28th September 1997 and 16th January 1998 between Glasbury and Cabalva.
1998:	Two at Glasbury on 9th and 10th May.
1999:	One at Glasbury and Pwll Patti from 19th January to 23rd May.
2002:	One to four at Glasbury between 28th March and 6th June..
2003:	One at Glasbury and Pwll Patti from 26th January to 26th March.
2005:	Two at Glasbury from 26th March to 16th April.
2006:	Three at Llowes and Glasbury from 3rd to 6th November.

After 2006 a pair frequented fields beside Penygarreg and Craig Goch Reservoirs from 6th April to 10th May 2008. In 2009 the same birds were seen in Rhayader, Nantmel and at Penygarreg Reservoir during April and May and in 2010 they bred at Llyn Gwyn raising one young and again in 2011, raising six. An adult with four Greylag x Canada Goose hybrid juveniles appeared at Glasbury in

October 2010 and one to four of these hybrids were seen at Llyn Gwyn, Llandrindod Lake and along the lower Wye on many dates during 2011-13.

A single bird was seen at Knighton on 21st April 2011, one was at Glasbury in February and March 2012 and a flock of eight was there on 20th March. A pair was again in the Elan Valley in April and May. An adult was at Glasbury from 12th to 16th March 2013 and at Llandrindod Lake on several dates between 18th March and 15th May. A pair bred on Dol y Mynach Reservoir in 2013 raising one young from five hatched.

Canada Goose *Branta canadensis* C2

Resident breeder.

Breeds North America and introduced into western Europe and New Zealand. Mostly resident away from North America.

Ingram and Salmon (1955) said that there was no definite record but that one had been reported from Pencerrig Lake but with no date. The first definite record was of a breeding pair in 1959. The first of eight eggs was laid on 4th April and three young fledged. So rare was the species that the name of the site was not published but is likely to have been Penybont Lake.

The next published records were in early 1963 when the very cold weather brought a flock of 63 to Maesllwch (Glasbury) on 10th January. Five or six were seen between Llowes and Glasbury on 27th January and 17th February and later in the year six were seen at Glasbury on 26th December. In 1965 there was a pair at Evenjobb in March and two birds at Glasbury on 6th August. The only records for 1967 were of six at Glasbury on 6th January and nine briefly at Hindwell Pool on 24th March whilst in 1968 there was just a single at Hindwell and three at Evenjobb in April. A pair raised five young at Penybont Lake in 1969 and one to four pairs bred there annually thereafter until 1989.

Throughout the 1970s records were mostly confined to Penybont and the Glasbury area with a pair breeding at Glasbury in 1975 and 35 seen there on 12th February. A flock of 17 seen at Llaithddu in August 1970 probably came from nearby Montgomeryshire where the species had been introduced in 1908 and where by 1970 there were some 300 birds in the Severn Valley. In the 1980s the increase in breeding records continued with pairs seen at Evenjobb and Llyn Heilyn from 1983, Llyn Gwyn and Pentrosfa Mire (two pairs – one shot) in 1985 and subsequent years, and at Howey and Park Farm (Maelinydd) in 1987.

The first nesting at Knill Pool took place in 1989 when two pairs attempted. Breeding took place at Cors y Llyn in 1991 and for the first time in the Elan Valley, at Penygarreg Reservoir, the same year - the first records having been there in 1988. Breeding has taken place at Cors y Llyn most years since and one to seven pairs have attempted on the Elan and Claerwen Reservoirs annually since 1999. One paired with a Greylag Goose at Pencerrig Lake in 1991 and pairs bred for the first time at Glan Llyn in 1993 and at Maelinydd in 1994. Although the first record at Llandrindod Lake was of three on 7th May 1984 the first breeding was not recorded until 1995. Pairs have bred at the new Rhogo Pool in most years since 1997 and at Llanbwchllyn since 1998. In 2000 a total of 28 pairs were found at 15 sites including a number on upland pools e.g. at Maelinydd (four pairs) and at Bwlchyfedwen. By 2011 the number had risen to 53 pairs at 37 sites with some on very small ponds.

Flocks have visited the lower Wye Valley in winter from Herefordshire for many years. Counts of over 200 have included 245 at Cabalva on 26th February 1986; 300 at Bronydd in January 1989; 400 between Bronydd and Cabalva on 19th January 1997; 280 at Pwll Patti on 13th November 1999; 250 at Pwll Patti on 11th November 2000; 300 below Glasbury in early January 2003, 200 there on 24th November 2007 and 265 on 15th December 2008.

Recent high counts at other sites have included 105 at Llandrindod Lake on 2nd February 2010, 40 on Craig Goch Reservoir on 4th July 2010, 38 at Llanbwchllyn on 14th October 2011, 53 at Llyn Gwyn on 26th July 2011 and 52 by the Wye at Llanelwedd on 17th January 2012.

Although mostly resident, most birds go annually to the Beauly Firth in Scotland to moult. There have been 40 recoveries in Powys of birds ringed elsewhere. They have come from Yorkshire (19), Cheshire (3), Cumbria (2), Derbyshire (2), Dyfed, Gloucestershire, Greater London, Highland (2), Shropshire (4), Staffordshire, Warwickshire (3) and the West Midlands. Also 301 birds ringed in Powys have been recovered elsewhere, going to: Hereford & Worcester (185), Shropshire (33), Gwent (28), Avon (5), Central Region, Cheshire (9), Derbyshire, Dyfed (2), Gloucestershire (4), Greater Manchester (2), Highland (4), Lancashire (6), Lincolnshire, Yorkshire (8), Northamptonshire, Nottinghamshire (3), Tayside, Warwickshire and one unknown in Britain. A gosling ringed at Penybont Lake in July 1982 was shot at Kington in October 1988 and another ringed at Penybont in July 1983 was shot at Lydbury, Shropshire, in October 1992.

Barnacle Goose *Branta leucopsis* AC2

Rare visitor

Breeds eastern Greenland, Svalbard, Novaya Zemlya and around the Kara Sea. Winters in north-west Europe.

Ingram and Salmon (1955) gives just a single record, 'One said to have been seen near Llandrindod Wells in 1919.'

There have been 16 records since:

1978:	One at Penybont Lake on 7th May.
1985:	One at Pentrosfa Mire and Llandrindod Lake from 12th to 21st March.
1985:	One at Pwll Patti on 1st September.
1986:	Seven at Cabalva on 26th February.
1987:	One at Pentrosfa Mire on 24th January joined three at Llandrindod Lake the same day.
1987:	One at Llandrindod Lake on 12th April.
1988-89:	Sixty at Bronydd from 29th December 1988 to 20th February 1989.
1992:	One at Glasbury on 15th November.
1994:	One at Llandrindod Lake on 22nd November.
1994:	Sixteen at Cabalva on 28th December.
1996:	One at Llowes on 2nd March.
1996:	One at Glasbury on 11th May.
1997:	One at Pwll Patti from 15th February to 16th April.
1999:	Seventeen at Pwll Patti from 11th to 22nd Otober.
2008-09:	One at Glasbury, Llowes and Pwll Patti on many dates between 6th October and 18th January 2009.
2012:	Two at Glasbury and Llowes on many dates in November and December.

The flock of 60 in the winter of 1988/89 were undoubtedly part of the flock which during the years 1984 to 1989 usually spent the early winter at Bittell Reservoir in Worcestershire and then January to April at Marloes Mere and Skomer in Pembrokeshire. These birds were almost certainly from the eastern Greenland population which usually overwinters on islands off the north and west of Scotland and in Ireland. Also almost certainly of the same origin were those at Cabalva in 1986 and 1994, and at Pwll Patti in 1999. Most of the others are likely to have originated from feral breeding of escaped birds elsewhere in Wales and England. A bird ringed in Greenland on 12th July 1963 was recovered at Pontrhydfendigaid in Ceredigion, just west of Radnorshire, on 13th November 1965.

Brent Goose *Branta bernicla* A

Rare winter visitor.

Breeds circumpolar on Arctic tundra. Winters on the Pacific and Atlantic coasts of North America, north-west Europe, northern China and Korea.

The only record in Ingram and Salmon(1955) is:'One was killed many years ago near The Skreen'.

Since then there have been seven records of the dark-bellied race *B.b.bernicla* which breeds in Arctic Siberia east to the Taimyr Peninsula.

1991:	Two at Glasbury from 14th to 24th February.
1991:	Five on the Royal Welsh Showground fields at Llanelwedd from 30th November to 12th December.
1991:	One at Glasbury from 7th to 25th December.
1997:	One at Glasbury on 19th March.
1998:	One at Glasbury on 5th and 6th April.
1999:	One at Pwll Patti on 13th November.
2005:	One at Glasbury on 8th April

Egyptian Goose *Alopochen aegyptiaca* C1

Very rare visitor.

Breeds across much of Africa where it is mostly resident. Introduced to England and the Netherlands.

The only record is of one seen in the Clyro, Llowes and Glasbury area on many dates between 8th May and 16th September 2008. A wanderer from the feral populations in England.

Shelduck *Tadorna tadorna*

A

Rare visitor

Breeds western Europe, northern Africa and central Asia. Resident and migratory as far as southern Asia and the Mediterranean.

Including the first record of one at Llanbwchllyn on 17th April 1949 there have been 49 records involving 72 birds.

A third of records were in the period 15th September to the end of January with all except one of the remainder from 1st February to 29th May and the most in April (13 records). There were two on Dol y Mynach Reservoir on 4th July 1991.

There have been 18 records in the lower Wye Valley from Pwll Patti and Glasbury to Bronydd, 10 on the Elan reservoirs, seven at Llyn Heilyn, five at Maelinydd, four at Llanbwchllyn, two at Pencerrig Lake and Llandrindod Lake and a single at Park Farm pool.

All records have been of one to two birds apart from three at Maelinydd on 3rd April 1972, three on Claerwen Reservoir on 17th May 1988, four on Caban Coch Reservoir on 14th May 1992, three at Maelinydd on 30th March 1996 and three at Llyn Heilyn on 20th February 2011.

Mandarin Duck *Aix galericulata*

C1

Rare visitor and breeder.

Mostly migratory in east Asia. Feral populations established in Britain, where mostly resident.

The first record was of four males and five females seen on the River Wye about 200 metres upstream of the bridge at Newbridge on 17th January 1985. The river was mostly frozen at the time with night-time temperatures down to -14 centigrade and maximum daytime temperatures also below freezing. It is likely that these birds arrived as a flock from feral populations in central England, where temperatures at the time were even lower in places.

River Wye at Glasbury: Sand Martin, Little Ringed Plover, Oystercatcher, Yellow Wagtail, Goosander, Common Sandpiper, Kingfisher, wildfowl, passage waders, terns and gulls. **Pwll Patti**, Radnorshire Wildlife Trust reserve, ancient oxbow of the Wye: Wildfowl, waders, Little Owl, Little Egret. Rarities have included Water Pipit and Red-crested Pochard.

River Wye; downstream from Erwood Bridge (above) and upstream of Pont Marteg: Dipper, Grey Wagtail, Common Sandpiper, Goosander and Mandarin.

River Wye; oxbows and backwaters between Glasbury and Llowes: Wildfowl, passage waders, Little Ringed Plover, Oystercatcher. Rarities have included Great White Egret, Avocet, Wood Sandpiper, Temminck's Stint and Garganey.

Elan Valley: Red Grouse, Hen Harrier, Merlin, Short-eared Owl, Teal, Golden Plover, Dunlin, Curlew, Goshawk, Crossbill, Tree Pipit, Wheatear, Stonechat, Whinchat, Goosander, Mandarin, winter Goldeneye and passage Ring Ousel. Rarities have included Roller and Blue Rock Thrush. **Maelinydd and Caergynan Pool**: Stonechat, Whinchat, Snipe and passage waders including the county's first and only Stone-curlew.

Henllyn and Llandeilo Hill: Red Grouse, Hen Harrier, Merlin, Golden Plover, Whinchat, Wheatear, Stonechat, Tree Pipit, Yellowhammer, passage waders and wildfowl.

Walton Plain (Basin): lowland mixed-farmland east of New Radnor; a nationally important area for archaeology inhabitated by man for 6,000 years: Yellow Wagtail, Tree Sparrow, Yellowhammer, Whitethroat, Hobby, Quail and Little Owl.

Llowes: Arable farmland in the lower Wye Valley: Yellow Wagtail, Tree Sparrow, Little Owl, Hobby, Yellowhammer, winter wildfowl and waders.
Gilfach R.W.T. Reserve: Area of ffridd with Wheatear, Whinchat, Stonechat, Yellowhammer, Tree Pipit and Meadow Pipit.

Llandrindod Lake Local Nature Reserve: Wildfowl, Reed and Sedge Warbler, Reed Bunting, Great Crested Grebe, Pied Flycatcher, Redstart, Wood Warbler, Tree Pipit, occasional passage gulls, terns and waders. Rarities have included Garganey, Slavonian Grebe and Great Northern Diver. **Llyn Heilyn**: Wildfowl, passage waders, terns and gulls. Rarities have included Wilson's and Red-necked Phalaropes.

Llanbwchllyn R.W.T. Reserve: Natural lake west of Painscastle: Wildfowl, Reed Warbler, Water Rail, woodland birds, occasional passage waders and terns. Rarities have included Bittern, Whiskered Tern, Smew, Red-crested Pochard, Long-tailed Duck, Garganey and Great Northern Diver.

Glan Llyn: Natural lake northwest of Rhayader. Wildfowl, Snipe, Reed Bunting, Sedge Warbler. **The Begwyns**: National Trust owned common with man-made pond: Wildfowl, passage waders, Golden Plover, Curlew, Whinchat, Wheatear, Stonechat, Hobby, Tree Pipit, Linnet and Yellowhammer. Rarities have included Red-backed and Great Grey Shrikes.

Radnor Forest: Coniferous forestry: Crossbill, Siskin, Goshawk, Long-eared Owl and Nightjar.

Radnor Forest: From Black Mixen (650m a.s.l.) looking towards Rhos Fawr, the highest point in Radnorshire at 660m, and (below) heather moorland near the Whimble looking towards Great Creigiau: Red Grouse, Hen Harrier and Merlin.

Harley Dingle: Dipper, Grey Wagtail, Hobby, Whinchat, Wheatear and Ring Ousel: and, below, forestry and young woodland at **Waun Marteg**: Grasshopper Warbler, Whitethroat, Willow Warbler, Whinchat, Redpoll, Nightjar and Long-eared Owl.

Cefncennarth R.W.T. Reserve: Sessile Oak-dominated upland woodland: Pied Flycatcher, Redstart and Wood Warbler; and, below, wet Alder-dominated woodland at **Burfa Bog R.W.T. Reserve:** Woodcock, Willow Tit, Redstart, Redpoll and Pied Flycatcher.

Coniferous woodland near Presteigne: Nightjar habitat above and, below, a Firecrest area.

Cors y Llyn National Nature Reserve: Water Rail, Snipe, Redpoll, Willow Tit, Reed Bunting, Hobby and Teal.

Courtship behaviour was seen from the first day and birds were seen frequently between Llanwrthwl and Brynwern Bridge in February and March. In April nest-site prospecting flights along the wooded river side were seen about a kilometre below Newbridge and a female with young were seen north of the village in June. Subsequently breeding was confirmed in each year from 1986 to 1992, except for 1988, with two pairs at least in 1987 and 1992. Birds were seen in the breeding season in 1993 and 94 and in 1996 two pairs bred and pairs were seen at two other sites. All this breeding activity was recorded along the Wye from Brynwern Bridge north to the Elan/Wye confluence although a male was seen regularly in May and June 1996 on the River Elan in the Dolafallen Bridge area.

One nest site was found in a hole 4.5 metres up in an oak tree about 15 metres from the river bank whilst one on the Brecknock side of the river was in a tree-hole two metres up and 200 metres from the bank. Birds were recorded in the breeding areas between 10th March and 10th August but became increasingly shy and elusive; the males usually leaving before early June and the females feeding amongst leaf litter in the quiet, riparian, broadleaved woodlands.

During this period the only records away from the Wye and Elan rivers were a drake at Llandrindod Lake from 14th October 1985 to 16th March 1987, a drake at Glasbury from 23rd February to 6th April 1986 and females at Dol y Mynach Reservoir on 25th July 1991 and 20th October 1992. No birds could be found in 1997 or 1998 and in 1999 just a single bird was seen on the Wye at Doldowlodd on 11th July. This was almost the same pattern of records as took place in neighbouring Montgomeryshire, where there was first breeding in 1985 but none after 1998 for five years.

The next records in Radnorshire were of a pair in the Newbridge area in April and May 2003, a female at Pwll Patti on 31st May 2006 and two drakes on the River Elan on 13th October 2007. Breeding took place around the Garreg Ddu and Caban Coch Reservoirs in 2008 when at least three drakes and two females were present from 10th February into May. One brood of at least two young were raised to fledging but one was taken by a Peregrine. Also in 2008, two birds were seen in the Glasbury area between 1st June and 1st August. In 2009 there were three pairs at Garreg Ddu Reservoir from 22nd March as well as a pair along the Elan, but no young were seen. Also in 2009 a drake from a wildfowl collection was released on Llandrindod Lake and was still present in 2013.

There was a noticeable increase in 2010 with pairs found in the breeding season at Garreg Ddu Reservoir (4), the Wye above Newbridge (3), between Newbridge and Brynwern Bridge (2), below Brynwern Bridge (2), near Llanstephan, between Erwood and Aberedw and at Boughrood. There were also at least two drakes on the River Arran, near Dolau, in April, two pairs on the Teme upstream and downstream of Knighton and at least three along the Ithon between Crossgates and Pont ar Ithon. The only young seen were four, fully fledged, with a female on the Elan on 2nd August. There were at least 15 pairs present in the springs of 2011 to 2013 and a female was with the released drake on Llandrindod Lake for two weeks in June 2011. Although a very difficult species to census, it is likely that the population of the county since 2010 has been at least 15-20 pairs.

Since 1989 a population has built up on and around ponds in the Forest of Dean, Gloucestershire. In 2013 this numbered some 250 birds and it is likely that the increase in records in Radnorshire in recent years originates from there, now the most important site for the species in Britain.

Wigeon *Anas penelope*

Winter visitor and passage migrant.

A

Breeds across northern Europe and Asia from Iceland, northern Britain and Scandinavia east across Russia to the Pacific coast. Winters in western and southern Europe, southern Asia, Japan and parts of North Africa.

Ingram and Salmon said that Wigeon were fairly numerous at times on Llanbwchllyn and occasional elsewhere in small numbers with a flock annually in winter at Llowes.

In the 1950s this flock was usually to be found in fields along the Wye between Boughrood and the bridge at Hay and numbered 80-100. In the 60s and 70s the average was lower with a maximum count of between 40 and 80, although 130 were present during very cold weather on 17th February 1963. Between the winters of 1980/81 and 1990/91 the maxima were in the range of 30-64 birds except for 200 at Glasbury on 26th January 1985 and 100-115 from mid-January to mid-March 1987. By now the flock was almost always to be found at Pwll Patti.

The highest counts were in the 1990s with 275 in January and February 1993 and 270 on 24th November 1999 – the last count of 200+ in the county. Between 2000/01 and 2009/10 the average high winter count was 144 (110-180) with a noticeable slow decline becoming apparent. The 2011/12 maximum count was 84 birds on 17th February 2012, although up to 40 birds were at other sites, and for 2012/13 it was 110 on 30th January 2013.

Elsewhere birds have been seen on five of the Elan reservoirs (the most being eight on Craig Goch Reservoir on 24th December 2000); at Rhulen mawn pool (five on 13th May 1951); St. Michael's Pool (13 on 15th April 1956); Beili Bedw Mawn Pools (five on 17th December 1954); Newbridge lower bog (two on 6th December 1985); Maelinydd (seven on 3rd October 1967); Llandrindod Lake (highest count: 16 from September to December 1997); The Begwyns pool (11 on 17th October 2005); Ireland Moor mawn pool (two on 31st October 1993); Hindwell Pool (five on 25th September 1969); Glan Llyn (drake on 14th October 2006); River Wye at Goytre Pool (drake on 9th March 1997) and at Hendregenny Pool (three on 8th November 2012).

At Llanbwchllyn there were just ten records between 1970 and 2001 but since then small numbers have been present, at least for a time, in most winters often feeding on aquatic vegetation pulled up by diving Coots. The highest count at Llanbwchllyn was 48 on 29th December 2003 when there was no water at Pwll Patti. The first record at Llyn Heilyn was of 13 on 22nd February 1952 and since then there have been a further 20 or so records. All have been of one to nine birds apart from up to 13 during January and February 2012 (and up to 35 for a few days in mid-January) and nine to 13 from October 2012 to March 2013. The only other regular site is Llandrindod Lake where up to eight have been seen for a time in recent winters feeding on an abundance of the aquatic macrophyte *Elodea*. A similar rich growth occurred between 1996 and 1998 when up to 16 were present before the lake was sprayed with a herbicide.

The first birds usually arrive during the last week of September, with sometimes a few from mid-month. The only earlier records have been two at Llanbwchllyn on 2nd September 1990 and one at Llandrindod Lake on 26th August 2013. Numbers usually peak during January and February and most depart in the second half of March. April records are unusual although there were 42 still at Pwll Patti on 8th April 2013, after the coldest March for fifty years, with the last lingering pair on 16th. Four were at Glasbury on 18th April 1953, six at Llyn Heilyn on 18th April 2005, a pair on Llandrindod Lake on 23rd April 1985 and a pair at Pwll Patti on 21st April 2001. Also there was the April record from St Michael's Pool and the May record from Rhulen, both mentioned above. A pair were present on the Elan reservoirs in June 2008 and a single bird, possibly injured, was below Glasbury during July and early August of the same year.

The breeding areas of the Wigeon which winter in Radnorshire are not known but birds ringed in Finland, Russia and Iceland have been recovered elsewhere in Wales. A first-year female ringed at Nosterfield, North Yorkshire, on 2nd October 2003 was shot at Aberedw on 7th December (262 km SSW).

Gadwall *Anas strepera* AC2

Mainly a rare autumn and winter visitor but which has bred.

Breeds locally across much of North America, western and central Europe and Asia east to China and Japan. More northerly populations are migratory wintering in the Mediterranean, southern Asia, parts of North Africa and the southern states of USA and Mexico.

The first record was of six seen on a small pool on Llandeilo Hill in August 1880 by Mr. H.N. Ridley of The British Museum. This was one of the first records for Wales and probably originated from the birds introduced at Dersingham, Norfolk, about 1850. Ingram and Salmon mention a pair in the Maesllwch

Castle collection said to have been taken at Llanbwchllyn, but with no date. These have recently been re-identified as a pair of Garganey.

There have been 65-72 records since. In 1964 a drake and two ducks were seen at Llyn Heilyn on 15th November and a drake again there from 22nd to 29th November. In 1966 a young bird of the year ringed in the Gualdaquivir Delta in Spain on 10th June was shot in Radnorshire near Builth Wells on 8th October. (*British Birds* Vol.62 No.2).

In 1971 and/or 1972 breeding was suspected at Llanbwchllyn and in 1973 a nest with three eggs was found at Rhosgoch on 19th May. The only other record in the 1970s was of one at Llyn Heilyn on 21st August 1979. A pair were at Hindwell Pool on 14th November 1982 and there were a further 10 records between 1985 and 1989, 18 in the 1990s, about 23 between 2000 and 2010 and another 10 or so in 2011/12.

Most records have come from Llyn Heilyn, Llanbwchllyn and the Pwll Patti/Glasbury area with a number of long-stayers and overwintering birds. A pair were at Pwll Patti for most of the period January to April 1988; two pairs were regular at Llyn Heilyn from November 1989 to January 1990 and one to two birds were at Llanbwchllyn for most of 1991 and 1992. Away from the main sites there have been several records at Llandrindod Lake since the first on 30th October 2002 (two pairs) with one to three birds present for a time in each year of 2010-12 due to the good growth of weed following the removal of large carp. As well as all the above there have been records at Dol y Mynach Reservoir on 30th November 1986; two records at Glan Llyn near Rhayader (10 on 19th February 1987 and a drake from 4th to 14th November 2001); on the Wye at Llanwrthwl (a pair on 4th February 1996); on the Wye at Bronydd (three in January and February 1997); one on a pool at Gigrin Farm near Rhayader from 4th to 15th January 2000; four on the Wye at Cabalva (10th December 2007) and a drake at Rhosgoch (22nd January 2012).

All records have been of one to four birds apart from the 10 at Glan Llyn, the first ever record given above, five at Pwll Patti in January 1993 and 10 at Llanbwchllyn on 16th November 2008. As well as the recovery in Radnorshire of the bird ringed in Spain, there have been recoveries of birds ringed in winter in Essex and Gloucestershire (2) found in Powys in subsequent winters.

Teal *Anas crecca*

A

Winter visitor, passage migrant and rare breeding bird.

Breeds across Europe and Asia from Iceland to Kamchatka and north-east Siberia. Resident in parts of western Europe but mostly migratory elsewhere wintering in southern Asia, south and west Europe, countries bordering the Mediterranean and parts of North Africa.

The first mention of the species as a breeding bird in Radnorshire was of a young bird found at Rhosgoch Bog on 30th May 1911 during a field meeting of the Woolhope Naturalists Field Club.

As a nesting bird the species has undoubtedly declined since the mid-1970s and this decline has probably been ongoing over the previous century. The loss of quiet ponds with vegetated margins, in both the uplands and the lowlands, seems to be the main reason.

Ducks with ducklings (the drakes desert the incubating females) are most frequently recorded on the Elan and Claerwen reservoirs and on the upland pools and lakes within the catchment. In recent years there have been up to seven such records annually and it is thought, judging by the pre-breeding season gatherings, that in the 1990s there were up to 10 pairs attempting and since 2000 probably four to eight. In the 1970s and 1980s records indicate some 10-15 pairs in the area. Positive breeding records were also much more frequent in the 1960s and 70s elsewhere in the vice-county than they are today. Records came from many upland pools as well as Rhosgoch Bog, Maelinydd, Llanbwchllyn and Llanwefr Pool but there have been no positive breeding records from these last four sites since 1990.

A few pairs still breed around some of the central upland mawn pools and lakes but although breeding took place at Pencerrig Lake, Penybont Lake, Pentrosfa Mire and Llyn Heilyn in the 1990s they have not done so recently. Although a difficult and secretive duck to census in the breeding season it is likely that in total about 10-15 pairs have probably attempted to breed most years in Radnorshire since 2000.

As well as the decline in breeding numbers there has been a noticeable reduction in the numbers at post-breeding season gatherings, on autumn passage and overwintering since the 1960s, 70s and 80s. Flocks of 20-50 were once much more widespread e.g. 50 Evenjobb on 2nd January 1971, 47 at Hindwell Pool on 30th August 1971 and 50 at Craig Goch Reservoir on 30th August 1971. Since the end of the 1980s much smaller numbers have been recorded overall and from fewer sites. The species is now rarely recorded outside of the breeding season on the Elan reservoirs whereas 20-60 birds used to be regular from August to January. The only recent flocks there have been up to 32 in late September and early October 2002 and 15-20 in the autumn of 2003.

Although small numbers may be found on any quiet pond in the autumn and winter the main sites in recent years have been Pwll Patti/Glasbury, Rhosgoch, Llyn Heilyn and Llanbwchllyn. Numbers in the Pwll Patti and Glasbury area are dependant on the water levels but since the mid-1990s the average winter count has been between 60 and 110 birds apart from 135 at Pwll Patti on 5th December 2005, 140 there on 18th January 2008 and 167 on 18th December 2012 as well as 210+ at Glasbury on 15th December 2008. There were 190-200 birds present from November 1995 to February 1996 and in the 1980s the winter high counts were mostly between 100 and 180.

The winter flock at Rhosgoch Bog was usually between 100 and 170 birds until the late 1990s with up to 200 in the winter of 1990/91. Recently the high has been between 50 and 90. Numbers at Llanbwchllyn vary greatly from year to year and there are obviously flock movements to and from Rhosgoch and Pwll Patti depending on levels of disturbance. High counts at Llanbwchllyn are usually in the range of 20-40 but 80 were counted on 4th October 1986, 150 on 17th October 1989 and 60-105 were present for much of the 2011/12 winter. Autumn/winter records from Llyn Heilyn usually peak at 30-65 birds but there were 75-115 present for much of September 1991, 70 on 28th November 2003 and 125 on 24th November 2011.

The species is rarely recorded at Llandrindod Lake, or the adjoining marshy areas, e.g. one on 18th November 1998, six on 31st December 2009, six on 1st January 2011 and four on 19th November 2012. Flocks elsewhere have included 60-65 at Penybont Lake during November and December 1997, 40 at Maelinydd in August 1959 and September 1972 and 1973, 36 at Pencerrig Lake on 14th February 1976, 32 at Penyclawdd Pool on 19th October 1964 and 6th January 1984, 30 on The Begwyns pool on 4th February 2000, 30 on the Beili Bedw Mawn Pools on 31st August 2001, 60 at Pentrosfa Mire on 16th January 2002, 30 at Hendregenny Pool on 18th October 2010, 31 on St Michael's Pool on 11th January 1964 and 30-40 at Crowther's Pool from October to December 1962. Records have also come from Glan Llyn, Llyn Gwyn, Newbridge lower bog, Cors y Llyn and the River Wye, although records from even slow-moving parts of the county's rivers are rare.

Winter gatherings form from the second half of September onwards with most birds usually departing during March. In late springs a few birds remain into early April with 30 still at Pwll Patti on 16th April 2013 being exceptional.

There have been 20 recoveries of ringed birds in Powys coming from Essex (6), Dyfed (3), Cambridgeshire (2), Cheshire, Dorset, Dumfries & Galloway, Gloucestershire, Shropshire, Suffolk, the Netherlands, France and Germany. Also two birds ringed in Powys have been found in Kent and Devon. A 'full-grown' bird ringed at Orielton, Pembrokeshire, on 5th January 1937 was recovered at Penybont in September 1937. An adult male ringed at Peldon, Essex, on 6th September 1960 was shot near Llanddewi on 2nd December 1962. A first-year male ringed in Suffolk on 25th September 1968 was shot at Rhosgoch Bog on 20th January 1970. A duckling ringed in Powys was shot in Kent in its first winter and another ringed in the upper Elan Valley on 8th July 1987 was found dead near the Tamar Lakes on the Devon/Cornwall border on 7th November. Teal ringed elsewhere in Wales have been found in Spain, Italy, France, Denmark, Scandinavia, Germany and Russia (including east of the Urals) and a duckling ringed in Iceland was recovered in November just over the border in neighbouring Herefordshire.

Mallard *Anas platyrhynchos* AC2C4

Widespread resident breeding bird, passage migrant and winter visitor.

Breeds across most of Europe, Asia and North America away from the high Arctic. Mostly migratory but resident in the more temperate areas of Europe and North America. Introduced to Hawaii, New Zealand and Australia.

Although by far the commonest duck, numbers today are overall about half of what they were in the 1970s and 80s. Counts such as 300+ on Craig Goch Reservoir on 30th August 1971, 240+ at Glan Llyn on 4th November 1970, 145 at Maelinydd on 26th August 1974 and 250 at Llanbwchllyn on 22nd August 1975 and 23rd October 1978 are unknown today. Recent counts at these sites would be usually only 10% of these totals. Increased predation of eggs and small young seems to be the main cause of the decline.

The major autumn and winter sites today are the Pwll Patti/Glasbury area, Llandrindod Lake, Llyn Heilyn and Hindwell Pool. The usual mid-winter total at Pwll Patti and Glasbury is 100-200 with high counts of 300 on 10th September 1994, 370 on 13th December 2008 and 450 on 22nd September 1996. At Hindwell there were 150 on 6th October 1979, 105 on 26th October 1986, 110 on 9th October 2001 and 170 on 4th July 2011. However, numbers at both these sites are greatly increased by releases for shooting.

Counts at Llandrindod Lake peaked when there was abundant aquatic vegetation in the late 1990s e.g. 200 on 21st September 1996 and 230 on 1st February 1998. Numbers declined after the vegetation was sprayed with counts ranging from 6-120 until 160 on 30th October 2003, 180 on 22nd July 2010 and 176 on 27th November 2011 as the weed growth was allowed to return. Counts at Llanbwchllyn in recent years have rarely exceeded 40 although there were 65 on 14th October 2011. At Llyn Heilyn there are often 50-80 present with a highest count of 110 on 28th November 2003. On the Elan reservoirs 20-30 have sometimes been seen since 2000 with 36 on Garreg Ddu Reservoir in November 2001 and 65 on the nearby Glan Llyn on 26th July 2009. Highest counts for other sites are 50 at the Beili Bedw Mawn Pools on 17th December 1954; 150 at Llanbister Bridge in January 1979; 80 at Llanwefr Pool on 24th June 1973; 60 at Pencerrig Lake on 30th August 1980; 50+ at Knill Pool on 27th December 1984 and 160 at Rhosgoch in October 1992. The River Wye Bird Survey of 1995/96 found 322 birds along the river bordering Radnorshire and Brecknock on 26th November 1995, 630 on 4th February 1996 and 209 on 31st March 1996.

Breeding takes place widely on all the major lakes and ponds, upland pools, farm ponds and most rivers although most young hatched usually quickly disappear.

There have been 47 ringing recoveries from elsewhere to Powys. These have come from Anglesey, Cambridgeshire (6), Cheshire, Dorset, Essex (3), Gloucestershre (19), Hereford & Worcester (7), Lincolnshire (2), Northamptonshire (2), Shropshire (2), County Wexford (Eire), Belgium and Denmark. Also 13 birds ringed in Powys have been recovered in Glamorgan, Gwynedd, Hereford & Worcester (6) and Shropshire (5). A female ringed at Slimbridge on 3rd October 1952 was shot at Gladestry on 24th January 1953 and a bird ringed at Meetkerke, Belgium, on 7th September 1958 was shot near Newchurch on about 15th January 1960.

Pintail *Anas acuta*

Rare autumn and winter visitor.

A

Breeds across most of North America, Europe and Asia wintering south to the Equator.

There have been about 27 records involving 47-50 birds. One was shot by Colonel Baskerville at Llanbwchllyn (undated - but before 1954) and one was shot by P.Lewis at Llandrindod Wells in 1919. All the records since are:

1962:	Pair at Glasbury on 18th February.
1964:	Drake at Llyn Heilyn from 29th October to 15th November.
1965:	Four at Glasbury on 3rd January.
1974:	Drake at Llanbwchllyn on 16th February.
1974:	Duck at Maelinydd from 4th to 7th April.
1977:	Pair at Llyn Heilyn on 20th February.
1979:	Singles at Glasbury in January and February.
1987:	Pair at Glasbury and Pwll Patti on 8th March.
1991:	Three drakes at Pwll Patti from 26th January to 4th February.
1991:	Four drakes and two ducks at Glasbury on 16th February.
1994:	Drake on a small pool above Llangunllo, on 30th January
1996:	Drake at Pwll Patti on 18th January.
1996:	Two drakes and a duck at Pwll Patti and Glasbury from 17th to 22nd February.
1997:	Pair at Llandrindod Lake on 11th March.
1997:	Drake on Dol y Mynach Reservoir fom 13th to 16th March.
1998:	Drake on Llandrindod Lake on 26th January.
2001:	Three at Llanbwchllyn on 11th November.

2003:	Drake at Llyn Heilyn from 1st January to 10th February.
2003:	One at Glasbury 26th October.
2006:	Pair on Llandrindod Lake on 5th December.
2007:	One on Llandrindod Lake 21st to 25th December.
2007:	One at Glasbury 16th to 31st December.
2008:	One at Llanbwchllyn on 24th September.
2011:	Duck at Llyn Heilyn on 3rd October and Llanbwchllyn on 14th.
2012:	Two pairs on Llandrindod Lake 4th January.
2012:	Drake at Bronydd on 15th January.
2013:	Drake at Llyn Heilyn from 5th to 28th December

Garganey *Anas querquedula* A

Rare spring and autumn visitor.

Breeds across Europe and Central Asia east to Kamchatka. Winters in West, Central and East Africa and southern Asia.

A pair in the Maesllwch collection were shot in the south of the county in the second half of the 19th century, probably at Llanbwchllyn.

There have been seventeen records since:

1962:	Drake at Rhosgoch Bog on 20th May.
1974:	Pair at Glasbury from 16th to 31st March.
1974:	Two pairs at Maelinydd from 4th to 7th April.
1987:	Drake at Llyn Heilyn on 19th May.
1991:	Drake at Dol y Mynach Reservoir on 16th May.
1992:	Drake at Glasbury on 4th April.
1995:	Juvenile at Llyn Heilyn from 28th to 30th August.
2008:	Duck at Llyn Heilyn on 17th August.
2008:	Drake at Llanbwchllyn 22nd to 23rd August.
2009:	Pair Rhosgoch 27th March to 11th April.
2009:	Drake Llandrindod Lake 31st May to 3rd June.

2009:	Pair Llanwefr Pool 13th to 14th April.
2009:	Drake Llyn Heilyn 30th May.
2009:	Drake Michaelchurch on Arrow 22nd April.
2010:	Drake Llyn Heilyn 4th May.
2011:	Drake Llanbwchllyn 2nd July.
2013:	Two juveniles at Llowes on 30th August.

Shoveler *Anas clypeata* A

Scarce visitor.

Breeds across North America, Europe and Asia. Winters western, southern and central North America, southern Europe and Asia and parts of North Africa.

There have been about 71 records involving approximately 152 birds. Llandrindod Lake has the most with c.20 records (maximum of six on 16th January and 1st August 2012); Llyn Heilyn, 14 (four from 6th to 15th March 1998); Pwll Patti/Glasbury, 14 (five on 25th February 2005); Elan/Claerwen reservoirs, five (two on three occasions); Maelinydd, five (six on 14th November 1983); Hindwell, four (three on 22nd December 1958). There have been three records from Llanbwchllyn and single records from Llanwefr Pool, Pencerrig Lake (seven on 5th and 6th April 1969), the Wye at Bronydd, Glan Llyn, Llyn Gwyn and Penybont Lake.

Records have come in every month: Jan(9);Feb(4);Mar(11);Apr(7);May(2);June(5); July(2);Aug(8);Sept(2);Oct(7);Nov(6);Dec(8).

Red-crested Pochard *Netta rufina* AC2

Very rare visitor.

Breeds from Spain and southern France locally north to Denmark. Also east from the Black Sea to northwestern China. Winters mostly around the European coast of the Mediterranean, the Black and Caspian Seas, northern India and Burma and the Nile Delta.

There have been three records:

1991:	Drake in eclipse plumage at Llyn Heilyn on 10th July.
1996:	Duck at Pwll Patti on 11th February.
1998:	Duck or juvenile at Llanbwchllyn from 23rd September to 7th October.

Pochard *Aythya ferina*

A

Uncommon but regular winter visitor and passage migrant. Very rare summer visitor.

Breeds across much of Europe and Asia. Winters in western and southern Europe, southern Asia to Japan and parts of North Africa.

Ingram and Salmon gave the species' status as, 'A regular but not numerous winter visitor to Llanbwchllyn, the Elan reservoirs and the River Wye'.

Birds are still regular at Llanbwchllyn with autumn/winter high counts usually between 10 and 20 but rarely more than one to four since 2010. Higher maxima have been: 72 on 22nd September 1971; 52 on 5th February 1998; 30 on 17th November 1995 and 22 on 8th November 1964 and 4th January 1999. Birds are most often present between November and February with extreme dates of 20th September 2001 and 5th April 1970. At Hindwell Pool counts of 15-30 were frequent in the late 1950s and throughout the 60s and 70s with the highest number recorded being 33 on 3rd January 1966.

Records were much less regular at Hindwell in the 1980s and 90s with the highest counts being 23 on 3rd January 1981, 38 on 24th January 1987 and 30 on 30th November 1994. There were only two records there between 2000 and 2013.

On the Elan reservoirs up to 15 birds were often counted in winter, usually on Dol y Mynach Reservoir, in the 1970s, 80s and 90s with a high of 18 on 1st March 1970 on Caban Coch Reservoir. There were nine records of one to two birds between 2000 and 2006, but none since 2007. First and last dates have been 21st September 1987 and 1st May 1960 although a duck was seen on Garreg Ddu Reservoir and at Llyn Heilyn at the end of June 2001. There have been about 20 records for Llandrindod Lake since the first in January 1987. These are usually of one to six birds but nine were present on 25th October 1994 and on 5th October 2005.

At Llyn Heilyn there have been just eight records, all of one to eight birds apart from 19 on 29th November 1970. In the Wye Valley from Boughrood to Cabalva there have been about 15 records, although the species is very rare at Pwll Patti. Highest numbers have been on the river during very cold weather e.g. 23 at Glasbury and Cabalva in February 1996 and 50 at Glasbury in February 1979. Mid-summer records are very rare, with a drake at Llanwefr Pool on 9th July 1955, the duck at Elan and Llyn Heilyn in June 2001, a drake at Llanbwchllyn on 29th June 2010 and one at Llandrindod Lake on 27th June 2011. Early autumn birds have been at Maelinydd on 29th August 1964 and The Begwyns pool on 13th September 1996. Other records have come from Glan Llyn (2) and a small pool on Beacon Hill. There have been no records of breeding. Birds ringed in many countries of Europe have been recovered in Britain as well as from Russia, including from well east of the Urals.

Ferruginous Duck *Aythya nyroca* A

Very rare visitor.

Breeds very locally in Europe but more widespread across Asia to western China and Mongolia. Winters in southern Europe, the Mediterranean, northern India, the Black and Caspian Sea lowlands and parts of North Africa.

There have been three or four records:
One, either a female or young bird of the year, was present on a pool at Boultibrooke, near Presteigne, from the latter part of 1859 until March 1860. (Mr Harford Brydges: *Zoologist* vol. 22 p.9047). This was the first record for Wales and the second record for Britain, after one in Scotland in 1857.

Three birds were seen on the River Wye at Builth by A.M. Gwynne-Vaughan and John Walpole-Bond on 19th April 1903.

One was seen on Hindwell Pool on 14th August 1973 and possibly the same bird was on one of the Elan reservoirs on 25th November the same year.

Tufted Duck *Aythya fuligula* A

Rare breeding bird and uncommon resident, passage migrant and winter visitor.

Breeds across Europe and northern Asia from Iceland to Kamchatka and Japan. Winters over much of western Europe, the Mediterranean, the Black and Caspian Sea lowlands east across northern India to China and Japan and a few places in North Africa.

James W. Lloyd in the Woolhope Naturalists' Field Club *Transactions* for 1869 said that two had been shot in Radnorshire 'about four years ago' and mounted by a Kington taxidermist.

The main site for this species has been Llanbwchllyn since at least the early 1900s when flocks of 30-50 were recorded. Up to 50 were also counted throughout the 1950s, 60s and 70s whilst there was a pronounced increase in the 1980s with a high of 80 in both 1982 and 1986 and 85 on 10th August 1985. In the 1990s the maxima fell back to 25-40 except for 50 on 19th August 1998. From 1999 to 2005 the highest counts were all between 25 and 33 birds and from 2007 to 2013 the range was 33-51 (30th August 2013). Some are present in all months of the year with the fewest from May to July when five to 20 are usual with the highest count being 30 on 26th July 2013.

Hindwell Pool has also long been a regular site with birds seen in all months. High counts have been 24 on 25th January 1959, 25 on 19th December 1980, 26 on 9th February 2004 and 38 on 25th February 2005. Since 2010 no more than 13 birds have been seen with just two to five being the norm. There are also birds usually present at Llyn Heilyn where up to 11 are often seen in any month. The highest count there was 18 on 21st October 1988. Other regular sites are Evenjobb (maximum of 15 on 24th November 1999), Stanage Park Lake (10 on 10th May 2000) and Llandrindod Lake (20 on 25th April 2012). Other lakes were frequented in the past but have been not so suitable in recent years, e.g. Penyclawdd Pool, up to 17 in the 1960s and 70s and Llyn Gwyn, maximum of 37 on 26th January 1957.

There have been 13 records from the Elan reservoirs since 1985, including possible breeding on Craig Goch Reservoir in 1985. All except two have been of one to two birds but there were three birds on Claerwen Reservoir on 21st June 2005 and seven on Craig Goch Reservoir on 14th March 2012. Many other lakes and ponds have attracted birds including The Begwyns pool (14 on 5th April 2006), Wern Fawr (Howey), Pentrosfa Mire, Beili Bedw Mawn Pools, Pilleth, Felindre, Gladestry, St Michael's Pool, Bwlchyllyn, Bwlchyfedwen, Womaston, Glan Llyn, Rhogo Pool, Pwll Patti, Cabalva, Pencerrig Lake, Park Farm pool, Penybont Lake and mawn pools on Glascwm Hill and Ireland Moor. Also up to 25 birds have been found along the Wye during very cold weather when still waters have been frozen.

The species was reported to have bred in Radnorshire before 1939. (*British Birds* vol. 32 p. 276). One to two pairs bred regularly at Llanbwchllyn up to1970 and occasionally until 1985 after which no young ducklings were seen at the site for many years (presumably due to the presence of large Pike) until four were raised in 2013. Also one to two pairs bred at Pencerrig Lake in the 1980s and 90s and breeding was regular at Penyclawdd Pool until the 1970s, after which the site became unsuitable. Young were raised at Llyn Heilyn in 1986 (9 young), 1992 (6), 1994 (10), 2012 (6) and 2013 (8 from two broods). Breeding has also taken place at Glasbury (1978 and 1986), Evenjobb (1987, 1989 and 2011), Stanage Park Lake (1991), Wern Fawr (1981), The Begwyns (2005), Pilleth (2005), Cabalva pond (2008), Knill (2011), Rhogo Pool (2008 and 2012) and Llandrindod Lake (1-3 broods each year 2008-13).

An adult male ringed at Amager, Denmark, on 17th May 1967 was shot at Womaston Pond on 31st October 1981 and a duckling ringed in Latvia in June 1984 was shot in Powys in December 1985. There have been many birds ringed in Iceland, Scandinavia, northern Europe and Russia west of the Urals which have been recovered in Britain and Ireland in winter.

Scaup *Aythya marila*

Rare autumn and winter visitor.

A

Breeds in sub-Arctic and Arctic North America, Europe and Asia. Winters mostly in temperate coastal waters, including the Caspian and Black Seas.

The first record was of one on the River Wye at Glasbury during the very cold weather of January 1963. There have been a further ten records since then:

1963:	Drake on Dol y Mynach Reservoir on 17th November.
1965:	Duck on the Wye at Glasbury from 3rd to 8th January.
1971:	Drake on Glan Llyn on 7th March.
1972:	Drake at Hindwell Pool from 11th to 13th March.
1976:	An 'immature' on Llyn Heilyn on 14th February.
1985:	'Immature' at Glasbury on 26th January.
1988:	Drake on Craig Goch Reservoir on 3rd October.
1992:	Drake on Caban Coch Reservoir on 24th March.
2001:	Duck on Claerwen Reservoir on 7th September.
2012:	Juvenile on Dol y Mynach Reservoir on 23rd October.

Probable ScaupXTufted Duck hybrids have been a duck with the drake at Hindwell Pool in 1972 and one at Llanbwchllyn on 18th April 1979.

Long-tailed Duck *Clangula hyemalis*

Very rare winter visitor.

A

Breeds circumpolar Arctic south to southern Finland, Labrador and southern Alaska. Winters on coastal waters south to Washington State, North Carolina, British Isles, Japan and Korea.

There have been two records: Ducks on Hindwell Pool from 30th November 1969 to 4th January 1970 and at Llanbwchllyn on 27th December 1983.

Common Scoter *Melanitta nigra*

Rare passage migrant.

A

Breeds from Iceland and northern Britain east across the tundra of Europe and western Siberia. Winters around the coasts of western Europe and North Africa.

The first record was of a first-summer male at Rhiw Pool on 16th August 1954 and in all there have been 38 records involving 183 birds. Thirty records have come from the Elan and Claerwen reservoirs: Caban Coch(11), Craig Goch(10), Claerwen(6), Garreg Ddu (2) and Penygarreg (1). Flocks of ten or more have been; 10 on Claerwen in August 1986, 19 Claerwen 4th November 1994, 10 Caban Coch 5th July 2003, 15 Craig Goch 11th July 2004, 14 Caban Coch 9th June 2005 and another 14 on Caban Coch on 11th July 2007.

Other records have come from Llandrindod Lake (2), Pwll Patti, Glasbury, Llanbwchllyn, Glan Llyn and one from the Afon Claerwen, downstream of the Claerwen Dam, a drake which was taking flies off the surface. Records have been in Jan(1), May(1), Jun(6), July(12), Aug(7), Sept(3), Oct(4), Nov(3) and Dec(1).

Nearly all records have been of birds 'grounded' during low-cloud or foggy conditions when they are migrating across the country from sea to sea. They usually rest for some hours and then leave. Most of the species' diet consists of mussels, cockles and other bivalves although freshwater insects and their larvae are eaten, especially by ducklings.

Goldeneye *Bucephala clangula*

Winter visitor and passage migrant.

A

Breeds across much of North America, Europe and Asia. Winters south to Central America, western Europe, the Mediterranean, the Caspian and Black Seas, Japan and Korea.

Ingram and Salmon(1955) said: 'One or two visit the Wye almost annually, about March. A pair, Elan valley Reservoirs, Jan.5th, 1954'.

The species has become a much more frequent visitor since then but there are only two regular sites: the Elan reservoirs, especially Dol y Mynach Reservoir, where birds have been present every winter since 1987 and in most years before that back to at least 1956, and on the River Wye between Boughrood and Cabalva where the species is much less frequently seen now than in the past.

At Dol y Mynach there were four to 11 birds between October and March/April each year until 2004. From 2005 to 2009 the highest counts were 13-16 (26th January 2005). For 2010-13 the maximum has been 10. On 29th October1993 there were four birds on Dol y Mynach and a flock of 13 migrants on the Claerwen Reservoir which quickly moved on. Records also come frequently from Craig Goch and Caban Coch Reservoirs (usually birds disturbed from Dol y Mynach) and occasionally from Penygarreg, Garreg Ddu and Claerwen Reservoirs. Most birds arrive during late October and November, with peak numbers nearly always in January, and leave before the end of March, although there is an increasing tendency to stay into April by which time much courting and pairing up has taken place. The earliest date was one on Dol y Mynach on 2nd October 2000 and the latest were pairs there on 29th April 1995 and on 1st May 1960 and a duck on Craig Goch Reservoir on 29th April 2001.

On the lower Wye 10-15 (26th January 1986) were found most winters in the 1980s and until 1993 since when birds have been fewer and much less frequent. Downstream of Llowes is the most favoured stretch, although birds occur up as far as Boughrood on the slower parts of the river and there are four records for Pwll Patti - the most being 10 on 24th January 1965. The earliest record was of one at Glasbury on 22nd September 1994 and the latest at Cabalva on 5th April 1970. At least two males have been shot on the Wye in recent years presumably having been mistaken for drake Goosanders.

Elsewhere there have been 16 records of one to two at Llanbwchllyn including a duck seen from 4th April to 16th July 1992; nine records of one to two from Llandrindod Lake, all except one since 2000; five records of one to two from Llyn Heilyn were all between 1971 and 1980; four records of one to two from Hindwell Pool included a bird from 12th December 1966 to about 8th January 1967 when it was shot along with some Pochard and appeared for sale in a local poulterers; two records from Glan Llyn included six on 14th January 2006; four birds were on The Begwyns pool on 30th November 1997; four on Pencerrig Lake in December 1992; three on the Wye north of Builth on 12th March 1986 and two drakes at Llyn Gwyn on 1st March 1984.

Smew *Mergellus albellus* A

Very rare winter visitor.

Breeds from northern Scandnavia east across Russia and Siberia to the Pacific coast. Winters inland and around coasts mainly in western Europe, the Caspian and Black Seas, China, Korea and Japan.

There have been six records:

1967:	Redhead on Garreg Ddu Reservoir on 15th January.
1968:	Redhead on Dol y Mynach Reservoir on 6th March.
1969:	Adult male on Dol y Mynach and Craig Goch Reservoirs from 1st March to 3rd April.
1971:	One on the River Wye at Erwood on 29th March.
1984:	Redhead at Llanbwchllyn from 7th to 14th April.
2007-8:	Redhead at Llanbwchllyn from 10th November 2007 to 26th March 2008 and the same at Llandrindod Lake early on 25th December.

Red-breasted Merganser *Mergus serrator* A

Rare visitor which has bred.

Breeds from Alaska east to Labrador and west Greenland, Iceland, Scandinavia, north Russia and Siberia to the Pacific coast. Winters Pacific and Atlantic coasts of north America, west Greenland, Iceland, northwest Europe, parts of south Europe and Asia east to China, Korea and Japan.

Ingram and Salmon writing in 1955 said that the species was, 'A regular winter visitor to the Wye, usually single birds, occasionally in twos or threes. There are a number of specimens recorded as having been shot in the county, but all lack data except one, shot on the River Ithon in December 1915 (*Field,* Dec. 18th 1915, p.1052)'.

One shot on the Wye at Erwood 'before 1882' was probably the bird referred to by John Williams-Vaughan (Woolhope *Transactions.* 1909 p.86) as being shot by Mr. H.T.Gwynne-Vaughan 'some years ago'. He also mentions a bird 'killed on Radnor Forest' and '..now stuffed at The Lion Hotel, Builth' but with no date. The species was also said to be occasional on the Wye in the 1920s.

Coinciding with the species rapid expansion as a breeding bird in Wales there were records of one to four birds in Radnorshire every year in the 1970s, e.g. four drakes on Caban Coch Reservoir on 22nd July 1971 and from 10th June to 24th July 1972, three on Penygarreg Reservoir on 25th July 1976 and four on the Wye at Brynwern Bridge, south of Newbridge, on 14th September 1978.

One to two pairs were present each April and May from 1983 to 1989 on the Wye between Builth Wells and Llanwrthwl with nest-site prospecting seen in 1985 and 1987. However, no resulting young were seen. In 1992 up to eight birds were seen between the Wye/Elan confluence and Newbridge between

22nd April and 18th May with a drake in moult on 7th June. In 1993 three pairs were present between Builth Wells and Llanwrthwl and a pair bred between Newbridge and Llanwrthwl raising three young from eight eggs. The nest-hole being in the riverbank on the Breconshire side of the river.

The only other records have been:

1987:	Drake, Llyn Gwyn on 25th May.
1988:	Drake, Claerwen Reservoir on 25th October.
1993:	Drake, Glasbury on 15th April.
1994:	Drake, Llanwrthwl on 10th April.
1994:	Drake on the River Wye at Boughrood on 6th May.
1997:	Pair on the River Ithon below Penybont on 20th April.
1998:	Drake, Caban Coch Reservoir on 8th May.
1998:	Redhead, Caban Coch Reservoir on 4th October.
2000:	Pair, Garreg Ddu and Penygarreg Reservoirs from 22nd April to 10th May.
2005:	Pair on the River Wye below Builth Wells on 16th February.

Goosander *Mergus merganser* A

Uncommon but regular breeding bird, passage migrant and winter visitor.

Breeds across much of the northern hemisphere. Resident in places, elsewhere a migrant wintering across the southern USA, western Europe, and parts southern Asia east to China, Korea and Japan.

Ingram and Salmon stated that the species was a regular visitor to the Wye in winter and early spring and that it was recorded in the Elan Valley before the reservoirs were made, which was between 1892 and1903. Twenty were at Cefncoed Pool on the Wye at Doldowlodd on 22nd December 1948.

Breeding has been recorded annually since 1972 and today birds may be seen on most of the larger still waters and rivers in any month of the year.

In the 1960s counts of 10-24 regularly came from the Elan reservoirs between December and early April. Breeding was first proved on 9th June 1972 when a female with nine young was seen on Garreg Ddu Reservoir. This closely following the first definite breeding record for Wales at Lake Vyrnwy in 1970.

The breeding population in Radnorshire increased rapidly in the 1970s and 80s reaching a peak of about 45-50 pairs in the mid to late 1980s. Since then there has been a very noticeable decline both in pairs present and, especially, young seen. This is probably due to shooting of full grown birds and predation of young although Otters have been seen catching full-grown birds on the Wye near Glasbury. In 2000 the number of pairs was about 32-35 along the rivers Wye, Elan, Ithon, Edw and Marteg and on the Elan reservoirs whilst 26-30 were found in 2010 when 20 broods/crèches were seen; six on the Elan reservoirs and 14 on the Wye and Ithon.

On the Elan reservoirs four to 10 pairs breed annually but with little success. Over 40 birds were counted there on 10th March 1973 and roost counts on Caban Coch Reservoir include 55 in October 1992 and 68 in September 1990. The choice of roost/gathering sites varies from year to year with Llanbwchllyn holding 50 birds on 3rd December 1990, 64 on 31st January 2006 and 110 on 16th January 2008 as well as 90-104 on several other dates in December 2007 and January 2008. Llyn Gwyn had 50 in January 1989 and there were 25 on Penybont Lake on 16th January 1995. On the Wye there were 50 at Glasbury on 12th August 1990 and 80 were counted between Glasbury and Boughrood on 12th December 1991. A female with a crèche of 53 young was seen on the Wye below Newbridge in June 1984.

Llandrindod Lake has become a favoured site in recent years with some birds readily taking bread thrown for the other wildfowl. The first record there was of four on 25th December 1965 with one to two seen on four dates in the 1970s and 80s. In March 1997, 24 were counted, 67 on 1st February 1998 , 52 were present on 12th December 2003 and 21st November 2004, up to 51 in November and December 2006, 46 on 29th October 2007 but much lower numbers since then. There have been very few records at Llyn Heilyn but up to 21 were present in January 2003. Other sites with records not already mentioned are the lower bog at Newbridge, Glan Llyn and St Michael's Pool.

The River Wye Bird Survey of 1995/6 found 55 birds on the Radnorshire sections on 26th November 1995, 109 on 4th February 1996 and 69 on 31st March 1996. A census in November 1990 found 120 birds in Radnorshire. Recent surveys along the length of the Wye in Radnorshire in February and March have produced high counts for February of 43 on 16th February 2005 and for March of 95 on 22nd March 2006. There is a noticeable passage of females and the season's young birds in August and September with flocks of 10-25 birds recorded most years in the Elan Valley passing through northwards.

A duckling ringed at Rhayader in July 1993 was found freshly dead 930 km NE in Rogaland, Norway, in October 1995 and another ringed in Powys was found 3,000 km NE in the far north of Norway in mid-September five years later. (Males moult in the far north of Norway). A breeding female ringed at Rhayader in June 1990 was retrapped, whilst flightless in moult, on the Eden Estuary, Scotland, on 16th August 1992. A duckling ringed in Powys in 1986 was found dead in Cumbria in its first winter and another duckling, ringed in Northumberland in July 1978, was shot in Powys in December.

Ruddy Duck *Oxyura jamaicensis* C1

Former rare summer visitor and breeding bird.

Breeds North America. Partly resident but also winters in southern USA, central and western South America. Introduced into Britain in 1960s, mostly culled since 2000.

The first record was a female at Llanbwchllyn on 21st November 1981. A pair was at the same place from 8th to 27th July 1985 and a drake on 1st April 1986. Two pairs were at Llyn Heilyn throughout July 1986 and a pair arrived there again in mid-May 1987 the female of which appeared with eight newly hatched young on 29th June. Six of the young eventually fledged and in July and August up to four drakes were also present. One to two drakes were also seen on the pond at Park Farm, Maelinydd, in the summer of 1987 and a juvenile, not from Llyn Heilyn, was seen there on 1st August.

A female returned to Llyn Heilyn on 30th April 1988 and up to five drakes and two ducks were present in May and June. A female with two small young appeared on 4th September which were abandoned by the parent (as is common) on 17th September and which fledged at the end of October. Two pairs were at Llyn Heilyn on 9th April 1989 and up to three drakes were present in August whilst a single drake was seen there in April and June 1990. The only record in 1991 was of two drakes at Llanbwchllyn in July.

In 1992 a duck and nine small young appeared at Llyn Heilyn on 18th July followed by a brood of four on 26th July and another of four on 29th August. Up to four drakes and three ducks were seen in July and August with high counts of 20 (including young) made on 1st and 29th August. In 1993 two broods of three were raised at Llyn Heilyn whilst between 1994 and 1996 there were just two records of two to three birds, both in May. In 1997 broods of three and two were raised and in 1998 one of six, although three pairs were present in April.

The only records since then have been of single drakes in 1999; at Llyn Heilyn on 25th May, Llanbwchllyn on 19th June and on The Begwyns pool on 3rd July. A female or juvenile was at Llanbwchllyn on 16th September 2000 and a drake at Llyn Heilyn on 27th June 2001 - the last county record before the government's nationwide cull took effect.

Red Grouse *Lagopus lagopus* A

Resident breeder.

Breeds from the British Isles across Scandinavia and east across Russia to Anadyr and Kamchatka; also in North America from Alaska to Newfoundland. Mainly resident with some altitudinal movements.

Ingram and Salmon said in 1955 that Red Grouse were,'Still resident and breeding in fair numbers on most of the heather moors...though numbers have declined from what they were.'

The game books from the Nantgwyllt Estate, west of Rhayader, for the years between 1859 and 1900 show a total of 2,822 Red Grouse shot in the period, an average of 67 per year. The Maesllwch Estate grouse moors included all those from Glascwm Hill to Llandeilo Hill, as well as The Begwyns and the hills around Newchurch. The game books, which cover 45 of the years between 1868 and 1935, give a total of 9,318 Red Grouse, an average bag of 207 per year, a best year total of 611 in 1904 and a biggest day of 220 on 9th September 1913. On Radnor Forest the average season total was 48 between 1926 and 1937 and 12 between 1938 and 1949. Although the heyday of grouse shooting on Beacon Hill was between the Wars, the only totals known are for the years 1951 to 2000. Totals shot were 875 in the 1950s, 690 in the 1960s, 781 in the 1970s, 534 in the 1980s, 168 in the 1990s and 6 in 2000. The highest year totals were 177 in 1959, 132 in 1957 and 128 in 1971.

In the 1950s,'60s and early '70s huge areas of heather moorland in Radnorshire were lost and replaced with improved grassland for intensive sheep production and coniferous plantations. Many heather moors were however kept for grouse shooting and some are still managed to that end today. These moors have included those at Beacon Hill, Radnor Forest, Rhulen Hill, Glascwm Hill, Gwaunceste Hill, Aberedw Hill, Ireland Moor, Llandeilo Hill and Llanbedr Hill. The heather moors of the Elan uplands have been largely unmanaged for grouse since the 1950s and have kept a population of about eight to 15 pairs whilst being by far the best in Radnorshire for other upland birds requiring mature heather.

In 1960 there were 25 birds counted on Glascwm Hill on 3rd September and the species was described as 'numerous' there the following year. In 1962 there were seven pairs located on Ireland Moor and the same in the Black Mixen/Whimble area of Radnor Forest. On those moors which were kept for shooting, numbers of Red Grouse were good throughout most of the 1970s with 1970 itself being described as 'the best for years' with 72 shot on one moor in the south of the county over the season whilst 100 were put up on one drive in 1972. 'About 20' were counted at the Black Mixen on 21st September 1977. Some moors have had at least some keepering from time to time up until the present day in an effort to produce enough birds to provide at least a day or two of shooting. On Ireland Moor, following a major effort to reduce crow, Magpie and Fox numbers, more than 120 Red Grouse were counted at the end of the breeding season in 2000.

The species is still very widespread in small numbers on all areas with extensive heather and is recorded annually from 25-30 sites, both managed and unmanaged. Between 2009 and 2011 counts included 12 on Beacon Hill on 8th September 2009, 16 on Glascwm Hill on 13th December 2010, 18 in three parts of the Elan uplands on 10th September 2010, 13 on Radnor Forest on 8th September 2010, 12 on Ireland Moor on 2nd December 2011 and noticeable increases on Gwaunceste Hill, Glascwm Hill and Aberedw Hill reported in 2010.

The main causes of local declines and extinctions today are diseases carried by sheep ticks, loss of heather moorland due to uncontrolled and slow burning, the encroachment of species-poor grasslands around the moorland edges due to heavy sheep grazing, the encroachment of bracken and predation by corvids and Foxes. Very cold winter weather and very wet summers, such as 2012, can also cause local extinctions and numbers found in the spring of 2013 were the lowest on average for at least 30 years.

Black Grouse *Tetrao tetrix* A

Former resident breeder.

Mostly resident and breeds from Britain, the Netherlands, Belgium, France, northern Italy, central Europe and Scandinavia east across Finland, Russia to the northern Balkans and south to Turkestan, northern Mongolia and North Korea.

On the Nantgwyllt Estate, west of Rhayader, 70 Black Grouse were shot between 1859 and 1900 and in the *Transactions* of The Woolhope Naturalists Field Club for 1895-97 the species was described as numerous in the same area. Two birds were shot at Dolberthog, near Llandrindod Wells, in October 1857 and the species was described as 'occasional' on the Radnorshire/Herefordshire border in 1860. The Maesllwch Estate records show a total of 52 birds shot in 14 of the years between 1868 and 1911 but none subsequently.

There was undoubtedly a great decline in Radnorshire between 1900 and 1940, as elsewhere in Wales. There were still a few birds in the 1920s on the Elan uplands, around Bwlch y Sarnau and in the south of the county. Ingram and Salmon said that one was shot near Presteigne in 1926, but this could have been a mis-heard record and perhaps refers to the bird shot on The Skreen shoot (mainly Llandeilo Hill) on 27th August 1926. Seven were seen near Beguildy on 16th April 1927 and a male was shot near Newchurch in about 1936. At least some of these records in the 1920s and 1930s may well have been the result of attempted reintroductions.

The species was said to have been unknown on Radnor Forest until at least 1930 when possibly a reintroduction attempt was made. Grouse shoot totals between 1926 and 1937 included no Black Grouse but one to two were shot each year on average between 1938 and 1949 and three birds were seen in September 1953. The new young coniferous plantations of the 1950s led to an increase in records mainly in the Waun Marteg area where birds were seen annually between 1955 and 1973 with six males and five females seen in 1960 and 1961, a covey of 10-12 birds in 1959 and 15 birds on 1st October 1961. The six males seen on 16th October 1960 were feeding in a stubble field and on hawthorn berries. The area was let for shooting from 1962 and numbers declined to three males in 1973. Further single records came from Blue Lins in April 1975 and from Waun Marteg in 1978.

Elsewhere there was a breeding season record in the Nantmel area in 1970 and on Llandeilo Hill on 17th August 1971. At Radnor Forest the first record since 1953 was on 16th November 1971 followed by a male and a female on 3rd February 1972. A male was seen on Llanbedr Hill on 16th February 1974 and one on the Elan uplands west of Penygarreg Reservoir on 30th June 1981. There was a male and a female on Radnor Forest in August and September 1981 and nearby at Black Mixen on 23rd October 1983. The last records for Radnorshire were of a male and two females near The Whimble, Radnor Forest, at dawn on 2nd June 1987 when a female Goshawk was seen to take the male.

Red-legged Partridge *Alectoris rufa* C1

Uncommon introduced and released gamebird which sometimes breeds.

Native resident in south-west Europe from north-west France and north-west Italy southwestwards across Iberia, formerly also the Channel Islands. Introduced into Britain from 1770 also to the Balearic Islands, Madeira, the Canary Islands and The Azores.

The species has been recorded in the Presteigne area since at least the early 1900s probably from birds released just over the border into Herefordshire. Breeding was reported near Presteigne in 1923 and one was caught in a garden and a covey seen in the main street of the town in February 1952. An injured bird was found near Knighton in 1953 when one was seen at Newchurch, a covey at Gladestry and 18 at Llan y Felin.

In 1968 birds were seen near Presteigne, at nearly 1,000 feet a.s.l., eight at Hill Farm, Presteigne, in the autumn and a single at Stanner Rocks on 28th April. In 1968 a pair and four young were seen at Dol Wilkin farm where the species had never been seen before. Breeding was reported from the Glasbury area in 1970 and 1971 and a single bird was seen at Llowes in 1970. Records came from Stonewall Hill and Knucklas in 1974, twelve were seen at Milton on 14th January 1979 and 11 at Bryngwyn on 11th

December 1979. A single bird was seen near Builth in May 1980 and one at Maelinydd on 30th August 1981. Birds were reported regularly throughout the 1980s and 90s from the Walton Plain with young seen occasionally. Also in the 1980s records came from Gladestry, Presteigne, Newchurch, The Begwyns, Nantmel, Bronydd, Elan Valley, Llandeilo Graban (adult and nine young on 9th July 1988), Dolau, Boughrood, Rhosgoch, Newbridge and Llanyre.

Records in the 1990s included several from the Glasbury area, breeding at St Harmon in 1995 and 1996, from between Clyro and Hay, near Rhayader, the Walton Basin, at Michaelchurch, a pair at Llyn Heilyn (1,214 feet) on 14th April 1998 and eight running across the Presteigne bypass on 15th September 1998. Since 2000 records have been more frequent especially from the east of the county due to more releases for shooting both in Radnorshire and just over the border into Herefordshire. Records have come from Crossgates, St Harmon, Elan Valley, Nant Glas, Felindre, Llanyre e.g. 13 on th November 2005, Presteigne area, Discoed, the Knighton area and Stanage Park e.g. 12 on 15th December 2006, Cregrina, Nantmel, Clyro, Glasbury, Boughrood, Beacon Hill and Pilleth.

Grey Partridge *Perdix perdix* AC2

Very rare resident breeding bird and released gamebird.

Breeds from the British Isles, Scandinavia, France and northern Spain east across Europe and Asia to central Russia and south to Italy, the Mediterranean, the Balkans and Iran. Mostly resident but migrates south from some parts of central Europe and Asia. Introduced into North America.

The Maesllwch Estate game books have records of Grey Partridge shooting on the lands between Llowes and Boughrood for 42 of the years between 1870 and 1935. A total of 12,980 birds for those years gives an average of 309 per season. The average annual totals for each decade were: 1870s - 281, 1890s - 568, 1900s - 530, 1910s - 235, 1920s - 101 and 1930s - 95. The highest season totals were 1,157 in 1898, 981 in 1902, 896 in both 1900 and 1901, 861 in 1905 and 791 in 1870.

The Doldowlodd Estate game books include shoot records for roughly the area bounded by Nant Glas, Llanyre, Llandrindod Wells and Newbridge for 58 of the years between 1858 and 1961. A total of 3,008 birds were shot in all with an average of 167 per year between 1896 and 1906. The highest season totals were 215 in 1897, 194 in 1899, 192 in 1902, 180 in 1903, 177 in 1898, 174 in 1904 and 135 in 1905 and 1914. However, the average for the years 1920 to 1961 was just 22 birds per season after which the successive cold winters of 1961/2 and 1962/3 wiped the species out locally.

Ingram and Salmon (1955) described the species as, '...thinly distributed, chiefly on the lower farms...decreased in numbers appreciably as compared with 25-30 years ago.' Today it may just be hanging on as a breeding bird in the south and east of the county but any population is the result of reared birds released for shooting.

Apart from the Doldowlodd shooting records, records in the 1950s included ones from Glascwm, Pantydwr and from near Rhayader (pair and nine young in 1955). In 1960 a pair was seen east of Penygarreg Reservoir at 1,500 feet and also in the 1960s at Cabalva, Doldowlodd, Llanfihangel nant Melan, Milton Hill, the Glasbury area, Penyfforest, Gladestry, Hendre Einon and the Presteigne area. Twelve were seen at Nantmel in 1970 and a pair at 1,200 feet on the Carneddau in 1979. Also in the 1970s birds were reported from Llowes, Glasbury, The Begwyns, Presteigne and the Four Stones area. Breeding was recorded annually around Glasbury between 1977 and 1991. In the 1980s records came from Glasbury, Aberedw, Michaelchurch, Four Stones, Llowes, Hundred House, Pwll Patti, Kinnerton, Llandrindod Wells, Discoed, Rhydspence, Maelinydd, Knighton, Penyclawdd and Boughrood.

Birds were released for shooting on some of the central heather moors in the early 1990s and these undoubtedly accounted for many records in the surrounding area including from Doctor's Pool, Rhulen Hill, Cwm Kesty and Glascwm in 1992 and Ireland Moor in 1993. Released birds probably also resulted in records from Nantmel, St Harmon and Rhayader in 1990. Adults with young were seen in 1990 at Glasbury and Llowes whilst records continued from the Walton Plain throughout the 1990s and also occasionally from the lower Wye Valley and from the Michaelchurch, Presteigne and Knighton areas.
Records since 2000 have been few with sightings at Kinnerton, near Newbridge, Presteigne, Knighton, Evenjobb, Heartsease, Huntington and, the most recent, a pair in the road at Boughrood on 10th May 2013.

Quail *Coturnix coturnix* A

Rare summer visitor which has occasionally bred.

Breeds on the Azores, the Cape Verde and Canary Islands, Madeira, north-west Africa, Iberia, France and southern Britain east across most of central and southern Europe and Russia east to Lake Baikal, south to northern India, Iran and Israel; also southern and eastern Africa and Madagascar. Most African and Indian populations are resident, others are migratory wintering in India, sub-Saharan Africa, parts of Iberia and north-west Africa.

'In the late 1860s and early 1870s a number were heard and some shot in the neighbourhood of Evenjobb' (Ingram and Salmon, 1955). The year of 1870 was one of particular Quail abundance in Britain and one was shot near Painscastle on 30th September. Today, 150 years later, the Evenjobb area is still the most likely place in the county to hear Quail.

A number of records between 1941 and 1946 probably refer to the Presteigne, Evenjobb and Hindwell areas being recorded as 'over the Radnorshire border' in Gilbert and Walker, *Herefordshire Birds* (1954). During the 1960s one or two birds were heard calling in the Hindwell area in several years and a nest with eight newly hatched young was destroyed by hay-mowing on 7th July 1965. One was heard calling on The Begwyns on 18th August 1962 but the only record in the 1970s was of one at 1,500 feet on Beacon Hill on 3rd June 1978. In the early 1980s records came from New Radnor on 1st June 1981, Bailey Hill on 9th July 1983 and Bryngwyn on 8th June 1984. Breeding took place at Hindwell in 1986 and in 1987 calling birds were at Builth Road for several days in early June, at Bettws on 23rd June, at Clyro on 4th July and at Four Stones from 1st to 10th July.

There were more records of Quail in Wales in 1989 than in any other year for at least the previous 50 years. Of the 237 records collated, 42 were in Radnorshire. The first was a female seen at close range on Yr Wylorn, Gilfach, on 25th May. Four were calling at Hawthorn Hill on 28th May and one at Boathouse Farm, near Hay, on 2nd June. The main arrival was in the period 18th to 25th June. At least 20 calling birds were located in rank *Molinia* grassland up to 1,720 feet on the Elan uplands on 23rd and 24th and three were in oats and barley at Four Stones on 23rd. In late June and July up to six were calling on a farm near Clyro and at least seven were found between Clyro and Glasbury.

In 1990 nine were located in *Molinia* on the Elan uplands during June and July, at least three birds were found in the Evenjobb/Four Stones area in early July and one was seen at Clyro on 15th July. In June 1992 at least three were in barley at Clyro, two or three at Four Stones and one on The Begwyns. Six birds seen together at Four Stones on 8th September were almost certainly a family party. In 1994 there were single records from Glasbury and Four Stones whilst in 1996 there were six records in May and June and a family party was seen at Walton in early September. In 1997 there were records from Knighton Racecourse in July and August, at Howey at the end of May and in May and June at Whitton, Walton, Clyro and Glasbury. The only records between 1998 and 2000 were from a farm near Clyro where single birds were seen or heard each year between 27th June and 25th September.

Records have been much more frequent since 2000. Three birds were calling near Glasbury on 14th July 2002 and one was seen on Red Hill on 15th September 2003. Two were on the Elan uplands in June 2007 plus two in the Glasbury area and two at Walton/Four Stones in July. Six birds were calling at five sites in 2008; Boughrood, Evenjobb, Burfa, Kinnerton and Gilwern Hill. In 2009 there were two near Knighton from 19th to 21st August, four were calling near Evenjobb on 16th July and two family parties were there on 22nd July. One bird was seen near New Radnor on 10th September. Six were calling from oats and wheat south of Evenjobb on 29th June 2010, one was calling at Four Stones on 14th May and two were on the Elan uplands on 6th July. Birds arrived early in 2011 with two near Evenjobb on 6th May and one at Hundred House on 12th. Six were in the Evenjobb area on 30th May and up to five heard in June. One to two birds were on the Elan uplands in late May and June and records in late May came from

Maelinydd and near Offa's Dyke, south of Knighton. In 2012 up to four were heard calling on the Walton Plain during June and July and two near Hawthorn Hill on 5th July. The only records in 2013 were singles near Four Stones on 15th July and Glasbury on 24th July. Most records have come from oats, followed by *Molinia*, barley, wheat, tall improved grassland and oil-seed rape.

Pheasant *Phasianus colchicus*

C1

Released gamebird which sometimes breeds.

Breeds indigenously from the Volga Delta and the Caucasus east to Mongolia and Amurland and south to China, Korea and Burma. Mostly resident but partly migratory in parts of eastern Asia. Introduced successfully across most of western and central Europe, north-west Africa, North America, Hawaii, Japan, Chile, Tasmania and New Zealand with many other attempts world-wide.

The Maesllwch Estate game books show a total of 28,558 birds shot over 31 years between 1870 and 1935 in the Wye Valley between Boughrood and Llowes with the highest years being 3,910 in 1905 and 3,479 in 1901 and the highest day total 638 on 4th November 1905. The highest ever day total for the county was the 751 birds shot by seven guns at Clyro Court on 10th November 1928.

Today the species is frequently seen in the lowlands of the east and south of the county where many birds are released for shooting each year. Elsewhere sightings are usually infrequent and are invariably due to small scale local releases for some informal rough shooting. Successful breeding in the wild is not common and where releases cease populations are not sustainable and the species disappears within a few years. Birds very rarely wander more than a mile from their place of release. A brood of 14 was seen at Pantydwr in May 1957 and a nest with 19 eggs found near Presteigne in 2009. Three hens with their young broods of five to eight chicks were in a wheat field below Glasbury in May 2011.

Red-throated Diver *Gavia stellata*

A

Very rare visitor.

Breeds circumpolar from high Arctic Canada, Greenland, Iceland, northern Scotland and Svalbard east across Fennoscandia and Russia to Kamchatka and the Bering Sea. Winters at sea in the Arctic Ocean, the North Atlantic and Pacific, south to the Mediterranean and Japan.

One was shot on a pool just down river of Erwood Bridge by Captain Hotchkis about 1889 and another was shot on the River Wye at Builth Wells on 5th February 1910.

Black-throated Diver *Gavia arctica* A

Very rare visitor.

Breeds from Scotland, Scandinavia and the Baltic countries east across northern Eurasia to Kamchatka and western Alaska and south to central Russia, Kazakhstan and Mongolia. Winters at sea south to the Mediterranean, the Black Sea and Japan.

The only record is of one believed to have been shot on the River Wye at Glasbury 'many years before 1882'.

Great Northern Diver *Gavia immer* A

Very rare visitor.

Breeds from Alaska east across Canada and along Arctic coasts to Greenland and south to Washington State and New England, also Iceland and occasionally Bear Island. Winters in coastal waters of the North Atlantic and Pacific south to Morocco, California and the Gulf of Mexico.

'Specimens' were 'obtained' on the River Wye near Hay and at Glasbury about 1860-1870 but there are no details.

Since then the have been eight records:

1929:	One on the Elan Valley reservoirs on 29th September.
1982:	An immature at Llanbwchllyn on 26th December
1986:	An oiled bird at Llandrindod Lake from 1st to 3rd January was taken to Newquay Bird Hospital but died later.
1997:	An adult on Craig Goch Reservoir from 15th November to at least 25th December was found long dead on the banks of the adjacent Penygarreg Reservoir on 14th March 1998.
1997:	A first-winter on Craig Goch Reservoir on 22nd November flew off north-westwards.
2000:	A first-winter on Llanbwchllyn on 9th January.
2000:	A winter-plumaged bird flew north-westwards high over Crugyn Llwyd, 4 km north of Bwlch y Sarnau, on 26th January.
2008:	One calling on Caban Coch Reservoir on 13th December.

Little Grebe *Tachybaptus ruficollis*

A

An uncommon breeding bird, which leaves most nesting sites for the winter months; passage migrant and winter visitor.

Breeds across Europe and southern Asia to Japan, India, Malaysia, the Philippines and New Guinea and throughout most of Africa. Mostly resident but northernmost birds move south in winter within the breeding range.

Ingram and Salmon described the species as very local giving just Hindwell Pool and possibly Llyn Heilyn as breeding waters. Later in the 1950s and throughout the 1960s the only breeding sites were at Llyn Heilyn (1-4 pairs), Penyclawdd Pool (1-3 pairs) and occasionally at Park Farm, Evenjobb, Maelinydd and Hindwell where up to 10-12 were present in winter. Twenty birds were present at Llyn Heilyn on 10th September 1968 and 19 on 17th September 1969. Six were on the Wye below Glasbury on 27th January 1963 when all still waters and much of the river were frozen. The only other sites with records were Llanbwchllyn with singles on 18th April 1964 and 27th September 1962 and Pwll Patti in March 1967.

In the 1970s breeding again took place at Penyclawdd until 1975 afer which the lake became unsuitable. One to two pairs continued to breed regularly at Llyn Heilyn and a pair bred at Glan Llyn in 1973. Records at Llanbwchllyn in March and early April were possibly birds passing through and breeding has never been proved there. In fact there have been only three records at the lake since 1979, single birds in 1992, 2000 and 2004 – perhaps because of the presence of large Pike. Winter records of one to five birds came from the Wye aroud Glasbury in the 1970s and single records also came from Pencerrig Lake, Llandrindod Lake, Glan Llyn, Pentrosfa Mire, the Wye north of Builth Wells, Dol y Mynach Reservoir, Caban Coch Reservoir and Llanwefr Pool.

Between 1980 and 1983 one to two pairs bred at Llyn Heilyn, Park Farm and Wern Fawr, Howey. Ten were on the Wye at Glasbury on 1st January 1981. In 1984 a pair bred at Dol y Mynach Reservoir for the first time and also probably at Knill Pool, Llyn Heilyn, Park Farm, Maelinydd, Pencerrig Lake and Womaston. Three birds were on Llyn Gwyn on 15th October. Ten birds were at Glasbury in January and February 1985. In 1986 a pair bred at The Begwyns Pool with others at Llyn Heilyn, Dol y Mynach, Park Farm pool and at Maelinydd. Breeding took place in 1987 at Llowes, Park Farm, Llyn Heilyn, Dol y Mynach and The Begwyns with records also from Glasbury, Llyn Gwyn and Glan Llyn. The pair at Llyn Heilyn hatched its third brood on 4th September. Two pairs bred at Dol y Mynach and at Llyn Heilyn in 1989 and a pair at Pencerrig Lake in 1991 and 1992 with two pairs there in 1993. A pair bred at Hindwell in 1994 raising two young, the first breeding there since 1959, and also at The Begwyns where three young were raised. At Dol y Mynach the reservoir was drained when the two young were half-grown and they perished.

The mid-1990s was a very noticeable low point for the species in Radnorshire with no proved breeding in 1995 or 1996. A pair bred on the newly created pond at the Rhogo in 1997 and at The Begwyns with two birds seen on Llandrindod Lake in October and November. Breeding again took place on the Rhogo pond in 1998 and two pairs at The Begwyns pool. There were records outside of the nesting season at Llandrindod Lake, Caig Goch Reservoir, Glan Llyn and Glasbury. Four pairs bred in 1999 and birds were seen on Claerwen Reservoir, Llyn Gwyn, the Goytre pool on the Wye below Newbridge, Glasbury, Dol y Mynach and Hindwell Pool (maximum of 11 on 22nd October).

Seven pairs bred at six sites in 2000 including one at Bwlchyllyn and two at The Begwyns. In 2001, outside of the breeding season, birds were seen at Craig Goch Reservoir, Llandrindod Lake, Goytre Pool, Hindwell Pool, Glasbury and Dol y Mynach. Thirteen birds were on Hindwell Pool on 11th January 2002 and one on the River Elan at Dolafallen Bridge in January and February. Two birds were on the now rarely flooded St Michael's Pool on 30th May 2003 and pairs bred on small ponds near Nantmel and Newbridge. Single pairs were found breeding at 13 sites in 2006 including at several recently excavated farm ponds as well as at Glan Llyn, Burlingjobb, Pentrosfa Mire and at Burfa Camp. Single pairs bred at 15 sites in 2007 including at Hindwell Pool where 18 birds were present on 4th September and 21 on 10th October. In 2008 breeding was at least attempted at 18 sites including at Pwll Patti for the first time, a site which is usually dry in summer. At Hindwell there were 23 birds on 11th September and 28 on 18th December and throughout the following January. Twenty-four pairs bred at 19 sites in 2009 including pairs at Llyn Heilyn and Glan Llyn. A further increase was noticeable in 2010 with 26 pairs found in a thorough survey. A pair bred at Llandrindod Lake and records came from Hendregenny Pool and Carregwiber Pool. Pairs bred at Llandrindod Lake again in 2011 and at Pilleth.

Breeding birds usually arrive on site between mid-March and mid-April and have mostly departed by October. The breeding season can be very long with newly hatched young seen from April to October and pairs making up to six attempts. Passage birds are frequent from late February to early April and between mid-August and mid-October. Usually records are of 1-2 birds but eight stopped for the day at Dol y Mynach Reservoir on 19th August 1989. Winter records from the lower Wye are fewer today than in the past with usually only one to four birds found, although six were present in January 2011. The Wye Bird Survey recorded no birds on the Radnorshire stretches on 26th November 1995, three on 4th February 1996 and two on 31st March 1996. In early February 1999 nine birds were counted on the Wye between Newbridge and Rhydspence.

Great Crested Grebe *Podiceps cristatus* A

Rare breeding bird, which leaves the nesting waters for the winter; passage migrant and winter visitor.

Breeds locally from Britain and southern Scandinavia south to Spain and east across Russia to China. Also parts of North, East and southern Africa, Australia and New Zealand. Mainly resident but many northern birds migrate south to the Mediterranean, northern India and southern China.

Breeding took place at Llanbwchllyn in 1926 and in several years before that although the national census of the species in 1931 found no birds in Radnorshire.(*British Birds* vol. 26 p.91). Apart from possible nesting at Hindwell Pool in the 1940s, Llanbwchllyn remained the only occupied site until 1966 when an occupied nest was found at Craig Goch Reservoir (1,050 feet) a site used nearly every year since but only raising young in 1986 (1) and 1992 (3) due mainly to human disturbance and fluctuating water levels.

Birds were recorded at Llandrindod Lake in 1969 and annually between 1972 to 1976 with nesting first noted in 1977 when two young were raised. Subsequently successful breeding took place there nearly every year until 1999 when four attempts all failed. Otters were seen at the lake for the first time in 1999. Two pairs bred there in 1985 raising eight young from two broods each. From 2000 to 2005 no young were raised although one to two pairs attempted most years. Three young were raised in each of 2006-8 but none in 2009. Three pairs were present for a time in 2010 but one of the two that did attempt raised three young from one brood. Three pairs (two nested) in 2011 raised no young; in 2012 three pairs attempted and two broods of two were raised but none in 2013.

At Llanbwchllyn there have been two pairs most years with three pairs found there, at least for a time, in 1979, 2003 and 2011. Four pairs bred in 1980 and raised seven young otherwise the site usually produces one to four fledged young most years although the presence of large Pike probably limits breeding success. Twelve birds were present , comprising adults and young, on 11th July 1982.

A pair attempted to breed at Glan Llyn most years from 1971 to 1985. Also perhaps at Llyn Gwyn in the 1970s and 80s and definitely there in 2009. Disturbance levels have greatly increased at Llyn Gwyn in recent years and the pair usually leaves soon after arrival for Llandrindod Lake. A pair raised one young at the top of Claerwen Reservoir (1,214 feet) in 1988 and one to three young have been raised there in at least four years since although attempts are made most years. Two pairs were present there in 1989. A pair attempted to breed on Dol y Mynach Reservoir every year from 1998 to 2005 raising two young in 1998, one in 1999 and three in 2002 but failing otherwise. Birds have been seen there rarely since 2006 when Otters became frequent in spring feeding mostly on frogs and newts.

Following the introduction of Rudd at Llyn Heilyn in the early 1990s the huge shoals of resulting fry and young fish resulted in a pair breeding successfully in 1994 raising three young. It was the only successful site in the county in 1996 and young were raised there in 1997(2), 1998(3), 1999(1), 2000(2) and 2001(1). The fish population suddenly crashed thereafter and there have been no records at the site since. Nesting was attempted at the Middle Gro oxbow lake below Glasbury each year between 1975 and 1981 but only sucessfully in two years. Attempts were also made along the slower reaches of the Wye below Llowes occasionally in the 1970s and 80s but were inevitably usually washed away by spates. The national census in 1965 recorded just two birds in the county and eight birds were found in the one of 1975. Three to six pairs have attempted to breed in Radnorshire each year since 2000.

Breeding birds usually arrive on site between mid-February and mid-March and are rarely present after October. As a passage migrant odd birds are seen most years on the Elan reservoirs in February and March and August to November and along the Wye. Nine adults were on Llandrindod Lake on 24th March 1986 and other records of migrants have come from Hindwell Pool and Park Farm pond as well as from the breeding waters. Along the lower Wye one to four birds are present most winters between November and February, otherwise records for December and January in the county are rare.

Red-necked Grebe *Podiceps grisegena* A

Very rare visitor.

Breeds from Sweden, Finland and northern Russia south to Germany, the Balkans and the Ukraine east to the Kirghiz Steppes, also from eastern Siberia south to Manchuria and Alaska, Canada and the northern USA east to The Great Lakes. Winters south to the Mediterranean, south-east China and the southern USA.

There has been one record: A first-winter bird was picked up on a small stream at Evenjobb on 7th November 2006 and put on a garden pond in the village where it ate several small goldfish and then flew off.

Slavonian Grebe *Podiceps auritus* A

Very rare visitor.

Breeds from Iceland, Scotland and Scandinavia east across Siberia; also Alaska, Canada and the northern USA. Winters mostly around the coasts of the southern parts of the breeding range.

There has been one record: One was on Llandrindod Lake from 11th to 14th February 1996.

Black-necked Grebe *Podiceps nigricollis* A

Very rare visitor.

Breeds locally across southern and central Europe east to central Asia, also Manchuria, parts of western-central USA, southern Canada, Colombia, parts of tropical, eastern and southern Africa. Winters mostly within its breeding range but also south-east Asia, South and Central America.

There have been just two records: One was seen by Mr A.M.Gwynne-Vaughan on the River Wye at Builth Wells on the 9th, 15th and 22nd April 1905 and one was on the Claerwen Reservoir on 25th October 1988.

Sooty Shearwater *Puffinus griseus* A

Very rare visitor.

Breeds on islands around the south of South America, including the Falklands, off south-east Australia and around New Zealand. When not breeding it is oceanic throughout most of the Pacific, Atlantic and Southern Oceans.

There has been one record: One was shot on the River Wye upstream of Glasbury 'a few years before 1899'. The specimen was examined by E.Cambridge Phillips.

Manx Shearwater *Puffinus puffinus*

A

Rare visitor.

Breeds Westmann Islands, the Faeroe Isands, islands around British Isles and off Brittany, the Azores, Madeira, off Cape Cod and formerly Bermuda. Winters off eastern South America and off the west coast of South Africa.

There have been 35 records most, if not all, of which are of young birds (many still have some nestling down) which have recently left their nest burrows on the Welsh islands, been blown inland by strong winds and crash-landed in Radnorshire at night sometimes it seems mistaking wet roads with street-lighting for open water.

1926:	Caught on a pool at Norton on 22nd September.
1944:	One at Crossgates and two near Llandrindod Wells 'in autumn'.
1954:	Found dead at Llandrindod Wells on 13th September having been ringed as a nestling on Skokholm four days before.
1967:	Two picked up in Llandrindod Wells on 15th and 16th September.
1968:	One picked up on the road in Knighton in October.
1970:	Found near Nantmel on 12th September having been ringed as a nestling on Skokholm five days before.
1970:	Found Llandrindod Wells on 18th September.
1977:	One picked up in Llandrindod Wells in 'early September' and later released off Skokholm was said to be an adult.
1984:	Flew into a window in Llandrindod Wells on 1st September and died later.
1985:	Found at Llanelwedd on 11th September.
1987:	Found at Llanbister on 5th September and released at Fishguard.
1987:	Found at Llanelwedd on 6th September and released at Aberystwyth.
1989:	Found dead at Gilfach, near Rhayader, in September.
1991:	One circling over the River Elan below Caban Coch Dam at 4:40pm on 15th October flew off high to the east.
1997:	Picked up at Abbeycwmhir on 30th August and released at Aberystwyth the next day.
1997:	Picked up at Llandewi at 10:15pm on 31st August during high winds and heavy rain.
2004:	Picked up at Crossgates on 11th September.
2008:	Picked up in Llandrindod Wells on 10th and 15th September, New Radnor on 14th and Knighton on 15th.

2009:	Picked up at Crossgates on 11th September.
2010:	Picked up at Crossgates on 20th September.
2011:	Five found over the 5th and 6th September at Llandrindod Wells, Presteigne, Craig Goch Reservoir, Claerwen Reservoir and Knighton.
2011:	Four found between 20th and 22nd September at Llandrindod Wells(2), Llanelwedd and Llanbadarn Fynydd.

Storm Petrel *Hydrobates pelagicus* A

Very rare visitor.

Breeds Westmann Islands, Faeroes, Burhou in the Channel Islands, islands off the coast of Britain and in the Mediterranean. Winters off western and southern Africa.

There have been two records: One was found on the Radnorshire side of the River Wye near Erwood in 1881 and one was picked up dead on the Wye at Clyro 'some years before 1899'.

Leach's Petrel *Oceanodroma leucorhoa* A

Very rare visitor.

Breeds on scattered islands around the North Atlantic inluding north-east USA and Canada, Westmann Islands (Iceland), Faeroes and Scotland. Also around the North Pacific from Japan and the Aleutians to Baja California. Winters throughout much of the north and central Pacific and Atlantic as well as off west and southern Africa.

There have been eight records involving nine or ten birds:

1877:	One was shot by Colonel Wood's keeper on the River Wye above Glasbury on 5th October following a storm from the south-west the night before.
1881:	One was found dead at The Skreen, below Erwood, after a storm in November.
1891:	One on the River Teme near Knighton in November.
1952:	One picked up dead at Howey at the end of October.
1952:	Two or three at Newbridge at the end of October.
1952:	One at Cabalva on 26th October. (29 were recorded inland in Wales at the end of October 1952).
1980:	One seen in flight at Llanyre on 15th September.
1989:	One on Craig Goch Reservoir on 26th December flew off north-west.

Gannet *Morus bassanus*

A

Very rare visitor.

Breeds on both sides of the North Atlantic including Newfoundland, Iceland, the Faeroes, Norway, British Isles, Channel Islands and north-west France. Winters in the North Atlantic and the Mediterranean.

There have been seven or eight records in total:

One was picked up by Mrs Lloyd of Nantgwyllt, Elan Valley, 'some years before 1899' and 'kept alive for some little time on fish and periwinkles'.
One was picked up dead near Dolyhir 'about 1895'.
One was seen flying west over Knighton on 6th June 1911 and one, probably the same bird, was shot at Penybont the same day.
One was shot at Knighton in 1916.
There have been four records since:

1987:	One was found in a field beside the Aberystwyth mountain road at Cwmdeuddwr, near Rhayader, on 4th January and taken to the RSPCA.
2000:	One flew high over Crugyn Llwyd, Bwlch y Sarnau, on 8th February.
2000:	One was seen flying over Rhodoldog, Cwmdeuddwr, towards the Elan Valley on 10th October.
2013	Immature at Llandewi on 13th October.

Cormorant *Phalacrocorax carbo*

A

Regular visitor in small numbers and passage migrant.

Breeds from Nova Scotia, western Greenland, Iceland, the Faeroes and British Isles eastwards on coasts and inland waters across the Palearctic to Japan, south to India and China as well as parts of north-west, central and southern Africa, Australia and New Zealand. Winters mostly within the breeding range.

Ingram and Salmon (1955) gave the species' status as an occasional visitor to rivers and lakes, together with a record at Womaston Pond on 3rd April 1953.

Throughout the 1960s and 1970s there were one or two records most years, usually from the Elan reservoirs and the Wye in the Glasbury area. There was a large increase in records from the late 1970s to the early 1990s directly correlated with the nationwide increase in inland fish-rearing operations and stocked waters for angling. Since the early 1990s there has been a noticeable decline in numbers.

Most records are for the period August to April although one to two immature birds may be found on the Elan reservoirs and the lower Wye throughout the summer. In the late 1980s the mid-winter population in Radnorshire was in the range of 35-45 birds. The Wye Bird Survey of 1995/6 found 12 birds along the Radnorshire parts of the river on 26th November 1995, 20 on 4th February 1996 and 10 on 31st March 1996. A repeat survey on 8th February 2000 found 12 birds. In the winter of 2001/02 the total population was about 20-25 birds. Between the years 2004 and 2010 the average Wye counts in February were 17 birds and 14 in March with highs of 34 on 13th February 2007 and 41 on 22nd March 2006 and lows of seven on 16th February 2010 and two on 16th March 2010.

On the Elan reservoirs there were often eight to 10 birds in winter during the 1980s and early 1990s but since 2000 the norm is three to six birds, which often roost on the island on Penygarreg Reservoir. Recent high counts have been 13 on 27th December 2005 and 12 on Penygarreg Reservoir on 7th January 2006 but most of these birds are passing through as are high flying flocks such as 13 north on 25th March 1988 and 12 south over Penygarreg Reservoir on 12th October 2001. Along the Wye roosts sometimes number 15-20 birds below Glasbury and five to eight above Builth Wells. Birds are often seen at Llanbwchllyn in winter in recent years with three to six birds usual and a highest count of 12 on 9th February 2004. One to three birds are sometimes seen on Llandrindod Lake and the nearby River Ithon although eight were on the Lake on 29th September 2010. There have also been records from Llyn Gwyn, Glan Llyn, the rivers Teme and Ithon, Hindwell Pool and Llyn Heilyn.

There have been 38 birds ringed elsewhere and found in Powys, including 23 from over 100km. Birds have come from Anglesey (8), Cumbria, Dublin (3), Dumfries and Galloway (2), Dyfed (16), Gwent (3), Northumberland, Leinster (Ireland), Strathclyde and France (2).

Most birds have come from colonies off the Welsh coast. A nestling colour-ringed on St Margaret's Island, Tenby, in June 1989 spent its first autumn and winter from 8th September on the Elan reservoirs and another ringed on Ireland's Eye, Dublin, on 23rd June 2006 was found dead on the Wye at Builth Wells on 28th January 2009. A nestling ringed on the Farne Islands on 10th July 1959 was shot at Llandrindod Wells on 5th June 1961 (391 km SSW). A nestling colour-ringed in northern France on 16th April 2009 was seen on the Wye near Hay on 2nd January 2010 (315 km NNW) and a nestling ringed at Penderi, near Aberystwyth, on 7th July 1987 was reported from the Elan Valley on 20th May 2012 (41 km E). Birds, especially first-winter, from Finland and Scandinavia are also likely to winter in Radnorshire occasionally. Although there have been no ringing recoveries to support this as yet, there have been in neighbouring Herefordshire.

Shag *Phalacrocorax aristotelis* A

Very rare visitor.

Breeds on the coasts of Iceland, the Faeroes, British Isles, southern Norway, the Kola Peninsula, north-west France, Iberia, the Mediterranean and the Black Sea. Mostly resident within the breeding range.

There have been two records: One, 'a young bird in fine plumage', was shot by Mr J.Williams-Vaughan's keeper on the River Wye at Erwood Pool 'a few years before 1899' and a first-winter bird on Craig Goch Reservoir on 1st November 2009 flew off strongly north-westwards.

Bittern *Botaurus stellaris* A

Rare winter visitor.

Breeds across Europe and Asia from British Isles, southern Sweden, France and Spain across Europe and Asia east to Japan, also locally in north-west and south-east Africa. Mostly sedentary in western Europe but birds from northern and central Europe and Asia migrate south as far as tropical Africa, China and India.

There have been 16 records:

1891:	Shot at Womaston in January.
1891:	Shot at Presteigne on 13th January.
1925:	Seen at Glasbury in December.
1926:	Seen at Newbridge-on-Wye in March.
1927:	Shot on the River Wye at Cabalva.
1937:	Caught near Penybont and kept in captivity for three years.
1968:	Shot (by mistake) near Lanbister Road on 26th December.
1983:	Seen at Pencerrig Lake on 22nd December.
1984:	Seen at Llanelwedd in December.
1988:	Seen at Middle Gro oxbow lake, Glasbury, from 25th November to 16th December.
1999:	Seen near Rhos Hirnant, Elan Valley, on 2nd January, flew towards Craig Goch Reservoir.

1999-2000:	One frequented dense riverside vegetation about a kilometre downstream of Glasbury bridge from 21st December 1999 to 20th January 2000.
2003:	Seen at Llanbwchllyn between 21st January and 4th February.
2006:	Seen at Middle Gro oxbow lake and beside the River Wye below Glasbury from 2nd to 11th January.
2008:	Seen by the Wye between Glasbury Bridge and Llowes on 6th December.
2011:	Seen at Bronydd on 6th and 21st January.

Squacco Heron *Ardeola ralloides*

A

Very rare visitor.

Breeds locally from southern Spain and France east through the Balkans and the south of Russia to Turkestan, south to the eastern Mediterranean and across much of Africa. European and Asian birds winter in Africa.

One was shot by Captain Hotchkis on the Radnorshire side of the River Wye near Hay-on-Wye on 3rd May 1867 and the specimen housed in Mr. Baskerville's collection at Clyro Court. It was the 2nd record for Wales.

Little Egret *Egretta garzetta*

A

Rare visitor and resident.

Breeds across western and southern Europe and southern Asia from the British Isles to India,China and Japan also through much of southeast Asia to Australia as well as Africa. Resident and migratory to the Mediterranean and Africa.

The first record was of one seen at several places in the Ithon and Aran Valleys, a mile or so north and south of Penybont, from 2nd to 31st January 1994.

Single birds were seen along the Wye around Glasbury on 4th May 1995 and 25th May 1996 and at Llowes on 17th December 1999 and 11th January 2000. One to three birds were present along the lower Wye between Glanwye and Cabalva from 3rd September 2001 to April 2002 and at least one, and usually two to three, have been seen in that area, including Pwll Patti, nearly every month since. Five were seen several times in 2008 and on 20th August 2011.

Away from the lower Wye, one flew up the Claerwen Valley below the Claerwen Dam on 3rd January 2004 and one was seen where the Milo Brook joins the River Edw on 15th August. Also along the Wye, there were singles at Llanelwedd on 30th April 2005 and between Brynwern Bridge and Rhayader from June to October 2006. A bird was seen regularly on ponds in the Howey area in December 2010, one was on the River Teme at Knighton on 12th March 2011 and further upriver at Lloyney and Knucklas on 3rd May 2012. One was by the Wye at Brynwern Bridge on 10th January 2012 and one along the Wye around Rhayader, the River Elan and the Elan Reservoirs between 20th April and 20th May 2013.

Great White Egret *Ardea alba*

Very rare visitor.

A

Breeds locally in Europe from France eastwards and around the Mediterranean, across much of central and southern Asia from the Caspian Sea and India east to southern Japan and China and across south-east Asia to Australia and New Zealand; also locally in sub-Saharan Africa, parts of southern Canada, much of the southern and western USA and South America. Partly migratory, wintering within the breeding range and south to southern Iran, southern Argentina and across most of sub-Saharan Africa.

There have been two records, both near the River Wye at Llowes, on 29th November 2012 and 10th - 20th October 2013. The first was probably the same bird which later settled at Wellington Gravel Pits in Herefordshire until at least March 2013. The species is expanding its range in western Europe and the first breeding record for Britain was in Somerset in 2012.

Grey Heron *Ardea cinerea*

Rare breeding bird; winter visitor.

A

Breeds from the British Isles east to Japan, south to Africa, India and Malaysia. Resident and migratory, some northern populations winter south to Africa and southern Asia.

Heronries have been found in Radnorshire at 16 sites over the past hundred years, although only four or five are occupied today.

The one at Stanage Park was deserted some time (perhaps a long time) before 1928 with no information on how many nests it held. Similarly Burfa Wood was occupied in 1904 but there are no later records. Bryndraenog Wood, near Beguildy, was deserted sometime between 1928 and 1954 whilst a site at Llandegley was occupied between about 1944 and 1946. One to three pairs nested in the Newbridge, Rhayader and Llangunllo areas in the 1970s and 1980s and the last pair at a colony between Knighton and Knucklas bred in 1986. One pair nested at Michaelchurch in 1954.

Over most of the last 60 years nesting has largely been confined to three sites. The heronry at Abbeycwmhir seems to have been occupied since about 1936; there were 18 occupied nests in 1952 and 20 in 1954. The wood holding the colony was felled in 1958 and there were just five nests in nearby larches in 1959 and two in 1960. Occasional pairs did nest there later, the last being in 1984.

The woods around Penybont Hall have been used since at least 1928, although the site seems to have been deserted after tree felling from about 1943 to the late 1960s. It is likely that the birds moved to Abbeycwmhir and back again. The colony had one to eight nests between 1969 and 2001, except for 12 in 1971, with low years after cold winters. As the colony moved into better trees a few hundred yards away numbers grew to 12 in 2002, 19 in 2005 and 23 in 2008. Since then successive winter cold spells have reduced numbers to just 8 in 2012 with only 3 raising young in 2013.

Cefndyrys, Llanelwedd, has been occupied since at least 1954 and possibly since before 1940. There were five occupied nests in 1954, 14 in 1961 and 16 in 1962. In 1963, after the very severe winter, there were only four. Numbers increased to 15 pairs in 1970 and peaked at 35 in 1975. Only 15 were found in 1982 following cold winters and the loss of some of the nesting trees in a gale. Although 18 nests were counted in 1984 there have been seven to10 every year since then, apart from 2007 when there were 12-15.

Since 2005 four colonies have been found along the Wye with one to 11 nests each and other small colonies may well exist elsewhere in the county. Also many birds that feed in Radnorshire come from heronries in the river valleys just over the county borders into Shropshire, Herefordshire and Breconshire. In recent years these colonies have held up to 60 nests in total. Attempts at nestbuilding have also been seen on the island on Llandrindod Lake in 2007 and in the Elan Valley in March 1993.

The species undoubtedly still suffers from persecution and disturbance of colonies to this day and some sudden increases and decreases are due to such activities with birds seeking safer and less disturbed sites, which are at a premium.

Birds shot at a trout hatchery near Michaelchurch in the 1950s and 60s included birds ringed as nestlings in Staffordshire (2), Oxfordshire and Holland and birds shot at Stanage Park, Llanelwedd, Womaston, Rhayader and Llandrindod Wells were also ringed as nestlings in Oxfordshire and Staffordshire. A nestling ringed in northern Germany in June 1963 was shot near Llandrindod Wells on 2nd October the same year. In total there have been over 50 recoveries in Powys of birds ringed elsewhere with nine of 100km+, including singles from Norway and the Netherlands. From within Britain in total birds have come from Cheshire, Cumbria, Dyfed, Gloucestershire (29), Merseyside, Norfolk, Oxfordshire (4), Shropshire (3) and Staffordshire (6). Nestlings ringed in Powys have been recovered in Dyfed, Glamorgan (2) and Gwent.

It is unusual to see more than five birds together away from the heronries but there were 14 together at Glasbury on 27th July 1994, 16 at Pwll Patti on 27th January 1994 and 22 in a field below Glasbury Bridge on 20th September 2010. Nine were feeding on hundreds of frogs at Glan Llyn on 10th April 2006 with one bird seen to swallow 15 in half an hour. River Wye Survey counts for 1995/6 were 17 on 27th November 1995, 35 on 4th February 1996 and 6 on 31st March 1996. Thirteen were counted along the Wye between Llyswen and Newbridge on 17th February 2009 and 17 on 13th February 2007.

Black Stork *Ciconia nigra* A

Very rare visitor.

Breeds central Iberia and from Poland and the Baltic countries south to the Balkans, Turkey and Iran east across central Asia to Korea and China, and in south-east Africa. Winters in tropical Africa and southern Asia.

An adult was seen at Felindre, Lloyney and Dutlas along the River Teme north-west of Knighton from 9th August to 10th September 1990. It was the second record for Wales after the first in early May 1989.

White Stork *Ciconia ciconia* A

Very rare visitor.

Breeds in north-west Africa and Iberia and from north-east France, the Netherlands, Denmark, Germany and the Baltic countries south to the Balkans, Turkey, Iran and Iraq as well as in Turkestan and from Korea and Manchuria to Sakhalin. Winters in sub-Saharan Africa, India and China.

There have been three records: Flying north near Rhayader on 2nd June 1986, flying east to west across the Elan Valley on 24th May 1993 and between Llandrindod Wells and Crossgates on 26th April 1999.

Honey-buzzard *Pernis apivorus*

A

Very rare summer visitor and passage migrant.

Breeds across much of Europe and central Asia from the British Isles, Iberia, France and much of Fennoscandia south to the Balkans and the Caucasus east to western Siberia. Winters in tropical and southern Africa.

One shot near Penybont in 1904 was seen by Professor J.H.Salter when in the possession of the station master at Llandrindod Wells Railway Station. One flew south over Pont ar Elan on 30th September 2000, one flew north up the Elan Valley on 12th June 2002 and one flew south-east over Llanyre on 13th July 2002. Since 1993 one to three pairs have attempted to breed in at least seven years up to 2012 with one to two young raised on five occasions. Frogs or Toads have been very significant constituents of the diet at times as well as wasp larvae.

Black Kite *Milvus migrans*

A

Very rare visitor.

Breeds from Iberia east across Europe to Siberia and Japan, India, China, south-east Asia, Australia and Africa. Northern populations winter mainly in Africa, India, southern and eastern Asia and Australia.

One was present at the Gigrin Farm feeding station and elsewhere in the Rhayader area from at least 16th December 2009 until it departed on 17th March 2010.

Red Kite *Milvus milvus*

AC3

Mainly resident breeder; passage migrant and winter visitor.

Breeds from north-west Africa and Iberia, the British Isles and France east to southern Sweden and across central Europe to western Russia and the Balkans. Northern populations migrate south as far as the Mediterranean.

The first mention of the species in Radnorshire was of birds at Cwm Elan in 1798. They were still common around Rhayader and the Elan Valley in the 1850s but between c.1860 and the 1890s most Red Kites in Radnorshire were either poisoned, shot or pole-trapped by gamekeepers in the Elan Valley, at Water-break-its-Neck (Radnor Forest), on the Maesllwch Estate and elsewhere. In the Woolhope Naturalists' Field Club *Transactions* of 1869, James W. Lloyd said that it bred at Radnor Forest and that two young were taken into captivity in 1868. Also he said that it was formerly common on the Forest and that numbers were trapped at the rabbit warren near Water-break-its-neck (Warren Wood) until the warren was recently destroyed and kites were now less common. In 1902, John Sharp, a retired keeper for the Maesllwch Estate, said that he had probably killed 30 kites during the 30 years that he was a keeper (c.1870-1900).

One or two pairs at least were still nesting in the first decade of the 20th century. One was shot by a gamekeeper near Llandewi in may 1903 and the oologist F.C.R.Jourdain had a clutch of eggs which were taken in the county in 1909. In the 1920s and early 1930s there were regular reports from the east and centre of the county most of which are thought to have resulted from attempts to introduce Spanish birds. In 1927 some 21 eggs from Spain were said to have been placed in Buzzard nests in Radnorshire and 53 eggs were brought into mid-Wales in 1928. Throughout this period birds still occurred in the Elan Valley but probably did not breed in the county but just over the border into Breconshire where the eggs were taken in 1930.

Ben Price, the Maesllwch gamekeeper, is recorded as having shot the female off a nest at Llanbwchllyn in April 1927 in mistake for a Buzzard and Ingram and Salmon writing in 1955 gave this as the last definite nesting in Radnorshire. There were rumours that a pair bred in 1940 and the Woolhope Society *Transactions* of 1946 recorded that kites had bred for the previous three seasons under protection, seemingly in the Radnor Forest area. There were several records in the early 1950s with sightings between January and March and in late June and July, but no proof of breeding.

Two young Spanish birds were ringed and released at Rhulen in July of both 1957 and 1958 and birds were still seen in the area, and between Aberedw and the middle of Radnorshire, until 20th July 1959.

Regular sightings came from the Elan Valley throughout the 1960s, with just a few records from elsewhere in the county. There was a definite increase in records in Radnorshire from c.1970 and it seems likely that attempted breeding took place in the Elan Valley in the early 1970s. In 1976 it was reported that a pair had bred successfully and was the first to do so in Radnorshire for over 40 years.

Five to seven pairs were breeding by 1989 and from 1990 there was a huge increase in records away from the west of the county with at least 15 pairs by 1998. A full survey in 2000 found 22 pairs out of an estimated 259 in the whole of Wales. There were 45 occupied territories in 2003, 84 in 2006, 130 in 2009 and 144 in 2010 - out of c.1,000 in Wales. A partial survey found 113 occupied sites/territories in 2011.

Winter roosts in the Elan Valley have reached 30-70 birds since 2000 and there are smaller roosts of 20-30 birds at several sites in the county. Feeding started at Gigrin Farm, near Rhayader, in 1994 with up to 15 birds being attracted. In December 2003 over 400 were counted and in the cold weather of early 2010 up to 600 were present.

There have been many recoveries of ringed Red Kites to and from Radnorshire, some of which show the pressures that the species still faces, even in the 21st century. A nestling ringed in Schleswig Holstein, Germany, on 8th June 1971 was found long dead (poisoned) at Pant y Dwr, near Rhayader, in July of the following year. Other nestlings ringed in Radnorshire and recovered elsewhere have included: ringed near Llanbadarn Fynydd on 1st July 2007 and found poisoned in Yorkshire on 3rd May 2008; ringed near Llangunllo on 29th June 2008 and found dead in 2009 near Burbage, Derbyshire, from Brodifacoum (a rodenticide) poisoning; ringed near New Radnor on 6th June 2009 and found freshly dead near Marlborough, Wiltshire, on 24th December 2010; ringed near Rhayader on 16th June 2009 and found freshly dead with a severed wing under the wind turbines at Bryn Tytli in April 2011; ringed near Painscastle and found long dead near the wind turbines at Talybont, Ceredigion, on 10th May 2010; ringed near Rhayader on 22nd June 2010 and killed by a car at Alton, Hampshire, on 14th April 2011.

Since 1996 there have been many sightings at Gigrin Farm of the wing-tagged introduced birds and their offspring from across Britain. The first was one from the south of England in1996 followed by birds from the East Midlands, Sussex and Central and Highland Scotland over the following two years. Since 2000 several birds have come from Yorkshire, including one found poisoned with alphachlorolase on Beacon Hill in September 2007 and another nestling ringed on 18th June 2005 was at Gigrin Farm on 13th July and then back in Yorkshire by 7th August.

As well as the ringed birds found poisoned at Beacon Hill in 2007 and at Pant y Dwr in 1972, another was found poisoned near Knighton in 1997, at least one bird was shot at Old Radnor in 1998 and another was poisoned near where it was bred at Pant y Dwr in 2005.

In total there have been 43 Red Kites ringed or wing-tagged elsewhere and recovered or seen in Powys, coming from: Buckinghamshire (8), Cambridgeshire, Dyfed (8), Hampshire, Highland, Leicestershire (5), Northamptonshire (7), Oxfordshire (2), Shropshire (1), West Yorkshire (5) and from elsewhere in Wales (5). Also a total of 21 birds ringed or wing-tagged in Powys have been found or seen elsewhere, going to: Dyfed (11), Gwent, Gwynedd, Hampshire (2), Lincolnshire, Northamptonshire (2), Somerset, County Wexford and Wiltshire.

Marsh Harrier *Circus aeruginosus*

A

Very rare visitor.

Breeds from north-west Africa, Iberia, Britain, France and southern Fennoscandia south to Iran and Iraq and east across Europe, Russia, northern Kazakhstan and Mongolia to Lake Baikal. Northern populations winter in sub-Saharan Africa, India and south-east Asia.

There have been five records:

1949:	One seen at Dolau on 18th April.
1971:	A female was at Rhosgoch Bog on 25th May.
1997:	A sub-adult male was near Llyn Heilyn on 21st October.
2000:	A juvenile male flew west about 4kms north of David's Well on 11th August.
2012:	Juvenile around Penygarreg Reservoir on 19th August.

Hen Harrier *Circus cyaneus*

A

Rare breeding bird, winter visitor and passage migrant.

Breeds from Iberia, France, the British Isles and Scandinavia east across Europe and Asia to Kamchatka, Sakhalin and Manchuria; also North America. Northern populations migrate to Central and South America, southern Europe and Asia.

The Woolhope Naturalists Field Club *Transactions* of 1895-7 stated that there were 'always a few' in the Elan Valley (but these may have been Montagu's Harriers) and Cambridge Philips (1899) said that a pair had nested for years near Nantgwyllt, Elan Valley, on the Breconshire side of the Wye. Also a pair was reported to have nested near Rhayader in 1903. An undated record from around this period was of a bird trapped on the hill above Llanstephan which may be the same as another, undated, of a specimen obtained in the county and in the Maesllwch collection.

A male was killed by a gamekeeper near Glasbury in January 1907 after which there were no records until a ringtail was seen at what is now the top end of the Claerwen Reservoir on 23rd October 1952. Another ringtail was seen near Womaston on 1st December 1953 and a ringtail and an adult male in the same area two weeks later.

There were a few records in most years in the 1960s and 70s gradually increasing to 11 in 1979. Throughout the 1980s and early 90s there were probaby at least six birds overwintering in the county mostly on the central hills from Beacon Hill and Radnor Forest south to Llanbedr Hill and occasionally on the Elan uplands. However, a roost at Rhosgoch Bog held up to 12 birds in the winter of 1986/7 and there were six roosting there regularly in January 1999. Favoured habitats are heather moorland, *Molinia* grasslands (especially in vole years), bogs, commons and extensive clearfelled areas of conifer plantation. Most autumn/winter records fall between late August and early/mid April with peaks at both extremes indicating the passage through the county when birds have been seen widely on farmland and sometimes purposefully flying high south or north.

Breeding seems likely to have taken place in at least one or two years in the 1970s with one to three pairs regularly from 1983 to 2001 and up to eight pairs annually since then with an increasing number of birds summering. Although the occasional nest has been in deep, tussocky, *Molinia*, a lack of rank, ungrazed and unburnt, heather moorland for nesting seems to be the major limitation on breeding numbers.

There have been four recoveries elsewhere of nestlings ringed in Powys and found in their first autumn or winter in Devon (hit overhead wires), Kent (caught by another ringer), Spain (shot) and Portugal (caught by another ringer). A nestling female ringed in Gwynedd was found breeding in Powys five years later.

Montagu's Harrier *Circus pygargus* A

Very rare passage migrant which may have bred in the 19th century.

Breeds from north-west Africa, Iberia, France, Denmark and the Baltic countries south to Italy and Turkey and east across Russia to the Yenisei. Winters in India and sub-Saharan Africa.

The birds referred to as Hen Harriers in the Woolhope Naturalists Field Club *Transactions* of 1895-7 as being present in the Elan Valley may have been of this species.

One, without details but likely to have dated from the 19th century, in the Maesllwch collection, was obtained in Radnorshire and John Walpole-Bond saw a female at Radnor Forest on 19th May 1928. A bird considered to be a first-summer male was seen in the Vron Valley on 31st July 1955 and a male was present in the upper Elan Valley from 29th May to 5th June 2002.

Other possible/probable records include males seen near Llyn Heilyn on 26th September 1953 and one seen down to 40 yards at Radnor Forest on 24th April 1966. A bird thought to be of this speces, but without sufficient detail, was seen at Abbeycwmhir on 3rd June 1971.

Goshawk *Accipiter gentilis* AC3

Introduced, mainly resident, breeder.

Breeds across most of Europe, northern Asia and North America. Resident with some populations in the extreme north wintering south to Central America and southern China.

The first reported record was of one seen in the west of the county in 1976 and breeding took place in 1979. However, the species was deliberately released on numerous occasions into the major mature conifer plantations of the county between about 1974 and 1989. At least some, and possibly all, of these birds came from Finland.

Breeding took place in Radnor Forest in 1980 and by 1986 birds were present in at least six localities across the county. There was a minimum of 12 pairs by 1990 and in 1991 probably 15-17 pairs nested. By 1999 this number had increased to 20-25 and probably 30 in 2000. Numbers have remained at about 20-27 pairs since then including some bigamous males with two females and two nests in close proximity to one another. Persecution seems still to be frequent with birds shot and nests and eggs destroyed.

Mature conifer plantations are the preferred nesting habitat although younger plantations have been increasingly used in recent years. Hunting takes place within plantations and in broadleaved woodlands, on open farmland and on hilltops and moorland. Most hunting in more open habitats takes place early in the morning and, especially, very late in the evening.

The most frequent prey items are racing pigeons, Grey Squirrel, Rabbits, Wood Pigeons and corvids but a very wide range has been recorded in the county including Barn Owl, Long-eared Owl, Short-eared Owl, Tawny Owl, juvenile Raven and Peregrine, Heron, including large young from the nest, Black Grouse, Red Grouse, Pheasant, Mallard, Teal, Tufted Duck, Goosander, Black-headed Gull, Lesser Black-backed Gull,

Starling, Green Woodpecker, Merlin, Kestrel, Sparrowhawk, Golden Plover, Curlew, Lapwing, Snipe, Woodcock, Crossbill, Mistle Thrush, Hare, silky bantams and chickens, especially from large free-range units.

There have been 11 ringed birds from other counties in England and Wales found in Powys: Dyfed (7), Gwent, Gwynedd and Herefordshire (2) - which were nestlings found near New Radnor and at Knighton. Five birds ringed in Powys have been recovered outside the county being found in Dyfed, Glamorgan, Gwent and Hereford & Worcester (2).

Sparrowhawk *Accipiter nisus* A

Common resident breeder, frequent passage migrant and winter visitor.

Breeds from north-west Africa, Iberia and the British Isles to northern Scandinavia east across Europe and Russia to Kamchatka, northern India, Manchuria, Japan and Korea. Northern populations are migratory to southern Asia and parts of North Africa.

Ingram and Salmon said in 1955 that the species was, 'Resident and breeds regularly, but is by no means as numerous as it used to be and numbers are relatively small.' With the new conifer plantations established in the county during the post Second World War period and the removal of organochlorine pesticides, which were in use from the late 1940s until the mid-1980s, numbers increased hugely from the late1960s into the 1990s by which time it was easily the commonest bird of prey. This is a position it still occupies today being found breeding throughout the county although much reduced in some plantations by Goshawks e.g. in the Elan Valley breeding numbers have been reduced by 80% since the early 1990s. Locally bred birds are mostly resident but numbers are increased in winter by birds from Scandinavia.

As well as coniferous woodlands, mixed and broadleaved woodlands are used for breeding although dense, unthinned, Sitka Spruce plantations are preferred. Bigamous males are frequent with two females and their nests often within 400 metres of one another. Birds are frequently attracted to garden bird feeding sites where birds up to the size of Collared Dove and Wood Pigeon have been recorded as prey although House Sparrow, Chaffinch and Blue Tit are the most frequent with the addition of Starling in the winter months.

A total of 40 bird species have been recorded as prey in Radnorshire including Dipper, Crossbill, Snipe, Common Sandpiper, Great Spotted Woodpecker, Reed Warbler, Willow Tit and Yellowhammer. A Green Woodpecker was attacked near Newbridge but escaped and nestlings are often taken, especially during spells of inclement weather. A brood of Pied Wagtails were seen taken from the nest one by one over a period of an hour on a very wet June day in the Elan Valley. Bats have often been seen chased at dusk and species identified as prey in the county have been pipistrelle sp., Daubenton's Bat (2) and Brown Long-eared Bat (3). The only other mammal identified from remains and pellets has been a Wood Mouse. Birds are frequently seen hunting over open moorland and commons sometimes several kilometres from woodland. This occurs mainly in autumn and may be local birds hunting Meadow Pipits and/or birds on passage.

There have been two recoveries in Powys of birds ringed in Dyfed and Shropshire and three Powys ringed birds found in Pembrokeshire, Glamorgan and Gwent. A first-autumn female ringed at the bird observatory on Heligoland, off the coast of northern Germany, on 14th October 2011 was found freshly dead at Pant y Dwr on 13th February 2012 (786 km WSW).

Buzzard *Buteo buteo*

A

Common resident breeder.

Breeds throughout most of Europe, the island groups off north-west Africa and across Russia east to Sakhalin, Manchuria, Korea and Japan. Resident over most of central and southern Europe, Japan and Korea; birds from most of Fennoscandia and Asia migrate south for the winter to Africa, southern Europe, Turkey and south-east Asia.

The Woolhope Naturalists Field Club *Transactions* of 1869 stated that the species was frequently trapped at the rabbit warren on Radnor Forest and was very common in the Elan Valley. Due to persecution, numbers were at their lowest immediately prior to World War1 but the war years themselves saw numbers increase rapidly as gamekeepers went to fight and many shoots ceased for the duration, most never to resume. By 1920 Buzzards were 'extremely common' in Radnorshire leading to the repopulation of Herefordshire, where the species had become extinct by about 1910.

There was a crash in the population in the mid-1950s due to the decimation of the rabbit population by myxamatosis. However, in 1958 17 pairs were found in a 30 square mile area embracing Erwood, Aberedw, Rhulen, Glascwm, Newchurch and Painscastle and by 1959 numbers were considered to be back to 75% of pre-myxamatosis levels. Persecution was still going on in some areas and in 1971 of 13 dead Buzzards found on one Radnorshire estate at least two had fatal doses of strychnine.

Newton (1982) found that mid-Wales had the highest density of breeding Buzzards in Britain with an average of 41 pairs per 100 square kilometres of farmland and today it is as common and widespread as ever with no noticeable decline due to the resurgence of Red Kite numbers. However with such a density of breeding pairs productivity is low and Newton found an average of just 0.6 young per pair per year and in Radnorshire the typical brood is a single young. In 1994 31 nests in east Radnorshire had an average clutch size of 1.8 eggs and 33 young fledged from 25 nests.

Nest sites are usually in mature broadleaved trees above 10 metres although mature conifers are often used. Nesting on cliffs seems to have been much commoner in the past but is rare today. A nest was found on the ground in an extensive flat area of rank *Molinia* grass moorland in the Elan uplands in 1990 from which two young were raised.

Groups of 10-20 birds are frequently seen soaring in thermals and worming in fields. Thirty-four were counted in a spiral over Nantmel on 22nd January 1982, up to 38 were worming in a field to the west of Rhayader in 1993 and up to 30 in the same field in December 2001. A newly sown field at the Middle Gro, Glasbury, attracted worming Buzzards throughout the late autumn and winter of 2012 with a highest count of 42 on 29th November.

Plumage colouration varies considerably with particular areas where pale birds and other variations are frequent such as the Llanwrthwl/Rhayader, Penybont/Crossgates and Llandrindod Wells/Hundred House areas. A number of these birds have been mis-identified as Rough-legged Buzzards over the years and even as Osprey occasionally. All white birds were seen in the Elan Valley in 1961 and 1971 and in the Llanbadarn Fynydd area from at least 1997-2002.

There have been 12 ringing recoveries in Powys of birds ringed in Dyfed (6), Gloucestershire, Shropshire (4) and 'Wales'. Also nine birds ringed in Powys have been recovered in Clwyd, Cumbria, Dyfed, Glamorgan, Gwynedd (2), Shropshire (2) and Staffordshire. Only two movements were of more than 100km; both ringed as nestlings, one of which was recovered in Cumbria about a year after ringing and the other, ringed near Newbridge in June 1971, was found long-dead in Staffordshire the following April.

Rough-legged Buzzard *Buteo lagopus* A

Very rare winter visitor.

Breeds circumpolar across Alaska and northern Canada and from Fennoscandia east across northern Russia to the Bering Sea and south to Kamchatka and the Aleutian Islands. Winters in southern Canada and USA and across central Europe and Asia to Korea and China.

The only definite record is of one photographed above Pont ar Elan, in the upper Elan Valley, on 11th April 1995. The same bird was also seen three times in Montgomeryshire: at Kerry on 4th March, at Carno on 20th April and at Lake Vyrnwy on 23rd April.

Past reports of birds near Llanbister in 1963, near Rhayader in 1964 and 1975 and in the Elan Valley in 1983 all lack detailed descriptions and are likely to have been unusually plumaged Buzzards, similar to ones which still occur in those areas today.

Osprey *Pandion haliaetus* A

Uncommon, but annual, spring and autumn passage migrant.

Breeds across North America, the West Indies, Europe and Asia, north-west and eastern Africa, Indonesia and the Philippines to Australia and New Zealand. Northern populations winter in South America, Africa and southern Asia.

The first records were of one shot on the River Wye in 1859 and one caught in a pole-trap at Clyro on 13th April 1867. There were at least two further records in the Clyro area between 1868 and 1908 as well as one shot near Penybont in May 1885. One was seen on the Wye at Boughrood on 23rd September 1934 and possibly the same bird was seen at Glasbury earlier in the month. Further early records, when the species had yet to return as a breeding bird to Scotland, were in the Elan Valley on 8th May 1938, on the Wye at Cabalva from 30th September to 15th October 1949 and over Downton and the Summergil Brook on 11th June 1953.

Two birds were seen at Cabalva on 22nd August 1959 and there were four records in the 1960s - two spring records on the Wye, one at Erwood in September and one at Llyn Heilyn on 13th October 1960. The only records in the 1970s were at Erwood on 4th May 1971 and near Knighton on the very unusual date of 28th December. There was another record on the River Teme near Knighton on 4th September 1982 and four other birds were seen between 1987 and 1989.

There was a huge increase in records in the 1990s coinciding with the increase in the breeding population in Scotland. In the 1990s and the 2000s the average number of records per year was about eight with 18 in 1993, 10 in 1996, 12 in 1999, 10 in 2006, 13 in 2008 and 12 in 2010. Altogether there have now been a total of about 197 records with the earliest being on 14th March 2004, at the Claerwen Reservoir, and the latest on the 3rd November 1995 seen heading down the Wye at Llanwrthwl. There have also been two late December records; the one at Knighton above and two birds between Boughrood and Llanstephan on 25th December 1995. Records have come from the lower Wye below Builth Wells (75 records), the upper Wye above Builth (35), the Elan and Claerwen reservoirs (48), the

River Teme, north-west of Knighton (5), Llandrindod Lake (5), Llyn Gwyn (3), Glan Llyn (2) and singles at Pencerrig Lake, Llyn Heilyn and Llanbwchllyn. The other 21 birds have been seen heading north or south overland at a variety of places.

The diet of birds which stay off-passage to hunt along the lower Wye, sometimes for a week or more, consists almost entirely of Chub. A carp was caught at Llandrindod Lake on 8th June 2005 and Brown Trout are sometimes taken on the Elan reservoirs, especially on the shallow Dol y Mynach Reservoir.

Satellite tracked birds that have passed through Radnorshire include a female ('Morven') which was ringed as a nestling in Morayshire on 8th July 2003 and fitted with a transmitter on 9th July 2008. She flew up the Elan Valley on 10th April 2009 having roosted near Barnstaple the night before and ended up near Prestatyn by the evening. A male ('Nimrod') flew over the Elan reservoirs on 13th April 2010 at a speed of 67 km/hour on its way from Blagdon Lake, Somerset, where it spent the previous night, to the Conwy estuary by dusk. It had been ringed as a nestling near Rothes in Scotland on 5th July 2001 and fitted with a transmitter on 1st September 2008. It left its wintering quarters, about 100 miles south of the River Gambia, on 21st March, roosted for two nights in the desert whilst crossing the Sahara by 28th, crossed into Spain on 1st April, crossed the Channel, at just 2 metres above the sea, on 12th April, flew over Lancashire at 3,000 feet on 15th, roosted at Kielder Forest on 16th and arrived at its nesting place in Scotland at 8pm on 17th. A nestling ringed in Scotland in June was found dead in Powys in September.

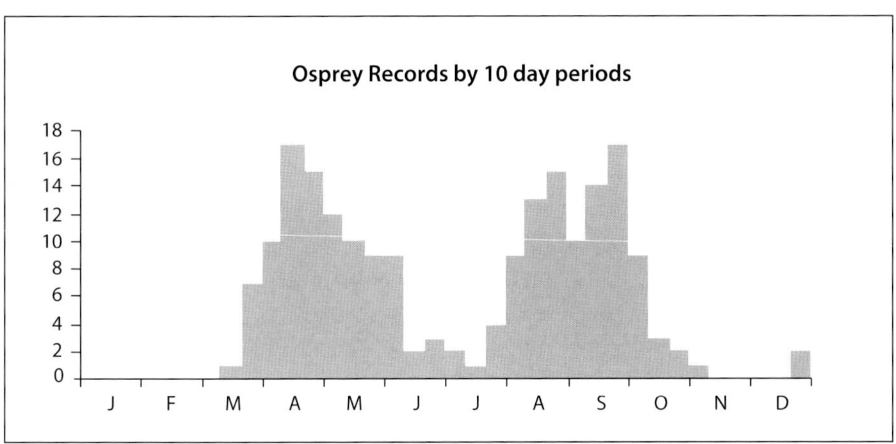

Kestrel *Falco tinnunculus*

A

Uncommon breeding bird; passage migrant and winter visitor.

Breeds over most of Eurasia and Africa, apart from Iceland and the far north from the Kola Peninsula to the Bering Sea parts of Africa and south-east Asia. Mainly resident but northern populations winter south to Central Africa, India, the Malay Peninsula and China.

Ingram and Salmon described the species in 1955 as 'fairly numerous and widespread.' There has been a huge decline since then, almost entirely since the introduction and spread of the Goshawk. In the Elan Valley area there were seven to nine pairs breeding each year between 1983 and 1988 but since then there has been a gradual decline to zero to three pairs since 2001, with no changes in land-use practices nor loss of suitable nest sites. The remains of adult birds have been found at Goshawk plucking places and remaining attempts at breeding are usually distant from Goshawk and Peregrine territories. Ian Newton in his studies on birds of prey cited 113 cases of Kestrels being taken by Goshawks.

In Radnorshire today pairs breed almost entirely around commons and moorland using mostly old corvid nests in trees and on crags as well as in nestboxes, barns and derelict buildings. A similar decline in numbers of 60% to 80% has been noted in other Welsh counties over the last 25 years or so. In 2008 at least nine pairs bred in Radnorshire, 11 occupied sites were found in 2010 and at least 14 in 2012 with some local reductions in predator pressure. It is unlikely that the present population exceeds 20 pairs compared to the 45-60 pairs of the early 1990s.

There is often a very noticeable passage of birds in August and September with birds sometimes staying for days or even weeks to feed on abundant Short-tailed Voles in 'vole plague' years. Ten were on the ridge between The Vron and Harley Valleys on 10th August 1953, 10 south-west of Llyn Heilyn on 5th September 1962, 11 at Pont ar Elan on 30th August 1998, 15 in the upper Elan Valley on 7th September 2001, 28 in the Elan and Claerwen Valleys on 6th September 2007, 24 in the same area on 2nd September 2008 and 12 on Beacon Hill on 12th September 2008. Doubtless some of these counts included locally bred birds. There were very few passage birds noted in the autumns of 2009-13. Some birds present in the county in winter are also likely to be from Fennoscandia or northern Britain, as well as ones locally bred. Some young, even from the same brood, will migrate south for the winter as far as the Mediterranean whilst others will stay locally.

Nestlings ringed in Powys have been shot or killed in their first autumns in France (2) and Spain. A nestling ringed in Buckinghamshire on 2nd June 1984 was found dead at Erwood on 22nd June 1985 and another nestling from the same county was killed by a car in August two years after ringing. A nestling ringed in Lancashire on 28th June 2005 was found freshly dead at Nantmel during a spell of cold weather on 25th November and another ringed near Abbeycwmhir on 27th June 1976 was killed by a car in Lincolnshire on 10th September (286 km ENE). Other birds ringed elsewhere and found in Powys have come from Clwyd (2), Dyfed, Gwent, Hereford & Worcester (3), Shropshire and Staffordshire and a Powys ringed bird was found in Gwent.

A nestling ringed at Keminmaa, Lappi, Finland, on 1st July 1996 was found dead for some weeks near Gilfach, north of Rhayader, on 23rd November (2,179 km SW).

Merlin *Falco columbarius*

A

Rare breeding bird; passage migrant and winter visitor.

Breeds from Iceland, the Faeroes, the British Isles and Scandinavia east across Russia to Kamchatka and the Bering Sea, south to Manchuria, northern Mongolia, Kazakhstan and Uzbekistan. Mostly migratory; wintering in USA, central and northern South America, southern, central and western Europe, the Arabian Peninsula, north-west Africa and from Afghanistan east to China and Japan.

Ingram and Salmon (1955) reported the Merlin's status as, 'a breeding bird in relatively small numbers ... thirty or so years ago its numbers were appreciably greater than they are today.'

There seems little doubt that the decline has continued due mainly to the huge losses of heather moorland in the 1960s which were replaced with improved grassland and, to a lesser extent, conifer plantations. Also corvid numbers have tripled since the mid-1970s and competition for nest sites in isolated moorland-edge trees and predation of eggs has increased as has the predation of adults and flying young by Goshawk and Peregine since the late 1980s. Organochlorine pesticides undoubtedly had some effect on Radnorshire Merlins as an egg analysed in the1970s had the highest concentration of PCBs (polychlorinated-biphenols) ever found in a Merlin's egg at the much higher than lethal level of 24.3 parts per million.

A complete and thorough survey has never been undertaken, and would be very difficult. However, in the late 1970s up to ten pairs were found whilst in the 1980s visits to previously used and likely places found six to eight in 1987, nine in 1988, 13 in 1991, seven in 1998 and 10 in 1999. Thirteen pairs were found in 2003, nine in 2006, seven in 2007, eight in 2008, 12 in 2010 but just six in 2011 and seven in 2012.

In the past nest sites were usually in old corvid nests in ffridd hawthorns and also, rarely, on the ground in extensive areas of rank heather moorland. Nesting in conifers started as early as 1956 when two nests were found in old Buzzard and Carrion Crow nests. Today, close to the edge of a conifer plantation bordering heather moorland is the commonest nesting site although hawthorns are still used, especially if the area is keepered, and nest sites have been found up to 300 metres into conifers. Old corvid nests in large, isolated, broadleaved trees such as oak or Beech in upland valley bottoms are also utilised. In 2007 a pair was found nesting in an old Magpie's nest in an overgrown hedgerow at 850 feet a.s.l. adjoining mixed farmland and bracken dominated common and another nested on the ground in an extensive area of very tussocky, rank, *Molinia* grassland.

By far the commonest prey species in the breeding season is Meadow Pipit but a surprisingly wide range of species have been recorded or remains found at plucking places including Wren, Linnet, Siskin, Redpoll, Skylark, Tree Pipit, Blackbird, Redstart, Wheatear and Whinchat, as well as Short-tailed Vole and Emperor Moth. Recently- fledged juvenile birds are very commonly taken as are young from the nest. In the autumn, flocks of Meadow Pipits are closely followed and in winter, thrushes and Starling are usually the main prey species.

Local breeding birds are usually absent from territories between August/September to mid-March. Passage birds are frequent from August to November and again in March and April and are often seen at lower elevations and along the river valleys. A few birds are recorded throughout the winter and these, and some passage birds, are more approachable, larger, darker and more heavily streaked underneath than local birds and are likely to come from the far north of Scotland, the Faeroes or Iceland.

There have been 19 recoveries elsewhere of birds ringed in Powys with birds going to Clwyd (4), Devon, Dorset, Dyfed, Eire, Glamorgan(3), Gwent, Gwynedd (2), Hampshire, Hereford & Worcester (2), Northamptonshire and Spain. Also six birds ringed elsewhere and found in Powys have come from Clwyd (2), Durham, Gwynedd, Lancashire and Northumberland.

A bird ringed as a nestling was found sick on board a ship about 200 km south of Cape Clear Island, Eire, in its first autumn. Another ringed as a nestling was found dead in Northamptonshire in its first winter and one ringed as an adult female in 1987 was found dead in early 1992 near Stamford, Lincolnshire. A nestling female ringed on 21st June 1976 was trapped and released by a bird ringer in Devon on 16th October that year and a second-year female ringed near Rhayader on 25th July 1983 was found 'shot or intentionally killed by man' at Beacon Hill, Hampshire, on 10th November. A nestling from Northumberland was found long dead in its first winter and one from Durham ringed in 2009 was hit by a car on 18th August 2010. Another nestling from Powys ringed on 18th June 2007 was hit by a car in Santander, Spain, on 13th October.

An adult female killed by a car in the Elan Valley on 13th March 1989 was found to have wet-weight concentrations in the liver of the following toxic organochlorines: 6.54 parts per million of DDE (the breakdown product of DDT), 6.75 ppm PCB (poly-chlorinated biphenols) and 0.37 ppm Dieldrin. Dry weight analysis also found 0.82 ppm of mercury, a level which can have a 10%-30% reduction in fertility. The bird could have been a migrant heading north or a local bird.

Hobby *Falco subbuteo*

Rare breeding bird and passage migrant.

A

Breeds from north-west Africa, Iberia, France and the British Isles east across most of Scandinavia, central and southern Europe, Asia east to Kamchatka and south to China. Winters in southern Africa from Tanzania and Angola to the Cape and in Burma and south-east China.

One reported by Cambridge Phillips(1899) as 'killed at Nantgwyllt' in the Elan Valley was probably the same as the one mentioned in the Woolhope *Transactions* for 1895-97 p.177.

The next record was of one seen flying across the Wye from Radnorshire into Herefordshire about half a mile upstream of Cabalva on 19th June 1954. In 1962 a pair bred in the Clyro/Bronydd area and again in 1963, but failed. At least one bird was present in the Clyro area in May and June 1964.

A bird frequented the Llandrindod Wells Golf Course area for several weeks in August and September 1970 but the next confirmed breeding was not until 1987, again in the Clyro area. Since then one to three pairs have been found each year in the lower Wye between Boughrood and Cabalva. Breeding was suspected on the Walton Plain in 1988 and 1989 and proved in 1990 since when one to five pairs have been found annually in the north-east of the county. In recent years pairs have been found in most other parts of Radnorshire including the Edw and Ithon Valleys. Although most sites are in the lowland areas, one nest site was at 1,600 feet, higher up than that of a neighbouring pair of Merlin.

Although a very difficult species to survey, three to seven pairs were found in the 1990s and since 2000 there has been a noticeable increase in summer records and a gradual increase in pairs found. In recent years birds have been seen hunting regularly in towns and villages and also nesting in and around parks and residential areas. Eight pairs were found in 2003, six in 2006 and 2007, seven in 2008, nine in 2010, 10 in 2011, just six in the awful summer of 2012 and five in 2013. Nest sites are usually in old corvid nests in isolated individual trees or clumps of conifers or mixed woodlands on lowland farmland but have also been found in Beech, oak and Sweet Chestnut and up to 100 metres into a conifer plantation. Nest sites which fail, or are disturbed, are rarely, if ever, used by the same pair in subsequent years. Birds usually arrive on territory in May and June and adults are often still bringing food to dependent young in September.

Passage birds are seen widely in May and September although records are rare in the uplands and the well wooded parts of river valleys. The earliest record was on 24th April 2010 near Presteigne and the latest on 18th October 2011 at Llowes.

Birds seen taken have included Sand Martin, Swallow, House Martin, Swift, Meadow Pipit, Tree Pipit, Skylark, Yellow Wagtail, Pied Wagtail, House Sparrow, Tree Sparrow, Linnet, Goldfinch and Redpoll as well as bats, craneflies, mayflies, dragonflies, flying ants, butterflies and moths.

A nestling colour-ringed near New Radnor on 27th July 2010 was seen at Minsmere, Suffolk, on 11th June 2011 whilst another from the same brood was found breeding in Wareham Forest, Dorset, on 2nd June 2013. Another nestling ringed near New Radnor on 29th July 2011 was found dead near Yeovil, Somerset, on 25th May 2013 and a nestling ringed near Glasbury on 5th August 2010 was found dead in the Pyrénées Atlantique, in the south-west corner of France, on 17th October of that year.

Peregrine *Falco peregrinus* A

Mainly resident breeding bird; winter visitor and passage migrant.

Breeds from Alaska and Greenland south to Tierra del Fuego and the Falklands and across most of Eurasia, Africa and Australia. Most North American, northern European and Asian birds migrate south to winter in coastal, central and South America, southern and western Europe, Africa, southern Asia and Australia.

Between 1930 and 1939 there was an average of seven pairs in Radnorshire, most ocupying sites used since the 19th century at least. In 1952 there were about six pairs but just one to two by 1955 and still only one to three in 1959. The nationwide decline shown by the B.T.O. surveys of 1961 and 1962 was found to be due to the use of organochlorine pesticides.

Following the ban on the use of most of these chemicals numbers started to recover in the early 1970s and by 1978 there were probably eight to10 pairs. Twelve pairs were found in 1985 and the same number in 1989. A thorough survey in 1991 found 22 occupied sites, 18 nesting attempts and 11 failures of which at least four were robbed of eggs or young and others lost to some very inclement weather. In 1999 18 occupied sites were found of which at least six raised young and in 2002 at least 15 pairs attempted to breed. There were 19 occupied sites in 2008, 16 in 2009, 13 in 2010 and 12 in 2011 and 2012. This recent decline seems to be due to the almost total cessation of racing pigeons passing through Radnorshire in recent years and possibly also the almost total loss of Black-headed Gulls as breeding birds in the county.

Most nest sites are in old Raven's or Carrion Crow's nests on cliff ledges or on wide ledges with some soil and vegetation or at least fine shale to hold the eggs. A huge variety of birds have been recorded as prey species in the county with a very noticeable increase in variety at some sites since the decline in racing pigeon numbers. Over 60 species have been recorded including Carrion Crow, Wood Pigeon, Feral Pigeon, Jackdaw, Magpie, Black-headed Gull, Starling, Fieldfare, Blackbird, Mistle Thrush, Cuckoo, Ring Ousel, Lapwing, Curlew, Snipe, Woodcock, Mandarin, Teal, Mallard, Goosander, Crossbill, Goldfinch, Whinchat, Great Tit, Meadow Pipit and Skylark as well as the nestlings and precocious young of several species. Rabbit, Grey Squirrel and bat sp. have been recorded and at one site the remains of a small Fox cub were found.

There have been nine recoveries of birds ringed in Powys and found elsewhere: in Avon, Cheshire, Cornwall, Dyfed, Glamorgan, Gloucestershire, Gwent, Gwynedd and Warwickshire. Also nine ringed elsewhere and found in Powys have come from Clwyd, Dyfed (2), Glamorgan (2), Gwent, Shropshire (2) and Co.Wicklow.

A nestling ringed on 9th June 1988 was found freshly dead on the Gower Peninsula on c.25th July 1988 and a nestling female ringed on 9th July 1995 was found sick or injured near Shipston-on-Stour, Warwickshire, on 22nd October 1995. Another nestling ringed on 18th May 1980 was found 'shot or intentionally killed by man' in its first winter at Dunmere Wood, Bodmin, Cornwall whilst one ringed in the Elan Valley was found dead there seven years later. A nestling was found long dead in Bristol eleven years after ringing and a nestling female ringed in County Wicklow, Eire, on 2nd June 1984 was found in Powys on 26th April 1989.

Water Rail *Rallus aquaticus* A

Rare breeding bird; passage migrant and winter visitor.

Breeds from the extreme north of Africa, Iberia, Iceland, France, the British Isles and southern Scandinavia east across much of Europe and Asia east to northern Japan, Sakhalin Island and the Lena River and south to Tibet and eastern China. Partly resident in western and southern Europe but migrates south over most of its range wintering in southern and western Europe and parts of southern Asia east to China and Japan.

Ingram and Salmon said that this species was, 'A somewhat scarce resident breeding species. Seen more often in winter.' The same can be said today.

A pair was found breeding in the county on 4th May 1903 but no site was given. A nest with 10 eggs was found at Rhosgoch Bog on 30th May 1930 and one with eight eggs there in 1950. One was shot at Michaelchurch-on-Arrow on 30th December 1950, another at Llandrindod Wells sewage farm in June 1952 with one seen nearby at Pentrosfa Mire in August.

Two nests were found at Rhosgoch in 1961 and another in 1966 when several were at Pentrosfa in December. Since 1985, breeding season records, including several of adults with young, have come from Llyn Heilyn (370 metres/1,214 feet a.s.l.), Pentrosfa Mire, Rhosgoch Bog, Llanbwchllyn, Glasbury, Clyro, Bailey Bychan, Colwyn Brook Marshes, Pencerrig Lake, the upper and lower bogs at Newbridge, Howey, Cors y Llyn, Glan Llyn, Llyn Gwyn, Nantmel and Penybont Lake. Most of these sites have also held birds in winter with several sometimes found at Newbridge lower bog (Aberithon), Rhosgoch, Llanbwchllyn and Pentrosfa e.g. seven at Llanbwchllyn on 20th December 1971 and six at Rhosgoch on 2nd February 1995. The most sites found occupied in the breeding season in any one year was 11 in 2010, with probably 14 pairs present in total. Four to eight occupied sites has been the usual number since 1990.

The species is more widespread in winter (November to February), although always scarce, with records coming over the years from all along the Wye below Rhayader (especially below Boughrood), Llandrindod Lake, Hindwell Pool, Evenjobb, Michaelchurch, the Teme and Ithon riversides and several other ponds, backwaters and lowland marshy areas as well as the breeding sites. Although several were reported to have been shot in the Elan Valley prior to 1896, the species has surprisingly not been recorded there since despite the seemingly suitable habitat around Dol y Mynach Reservoir. However, records have come from nearby at Glan Llyn, the Wye at Rhayader and beside the lower River Elan.

Spotted Crake *Porzana porzana* A

Very rare visitor which has bred.

Breeds from Spain and France to southern Fennoscandia east across Europe and Asia to north-west Mongolia. Winters in Africa south of the Sahara and northern India.

All breeding records have come from Rhosgoch Bog where it was first found in the 19th century. Following a widespread decline in north-west Europe during the late 19th and early 20th centuries the species was not recorded in Radnorshire again until 1923 when the ornithologist E.P.Chance found a broken eggshell at Rhosgoch and took a clutch of nine eggs there the following year. Two birds were also reported as being shot at Rhosgoch Bog in October 1923. A nest was found in 1929 and young were seen in 1939. There is also an undated record of breeding and of two young birds being 'procured'.

The only definite record since then was of a male calling from a rushy field at Colwyn Bridge, Hundred House, between 20th May and 15th June 1993. The rhythmic, electrical, whiplash like calls went on all night and for much of the day and local residents first contacted the electricity board as there was a sub-station nearby. When they disclaimed any responsibility the army were called in as there was a military exercise in the area at the time and perhaps the noise was coming from some sort of beacon or transmitter. The strange sound made the front page of a national newspaper. Soon after the county bird recorder was contacted and the mystery was solved. The bird remained calling from the very ordinary area of a wet field with willows and rushes for a further fortnight and was occasionally seen by visiting birdwatchers as it fed out in the open at dusk. A bird, almost certainly of this species, was seen in front of the hide at Llanbwchllyn on 9th September 1995.

(A very small crake, either **Little or Baillon's Crake**, *Porzana parva/pusilla,* was flushed at close range in an area of willows and *Phragmites* beside the River Wye about half a mile below Glasbury Bridge on 10th January 1989 but views were frustratingly poor and brief and the species could not be determined.)

Corncrake *Crex crex*

A

Former breeding bird now a very rare visitor.

Breeds from France and the British Isles and southern Scandinavia east across central Europe and Asia to Lake Baikal and the Lena River and south to Kazakhstan. Winters in eastern and south-eastern Africa.

Ingram and Salmon, writing in the mid-1950s, said that the species formerly bred commonly. Single birds were shot on Grey Partridge shoots at Cilgwyn, near Boughrood Brest, on 15th September 1897, at Llowes on 15th September 1902 and at Rhosgoch on 8th September 1902.

There were no positive breeding records in the BTO survey of 1938/39 although it was reported in 1945 that the species, 'breeds in three different localities just inside the Radnorshire border' (from Herefordshire) (*British Birds* vol.38 p.279). It is likely that this would be on the Walton Plain between New Radnor, Old Radnor and Evenjobb, and/or possibly in the lower Wye Valley.

Single birds were seen at Whitewall, near Presteigne, in September 1941 and September 1952 whilst in 1950 a pair were seen at Crossgates with calling there in July.

There have been eight records since:

1955:	One flushed in the Vron Valley on 30th April.
1955:	Pair seen and almost certainly bred successfully on a farm in the Edw Valley.
1958:	One calling in a meadow north-west of Presteigne in May.
1965:	One picked up dead at Howey on 5th May.
1966:	One calling around Dolassey, Bleddfa, for about six weeks from June to August.

1970:	One calling from a hayfield on Bryndraenog Farm, Dutlas, from late July.
1982:	One calling near Cors y Llyn, south of Newbridge, on 14th June.
1996:	One seen and heard near Painscastle on 30th April.

Moorhen *Gallinula chloropus*

A

Widespread breeding resident and winter visitor.

Breeds across much of Europe, Asia, Africa, North and South America. Resident in most parts but many northern populations are wholly migratory to within the breeding range.

The entry in Ingram and Salmon said that the species was, 'A widespread resident and breeds regularly on most lower bogs, lakes and pools, as well as on farm ponds, but rarely above 1000 feet.' Exactly the same could be said today, although this would hide the low numbers reached in the 1980s and 1990s due mostly to predation by mink.

During the late 1970s and the 1980s breeding records declined, particularly along the lower Wye and nearby ponds and backwaters, and later in the catchments of the Ithon, the upper Wye and the Elan reservoirs. On the plus side during the late 1980s and 1990s many new ponds were being created and these were gradually colonised as their vegetation developed. Also during the late 1990s major improvements were made to the attractiveness of Llandrindod Lake for wildlife resulting in lots of aquatic vegetation and four pairs of Moorhen breeding in 1997 followed by counts of up to 48 birds in December. However, the lake was sprayed later to kill the weed and this resulted in all the birds leaving for other waters. Numbers at Llandrindod Lake have now increased again with counts of 25 on 30th October 2003, 29 birds on 17th November 2007 and 23 in January 2010 and February 2012.

In the 1950s and 60s Hindwell Pool was the favoured site for Moorhen with 31 present on 4th October 1969, 42 on 25th October 1955 and 40-50 on 1st November 1959. Autumn and winter high counts reached 16-29 throughout the 1970s but mink caused a major decline at Hindwell, as elsewhere, in the early 1980s. There was a concerted round of trapping there in 1985/6 resulting in a return to counts of 15-20 birds , apart from 24 on 10th October 2005 and 22 on 10th October 2013, until 2010 since when numbers seem to have tumbled.

In the 1950s Rhosgoch Bog had up to six pairs breeding but there is little open water there now. Also some other waters have lost their attractiveness, such as Penyclawdd (1,239 feet a.s.l.) and St Michael's Pool (1,170 feet), although both still have pairs occasionally. Breeding is rare along the rivers these days and birds are also less frequently seen in the winter months. The last count of any note being 11 found along all of the river in Radnorshire by the River Wye Birds Survey on 4th February 1996. Also there have been no records in the Elan Valley in recent years since the last breeding on Dol y Mynach Reservoir in 1994 and on the hill pond at Wenrhydd (1,510 feet) in 1998.

Since 1990 breeding has been found at 48 sites in the county with at least one pair at 33 of those in 2010. In recent years up to six pairs have bred at Llandrindod Lake and, although up to three to four pairs have been found in some past years at Pencerrig Lake, Bwlchyllyn, The Begwyns Pool and St Michael's Pool, most sites just hold a single pair. One to two pairs breed annually at Llyn Heilyn (1,214 feet) but at Llanbwchllyn, where large Pike are a problem, there is usually just a single pair although it is a large and very suitable site.

Other than the counts at the major sites given above, double figure gatherings are rare with 14 at Knill Pool on 4th January 1999, 10 at Pwll Patti on 13th December 1980 and from January to March 2000, and 11 at Llanbwchllyn on 9th February 2004 and 15 at Llyn Heilyn on 19th August 2013.

A young bird of the year ringed in Denmark on 12th September 1961 was shot in Powys on 5th November and a chick ringed in the Netherlands on 19th July 1951 was found dead beside the River Wye at Erwood on 4th December 1955.

Coot *Fulica atra* A

Widespread breeding resident and winter visitor.

Breeds from north-west Africa, Iberia, France, the British Isles and southern Fennoscandia east across central Europe and Asia to the Lena River, Sakhalin, Japan, China and Korea and south to the Nile Delta, Iraq, Iran and India; also in New Guinea and Australia. Most northern European and Asian birds are migratory as far south as North Africa, India, south-east China and Indonesia.

The species was undoubtedly a much rarer breeding bird in the 1950s and 1960s than it is today although numbers were greatly increased in winter by immigrants. As with the Moorhen and some other waterbirds, feral Mink had a major impact on the local breeding population at some stes in the 1970s and 80s.

In the 1950s there were up to eight pairs at St Michael's Pool, a site which today rarely has any water, and four to five pairs at Penyclawdd Pool, a site which is also much less attractive to waterfowl today. There were also one to two pairs at Hindwell Pool, Evenjobb and Llyn Heilyn and three to four at Llanbwchllyn. In the 1960s up to six nests were found at Llyn Heilyn as well as one to two pairs at Llanwefr Pool and up to three at Pencerrig Lake. The only new breeding site found in the 1970s was at Penybont Lake. During the 1980s there were up to 12 pairs at Llyn Heilyn, seven to eight at Hindwell Pool and up to eight pairs at Pwll Patti in wet springs. Other sites with one to four pairs were Dol y Mynach Reservoir, Llandrindod Lake, Wern Fawr (Howey), Pentrosfa Mire, Stanage Park, Llyn Gwyn, Knill Pool, Glan Llyn and Park Farm Pool. Thirty nesting pairs were found in total in1981.

In the 1990s up to four pairs nested on The Begwyns pool, at Pwll Patti and at Pencerrig Lake, six pairs at Llanbwchllyn, seven at Llandrindod Lake and eight at Llyn Heilyn. One to two pairs also nested at Dol y Mynach Reservoir (until 1991) and at Llanwefr Pool with singles at Gilwern, Downton, Womaston, Llyn Gwyn, Claerwen Reservoir, Park Farm Pool, Penybont Lake and at a new farm pond on the Rhogo for the first time in 1997. A fairly complete survey in 2000 found 35 pairs at 20 sites with new sites at Brilley Common and Bwlchyllyn, as well as at several of the larger new farm ponds. Breeding attempts were occasionally reported from the slower stretches of the River Wye in the past, but not since 1989.

Although seven pairs bred on Llandrindod Lake in 1997 when there was a healthy aquatic vegetation, none did so after it was sprayed with herbicide until 2010 when two pairs attempted, rising to six in 2012 and 2013. Since 2000 pairs have bred at St Michael's Pool (2003), Gladestry, Rhosgoch Bog, Llansantffraed, Penyclawdd Pool, Hendregenny Pool and Park Farm Pool as well as five to eight pairs at Llyn Heilyn and Llanbwchllyn although production of young is usually very low at both of these sites e.g. in 2012 five pairs raised three young at Llanbwchllyn and eight pairs raised seven young at Llyn Heilyn. However, there was an unprecedented growth of Pond Water-crowfoot at Llyn Heilyn in 2013 and as a result 30 young were raised by nine pairs. A thorough survey of the county in 2010 found 36 pairs at 19 sites.

From late July and throughout August and September many birds, particularly young of the year, disperse from most breeding sites, especially the smaller ones. As a result they may turn up on non-breeding waters briefly or for the autumn and winter increasing counts at some of the larger lakes and ponds. The highest post-breeding season and winter counts at Llyn Heilyn have been 78 on 23rd November 1969, 71 in July 1970, 72 in August 1979, 70 in October 1985, 35 in October 1998, 47 on 6th August 1992, 20 in July 2001, 30 in October 2009, 33 in September 2012 and 56 on 9th August 2013. At Hindwell Pool there were 70 in mid-November 1959, 73 alive and 11 dead on 25th February 1963 (during the extremely cold weather) and 60 in November 1988. There have rarely been double-figure counts there in recent years. Llanbwchllyn held 70 birds on 31st October 1977, 48 on 21st August 1991, 40 in February 1999, 56 on 9th February 2004 and 73 on 12th September 2010.

At Llandrindod Lake the first birds were seen in 1982 after a cold winter but numbers were low until the carp were mostly removed and the lakes aquatic vegetation was allowed to develop. In 1997 there were 25 in July rising to a peak of 94 in December, the highest ever site count for Radnorshire. After the herbicide spraying of the lake in 1998 there were just 14 in December 1998 and in 2001 just a single bird was seen from 10th September. Two birds were there in February 2006 and in April 2009, six in December 2009, 14 in October 2010, up to 45 in November 2011, 53 on 23rd September 2012, 58 on 15th October and 55 on 18th December. Other notable counts have been 42 at Pwll Patti on 24th February 1981, 36 at Park Farm Pool on 13th September 1980 and 32 on the River Wye below Glasbury during very cold weather in February 1979. A county-wide count on 6th/7th January 1984 found 105 birds at 8 sites.

A young bird of the year ringed in the Netherlands on 6th December 1969 was found dead in Powys two weeks later.

Oystercatcher *Haematopus ostralegus*

A

Very rare breeder and uncommon passage migrant.

Breeds from Iceland, the Faeroes, the British Isles and the coasts of Europe from Russia to Portugal and east to Turkey. Also inland in Russia and Asia east to the Pechora River and Turkestan as well as Kamchatka and eastern China. Resident in western Europe otherwise migratory to coastal northern Africa, the Arabian Peninsula, India and southern China.

The first record was of three birds beside the River Wye at Erwood on 2nd September 1903 and the second was along the Wye four miles above Rhayader in March 1927.

There were three records in the 1950s, at Rhiw Pool, Pant y Dwr and in the Elan Valley; seven in the 1960s (including six beside Penygarreg Reservoir on 1st August 1961) and five in the 1970s. It seems likely that breeding first took place along the Wye below Glasbury in the 1980s but was first proven in 1990. Since then one to three pairs have attempted along the lower Wye between Boughrood and Cabalva annually but with poor breeding success mainly due to the almost daily disturbance by groups of canoes landing downstream of Glasbury. Breeding birds usually arrive from mid-January to early March and have usually departed by late August.

Away from the lower Wye there were 13 records in the 1980s including seven at Llyn Heilyn on 29th July 1986. The nine records in the 1990s included one at Llyn Heilyn on 19th April 1993 which was killed by a pair of Coot. Between 2000 and 2013 there were 20 records away from the lower Wye including a flock of 22 at Llyn Heilyn on 13th March 2011, by far the largest group seen in the county.

There have been 32 records from the Elan and Claerwen reservoirs and six from Llyn Heilyn. Other records have come from Howey, Llanyre, Landrindod Lake, Llandrindod Wells, the River Ithon at Penybont, the Wye at Llanelwedd (2), Nantmel, Doctor's Pool, Llyn Gwyn, Presteigne and Abbeycwmhir. Records have come in every month with the most in July(10) and August(9).

A chick ringed in Shetland was found freshly dead in Powys in July four years later.

Avocet *Recurvirostra avosetta*

Very rare visitor.

A

Breeds in parts of Africa, Europe and Asia east to Mongolia. Winters in Africa, India and China.

The only records are of three on a backwater of the River Wye between Glasbury and Llowes on 6th July 2010 and two at the same place on 8th August 2011, which were almost certainly two of the birds seen the year before. It seems likely that these birds originated from the small breeding population recently established at Upton Warren, Worcestershire.

Stone-curlew *Burhinus oedicnemus*

Very rare visitor

A

Breeds from northern Africa, Iberia, France and England east across southern and central Europe and south-west Asia east across Kazakhstan, also India, Sri Lanka, Burma and Thailand. Most European and central Asian birds migrate to Africa.

The only record is of one at Maelinydd on 20th August 1980.

Cream-coloured Courser *Cursorius cursor*

Very rare visitor.

A

Breeds on the Canary Islands, parts of northern Africa, Syria, Turkey and Iraq east to Afghanistan. Partly migratory to sub-Saharan Africa, Saudi Arabia and north-west India.

There has been one record. An adult was present on Bradnor Hill Golf Course, Herefordshire, from 18th to 23rd May 2012 when it left at about 11.30am flying high south-west over Stanner into Radnorshire. The third record for Wales.

Little Ringed Plover *Charadrius dubius* A

Very rare breeding bird and passage migrant.

Breeds from north-west Africa, Iberia, France, the British Isles and Fennoscandia east across Europe and Asia to China, Japan, India, the Philippines and New Guinea. Winters across central Africa south of the Sahara and south-east Asia.

The first record was of a pair below Glasbury in May 1977 after which one to two pairs bred in the same area in most years until 1990. During the 1990s, three to five pairs were found in suitable areas along the lower Wye rising to six in 2001 and eight in 2002. Seven pairs were found early in the season in 2003, four to five from 2004 to 2011, three in 2012 and three in 2013. Not all pairs attempt to breed and breeding success is low due mainly to the increasingly frequent landing of groups of canoes on shingle banks. Young from repeat clutches have been hatched as late as the first week of August.

Most birds arrive in the second half of April and have left by mid-August. The earliest arrival was on 15th March 2009 and the latest was seen on 14th September 1991.

Away from the lower Wye there have been just ten records: Maelinydd on 2nd April 1988, Llyn Heilyn on 17th June 1991 and 1st September 1995, a pair at The Begwyns pool on 13th June 1996, by the Wye at Llanelwedd on 12th April 2004 and five records from the Elan Valley. Four of those were in late May and early June 1997 and came from the upper River Elan above the reservoirs between 22nd and 27th May (one to two birds at two sites), beside Craig Goch Reservoir on 23rd May and from the north end of the Claerwen Reservoir from 30th May to 4th June. The other record was at Pont ar Elan on 3rd June 2006.

Ringed Plover *Charadrius hiaticula* A

Rare passage migrant.

Breeds from north-east Arctic Canada and Greenland, Iceland, the Faeroes, the British Isles and Scandinavia east across Russia to the Bering Sea. Partly resident in Britain, other populations are migratory to Britain, the Mediterranean, Africa and the Persian Gulf.

The first record was of one shot at Rhiw Pool on 3rd September 1926 and the second was found dead near Knighton on 19th May 1930.

There were three in the Elan Valley on 1st May 1960 and since then there have been a further eight records from there, 31 from the Glasbury/Llowes area, four from Llyn Heilyn and others from Llyn Gwyn, Ireland Pool, Llanbwchllyn, Aberedw Hill and Maelinydd (2).

Most records have been of one to three birds apart from four at Glasbury on 18th April 1977, five at Llanbwchllyn on 19th and 20th August 1967 (when the lake was being drained), six to nine at Glasbury/Llowes between 22nd and 30th April 2012 (involving at least 12 birds) and five there on 4th May 2012 which showed the characters of birds which breed in north-east Canada and Greenland, as did another three there on 12th May.

The total of 53 records have been in February (2), April (13), May (18), June (4), July (4), August (6) and September (6). The earliest record was of a bird found freshly dead beside the River Wye near Hay on 10th February 1991 which had been ringed as a young bird of the year in Norway on 31st August 1980. The only other February record was also in 1991, at Llyn Heilyn on 25th. The latest record was one at Glasbury on 16th September 2009.

Dotterel *Charadrius morinellus* A

Rare passage migrant.

Breeds locally in Scotland, the Netherlands, Fennoscandia, Austria, Poland and Italy across Arctic Russia to the Bering Sea, also central Russia from the Altai Mountains east to the Stanovoy Range. Winters from north-west Africa and the Mediterranean east to Iraq and the Persian Gulf.

There have been 14 records:

1952:	Five at Penrhiw-wen, east of Craig Goch Reservoir, on 10th May.
1987:	Six above the Claerwen Dam on 26th April.
1987:	Three on Llanbedr Hill on 29th April.
1987:	Four above Rhulen on 2nd May.
1993:	Ten near Llanbedr Hill on 10th May.
1999:	Six east of Ireland Well from 2nd to 4th May.
1999:	Two east of Ireland Well on 22nd May.
1999:	Two on Beacon Hill on 22nd May.
2004:	One west of Garreg Ddu Reservoir on 15th September.
2008:	Three on Red Hill on 9th May.
2010:	Three on Aberedw Hill on 10th May.
2011:	Four near Black Mixen on 30th April.
2011:	Two on The Begwyns on 4th May.
2011:	Four above Llyn Heilyn on 10th May.

Golden Plover *Pluvialis apricaria* A

Rare breeding bird; widespread passage migrant and winter visitor.

Breeds from Iceland, the Faeroes, the British Isles and Fennoscandia east across northern Russia to the Yenesei and the Central Siberian Plateau. Winters in parts of north-west Europe and around the Mediterranean.

Walpole-Bond writing in his book '*Bird Life in Wild Wales*' (London, 1903) records a pair breeding on Aberedw Hill in May 1902 and finding a pair with a young bird there on 29th June 1903. Ingram and Salmon(1955) said that occasional pairs had been seen on the moorlands above the Elan Valley. This, coupled with the lack of any reference to birds seen or shot in the summer in the 19th century suggests that the species has always been a rare or very rare breeding bird in the county. They also stated that it was 'frequent on the hills north of Painscastle in winter' – as it is today. Occasional birds were shot in that area between 1872 and 1934 on The Begwyns, Ireland Moor and at Rhosgoch Bog. One to four birds were shot on 11 dates, eight were seen on The Begwyns on 22nd October 1927 and 13th October 1930, and 13 on 6th February 1872.

A nest with eggs was found above the Claerwen Reservoir on 6th June 1971 and surveys carried out between 1975 and 1978 found 30 pairs in the Radnorshire part of the Elan uplands in 1976 as well as two pairs on Aberedw Hill, one on Llanbedr Hill and two in the far north of the county. Surveys since then in the Elan uplands found 24 pairs in 1990, 19 in 1991, 11 in 1992, 19-22 in 1995, 14 in 2001, 11 in 2002, seven in 2007 and eight in 2009 and 2010. Figures for the eight square kilometres of the most suitable habitat have been eight pairs in 1976, 15 in 1982, eight in 1990, six in 1991 and 1992, five in 1993, 15 in 1995, five in 2004 and 2007 and six in 2009 and 2010. Accurate surveying is far from easy and sequential breeding has been recorded.

The two high count years of 1982 and 1995 were following more than usual large-scale burning of the upland grasslands during the late winter which created a lot of suitable short habitat for the following spring. Other than those two years, numbers in the core areas have therefore been remarkably stable. Declines elsewhere are undoubtedly due to less heavy grazing and burning than in the 1970s and 80s, a threefold increase in Carrion Crow and Raven numbers since the mid-1970s, increased predation by birds of prey, diseases carried by (and heavy infestations of) sheep ticks which can kill small young, and a very noticeable reduction in crane-fly larvae in recent decades.

Away from the Elan uplands one to six pairs are recorded in total in most years from Aberedw Hill, Llanbedr Hill, Glascwm Hill, Ireland Moor and Radnor Forest. An old report from 1902, without detail, of breeding at Penybont could possibly refer to the nearby Llandegley Rhos rather than the less likely Penybont Common. As well as the declines in breeding numbers there are also lower passage and winter numbers today than in the past. Examples of counts from the 1960s include 300+ on Maelinydd on 31st March 1961 (of which about half showed characters of the northern type '*altifrons*' which predominate from northern Scandinavia eastwards), 300 at Four Stones on 29th November 1964, 300 at Boughrood on 10th November 1968, 600 at Four Stones on 8th October 1969 and 500 at Llowes on 23rd December 1969. There were also widespread sightings of flocks of 30-150 birds elsewhere.

Counts throughout much of the 1970s were similar e.g. 60 at Four Stones on 13th December 1971, 350 at Crossgates on 1st February 1974, 250 at Maelinydd on 31st March 1974 and 3-500 at Glasbury in November 1977. The late 1970s however saw a dramatic decline with the only significant counts being 350 at Four Stones in November 1978 and 200 at Glasbury in late October 1979. In the 1980s there was just a single three-figure count (100 at Brynthomas on 5th December 1981) with 30-70 seen occasionally at Maelinydd and Four Stones. In the 1990s a flock of 50-80 was sometimes seen on the hills north of Painscastle in winter but the only counts of over 100 were 150 flying south over Disserth on 17th November 1995 and 120 heading west over Radnor Forest on 28th December 1995.

Since 2000 there has been a very noticeable increase in winter records with some larger flocks and much more widespread smaller groups. There were 350 near the source of the River Teme on 20th March 2001, 300 on The Begwyns on 25th October 2001, 140 at Drysgol Fields on 10th October 2003 and 2-300 on The Begwyns on 5th November 2004. Rhos Hill held 200 for much of November 2005 and there were 270 at Rhos y Meirch, near Knighton, in February 2006. There were 130 on Rhulen Hill on 13th February 2007 and 270 on Hergest Ridge on 8th November 2008 – a flock which was usually just over the border into Herefordshire. In 2009 a flock of 140 flew over Llandrindod Wells on 12th February and in 2011 there were 240 were on Llandeilo Hill on 18th October 2011, 140 at Waun Hirwaun on 22nd March and 100 on Llandeilo Hill on 16th February. There were 110 at Bwlch y Sarnau on 20th March 2012 and of the 166+ on The Begwyns on 22nd April 2012 and the 250 there on 20th April 2013 many were northern type birds in full summer plumage, as indeed are many of the birds seen on passage through the county in March and April flocks.

Favoured feeding grounds are the extensive areas of flat or gently sloping, short, semi-improved, acid grasslands of the hills and commons with areas cut for bracken baling being particularly attractive. On passage and in cold, snowy, weather, large lowland improved grassland and arable fields, such as on the Walton Plain and in the major river valleys, are sometimes visited, often in the company of Lapwings. Very short heather moorland is also occasionally frequented, especially where burning has taken place within the previous few years. There is undoubtedly a lot of movement of flocks around the county during the autumn and winter months and exchange of birds with Montgomeryshire to the north and Herefordshire to the east. The most settled flocks are those where human disturbance, in all its forms, is low and where attacks by birds of prey are infrequent and nocturnal predation by Foxes is rare. Like the winter visiting thrushes, many Golden Plovers leave the county from December onwards, especially as a result of very cold and/or snowy weather. As ringing has shown elsewhere in Britain, they move on as far south as France, Iberia and Morocco.

A first-winter bird ringed in the Netherlands on 14th March 2009 and re-caught near Llaith Ddu on 12th December 2009 was the first Dutch ringed Golden Plover to be found in Wales and another ringed in Belgium on 22nd March 2011 was caught near Bwlch y Sarnau on 23rd October 2011 (442 km WNW). A bird ringed in north Powys in November 2012 was found in Spain in December. It is likely that wintering and passage birds to Radnorshire are a mixture of Fennoscandian and Russian breeders plus some British and Icelandic birds.

Grey Plover *Pluvialis squatarola* A

Very rare visitor.

Breeds on Arctic tundra from the Kanin Peninsula in Russia east across Siberia to the Bering Sea and in Arctic North America from Alaska east to Baffin Island.

There have been two records, both along the River Wye betwen Glasbury and Llowes. One on 14th May 1994 and four on 4th November 1996.

Lapwing *Vanellus vanellus*

A

Rare and declining, mostly resident, breeding bird; uncommon passage migrant and winter visitor.

Breeds from the Faeroes, the British Isles, Iberia and Scandinavia east and south across most of Europe and Asia south to Turkey, Georgia and northern Iran and east to Mongolia and Manchuria. Northern and central continental populations are migratory south and west to the British Isles, France, Spain and parts of North Africa and north-west India to southern China and Japan.

Ingram and Salmon (1955) reported that numbers had, 'diminished greatly in the past 25-30 years' and that the species was widely distributed from the lower farms and bogs up to moorland at about 1,500 feet.

In the 1960s and 70s there were still at least 900-1,000 pairs breeding in Radnorshire although the decline was continuing year on year. Impressive flocks were still frequent: 650 at Four Stones in November 1960, 1,200 at Llowes in August 1962, 600 on Glog Hill in October 1964, 300 on Stonewall Hill in July 1965, 200 beside Craig Goch Reservoir in early September 1968, 1,500+ near St Michael's Pool following the plough on 28th June 1969, 1,000 on Maelinydd in August and September 1969, 1,000 at Llowes in December 1969, 500 near Craig Goch Reservoir on 2nd August 1970, 1,000 at Maelinydd and 800 near Rhayader in August 1970, 1,200 at Crossgates in November 1971, 1,100 near Walton in December 1972, 2,300 at Crossgates in February 1974, 2,000 at Maelinydd in August 1974, 1,500 at Crossgates in January 1975, 1,000 at Glasbury in August 1978 and 1,000 at Llandrindod in August 1979.

By the mid-1980s breeding numbers had declined to between 350 and 450 pairs. Large flocks were rare with the only four-figure counts in the 1980s being 1,000 at Boughrood in July 1980, a cold weather movement of 1,400 flying south-west over Glasbury in January 1987 and 1,000 near Cabalva in January 1989. Post-breeding season flocks of several hundreds were still often seen: 500 at Dolau in September 1981, 500 at Penybont in August 1982, 500 at Maelinydd in August 1983, 450 at Glasbury in August 1985, 325 at Glasbury Farm in August 1987 and 250 at Glasbury in August 1989. The speed of the decline in the mid-1980s is well shown by a survey of a large sample area which found 102 pairs in 1984 but just 63 pairs when repeated in 1986.

The decline continued throughout the 1990s with only about 140 pairs in the county in 1997 and barely 100 in 1998. Fewer than 85 pairs were found in the early season of 2000, below 50 in 2003, 35-40 in 2005, 22 in 2007, 24 in 2008, 22 pairs on territory in April 2009, 26 pairs in 2010, 19 in 2011 and just 17-21 in 2013. Since the early 1990s many pairs have not stayed long on territory in the early spring, often only a week or two, made no attempt at breeding and left before early May.

Large, post-breeding season flocks are now a thing of the past with the last of three figures being 150 at Glasbury in July 1992. There are still occasional records of late autumn and winter flocks of more than 100 comprised of visiting or passage birds, often during cold and snowy spells of weather: 600 flew south over Llandrindod on 15th February 1994, 300 flew south over Bettws on 5th February 1996, 600 flew south over Crossgates on 28th December 1995 and 150 south over Rhayader on 24th December 1995. From January to March 1996 there were 200 at Glasbury/Llowes, 100 at Glasbury in November 1997, 370 at Glasbury in November 1995, 250 at Glasbury in late January 1995 and 200 at Llowes in late October 1993.

Since 2000 there have been some sightings of flocks of between 50 and 95 birds most years, usually during cold weather, and a flock of 310 in a field near Kinnerton in cold weather on 2nd January 2010: 95 were at Glasbury on 14th December 2002, 70 flew west over Gladestry on 4th January 2001, 60 were on Stonewall Hill on 7th December 2001, 60 at Evenjobb in snowy weather on 25th February 2005, 60 at Llandrindod Wells on 16th December 2007, 80 flying high over Llanyre on 4th January 2008, 70 west over New Radnor on 12th February 2009, 75 heading south there during cold weather on 22nd December 2009, 65 at Pwl Patti on 30th December 2009 and 60 at St Harmon on 30th January 2012. A flock of local breeding birds has spent the winter in the Crossgates/Llanyre/Llanelwedd area for many years but has declined from 40-60 in the 1980s and 1990s to 12-18 in 2011/12.

Local declines in breeding populations have been documented for several areas: Around the Elan reservoirs there were 26 pairs in the Radnorshire part in the mid-1970s, 12 in 1989 and just one in 1994. From 1995 to 2012 there were just four years when a single pair held territory or attempted breeding and the species is not recorded at all there in most years. On Maelinydd there were 33 pairs in 1981, 26 in 1983, 20 in 187, 15 in 1991, 12 in 1996, four in 1999, three in 2002 and one to two pairs have held territory or attempted to breed most years from 2005-2013. In the Gladestry area there were six to 10 pairs in the late 1970s and early 1980s, two in 1987 but none after 1991. In the upper Edw Valley above Hundred House there were 18 pairs in 1987, six in 1992, one in 1995 but none since 1996. A study in the area south and west of Llandrindod Wells found 25 pairs in 1994 but just four or five in 2000 with no young raised and just 12-18 young fledged in the seven years. At Plas Warren there were 10 pairs in 2000, eight in 2001 and one in 2002. However, careful mixed farming with a significant and appropriate arable content can reverse the trend locally, at least for a time. At Penywrlodd, Clyro, there was a single pair in 1996, two in 1997, at least four in 1998, six in 1999, four in 2003 and 2004, two or three in 2005 but none since. Also intensive gamekeeping on grouse moorlands resulted in temporary local increases in breeding numbers in the 1990s.

The causes of these declines include the widespread drainage of damp, rushy fields, the huge increase in sheep numbers, loss of mixed agriculture and, especially, the reduction in cattle numbers. Perhaps most significant has been the threefold increase in corvid numbers and other ground predators since the mid-1970s.

A chick ringed in the Elan Valley in 1988 was 'found dead' in the Gironde, France, in its third winter whilst two ringed near Llandewi in 1927 were both shot in Spain – one in its first winter and the other in its seventh. A chick ringed in Sweden has also been found in winter in mid-Wales.

Knot *Calidris canutus*

A

Very rare visitor.

Breeds near the coast in parts of the high Arctic of Canada, Greenland, central and eastern Siberia. Winters, usually in high concentrations, from the British Isles and Iberia south around the West African coast to South Africa, also the southern USA, Chile and Argentina, New Guinea, Australia and New Zealand.

There have been two records: A winter-plumaged bird beside the Claerwen Reservoir on 19th February 2009 and an adult in summer plumage at Llyn Heilyn on 18th May 2011.

Sanderling *Calidris alba*

A

Very rare visitor.

Breeds in the high Arctic of Canada, Greenland and the northern Taimyr Peninsula in Siberia. Winters around coasts of the British Isles, Denmark, France, Iberia and the Mediterranean, Africa, southern Asia, Australasia, North and South America; also inland in parts of central and East Africa.

Thee have been four records:

2000:	Beside the River Wye below Glasbury on 13th May.
2008:	Between Glasbury and Llowes from 16th to 18th May.
2009:	Between Glasbury and Llowes on 14th May.
2010:	A juvenile at the top of Craig Goch Reservoir on 29th August.

Little Stint *Calidris minuta*

A

Very rare visitor.

Breeds from northern Norway and the Kola Peninsula east across Arctic Russia to the New Siberian Islands. Winters from Iberia and the Mediterranean throughout much of Africa and around the coasts of the Arabian Peninsula east to Bangladesh.

There have been ten records:

1968:	One by the River Wye near Llowes on 26th May.
1971:	One beside Caergynan Pool, Maelinydd, on 8th August.
1991:	A juvenile at Llyn Heilyn on 7th and 8th September.
1992:	One below Glasbury on 2nd June.
1993:	Two by a pool on Aberedw Hill on 6th September.
1993:	One at Llanbwchllyn on 7th September.
1993:	One at Caergynan Pool, Maelinydd, on 16th September.
1995:	Two at Llyn Heilyn on 24th August.
1996:	Two on 21st and three on 22nd September between Glasbury and Llowes.
2011:	A juvenile at Llanbwchllyn on 7th September.

Temminck's Stint *Calidris temminckii*

A

Very rare visitor.

Breeds from Norway and northern Sweden and Finland east around the Kola Peninsula and across Arctic Russia to the Bering Straits. Winters around parts of the Mediterranean and the Nile Valley and Delta and central Africa east to south-east China and the Malay Peninsula.

There have been two records: One by Caergynan Pool, Maelinydd, on 19th May 1993 and one around an oxbow of the River Wye near Llowes on 2nd and 3rd May 2010.

Curlew Sandpiper *Calidris ferruginea* A

Very rare visitor.

Breeds in Arctic Russia from the Taimyr Peninsula east to the Kolyma Delta. Winters in sub-Saharan Africa, including coastal Madagascar, and along coasts from the Arabian Peninsula east to south-east China, Indonesia and Australia.

There have been two records: One in near full summer plumage was at Caergynan Pool, and a nearby smaller pool, at Maelinydd on 23rd July 1961 and a juvenile was at Dol y Mynach Reservoir on 20th August 1989.

Purple Sandpiper *Calidris maritima* A

Very rare visitor.

Breeds north-east Arctic Canada, Greenland, Iceland, the Faeroes, northern and western Fennoscandia and the north coast of the Kola Peninsula, Bear Island, Svalbard, Novaya Zemlya and the northern coast of the Taimyr Peninsula. Winters on the coast around northern and western Scandinavia, the Kola Peninsula, Germany and Denmark, the Faeroes, and the British Isles south to north-western Spain and Portugal.

There have been four records:

1987:	One around Llandrindod Lake on 25th March.
2002:	One by the River Wye underneath Glasbury Bridge on 22nd March.
2002:	One by the River Wye beween Glasbury and Llowes on 15th April.
2011:	One below the Claerwen Dam from 14th to 16th September.

Dunlin *Calidris alpina* A

Rare breeding bird and scarce passage migrant.

Breeds from eastern Greenland, Iceland, the Faeroes and the British Isles east across parts of Fennoscandia and Arctic Russia east to the Bering Sea, north-west Alaska and parts of north-east Canada. Winters mainly around the coasts of north-west Europe, the Mediterranean, North Africa and the Arabian Peninsula to north-west India and south-east China.

'Young birds' were 'found on the hills above Llanfaredd' (Aberedw Hill) on 29th June 1903 and the species was recorded as having bred on the hills above the Edw Valley in 1939, which would have been either Aberedw Hill, Llandeilo Hill or Llanbedr Hill. One was found dead at Llanwefr Pool on 27th April 1929 and in 1930, 1932 and 1934 there were records there in late April of adults in breeding plumage, and at nearby Llyn Heilyn on 3rd May 1935, which suggested breeding on Llandegley Rhos. Although there were no records in between, a nest and four eggs was found at Llandegley Rhos on 12th May 1974. The only other breeding records have come from Radnor Forest in 1994,1995 and 2011 and from the Elan uplands where 13 pairs were found in the Radnorshire part in 1976, 18 pairs in 1982, 12 in 1990, 14-18 in 1995, six to eight in 2002, five to 11 in 2003, six in 2007 and 2010, four in 2008 and five in 2009. As with Golden Plover, numbers in the best habitat have changed little in recent years.

Passage birds have been recorded in every month with six records in January, three in February, six in March, nine in April, 28 in May, three in June, 19 in July, 27 in August, 14 in September and singles in October, November and December. By far the most records have come from the Glasbury to Llowes area (70), especially in recent years since changes in the route of the River Wye has created some new backwaters. Other records have come from Maelinydd (14) and Llyn Heilyn (10) with others at The Begwyns (4) and Llanelwedd (2), as well as several around the Elan and Claerwen reservoirs probably not related to local breeders.

Most records are of single birds with about a third of two to five together. There have been 12 records of 10 birds or more:

1975:	21 at Maelinydd on 7th September.
1995:	30, all adults, at Maelinydd from 26th July to 2nd August.
1999:	50 rested briefly on the hilltop north of Pont ar Elan on 23rd November.
2003:	10 at Glasbury on 31st March.
2009:	12 between Glasbury and Llowes on 14th May.
2009:	11 as above on 15th September.
2010:	11 as above on 12th August.
2011:	14 at Maelinydd on 16th July.
2011:	14 between Glasbury and Llowes on 22nd July.
2011:	15 as above on 18th September.
2012:	32 as above on 29th April.
2012:	11 as above on 11th May.

Passage birds have shown a wide variety of plumage types and biometrics and it is likely that they include birds of the three subspecies, *arctica, alpina* and *schinzii.*

Ruff *Philomachis pugnax*

Very rare visitor.

A

Breeds from the British Isles (rarely), the Netherlands and Scandinavia east across northern Europe and Asia to the River Kolyma. Winters around the coasts of India and the Arabian Peninsula, central Turkey, locally around the coasts of the Mediterranean and north-west Europe and throughout much of sub-Saharan Africa.

There have been five records of single birds:

1970:	On an exposed mud bank at top end of Craig Goch Reservoir on 2nd August.
1986:	By the River Wye between Glasbury and Llowes on 28th August.
2009:	On a backwater of the Wye near Llowes on 6th July.
2010:	As above on 26th July.
2011:	On exposed mud during drought at Llanbwchllyn on 7th September.

Jack Snipe *Lymnocryptes minimus*

Uncommon winter visitor and passage migrant.

A

Breeds from northern Fennoscandia east across northern Russia to the Kolyma Peninsula. Winters from the Britsh Isles and Denmark south to Iberia and around the Mediterranean, parts of northern and sub-Saharan Africa, around the Persian Gulf and the southern end of the Caspian Sea, also locally east to India, the Malay Peninsula and south-east China.

Ingram and Salmon(1955) gave its status as,'a regular but not numerous winter visitor.' The same could be said today for this inconspicuous wader but there is no doubt that it has been increasing here since about 1990 and judging from shooting records of the late 19th and early 20th centuries it was perhaps much commoner then.

The species has been recorded from over 50 sites from the lower Wye Valley to over 2,000 feet on Radnor Forest and is particularly widespread in the north of the county. Typically most records are of single birds flushed at very close range on open, wet and rushy, ground but birds have been put up from a wide variety of wet places including roadside ditches and around garden ponds. Daytime roosts, usually with Snipe, are regular at a number of very wet sites including Rhosgoch Bog, Rhiw Bottom and Pentrosfa Mire.

Although 90% of records are of single birds, three to eight birds have been recorded from one to four sites each winter since 1994 and prior to then three were below Glasbury in March 1980 and four were at Nantmel on 5th December 1971. Double-figure counts made using dragged ropes have been; at Rhiw Bottom, 14 on 22nd December 2011 and 10 on 8th January 1999; at Pentrosfa Mire, 16 on 3rd December 2000 and 12 on 21st November 2004; and at Rhosgoch Bog, 14 on 10th January 1993. Other regular sites are Beacon Hill, Maelinydd, Garreg Llwyd, The Begwyns, the upper Elan Valley, Pwll Patti and the lower Wye, Llanbwchllyn, Llyn Heilyn and Moelfre. Individual birds are often very faithful to very small sites. One bird returned to a short length of rushy wet ditch on The Begwyns for three successive winters.

The majority of records come from the months of November to March. There have been just three records in the first half of October, with the earliest being one on Maelinydd on 1st October 1971, and two in the second half of April, the latest being on Beacon Hill on 29th April 1962.

Snipe *Gallinago gallinago* A

Uncommon but widespread breeding bird; frequent passage migrant and winter visitor.

Breeds from Iceland, the British Isles, France and Scandinavia east across Europe and Asia to far eastern Russia and south to Kazakhstan and northern China. Also much of Canada, the northern USA, South America and eastern and southern Africa. Northern populations are migratory to South and Central America, southern and western Europe, sub-Saharan Africa and southern Asia east to Japan and the Philippines.

The Maesllwch Estate game books record that several visits were made most years between 1870 and 1935 to Rhosgoch Bog to shoot Snipe. A total of 1,610 birds were shot over 41 seasons with the most being 112 in 1871 and 86 in 1910. The most shot in a day was 26 on the opening day of the Snipe season (1st August) in 1902 with 15-19 on eight other August dates and 19 on 12th December 1911. It is likely that well over 100 birds were often present at Rhosgoch Bog during the autumn and winter in those days. The site was also important for breeding birds as 'considerable numbers', as well as a nest with eggs, were found there by members of the Woolhope Naturalists Field Club on 30th May 1911.

The species was also undoubtedly a much commoner breeding bird in the past than it is today due to the widespread drainage of land which has taken place, especially since the 1950s. However, it is still frequent in the wetter areas of upland moorland and bog throughout the county, as well as on most lowland bogs, mires and wet commons.

The largest population today by far is in the Elan uplands, a large unimproved drinking water catchment area which has not been subjected to the extensive drainage works elsewhere. In a survey in 1995 there were 25 territory holding birds found in the Radnorshire parts, 22 in 2008 and 26 in 2009. Within this wider area, a survey of the area around Craig Goch Reservoir and along the upper River Elan found at least 12-15 drumming birds in 2005 and 12 there on 6th May 2008. A survey of 12 of the best sites in the county in April and May 2010 found 44 drumming birds. At least 100 pairs probably breed in Radnorshire today.

On Maelinydd Common seven to eight pairs were regular in the 1970s and early 1980s but only three to four were found in 1998 and 2010. Similarly Penybont Common was more attractive in the past with several pairs in the 1960s and 70s but just one to two since 2000. Rhosgoch Bog had eight to 10 drumming birds in 1998 and seven in 2010 although the encroachment and growth of willows is slowly reducing the area of suitable habitat. This is also a problem at a number of other lowland sites where Snipe breed including Pentrosfa Mire and Llanbwchllyn which both still had single drumming birds in 2010. A few pairs also breed annually at Moelfre Turbary, the St David's Well area, Rhosfallog, Cwmmaerdy and Rhiw Bottom. Many wetter, rushy areas with wet flushes and impeded drainage also have breeding birds, including Beacon Hill, The Begwyns, Gwaunceste Hill, Disgwylfa Hill, Aberedw Hill, Llanbedr Hill and at Radnor Forest up to 1,900 feet.

Post breeding season groups are sometimes encountered, e.g. 32 at Penyclawdd on 29th August 1970 and 13 on Maelinydd on 2nd August 1988. Autumn passage and the influx of winter visitors from the north and east is not usually noticeable until the end of September with the peak in October and early November. Many birds undoubtedly pass through quickly whilst others stay for the winter unless severe freezing weather arrives and they move off south or to the coast.

High counts are mainly recorded in late autumn and mid-winter when the species is much more widely distributed and numbers are increased several fold by immigrants from the Continent and northern Britain. At Rhosgoch Bog there were 90+ on 10th October 1991, 95 there on 16th December 2007, 85 on 22nd November 2008 and there have also been many other counts there of 40-75. As well as at Rhosgoch there have also been winter roosts regularly in the Glasbury area of 30-70 birds, at Rhiw Bottom of 20-45 and at Pentrosfa Mire of 15-80. There was a count of 'about 100' put up by a shoot in the Llandrindod Wells area on 3rd November 1979 which was probably at Pentrosfa Mire. Other notable counts have been 40 in marshy fields near Gladestry on 25th November 1966, 20 on the Blue Lins on 26th October 1969, 40+ on Penybont Common on 27th February 1971 and 20 at Brynderllwyn Bog on 29th December 1979.

Daytime winter feeding flocks are rare with birds usually dispersing widely from roosts but 25 were found feeding on a stubble field at Clyro on 18th February 2004 and 10-15 there on 22nd March 2007. Single birds are often flushed from dry areas of bracken and rank grass in autumn and winter as well as from wet places a small area of which can often hold a bird or two for long periods.

A bird ringed in Sweden was found dead near Llandrindod Wells on 31st December 1971. Two other young birds of the year ringed in Sweden in July have been found in mid-Wales in late September and December and a bird ringed in Germany in October was shot here in late November.

Woodcock *Scolopax rusticola* A

Rare breeding bird; widespread and not uncommon passage migrant and winter visitor.

Breeds from Scandinavia, the British Isles, northern Iberia, the Azores, Canaries and Madeira, east across Europe and Asia to Sakhalin, Manchuria and Japan and south to include parts of the Crimea, Georgia, Kazakhstan, north-east China and northern India. Resident in milder parts of its range but most populations are migratory to western and southern Europe and the Mediterranean east across India and China to the Malay Peninsula and the Philippines.

The earliest records come from the game books of the larger estates where birds were sometimes shot during Pheasant drives. The Maesllwch game books show that the species never seems to have been common, even in winter, in the woodlands and dingles between Boughrood and Llowes with just 359 birds shot over 40 years between 1870 and 1935, and no more than 19 in any one year.

On the Doldowlodd beats in the Nant Glas, Llanyre, Llandrindod Wells and Newbridge areas a total of 1,872 birds were shot over 81 years between 1897 and 1990. The most in a year was 87 in 1982 and the highest day total was 28 on 23rd January 1981. Counts made on these Pheasant drives have included 30+ on 30th December 1968, 38 on 27th January 1977 and over 100 on 27th and 28th December 1984.

Ingram and Salmon said in 1955 that the species bred regularly in a few suitable localities and was fairly numerous in winter whilst W.B.Alexander in his papers in *Ibis* between 1945 and 1947 on *'The Woodcock in The British Isles'* said that it was confined as a breeding bird to east Radnorshire, based on the national survey of 1934/5. Although never a common breeding bird in the county, and unknown as such until towards the end of the 19th century, there has undoubtedly been a reduction in some areas since the early 1980s and perhaps an increase in others.

The huge increase in new conifer plantations between 1950 and 1980 led to more widespread breeding season records by the end of the 1960s, albeit at low densities. The drainage and felling of many wet native woodlands on the other hand reduced suitable habitat at the same time. Breeding season records in the 1950s, 60s and 70s were typically just one to two per year e.g. four roding birds at Stanage Park on 12th June 1971, nest and two eggs at Cwmcynydd on 5th May 1958, two roding near Newbridge on 27th June 1976. Up to seven roding males were found in the woodlands on the Radnorshire side around the Elan reservoirs in 1976 but there have been no breeding season records there since 1988, when two roding birds were found, probably due to predation by introduced Goshawks. Remains of Woodcock have also been found at Peregrine and Goshawk sites elsewhere in Radnorshire, especially in the winter months.

More effort has been made in recent years to survey for roding birds and breeding season records since 2005 have come from across much of the county including the Doldowlodd/Nant Glas area, the Wye Valley woodlands between Newbridge and Boughrood, the Cwmbach/Llanelwedd area, Burfa Camp, woodlands around Presteigne and Knighton, Stanage, Cwm Byddog, Rhosgoch, Hundred House, Llowes, Clyro, New Radnor, Old Radnor, Penybont, Gladestry, woodlands in the Ithon Valley, Newchurch, Llandrindod Wells and Radnor Forest. Four roding birds were found at four sites in 2002, six at four in 2003, 12 in a wider search in 2004, 15 at 11 sites in 2008, 14 at seven in 2009 and nine at six in 2010.

Although this usually quiet, crepuscular, and polygynous bird is very difficult to census with any great accuracy, it is likely that at least 15-25 roding males currently display annually in Radnorshire over coniferous woodlands with clearfelled areas and wide rides as well as various types of broadleaved woodland. Flat, ungrazed, woodlands with at least some ground cover and low aerial predator pressure are preferred for roding and nesting, and damp woodlands and fields for nocturnal feeding.

The first autumn arrivals usually coincide with the onset of cold weather to the north and east and this is usually in the first week or so of November. These influxes are very sudden and noticeable with large falls of birds appearing overnight often during the days around the full moon, the 'Woodcock Moon' as it is known in many rural areas. Such big arrivals in the past have been on 6th November 1989, 18th November 1995, 6th November 2000, 8th November 2004 and 7th November 2010. The first arrivals can rarely be much earlier such as in 1993 when a cold northerly blast brought a big arrival over the 15th and 16th October. Twenty were put up on a short walk through Cwm Coel in the Elan Valley on 9th November 1989 and 30 in woods around Aberedw on 8th November 2004. Later in the winter, when most birds have either moved on or settled down, records are usually of one to three birds.

In November and December most birds move on to Ireland and other points south and west but many stay throughout the winter and are widespread in many wooded habitats, especially broadleaved, in the daytime and when worming on neighbouring damp grasslands at night. High counts have been 70 birds (34 shot) in a shoot within an eight mile radius of Llandrindod Wells in February 1967. Dusk flight counts to night-time feeding areas have included 45 near Hundred House on 18th December 1988 and 36 there on 5th January 1992, 48 near Newbridge on 1st February 1994, 30 near Llandrindod on 19th January 1995, 24 in the Elan Valley on 22nd February 1999 and 45 near Rhayader on 16th December

2008. Most winter visiting birds leave for points east in the second half of March but some are still present in the first week or so of April.

Winter visitors come mainly from southern Fennoscandia, the Baltic countries and Russia as far east as the Urals. A bird ringed at Bwlch y Sarnau on 29th November 2009 was shot on 15th April 2010 in Novgorod, Russia (2,267 km E). However, some birds winter in western Britain from breeding grounds as far east as the Yenesei Valley in central Russia, a distance of some 6,000 km.

Other recoveries include: One ringed at St Harmon on 7th November 2010 was shot in County Wexford on 2nd January 2011; an adult ringed at Nantmel on 17th November 2008 was shot in the Rhondda on 3rd January 2011; a bird ringed near Llaithddu on 12th December 2009 was shot on the Gower Peninsula on 28th January 2012 (99km SSW); two birds ringed at Doldowlodd on 7th February 2011 were both shot a few miles away at Newbridge on 30th December 2011 and a nestling ringed in Sweden was shot in mid-Wales in November. An adult ringed near Bwlch y Sarnau on 8th February 2011 flew into a window in southern Finland on 2nd July 2012 and a first-year bird ringed at Doldowlodd on 1st December 2011 was also recovered in southern Finland – killed by a cat on 25th September 2012.

In total birds ringed elsewhere and found in Powys have come from Dyfed (3), Russia, France (2) and Sweden whilst ones ringed in Powys have gone to Glamorgan (2), Dyfed, County Wexford (Eire), Finland (2), France (2), and Russia (4). Winter visitors are often faithful to the same area year on year with one bird in the Elan Valley returning to a small site for an exceptional seven successive winters.

Black-tailed Godwit *Limosa limosa* A

Very rare passage migrant.

Breeds from Iceland, the British Isles, France and the Netherlands east across Europe and Asia from southern Sweden south to the Crimea and east to Kazakhstan; also other populations in north-east Siberia, the Central Siberian Plain and parts of north-east China. Winters in the British Isles, France, Iberia, the Mediterranean, parts of northern Africa and across sub-Saharan Africa, the Persian Gulf, India, south-east Asia to New Guinea and Australia.

There have been sixteen records involving 39 birds:

1965:	One by a roadside pool at Maelinydd from 3rd to 4th April.
1966:	Two at Black Pool, Maelinydd, on 7th May.
1967:	One in summer plumage at Llyn Heilyn on 16th May.
1978:	One at Rhosgoch on 14th May.
1985:	One at Llyn Heilyn from 14th to 16th June.

1986:	One in a field just west of Craig Goch Reservoir on 20th April.
1996:	Eight in a field beside the River Wye near Llowes on 23rd April.
2002:	Three at Llyn Heilyn on 30th April.
2008:	One near Llowes on 12th November.
2009:	One at Llyn Heilyn on 16th and 17th March.
2010:	Two near Llowes on 30th April.
2010:	Eight near Llowes on 1st July, 4 remaining on 2nd.
2010:	One,different, (site as above) on 6th July.
2012:	Four in a flooded field near Clyro on 30th April.
2012:	One with Curlew near Caergynan Pool, Maelinydd, on 18th July.
2013:	Three near Llowes on 31st July.

Bar-tailed Godwit *Limosa lapponica* A

Very rare passage migrant.

Breeds from northern Fennoscandia east across northern Europe and Asia to Siberia and western Alaska. Winters from the British Isles and the Netherlands south around the coasts of Africa, southern Asia, Australia and New Zealand.

There have been ten records:

1971:	A first-summer bird at Maelinydd on 8th and 9th May.
1977:	One at Maelinydd on 28th August.
1987:	One in a field just west of Craig Goch Reservoir on 15th May.
1993:	One near Llowes on 1st and 2nd May.
1995:	Four near Llowes on 30th December.
1997:	One at Glasbury on 3rd May.
2002:	Two adults at Llyn Heilyn on 16th August.
2012:	Two in a flooded field near Clyro from 28th to 30th April.
2012:	Two (site as above) on 6th May.
2012:	Six (site as above) on 11th May.

Whimbrel *Numenius phaeopus* A

Rare passage migrant.

Breeds from Iceland, the Faeroes, Scotland and Fennoscandia east to western Siberia and locally south to the Caspian Sea and east to north-east Siberia, also Alaska and parts of northern Canada. Winters along coasts of USA, South America, southern Iberia, Africa, Arabia, India, south-east Asia and Australia.

Since the first record of one at St Michael's Pool on 30th April 1935 there have been about 59 further records involving approximately 155 birds. There were two records in the 1950s, one in the 1960s, five in the 1970s, six in the 1980s, 23 in the 1990s and 23 between 2000 and 2013.

Records have come from every month between February and November with 15 in April, 19 in May, 12 in July, six in August, three in June, two in November and singles in February, March, September and October. Sightings have come from 20 sites with the most coming from the Glasbury/Llowes/Clyro area along the lower River Wye (23), Maelinydd (10) Llanbedr Hill/Ireland Moor (5) and Llyn Heilyn (5). Other records have come from The Begwyns, Pwll Patti, Howey, Doldowlodd, Glascwm, Beacon Hill, the Elan Valley reservoirs, Aberedw Hill and Gladestry.

The majority of records have been of single birds but two to four have been seen on 20 occasions with higher counts of six at Llanbedr Hill/Ireland Moor on 6th May 1988 and 4th May 2008, six at Maelinydd on 28th April 1993, eight at Maelinydd on 19th August 1987 and nine at Gladestry on 21st May 2000. In April and May 2012 cold, wet, and windy weather held up many northern waders and other migrants to an unprecedented extent. This resulted in several Whimbrel records in partly flooded fields in the Llowes and Clyro area of the lower Wye Valley. A flock of 16 was present on 28th April, four were seen on 29th and eight on 30th. On 3rd May there were six and on 10th a total of 17 in three groups.

An adult bird ringed in Belgium on 27th April 1975 was found long-dead at Llandewi on 15th June 1977 and a nestling ringed in Iceland has been recovered in Powys.

Curlew *Numenius arquata* A

Uncommon breeding bird, passage migrant and winter visitor.

Breeds from France, the British Isles and Scandinavia east across Europe and Asia to Manchuria and south to the Caspian Sea. Winters Iceland, the British Isles and the Netherlands south to southern Africa and east to China and Indonesia.

In the late 19th and early 20th centuries the species was a widespread breeder on upland moorland. Mr R. Lewis-Lloyd reported to the Woolhope Society in 1896 that it was 'very numerous' in the Elan Valley. The species was seen 'in considerable numbers', and a nest with eggs found, at Rhosgoch Bog by members of the Woolhope Naturalists Field Club on 30th May 1911. From the 1920s to the end of the 1940s there was a very noticeable change in Radnorshire, as elsewhere, to breeding in the river valleys and on lower ground including rough, marshy and rushy fields as well as cultivated land. Overall there was a huge increase in numbers.

However, by 1957 numbers had already 'decreased noticeably' in the Pant y Dwr area and since the late 1970s and early 1980s there has been a continuing decline county-wide due to the widespread drainage of, and 'improvements' to, farmland, the shift to silage making from hay-making and a huge increase in predator pressure.

The population between the mid-1950s and the 1970s was about 300-400 pairs. In 1998 a survey in eight of the 21 10-km squares wholly or partly in the county found 82 pairs and in 2003 a survey found 88 pairs where there were 130 in 1997. Since then there have been further declines with sample sites visited in 2005 indicating a population of just 55-65 pairs. The decline seems to have slowed since then with most of the sites occupied being less prone to disturbance and predation and with safer nesting sites and better feeding areas. In 2008 there were at least 41 pairs on territory in April, 48 in 2009 and 38 in 2010 with unimproved and semi-improved grasslands and moors in the north of the county the stronghold areas. In the whole of Wales, surveys suggested a population of about 5,700 pairs in 1993 and 1,100 pairs in 2006. A decline of over 80%, very similar to that in Radnorshire over the period. Eggs not surviving to hatching has been the basic reason.

In the Radnorshire part of the Elan Valley there were 18 pairs in 1976, eight to10 in 1987 and two to five from 1995 to 2013. On Maelinydd there were seven to 10 pairs in the1980s and 1990s and two to four since 2004.

Spring passage is difficult to distinguish from birds arriving on territory which usually takes place in February and March. The earliest displaying bird was at Newbridge on 11th January 1990. However, late-winter flocks of 70-100 at Rhosgoch on 4th March 1999 and 50 on Aberedw Hill on 22nd March 2004, which flew off west, may well have included birds on passage through the county.

Autumn passage starts as early as late June with birds often heard calling at night flying over southwards. Post breeding season groups are seen soon after; at Maelinydd there were up to 112 birds present during July and August in the 1960s and 1970s, 30-40 in the 1980s and 1990s, and eight to 15 in the years 2005-2013. At Rhosgoch there were 200 on 21st July 1962, 35 on The Begwyns on 8th July 2000 and 25 on Beacon Hill on 4th August 1984.

Inland wintering by Curlew is a relatively recent phenomenon being first recorded in neighbouring Montgomeryshire and Herefordshire in the winter of 1954/55. In 1957 a flock of 60-70 was reported from below Glasbury in the winter with locals saying that up to 150 had been seen there 'for many years'. This flock, which wholly or partly sometimes visited The Begwyns and Rhosgoch, was often of more than 100 birds in the 1960s, 70s and 80s with 150 there in August and September 1961, 240 on 26th February 1977, 180 on 28th January 1978, 120 on 4th October 1981 and 100 on 17th December 1989. Up to 50-80 were counted during the autumn and winter in the1990s, 35 in 2004/5, 23 in 2007/8, 18 in 2009/10, 15 in 2011/12 and nine in 2012/13, although up to 31 were present during unseasonably cold weather in mid-March 2013. It seems likely that the birds which gathered on Maelinydd formed part of this lower Wye flock.

An adult ringed at Maelinydd in early May 1984 was found dead in October of the same year near Brecon and a bird ringed in October in mid-Wales was found breeding in Munster, Germany, in May 13 years later. Ringing also shows that some birds from southern Fennoscandia, Germany and the Baltic countries winter in the south-west of the British Isles, including Wales.

Common Sandpiper *Actitis hypoleucos* A

Widespread breeding bird and passage migrant which occasionally overwinters.

Breeds from Iberia, the British Isles and Scandinavia east across Europe and Asia to Kamchatka and south to the Mediterranean, Iraq, north-west India, northern China and Japan. Winters mainly from southern Iberia and the Mediterranean, throughout most of sub-Saharan Africa and the Nile Valley east across south-east Asia and Australia.

Ingram and Salmon (1955) said that the species was very much reduced as a breeding bird compared with 30 years ago and they referred to a large reduction in numbers between Erwood and the upper Edw Valley between 1945 and 1955, down from 9-10 pairs to only one to two. There has undoubtedly been a decline in some parts of Radnorshire since the mid 1980s due to increased recreational disturbance in places and increased predation, especialy from feral Mink.

In the Radnorshire part of the relatively undisturbed Elan Valley up to 30 pairs(1997) have been found around the reservoirs and lakes and along the rivers since the first survey in the mid-1970s. There have been regular, complete and partial, surveys there since and, for the same core area, counts have been 20 in 1976, 18 in1992, 24 in 1993, 26 in 1994, 18 in 1995, 25 in 1997, 25 in 2002, 22 in 2006, 21 in 2008 and 19 in 2011. Breeding success from year to year varies greatly with high reservoir levels producing the best years due to reduced disturbance levels.

The species breeds around most of the Elan reservoirs, along most rivers down to many quite small streams, and around some of the upland lakes. In 1998 a survey of the River Wye between Llanwrthwl and Cabalva (c. 40km) found 32 pairs and in 2003 an incomplete survey of the Wye and its major tributaries, the Ithon, Marteg and Edw, found 67 pairs which suggested a total county population of 110-120 pairs. However, an exact repeat of that river survey in 2010 found only 44 pairs.

The first returning birds are usually seen about the 12th to 15th April with the earliest record being at Glasbury on 29th March 1990. Birds on passage, presumably heading for Scandinavia from West Africa, are recorded as late as mid-May and returning birds are seen from the end of June. The peak autumn passage period is at the end of July and in early August with a few records again in late September and October being nearly all of juveniles of presumably continental origin judging by ringing recoveries elsewhere.

Passage birds are regular at non-breeding lake sites including Llandindod Lake and Llyn Heilyn and occasionally at Hindwell Pool, Maelinydd and Llanbwchllyn. Six birds were at Llandrindod Lake on 5th May 1990 and on 8th July 2008. Many more stop off along the rivers but are difficult to distinguish from local breeders. Along the Wye between Glasbury and Llowes there were 18 on 13th July 1996 and 22 on 24th July 2013.

Late records have been in the Elan Valley on 10th October 1989 and at Glasbury on 16th October 2004 and 28th October 1995 with a bird seen there on 20th November 1999 perhaps going to overwinter locally. Overwintering birds have been recorded along the lower Wye in the Glasbury and Pwll Patti area in 1964/65, 85/86, 87/88, 88/89, 89/90, 95/96, 2002/03, 05/06 and 08/09. The same returning bird was responsible for the four records in the 1980s. Other mid-winter records have come from the River Wye at Bronydd on 7th January 1990, Erwood on 17th January 1993, Llanelwedd on 4th February 1996 and Llandrindod Lake on 18th February 1999. It is not known whether the overwintering birds are local breeders or immigrants from the continent.

An adult ringed at Rhayader on 2nd July 1993 was recovered in Morocco 'about April' 1996 and a chick ringed at Rhayader on 11th June 1970 was found dead at Trawsfynydd (75 km NNW) in May 1971 where it was probably breeding. The wintering areas of British breeding birds are as yet unknown, as there have been no ringing recoveries in Africa between October and March, but is likely to be West Africa.

A yellow-legged bird was present at Llyn Heilyn from 15th to 19th August 1989 and any winter birds should be carefully looked at for the possibility of the closely related, Nearctic, Spotted Sandpiper, *Actitis macularius.*

Green Sandpiper *Tringa ochropus* A

Regular autumn passage migrant and winter visitor; rare spring migant.

Breeds from Scandinavia and the Baltic countries east across Russia to the Kolyma Peninsula and south to Lake Baikal and northern China. Winters in western and southern Europe, north-west and sub-Saharan Africa east across most of southern Asia to Japan and the Philippines.

Davies (1912) stated that the species had been recorded in the county but gave no detail. The first dated record was at Llyn Heilyn on 8th September 1939 and the second at Rhiw Pool, Radnor Forest, on 3rd August 1948.

Autumn passage usually extends from July to October with the peak in August. There have also been several records of returning birds in June with the earliest being by the River Ithon at Penybont on 13th June 1970 and at Llanbwchllyn on 14th June 1958. The Pwll Patti and Glasbury to Llowes area of the River Wye attracts the most birds with at least 12 present in August 1965, 11 on 22nd August 1978 and 16th August 2008, 10 in July and August 1964, nine on 21st July 1963 and eight on 19th August 1991, 20th July 2002 and 24th July 2013.

Other records have come from many widespread wetland sites including Llyn Heilyn (21 records), the Elan reservoirs (20), Maelinydd (8) and Penyclawdd Pool (5). One to three records have come from Llanbwchllyn, the River Ithon, The River Edw, The Begwyns pool, Beili Bedw, the River Teme valley, Hindwell Pool, Ireland Pool, Llanbedr Hill, Henllyn, Glan Llyn, Llyn Gwyn, Rhulen Hill, Gwaunceste Hill, Rhosgoch Bog and several other small mawn pools, garden and farm ponds and lakes. Records are usually of single birds but there were six at Llanbwchllyn on 22nd August 1975, five at the Beili Bedw Mawn Pools on 10th August 1980, four at The Begwyns pool on 13th August 2000 and six near Llowes on 24th July 2013.

One to three birds have overwintered along the lower Wye most years since at least the early 1960s with four present in January 1966. These birds usually arrive in July and August and depart during the first two weeks of April. Winter records elsewhere are rare but have come from the River Teme at Knighton on 26th December 1967, Brynthomas on 20th February 1981, the River Ithon at Penybont on 24th January 1984, the Ithon at Llandrindod Wells in December 1987 and January 1988, Hindwell Pool on 28th

November 2003 and December 2008, the River Ithon at Llanbister Road in November and December 2003, Llyn Heilyn on 3rd December 2007, Rhosgoch on 21st February 2010 and 16th January 2012, and Llanbwchllyn in December 2011. About 500-1,000 birds are estimated to overwinter in the British Isles as a whole but where they come from is as yet unclear as there have been no ringing recoveries but judging by the late departure dates is likely to be in the north of the species range.

Birds often return to the same site or small part of the River Wye each winter for several years and passage migrants doubtless also use the same stop-over sites in successive autumns. One ringed at Glasbury on 5th August 1964 was shot three kilometres away downriver on 2nd September 1965.

Spring passage is obscured along the Wye by wintering birds but elsewhere birds have been seen on passage at Llyn Heilyn on 21st April 1989, by the River Elan near Rhayader on 24th April 1990, by Caban Coch Reservoir on 2nd May 1995 and beside the River Ithon near Llandrindod Wells on 8th May 2012.

Spotted Redshank *Tringa erythropus* A

Rare autumn migrant and very rare winter visitor.

Breeds from northern Scandinavia and inland east across northern Russia to 180 degrees east. Winters mainly from the Mediterranean and sub-Saharan Africa east to India, southern China and Indonesia.

One in the Maesllwch collection in the early 1900s was likely to have been shot in the south of the county.

There have been 16 records since:

1968:	Llyn Heilyn on 6th August.
1969:	On the Maelinydd pools on 8th and 9th August.
1969:	At Glasbury on 17th September.
1970:	Maelinydd on 1st August.
1972:	Maelinydd on 26th August.
1986:	Between Glasbury and Llowes on 28th August.
1989:	Dol y Mynach Reservoir on 20th August.
1991:	Two juveniles at Llyn Heilyn from 20th to 26th August.
1995:	Hindwell Pool on 22nd August.
1996:	Pwll Patti on 8th February.
1996:	Between Glasbury and Llowes on 4th August.

1996:	Caergynan Pool, Maelinydd, on 25th August.
2009:	Glasbury on 1st October.
2010:	Adult near Llowes on 8th July.
2010:	Juvenile at Llandrindod Lake on 27th August.
2011:	Juvenile near Llowes on 6th August.

Greenshank *Tringa nebularia*

A

Regular but declining autumn passage migrant; very rare spring migrant.

Breeds from northern Scotland and Scandinavia east across Europe and Russia to Kamchatka. Winters from south-west British Isles, Iberia, the Mediterranean and Africa east across southern Asia to China and southern Japan, Indonesia, the Philippines and Australasia.

The first county record was of one at Llyn Heilyn from 24th to 31st August 1952 and the second at the same place on 8th September 1954.

Since then there have been about 150 records with sightings for most years from the lower River Wye between Boughrood and Bronydd, especially the Glasbury to Llowes stretch. There have been noticeably fewer sightings since c.1996.

Most records are of single birds but two or three together in a small area are sometimes found. Ten were in the Glasbury area on 23rd August 1963, eight were there on 27th August 1976 and 12 on 17th August 1982. Five were by the River Wye at Erwood on 1st September 1984 and five at Llyn Heilyn on 14th August 1995.

Although the vast majority of records have come from the lower Wye there have been 15 records from around the Elan and Claerwen Valley reservoirs, 12 from the Maelinydd pools and nine from Llyn Heilyn. Other records have come from The Begwyns pool (4), Llanbwchllyn (2), Llanwefr Pool (2), Llyn Gwyn, the River Ithon at Llanbadarn Fyndd and Penybont, the River Wye at Llanelwedd and a flooded field at Kinnerton.

There have been seven spring records, mostly of summer plumaged birds; Maelinydd on 4th April 1965, two by the Claerwen Reservoir on 6th June 1987, at Glasbury on 26th May 1997, 20th May 2001, 5th and 6th June 2008 and 14th May 2009, and one at Llyn Heilyn on 14th May 2006. The earliest autumn record was on 13th July 1990 beside Garreg Ddu Reservoir and the peak passage period is in the second half of August, when most of the year's juveniles pass through. Many birds often stay for some days, or even weeks. Passage continues for much of September and there have been three records in October and singles in November and February. Summer-plumaged adults were at Llyn Gwyn on 28th July 1993 and at Llyn Heilyn on 15th July 1994 and 18th July 2011. Birds seen in Radnorshire are likely to be breeding birds from Scotland and Scandinavia on their way to and from West Africa.

Wood Sandpiper *Tringa glareola* A

Rare passage migrant.

Breeds in Scotland (a few pairs) and from Scandinavia east across Russia to Kolyma and Kamchatka and south to Lake Baikal and Sakhalin. Winters in sub-Saharan Africa, southern Asia and Australasia.

There have been eleven records:

1951:	Two at Llyn Heilyn on 10th August.
1965:	On an island below Glasbury bridge on 16th and 17th August.
1987:	Newbridge-on-Wye on 8th May.
1988:	Llyn Heilyn on 8th August.
1993:	Beside the River Elan near Rhayader on 19th May.
1994:	Along the western shore of Craig Goch Reservoir on 21st May.
2001:	Near Llowes on 7th September.
2009:	as above on 10th May.
2009:	as above on 14th May.
2012:	as above on 30th May.
2013:	as above on 24th July.

Redshank *Tringa totanus* A

Former breeder in small numbers, rare passage migrant.

Breeds from Iceland, the Faeroes, the British Isles, France, Iberia and Scandinavia east across central Europe and southern Russia to western China, Mongolia and Manchuria. Winters in Iceland and the British Isles to Iberia, the Mediterranean and Africa east to India and south-east Asia.

The species was unknown as a breeding bird throughout most of Wales until the 1920s and nesting was first recorded in Radnorshire on Radnor Forest in 1914. On 4th May 1915 a pair, apparently with young, was found at Llandegley Rhos and a pair also bred at Rhosgoch Bog in that year. Pairs were found near Llanbwchllyn on 3rd May 1927 and at Llyn Heilyn on 3rd May 1935. The Redshank enquiry of 1938/9 found four to six pairs in the county.(*British Birds* vol. 34 p.14).

In the 1950s and 1960s pairs were reported in the breeding season from Maelinydd (1-3 pairs), Penybont Common (1-3), The Begwyns, Llyn Heilyn, Rhosfallog, Doctor's Pool, Litton Hill, St Michael's Pool and Llanwefr Pool. In the 1970s records came from Maelinydd (1-4 pairs), Penybont Common (1-3), the lower Wye Valley (1-3), Glan Llyn, the Elan and Claerwen Valleys (1-4), Rhulen Hill, Rhosgoch Bog, Llyn Heilyn and Moelfre whilst in the 1980s occupied sites were Maelinydd (1-3), Elan and Claerwen Valleys (1-2), Llanbedr Hill, Rhosgoch Bog, Llyn Heilyn and Moelfre.

By the 1990s there were just two regular breeding places; Maelinydd (1-2 pairs) and Moelfre (1-2), with a pair also at Llyn Heilyn in 1990 and 1991. In 2003 single pairs were found at Maelinydd, Moelfre and along the lower Wye but there have been no breeding records since. Overall it seems that there were 10-15 pairs, and perhaps as many as 20, breeding during the 1950s, 60s and 70s. By the end of the 1980s this was down to three to five pairs and to zero to three pairs between 1995 and 2003. This decline is inline with the national trends which showed an 80% decline during the period, especially at inland sites. However, the reason at Radnorshire sites was not the drainage of wet grasslands as at national level but rather increased grazing pressures and predation.

There have also been regular records of migrants, as well as of pre and post breeding season groups, e.g. eight at Boughrood on 21st March 1965, 12 at Maelinydd on 25th March 1978, 11 beside Craig Goch Reservoir on 2nd August 1970 and four below Glasbury on 30th April 2012, 22nd August 1962, 19th August 1991 and 27th October 1995 – the only October record. From the 1950s to the 1990s there were also widespread annual records of one to two birds on passage in March and April and from late June to September.

The only winter records are of one to two in the Glasbury area in January and February 1987 and at the top end of Craig Goch Reservoir on 24th February 2009. Including this last record, there were just 20 records from 2006 to 2012, 10 in spring and nine in autumn, involving 28 birds. Redshanks seen in Radnorshire are likely to be British breeding birds or from Iceland and the Faeroe Islands.

Turnstone *Arenaria interpres* A

Very rare visitor.

Breeds circumpolar mostly on the coasts in the high Arctic of North America, Greenland, Europe and Asia. Winters on coasts from the British Isles and southern USA south around South America and Africa east across southern Asia to Australia and New Zealand and around most of the larger oceanic islands.

There have been three records of summer-plumaged birds: At Llanbwchllyn on 10th May 1979 and along the River Wye between Glasbury and Llowes on 7th June 1992 and 14th May 2009.

Wilson's Phalarope *Phalaropus tricolor* A

Very rare visitor.

Breeds from southern Canada south to central USA. Winters in southern Chile and Argentina.

The only record is of one at Llyn Heilyn on 6th September 1975 which was found and watched busily feeding for half an hour by a Herefordshire Ornithological Club group.

Red-necked Phalarope *Phalaropus lobatus* A

Very rare visitor.

Breeds circumpolar in tundra and boreal regions of Iceland, the Faeroes, northern Scotland and Scandinavia east across northern Russia, including Kamchatka, the Aleutian Islands, Alaska, northern Canada and Greenland. Winters at sea in tropical areas off western South America, West Africa, Saudi Arabia and south-east Asia but distribution is poorly known.

The only definite record is of one partly in summer plumage at Llyn Heilyn from 30th April to 2nd May 2012. A phalarope watched for ten minutes beside the River Wye below Glasbury on 17th September 1977 was almost certainly of this species.

Grey Phalarope *Phalaropus fulicarius* A

Very rare visitor.

Breeds Iceland, Svalbard, Arctic Russia, Alaska, Arctic Canada and Greenland. Winters at sea off the west coasts of South America, central and southern Africa.

There have been three records of storm-driven birds:

One was shot in September 1866 'by a gamekeeper of W.de Winton, Esq. on his grouse moors in Radnorshire, swimming and diving on an artificial dam near some dwelling houses'. (Woolhope Society *Transactions*, vol 1870 p.254). One was seen on a small pond near the house at Boultibrooke, Presteigne, on 28th September 1871. (*Zoologist*, 2nd series; vol.6 p.2852) and one was on the Craig Goch Reservoir, near the dam, on 7th September 2008.

Pomarine Skua *Stercorarius pomarina* A

Very rare visitor.

Breeds in Arctic Russia, Alaska, Canada and Greenland. Winters at sea in the Arctic Ocean, around the Pacific to Australia, the east and west Atlantic and the northern African coast of the Indian Ocean.

There have been two records:

One from Radnorshire in Mr A.Gwynne-Vaughan's collection, a specimen exhibited in 1895 'from Radnorshire, just on the borders of Herefordshire' (Woolhope Society *Transactions* 1895-97 p.103) and 'one in Radnorshire' (Woolhope Society *Transactions* 1909 p.84), probably all refer to the same bird. The remains of one were found near Glasbury in 1926.

Great Skua *Stercorarius skua* A

Very rare visitor.

Breeds in Scotland, the Faeroes and Iceland. Winters at sea in the North Atlantic south to northern South America.

The only record is of one picked up exhausted at Lower Cwm Farm, Llandegley, on 20th December 1989. After eating two tins of sardines and half a pound of sprats it was released on the coast at Ynyslas, Ceredigion, two days later.

Kittiwake *Rissa tridactyla*

A

Rare visitor.

Breeds from the coast of north-west Iberia, France, the British Isles, Iceland and the Faeroes east around the coasts of the islands and mainland of northern Europe and Russia east to Kamchatka, the Aleutians, Alaska, northern Canada and Greenland. Winters in the North Atlantic, North Pacific and Arctic Oceans.

There have been fifteen records:

1976:	Fourteen adults on Caban Coch Reservoir on 14th May.
1988:	Two adults on Llyn Gwyn on 17th and 18th March.
1992:	Adult on Dol y Mynach Reservoir on 27th January.
1993:	Ten adults on Craig Goch Reservoir on 1st June.
1997:	Adult at Llandrindod Wells Lake on 27th February.
1997:	First-winter Caban Coch Reservoir on 24th November.
1999:	Adult Caban Coch Reservoir on 19th January.
1999:	Adult Caban Coch Reservoir on 8th April.
1999:	Adult Craig Goch Reservoir on 6th November.
2000:	Adult Caban Coch Reservoir on 1st January.
2002:	Adult Garreg Ddu Reservoir on 7th February.
2002:	Adult Penygarreg and Craig Goch Reservoirs on 10th March.
2007:	Adult Penygarreg and Craig Goch Reservoirs on 8th November.
2008:	Adult Llandrindod Wells Lake on 10th and 11th March.
2009:	Second-winter Garreg Ddu Reservoir on16th October.

Black-headed Gull *Chroicocephalus ridibundus* A

Scarce, but formerly common, breeding bird; regular passage migrant and winter visitor.

Breeds Iceland, the Faeroes, the British Isles, France and Scandinavia east across Europe and Asia to Kolyma and Kamchatka and south to Italy, Turkey, the Caspian Sea and Lake Baikal. Winters north-west Europe, around much of the North Atlantic, the Mediterranean, coastal North Africa and east to around southern Asia and the western Pacific.

The first breeding in the county probably took place at Llanwefr Pool about 1900, although this date was on recollection in 1939. A few pairs nested on the mawn pools to the south of Glascwm Hill in 1904, Rhosgoch Bog was colonised in 1908 and nesting at Rhiw Pool (Radnor Forest) and at Llanwefr Pool started about 1910. These, and about 30 other colonies, large and small, have become established and been abandoned over the last 100 years or so.

There have been three national surveys in England and Wales; in 1938, 1958 and 1973. In 1938, four colonies were found in Radnorshire with a total of 342 pairs; in 1958, six totalled 250-300 and in 1973 nine colonies were counted which held 251-265 pairs. However, 1938 was a very dry year with some colonies hardly used and 1958 was another low point. Between the census years there were many ups and downs.

At Llanwefr Pool there were c. 750 pairs in 1934, 150-200 in 1937 and about 300 in 1938. Many eggs were taken for food in the WWII years but there were still 250-300 pairs in 1954 and this was the norm in that decade with occasionally very low numbers e.g. only about 25 pairs in 1957. In 1960 there were 60-70 nests, 250 pairs in 1963 and 100 pairs in 1969. Only 25-60 pairs were found in the 1970s but 180-200 bred in 1983. There was a rapid decline thereafter with only 20-40 pairs in the late 1980s and early 1990s and since 2000 only the occasional few pairs nest there as the site reduces in size and attractiveness.

At Rhosgoch Bog 50-60 birds and several nests with eggs were found by members of the Woolhope Naturalists Field Club on 30th May 1911. Three hundred pairs were found in 1934 but the site was very dry in 1938 and just 12 were counted. On 10th May 1932 the ornithologist F.C.R. Jourdain (in search of Spotted Crakes) counted 5,000 birds – the highest ever count in Radnorshire. About 500 pairs bred in 1948 rising to over 2,000 in 1954 but down to 30-40 in 1958 and 1959. There were some 500 pairs in the early 1960s, with 1,500 adults present on 21st April 1960, but none in 1968 and 1969. In 1977 a nest count of 306 was made and 250 pairs were recorded in 1979 but by 1983 there were just 10 pairs. Breeding has taken place occasionally there since with 20+ pairs raising seven young in 2008 but none there in 2010.

A colony at the mawn pools south of Glascwm Hill was only occupied in wetter years when they held water. None bred in 1938, 1952 or 1955 whereas there were 480 pairs in 1954, 200-250 in 1965, 40-60 in 1973,100 in 1983 and 80 in 1984. Since then five to10 pairs have nested in some years but with little success. At Penyclawdd Pool there were 200 pairs in 1954 and 200-250 was the usual number in the 1950s and 1960s. Eighty young were counted on 26th June1971 and there were still about 150 pairs in the mid-1970s but none in 1979 and none since following the site being made unsuitable. At nearby St Michael's Pool there were c. 200 pairs between 1925 and 1930 but numbers dwindled due to egg collecting to just six pairs in 1937 and none in 1938. In the 1950s there were 25-75 pairs, about 500 birds were counted there in 1966 and100 pairs bred in 1963. The site has become increasingly dry and the only breeding record there recently was of a pair in 2003. At mawn pools just to the south of St Michael's Pool there were a few pairs in 1938 and at Rhiw Garn there were 200 pairs in 1979 and 1980 only.

At the ponds on and around Maelinydd there were 5-12 nests between 1958 and 1963, 48 pairs in 1973 and 100 nests in 1979. In 1987 there were 40 pairs at nearby Park Farm Pool and 'several' there the following year. Pentrosfa Mire held six to 10 nests in the eary 1970s, 20 in 1988 and up to 150 in the early 1990s. The all night noise from the colony however disturbed local residents and the birds were 'moved on with a shot-gun'. At nearby Wern Fawr, 150 pairs were counted in 1986 and occasional pairs have bred there since.

The first two pairs were noted at Llanbwchllyn in 1958 gradually increasing to over 100 in 1980 but declining thereafter due to the growth of willows. None have bred there since the mid-1980s. In the Claerwen Valley a colony at Dol y Mynach Reservoir started in 1987 with 40 pairs raising 30 young. In 1988 numbers rose to 140 pairs raising 200 young and in 1989 at least 200 pairs nested raising 250 young. The peak came in the following year with about 400 pairs fledging over 440 young and with 1,550 adults present on 18th June. In 1993 there were 240 nests but none the next year and none since.

At nearby Wernrhydd, on the heather moorland east of Garreg Ddu Reservoir, there were 100-200 pairs throughout the 1990s then a rapid decline to just a few pairs in 2006 which raised two young. At Llyn Cerrigllwydion Isaf there were 10-20 pairs in the early 1970s but only occasional pairs nest there today. Single pairs bred at the top ends of Craig Goch and Claerwen Reservoirs in 1995 and 1999 respectively. Predator pressure seems the main reason why the Elan and Claerwen colonies have died out.

At Llanwentre Pool there were up to 500 adults and many nests in 1970 and 113 pairs in 1973, but no records of breeding there subsequently. The Rhiw Pool colony held 200 pairs in 1912, none in 1933, 150-200 in 1934, a few in 1935 and 20-30 in 1937 and 1938. One or more of the mawn pools on Llanbedr Hill, Ireland Moor and Aberedw Hill are sometimes occupied with 100 nests at Aberedw Hill in 1979 and 50-100 nests in the area in recent years. Since 1986 a few pairs have attempted to breed around Llyn Heilyn in some years with 40 pairs in 1988 but typically just a few e.g. four young were raised from four nests in 2013. At Felindre there were 40 pairs in 1961 and at nearby Bwlchyllyn there have been one to five nests some years since 2000.

One to six pairs have bred at The Begwyns pool in some years since 1986 and up to five pairs at Llandrindod Lake since 1997. A pair bred at Llyn Gwyn in 1987, at Glan Llyn there were 16 nests in 2005 and 15 in 2006, and at Bwlchyfedwen there have been 3-10 pairs since 2004.

Despite probably fewer than 200 pairs in total nesting in the county in recent years there are still some flocks passing through in spring, although in far lower numbers since 2000. At Caban Coch Reservoir there were 380 on 1st April 2003 and 100-165 have been counted at Llandrindod Lake in April of most recent years with high counts of 250 on 23rd March 1997, 200 on 15th April 1998 and on 17th April 2000. March and April passage flocks on Caban Coch Reservoir often numbered up to 1,000 birds in the 1980s and 1990s and over 500 were at Glasbury in early April 2009. Other high counts have been 120 at The Begwyns on 30th March 2000, 2,000 at Llanbwchllyn on 22nd March 1981, 1,000 there on 10th April 1982, 500 at Llyn Heilyn on 26th April 1987, 400 at Llyn Gwyn on 17th March 1989 and on 8th April 1992, 650 at Cabalva on 20th March 1987 and 1,000 flew west there on 15th February, 400 at Llowes on 29th March 1995 and 15th December 1999 and 700 there on 31st October 1993. Any sighting of Black-headed Gull in Radnorshire is noteworthy today, especially away from the lower Wye Valley.

There have been more than 140 recoveries of chicks ringed at Radnorshire colonies including one shot near Barcelona in its first winter, singles to France, Portugal and the Netherlands and 19 to Ireland. Several have been recovered in Lancashire and Yorkshire in the autumn and winter and others have gone to East Anglia, elsewhere in Wales, Cornwall, Cheshire, Staffordshire, Kent, Northumberland, Lincolnshire, Middlesex and Somerset. There have been 14 birds ringed elsewhere and found in Powys including chicks ringed in Norway, Sweden (3) and Lithuania (2) recovered in August, October and January. A nestling ringed at Rhosgoch Bog on 17th June 1962 was found freshly dead at Llanwefr Pool on 1st July 1982, 12km to the north-west and just over 20 years of age.

Little Gull *Hydrocoloeus minutus* A

Very rare visitor.

Breeds from Finland and the Baltic countries discontinuously east across central Asia to the Sea of Okhotsk in three discrete populations; also small numbers in north-east USA and Canada. Winters around the coasts of much of Europe and north-east North America as well as the Mediterranean, Caspian and Black Seas.

There have been eleven records of this small gull which has greatly increased in numbers around the Baltic over the last fifty years.

1982:	Immature at Maelinydd on 2nd August
1985:	Sub-adult at Llyn Heilyn on 24th October.
1990:	First-summer at Llyn Heilyn on 10th May.
1991:	Second-winter in the Glasbury and Llowes area from 11th March to the 22nd April.
1992:	First-summer at Dol y Mynach Reservoir from 25th to 30th May.
1997:	Adult on Penygarreg Reservoir on 23rd November.
1998:	One at Llyn Gwyn on 24th March.
1999:	Glasbury and Llowes area of the River Wye;1 from 20th September to 4th October and two present from 24th September to 28th September.
2010:	First-summer near Llowes on 11th July.
2011:	First-summer on Craig Goch Reservoir on 16th May.

Mediterranean Gull *Larus melanocephalus* A

Very rare visitor.

Breeds locally from the western Baltic, Denmark, France and the south-east of England to the Mediterranean, Romania, the Black Sea and Georgia. Winters around the coasts within the breeding range as well as Iberia and north-west Africa.

The only record of this species, which is increasing in the British Isles and north-west Europe, was an adult with Black-headed Gulls at Rhosgoch Bog on 1st July 2008.

Common Gull *Larus canus* A

Scarce passage migrant and winter visitor.

Breeds from Iceland, the Faeroes, the British Isles and France east across most of northern Europe and Asia to the Bering Sea, south to northern Iran, Lake Baikal, Sakhalin and Kamchatka, also in north-west North America. Some birds are largely resident others winter at sea as far south as the Persian Gulf, the Black and Caspian Seas, Japan, China and California.

Ingram and Salmon (1955) described the species as an occasional winter visitor to the lower Wye Valley with no other detail. The first dated records were four near Kinnerton on 21st July 1955 and one near Cwmbach Llechrhyd on 7th August 1955.

Up to 2013 there have been about 79 records with noticeably fewer in recent years. There were four dated records in the 1950s, six in the 1960s, eight in the 1970s, 29 in the 1980s, 20 in the 1990s but just 12 from 2000 to 2013. Records have come in every month except June: Jan(8), Feb(12), Mar(13), Apr(5), May(5), Jul(7), Aug(5), Sept(1), Oct(6), Nov(10), Dec(7). Most have come from the lower Wye Valley (20) and from the Elan and Claerwen reservoirs (15). There have also been 10 records in the Hindwell, Kinnerton and New Radnor area (the Walton Plain), four from Llandrindod Lake including five birds on 23rd March 1997, three from elsewhere in Llandrindod, four from Llanelwedd, two from Newbridge and others from Glascwm Hill, Llanwefr Pool, Llyn Gwyn and Norton.

In the 1960s, 70s and early 80s the large arable fields of the Walton Plain attracted occasional flocks wandering westwards from their usual haunts in Herefordshire and the Severn Valley. There were 'just over 200' near Hindwell on 2nd April 1961, c. 30 at Four Stones on 7th February 1970, 21 at Hindwell on 14th February 1976 and 12 there on 18th August 1976. On 20th February 1973 at Hindwell a flock of about 800 gulls 'were mostly Common'. Elsewhere there were 200 at Crossgates on 1st February 1974, c. 100 between Bronydd and Clyro on 17th March 1987 and 12 at Glasbury on 3rd March 1990.

Ringing recoveries show that birds visiting Wales come from Scotland, Scandinavia, the Baltic countries and western Russia.

Lesser Black-backed Gull *Larus fuscus* A

Frequent passage migrant and winter visitor.

Breeds from Iceland, the Faeroes, the British Isles, France and Denmark east across Scandinavia and north-west Russia. Winters within the breeding range and south to the coasts of western Africa, Saudi Arabia and the Persian Gulf.

Until the early 1930s there was a colony of up to 50 pairs on Cors Caron (Tregaron Bog), Ceredigion, and this was probably the source of the 'several pairs' of birds regularly seen by John Williams-Vaughan in the Wye Valley in spring and summer in the early years of the 20th century (Woolhope Society *Transactions* 1909 p.86).

The species declined greatly as a breeding bird in Wales, and elsewhere in the British Isles, during the 1940s and early 1950s due to egg collecting for human consumption, especially during the WWII years. However, there was a 15-fold increase in breeding numbers in the British Isles between the mid-1950s and the mid-1970s due to a huge increase in inland refuse tips and wasteful fish-trawling practises. This also resulted in birds overwintering in the British Isles rather than migrating to Iberia and north-west Africa as they all used to do.

From 1950 to the mid-1970s there were just a handful of records in Radnorshire of one to two birds most years. Since then double and triple figure counts have not been rare although since the closure of refuse tips in the 1980s and 90s e.g. at Nantmel and Clyro, flocks are less regular, especially along the lower Wye. Changes in the sea-fishing industry have also resulted in large declines in breeding numbers in Wales and elsewhere in recent years.

Spring passage northwards is noticeable from late March to the end of May whilst autumn movements south take place between mid-June and the end of September with the peak in July. At Gladestry in 2003 birds were seen flying south-east on ten dates between the 14th June and the 21st September with one to 12 on eight dates, 22 on 15th June and 274 on 5th July. There are regular sightings of flocks in the late autumn and winter months in the lower Wye Valley and surrounding area and also small flocks flying south from the Severn Valley over the north of the county and down the Wye, Ithon and Teme valleys. The vast majority of all birds seen in Radnorshire are in adult or near-adult plumage with usually only small numbers of juveniles seen in autumn.

High counts have been; 230 below Glasbury on 12th January 1992, 180 at Llowes on 6th February 1992, 80 at Maelinydd on 14th May 1980, 450 following the plough at Llanfihangel nant Melan on 24th June 2010, 347 at Llyn Heilyn on 29th July 1988, 100 at Dolau on 1st August 1979, 200 at Glasbury on 26th September 1999, 800 at Llowes on 5th October 1999, 300 at Glasbury on 8th October 2000, 220 below Glasbury on 16th November 2008, 180 near Boughrood on 2nd November 2007, 160 near Painscastle on 24th November 2011 and 160 near Ffynnon Gynydd on 15th December 2000.

Birds showing the characteristics of the race *intermedius* (dark blackish-grey mantle and wings when adult) which breeds in south-west Scandinavia are occasionally seen as far west as Radnorshire. Of 100 in the Glasbury area in early December 1991 most were *intermedius*; of 90 at Llowes on 28th December 1991, 25 were *intermedius* and a flock of 110 birds at Glasbury on 4th October 1994 comprised 85 *intermedius* and 25 *graelsii* – the race which breeds in the British Isles and elsewhere in north-west Europe and generally has noticeably paler upper parts.

Colour ringed birds from Trawsfynydd (Gwynedd) and Gloucestershire have been seen in flocks and it is likely that the flock present at Llyn Heilyn for much of July 1988 came from North Wales. Thirteen birds ringed as chicks elsewhere have been recovered in summer and autumn in Powys and have come from Bardsey Island, Gwynedd (3), Skomer and Skokholm (4), Walney Island (2), the Farne Islands and Gloucestershire (2). A chick ringed on South Walney, Cumbria, on 9th July 1999 was found long dead at Cascob on 1st October 2003 (197 km S).

Herring Gull *Larus argentatus*

A

Uncommon, but increasing, passage migrant.

Breeds from Iceland, the Faeroes, the British Isles, France and Scandinavia across Russia and northern North America. Winters mostly inshore around most coasts of the Northern Hemisphere.

The first record was of 'some' passing over St Harmon on 6th August 1952 – still the most likely place to see the species in Radnorshire. The second record was of a flock of 10 adults and two immatures flying east over Penybont on 18th June 1955.

Up to 2013 there have been about 165 records; three in the 1950s, four in the 60s, 13 in the 70s, 12 in the 80s, 32 in the 90s and 101 since 2000. Records have come in every month: Jan(15), Feb(2), Mar(10), Apr(22), May(18), Jun(12), Jul(9), Aug(7), Sept(8), Oct(4), Nov(28), Dec(30). Most of the November and December records have come since 2009 from the St Harmon area and have been of birds mostly travelling north to south from the Severn Valley to the Wye Valley and on to South Wales.

Of 19 records along the lower Wye 13 have been in the months of November to January whilst of the 32 records on the Elan and Claerwen reservoirs just 3 have been in that period and 21 between April and June, mostly on passage northwards.

Most records have been of one to three birds with high counts being 16 flying west over Caban Coch Reservoir on 24th May 1988, 10 flying south over Rhayader on 7th August 1997 and a flock of 90 doing the same on 12th January 2002. At St Harmon in 2009 there were flocks of 125 and 210 seen heading south on 5th December, 37 on 28th November and 63 heading north on 29th November. In 2012 high counts there were 80 on 2nd January, 150+ on 12th November flying north-east, 150+ in fields on 23rd November, c.100 on 28th November and 5th December, 75 on 9th December and 43 on 27th December.

Records have also come from Llandrindod Lake (8), Bettws (3), Llanbwchllyn, Maelinydd, Llyn Gwyn, Llyn Heilyn, Beacon Hill, Gilwern Hill, Howey, Llanbedr Hill, Llangunllo and New Radnor. Most sightings have been of adults, but a higher proportion of juveniles and immatures occur than for Lesser Black-backed Gull, with which species they are sometimes seen.

Birds showing the characters of the nominate race *argentatus* (which breeds in Fennoscandia, around the Baltic and in western Russia) were seen on Craig Goch Reservoir on 8th December 1998 and at Glasbury on 1st December 2007.

Chicks ringed on Anglesey and Skokholm have been found dead in Powys in January and July.

Yellow-legged Gull *Larus michahellis* A

Very rare visitor.

Breeds in the Mediterranean and the west of the Black Sea. Disperses north-westwards in autumn and winters within the breeding area as well as off north-west Africa.

Formerly considered a race of Herring Gull but now given specific status, this species was first identified in Radnorshire on 22nd November 2007 along the River Wye near Llowes. This bird was subsequently seen in the same area, on and off, until 26th June 2008. In 2009 there were two birds seen in the same Glasbury/Llowes/Clyro area between 2nd and 12th July and one of those birds was also seen occasionally between 22nd April and 27th August 2010.

Glaucous Gull *Larus hyperboreus* A

Very rare visitor.

Breeds on Arctic islands and tundra in Iceland, Arctic Russia, Alaska, Arctic Canada and southern Greenland. Winters in the Arctic Ocean, the North Pacific and North Atlantic.

The only record is of an adult on Craig Goch Reservoir on 30th October 1993.

Great Black-backed Gull *Larus marinus* A

Rare visitor.

Breeds from Iceland, the Faeroes, the British Isles, north-west France and Scandinavia east to Murmansk, Svalbard and Bear Island; also eastern North America. Winters within the breeding range and south to the Mediterranean and the Black and Caspian Seas.

The first record was of one passing over Llyn Heilyn on 22nd August 1953 and the second was one on the River Wye at Llanfaredd on 25th April 1954.

The majority of records have come from the lower Wye below Glasbury where the attraction is usually washed up dead sheep or Salmon. One to two birds have been present, at least for a time, in many winters since 1973, especially during January. There have also been several records in the area in April and May and one to two in July, August and September. Eight were present in January 1992, six at the end of December 1991 and five in May 1982 and January 1989.

Away from the lower Wye Valley there have been about 52 records of which 36 have come from the Elan and Claerwen reservoirs. Records have been in every month with the same pair visiting mainly Craig Goch Reservoir regularly from 2002 to 2010 and in 2011 and 2012 just a single adult. A juvenile accompanied the pair in August 2005 and three birds were at Claerwen Reservoir on 17th May 2013. Dead sheep around the reservoir shorelines is usually what holds the birds, often for many days, before they head off west, back towards Cardigan Bay.

Records have also come from Llandrindod Golf Course (five on 6th November 1971), the Wye at Llanstephan, Rhayader, Bettws, St Harmon, The Begwyns pool, over Gilfach Nature Reserve, at Llandrindod Wells and near Painscastle, where a bird ringed as a chick on Flatholm in the Bristol Channel on 14th June 1969 was found dead on 3rd July 1972.

Most records have been of birds in adult or near-adult plumage but immatures of all ages have been seen.

Little Tern *Sternula albifrons*

A

Very rare visitor.

Breeds discontinuously across much of Europe and western Asia north to Finland and south to the Caspian Sea and the Persian Gulf; also south-east Asia, parts of Africa and Australia. Northern populations are migratory to coastal waters around Africa, south-east Asia, Australia and New Zealand and the western Pacific.

There have been four records:

One was picked up exhausted near Knighton on 23rd September 1915. One was seen flying up and down the River Wye at Erwood Bridge during a severe gale on 29th July 1956. One was seen flying along the Wye below Glasbury on 29th April 1979 and another in the same place on 22nd August 1991.

Whiskered Tern *Chlidonias hybridus* A

Very rare visitor.

Breeds locally across southern Europe, western Asia, northern India, Australia and south-east Africa. Winters in sub-Saharan Africa, India, south-east Asia and the Philippines to Australia.

One was seen at Llanbwchllyn on 21st April 1956 and on the morning of the 22nd. At the time it was the first record for Wales and the 26th for the British Isles.

Black Tern *Chlidonias niger* A

Rare passage migrant.

Breeds locally from France and southern Sweden east across central Russia to the Yenesei and Lake Balkhash; also across much of Canada and parts of northern USA. Winters around the coasts of tropical West Africa and northern South America.

The first record was at Llanwefr Pool on11th May 1949 since when there have been a further 44 records. There have been three records in April (the earliest being at Llanbwchllyn on 14th April 1981), 26 in May, one in July, 10 in August, four in September and one in October - at Llandrindod Lake on 3rd October 1966.

There were four records in the 1950s, six in the 1960s, one in the 1970s, four in the 1980s, 12 in the 1990s and 17 between 2000 and 2013. Records have come from Llyn Heilyn (9), the lower Wye (15), Llandrindod Lake (8), Llanwefr Pool (4), Llanbwchllyn (3), Dol y Mynach Reservoir (2), Bwlchyfedwen, Glan Llyn, Rhiw Pool and Cabalva.

There have been 28 sightings of single birds, seven of two together, two of three birds and four of four birds. Nine were at Glasbury on 7th May 1988, 16 flew west up the Wye at Clyro on 31st August 2008, 17 flew up the Wye below Glasbury on 30th August 2005 and 30 similarly on 8th August 1992 flew over an RSPB warden on a canoeing holiday.

These birds almost certainly come from the breeding populations in the Netherlands, and also possibly Denmark, on their way to and from their wintering areas off West Africa.

Sandwich Tern *Sterna sandvicensis* A

Very rare passage migrant.

Breeds locally around the British Isles, France, the Baltic, the Mediterranean and Black Seas, eastern North and South America. Winters around Africa, Saudi Arabia, Central and South America, the Mediterranean, Black and Caspian Seas.

There have been nine records:

1993:	One long the River Wye near Hay on 29th April.
1994:	Three along the Wye below Glasbury on 31st March.
1994:	Two on the Wye near Llowes on 22nd April, one remaining until 3rd May.
1994:	Five flying north-east over Howey and Llandrindod Wells on 19th June.
1999:	Two resting on Garreg Ddu Reservoir on 10th April.
2003:	One flying north over Garreg Ddu Reservoir on 7th May.
2003:	One at Caban Coch Reservoir on 3rd August.
2010:	Two on Llandrindod Lake on 30th September.
2011:	Two between Glasbury and Llowes on 22nd August.

Common Tern *Sterna hirundo* A

Rare passage migrant.

Breeds from the Azores, Madeira, Iberia, France, the British Isles and Scandinavia east across northern and central Europe and Asia to north-east Siberia, south to Iran, Iraq, the Himalayas, Kazakhstan and northern China; also much of central and eastern Canada and north-east USA and locally in the Caribbean. Winters mostly around the coasts of Africa, South America, south-east Asia and Australia.

One was killed on the River Wye near Hay in 1864 or 1865 (Woolhope Society *Transactions* 1869). The next record was of an immature at Llyn Heilyn on 7th September 1956, since when there have been a further 48 records involving 76 birds.

All records have been between 22nd April (Glasbury,2011) and 24th September (Glasbury,2010) and monthly totals are; six in April, 15 in May, seven in June, four in July, 10 in August and seven in September. Twenty-one records have come from Llandrindod Lake, seven from the Elan and Claerwen reservoirs (mostly Dol y Mynach), 15 from the lower Wye Valley, three from Llyn Heilyn and singles from Pentrosfa Mire, Llyn Gwyn and Llanwefr Pool.

Records are usually of birds passing quickly through north or south and/or resting briefly. Most sightings have been of single birds with two to three together seen on 10 occasions. Four were at Glasbury on 13th May 1993, five there on 5th September 1967 and eight in the Elan Valley on 1st July 1978. A pair were present, and mating was seen, around large shingle banks along the Wye between Glasbury and Llowes at the end of April 1994 and again from 3rd to 11th May 1995.

Arctic Tern *Sterna paradisaea* A

Very rare passage migrant.

Breeds circumpolar from Iceland, the Faeroes, the British Isles and Scandinavia east across northern Russia including the Arctic islands, the Aleutian Islands, Alaska, northern Canada and Greenland. Winters in the South Atlantic, Indian and Pacific Oceans south to Antarctica.

There have been eight definite records:

1977:	Four at Llandrindod Lake on 7th August.
1991:	Two at Llyn Heilyn on 11th June.
1997:	Five flew over Caban Coch Reservoir on 20th September.
2001:	One flew up the River Wye at Glasbury on 21st May.
2008:	Two along the River Wye at Clyro on 31st August.
2012:	A flock of thirteen at Llyn Heilyn on 25th April flew off north.
2012:	A flock of twelve terns which flew north-west from Craig Goch Reservoir on 25th April included at least four Arctic.
2012:	Two flew upstream at Glasbury on 25th April.

Common or Arctic Tern *Sterna hirundo/paradisaea*

There have been 17 records involving 34 birds not seen well enough to assign to one species or the other. Most are likely to have been Common Terns.

Records have been between 25th April and 2nd October and for each month have numbered one in April, three in May, three in June, two in July, six in August and one each in September and October. Six of the records have come from the lower Wye Valley, four from Llandrindod Lake, three from Llyn Heilyn, two from Llanbwchllyn and singles from ponds at Maelinydd and Michaelchurch. Four birds were at Glasbury on 30th August 1991, six were at Llanbwchllyn on 18th May 1965 and eight heading north-west from Craig Goch Reservoir on 25th April 2012 were with four Arctic Terns and were almost certainly also of that species.

Guillemot or Razorbill *Uria aalge/Alca torda*

An auk seen flying fast down the River Wye at Llanelwedd on 6th October 1989 was either a Razorbill or, more likely, a Guillemot of the more northern, nominate, race *Uria aalge aalge* with very dark upperparts.

Little Auk *Alle alle* A

Storm-blown vagrant.

Breeds on Arctic islands in north-east Canada, Greenland, Iceland, Franz Josef Land, Jan Mayen, Svalbard, Novaya Zemlya and Bear Island. Winters in the North Atlantic and Arctic Oceans south as far as Nova Scotia and the North Sea, rarely in the Mediterranean and the Bering Sea.

There have been two records. One was picked up alive in a garden in Llandrindod Wells on the evening of 23rd December 1991 and the other was also picked up alive at Crossgates on 21st January 2007. It was released the same day at Ynyslas, Ceredigion, where it promptly flew eastwards, inland – suggesting, perhaps, that it had been blown in from the North Sea rather than from the Irish Sea.

Rock Dove *Columba livia* AC4

Probable former native breeder; uncommon feral breeder today.

Breeds naturally on some islands off western Scotland and Northern Ireland and in many remote places of Europe and Asia and possibly elsewhere. Feral birds are widespread around the world especially in towns and cities. Largely resident with local seasonal and altitudinal movements.

The species has been domesticated since at least 4,500 B.C. and dovecote birds were probably first brought to the British Isles by the Romans. In the Woolhope Naturalists' Field Club *Transactions* of 1869 James W. Lloyd stated that the species bred at Stanner Rocks. Breeding feral populations, which are regularly supplemented by lost racing birds, are found in many places with 10-20+ present in recent years at Glasbury Bridge, Llandrindod Wells, Knighton, Llanelwedd, Presteigne and Rhayader.

Stock Dove *Columba oenas* A

Widespread, but not common, resident breeder.

Breeds from Iberia, north-west Africa, the Mediterranean area, the British Isles and Scandinavia east to central Russia, Turkestan and Iran. Northern populations are migratory as far south as the Mediterranean area and Iraq.

The species spread throughout much of Britain from the south-east of England in the early and mid-19th century. On an excursion of the Woolhope Naturalists' Field Club to the Elan Valley on 23rd June 1896 at least a few Stock Doves were found breeding on the cliffs at Caban Coch despite all the noise of the construction of the dam below. The species bred on the same cliffs until 1988.

Ingram and Salmon in 1955 described the species as widespread and still fairly common although decreased appreciably compared with 40-50 years ago. The species suffered big declines, and local extinctions, across the British Isles between 1950 and 1961 due to the use of toxic cyclodiene-based (organochlorine) seed dressings.

Although still widespread today it could not be described as 'fairly common'. It is much less common in the west and north of the county, especially on the high ground, preferring the lowlands of the east and south where most of the arable land is. The breeding season Atlases of 1968-72 and 1988-91 found Stock Doves in all but one of the 21 hectads wholly or partly in Radnorshire whilst the winter Atlas of 1981-84 had records in all but the two in the far north-west (the upper Elan and Claerwen Valleys) and the same has been the case in summer and winter since 2005.

However, there has undoubtedly been a decline in numbers in some areas since about the mid-1980s and noticeable increases in other places since about 2005 due to increases and changes in arable crops. There were formerly six to seven pairs in the woodlands around the Elan reservoirs but all disappeared between 1976 and 1989 and the species is rarely recorded there today, although present nearby towards Rhayader. Predator pressure would seem to be the reason, although since c.2010 this has declined a little. Such declines have also occurred locally elsewhere in the county and the population in 2012 was probably between 250 and 300 pairs.

Until the mid-1990s flocks of 30-50 birds were quite frequently seen on arable fields in winter, especially in the south and east of the county, with an exceptional 140 present near Howey from January to March 1987. There were 50 at Four Stones on 3rd February 1968, 50 at Hundred House on 8th January 1978, 40 at Llyn Heilyn on 18th April 1979, 50 at Glasbury on 2nd September 1989 and about 50 were near Llowes in November and December 1999. Between 2000 and 2005 double-figure flocks were scarce and the highest count was of 25 at Llanbadarn Fynydd on 22nd June 2002.

Arable weed seeds are a major part of the species' diet and since 2005 numbers have noticeably increased in line with an increase in, and more widespread growing of, autumn sown grain crops and oil-seed rape. Autumn-sown oil-seed rape provides an important winter and early spring feeding area. Recent feeding flocks have included 45 near Cwmbach on 6th July 2009, 45 at New Radnor on 3rd October 2011 and 52 at Clyro on 21st January 2011. Cold weather induced passage and influxes from the north and east of Britain occur occasionally, usually with Wood Pigeons, e.g. 17 flew south over Franksbridge on 7th February 1996.

Breeding areas include older broadleaved woodlands and individual trees in hedgerows with suitably large natural holes, farm buildings (old and new) which have nesting ledges, and cliffs and quarries - although less so than in the 1980s and before. The lack of suitable nest sites undoubtedly has a limiting effect on the population and the species is a regular occupier of nestboxes put up for owls. Three broods are often reared and young in the nest have been found in the county in all months between May and October.

Wood Pigeon *Columba palumbus* A

Common resident breeding bird, passage migrant and winter visitor.

Breeds throughout most of Europe including the Azores and Madeira and north-west Africa east to Iran, western Siberia and the Himalayas. Northern populations are migratory to within and to the south of the species' breeding range.

The species increased greatly in numbers in the 19th century due to the increase in arable farming acreage and in particular the growing of clover. The growing of oil-seed rape since the mid-1970s has also been a huge boost to winter survival rates. Very cold winters have taken their toll, especially the spell from January to March 1963. Today the species is found breeding in most types of woodland, especially young conifer plantations, with nearby improved grasslands and/or arable land. Tall hedgerows and dense areas of broadleaved scrub are also widely used as breeding sites with nests often found in the county as low as two metres.

The densest breeding populations in Radnorshire occur in the east and south of the county where there is mixed farming with scattered woodlands and tall, dense, hedgerows. Upland areas such as Radnor Forest (up to 600 metres) and the Elan uplands, where there is high predator pressure, are occupied in low numbers with birds often flying some distance to feed on improved pastures and, in the early autumn, on bilberries. Also many birds breed within towns and villages and are commonly recorded at garden feeding stations.

Although nesting in Radnorshire has been recorded in every month from March to November, the peak of the breeding season is very late, between July and September. Three broods are often raised in the most suitable parts of the county with just a single brood in many higher areas of the north and west where the populations are doubtfully self-sustaining and probably dependant on immigration from the more productive lowlands. A nest with four young was found in a Presteigne garden on 8th May 1940 – doubtless the product of two females laying in the same nest. (*British Birds* vol. 34 p.22). Birds are found in every hectad in the county and the breeding population in 2012 was likely to be between 1,500 and 2,000 pairs.

There are annual autumn influxes into Radnorshire fom the north and east usually coinciding with the first cold weather in late October and November. Flocks either move on quickly or stay depending on how heavy the acorn and Beech mast crop is or whether there are young oil-seed rape fields to hold them.

Cold-weather movements also occur later in the winter if there are very hard frosts and/or snow. Flocks of a few hundred birds are frequent but four-figure counts are unusual: 1,000 were at Glasbury on 21st November 1981; 3,500 flew down the Marteg Valley at Gilfach in two hours on 9th November 1996 and 1,000 flew down the Edw Valley near Franksbridge on the same day; 1,000 flew south at Newbridge on 4th November 1998; 1,000 were in the Elan Valley on 2nd December 2000 and 2,000 were there on 5th November 2001; 3,000 flew south in an hour over Radnor Forest on 28th October 2009 and counts of 1,000 were made at Glasbury and in the Elan Valley the following day; 4,400 flew south-east over Radnor Forest in three hours on 29th October 2011.

There has only been one ringing recovery of more than 20 km from Powys and that was ringed in June and shot in Cornwall in November.

Collared Dove *Streptopelia decaocto*

A

Widespread and common resident breeding bird.

Huge range expansion since about 1930 and now breeds across Europe and Asia to Sri Lanka, Turkestan and Korea and also many parts of North America. Largely resident apart from altitudinal movements to lower ground in some places in winter.

The first record was of one at Presteigne on 31st March 1965 (ten years after the first British record in Norfolk) and the first breeding record was at Knighton the following year. On the 15th October 1967 there was a flock of 24 at a corn merchant's yard in Knighton and colonisation of the county was rapid thereafter.

The heyday of the species in Radnorshire was in the 1970s and 1980s with flocks of 20-40 often reported and a highest ever count of 56 at Glasbury on 17th January 1979. There was however a marked reduction in numbers and a contraction in distribution range in the county from the late 1980s to about 2000 followed by a levelling out since then. Heavy predator pressure was undoubtedly the reason. It formerly bred at several places on the farms and around the reservoirs in the Elan and Claerwen Valleys but none have done so since 1991 and there have only been a few records of single birds passing through since. Similarly it has disappeared from several other areas, mostly in the uplands.

The breeding Atlas of 1968-72 found birds in 10 of the county's 21 hectads; by the winter survey of 1981-84 this rose to 13 and by the summer Atlas of 1988-91 records came from 17. Since 2006 birds have been recorded in 17 in both winter and summer and the breeding population in 2012 was probably within the range of 550 to 750 pairs.

In Radnorshire the species nests mostly in amenity conifers, shelter belts and young plantations in and around villages, towns and farms, especially the larger mixed and arable ones in the lowlands of the east and south where small flocks of 10-20 may be present year round. Smaller numbers are also often attracted to garden feeding stations, especially since the late 1990s with the increased availability of lower cost birdseed. Young in the nest have been found in the county in every month from March to November and three or more broods are frequent in favourable areas although predation of the usually conspicuous eggs and young is often very high.

One was found sick in Powys in May 1982 having been ringed at a site in Hampshire in April 1981 where several hundred used to be ringed each year.

Turtle Dove *Streptopelia turtur* A

Very rare summer visitor and passage migrant which has bred.

Breeds aross Europe and Asia and parts of North Africa from the British Isles, Iberia and the Canary Islands east across the Baltic countries and Russia to Mongolia and Afghanistan and south to the Nile Valley, Iran and Saudi Arabia. Winters in central, sub-Saharan, Africa.

In the late 19th century the species was scarce and known only from the Boughrood area of the Wye Valley. Ingram and Salmon reported in 1955 that the species was considered to be not uncommon in the county 40-50 years before (c.1905-1915) but that it was certainly a scarce bird now. They had not seen one in Radnorshire for five years and had heard of only two - at Rhosgoch on 1st July 1951 and at Rhiw Pool on 28th July 1953.

These observations fit in well with the facts that Turtle Doves spread into Wales in the mid-19th century and experienced another upsurge in numbers in the first decade or so of the 20th century. The species is largely a weed-seed eater which generally flourishes in agricultural recessions and declines in the face of intensive farming. The species had a high point in Radnorshire during the late 1950s and the 1960s when there were obviously several pairs nesting in the Rhiw Pool area of Radnor Forest, presumably in young conifers, and in the Glasbury/Llowes/Clyro area. In the conifer plantations above Rhiw Pool at least six were seen and others heard on 20th May 1956 and there were other sightings there between 1953 and 1963 after which, presumably, the forestry became too mature and so unsuitable for nesting.

In the lower Wye Valley there were pairs at Clyro and Llowes in June 1961 and about 30 were feeding in a field at Llowes on 21st June 1963. Just south of Llowes there were about 10 pairs in the Glasbury area in 1964 which undoubtedly included some towards Hay in the Llanigon area of Breconshire. There was also a record down river at Cabalva in July 1964 and a pair bred up river near Erwood in 1968. A few birds were found in summer in the Glasbury/Clyro/Llowes area in several years until 1974. A pair bred at Glasbury in 1981 and an adult and a juvenile were seen there on 11th July. One was seen at Llowes on 11th September 1982 and one at Boughrood on 28th June 1983. A pair bred at Boughrood in 1987 and one was seen nearby at Glanwye in May of the following year. Four birds were seen at Clyro on 8th June 1992 and pairs bred in dense willow carr between Glasbury and Llowes in 2005 and in young, dense, conifer plantation near Presteigne in 2011. These two pairs mostly fed in large horse paddocks/pastures, headlands planted with seed mixtures for game birds, on recently harvested oil-seed rape fields and with Collared Doves around the farm yards and buildings of large mixed farms.
Other records have included: a pair near Presteigne railway bridge in 1959; three at Whitton on 6th August 1962; a pair near Knighton on 30th June 1963; one above Llanelwedd Quarry on 19th June 1971;

one at St Harmon from 12th to 15th May 1972; at Presteigne on 26th July 1976; at Penybont on 8th May 1980; one at Evenjobb on 22nd July 1988; at Bwlch y Sarnau on 25th May 1994; near Newbridge on 14th May 1996; at Penywrlodd, Clyro, on 18th September 2000; at a garden feeding station in Rhayader on 10th June 2005 and at Llowes on 20th September 2010 – the latest county record.

As well as the breeding record for 2011, there were also individuals from May/June to August at Llandegley, Llanfihangel nant Melan and New Radnor – all were associated with garden feeding stations. The bird at New Radnor returned from mid-May 2012 staying to the end of June and the same Llandegley individual was present from at least 10th May to 28th August 2012 and from 19th April 2013 (the earliest Radnorshire record) to at least 9th July. These records since 2011 are probably derived from several pairs then breeding just east over the border into Herefordshire.

Ring-necked Parakeet *Psittacula krameri* C1

Very rare visitor.

Breeds naturally in sub-Saharan Africa and southern Asia. Introduced to England, the Netherlands, Belgium, Germany, Israel, Kenya, Mauritius, Egypt and south-east USA. Resident.

The first record in the British Isles was in 1969 and the first breeding record was in Surrey in 1971. Both arose from avicultural escapes and deliberate releases. The population reached 500-1,000 birds by the early 1980s and about 30,000 by 2010. Most birds are still in south-east England and it is the most northerly population of breeding parrots in the world. They are an agricultural pest in Africa and Asia and are beginning to be so in Britain where they are also noisy and vigorous attendees at garden bird feeders.

There have been four records of single birds in Radnorshire: Near Knighton on 28th June 1986; near the car park for Water-break-its-neck on 4th December 1987; one around Caenbrook Meadow, Presteigne, on 2nd July 2001 and one at Norton on 21st July 2010 was seen in Rhayader and Llandrindod Wells in July and September and then back to Rhayader in November.

Cuckoo *Cuculus canorus*

A

Widespread but uncommon breeding bird.

Breeds from north-west Africa, Iberia and the British Isles east across Europe and Asia to Kolyma, Kamchatka and Japan, north to beyond the Arctic Circle and south to Turkey, Iraq and China. Winters in sub-Saharan Africa and south-east Asia.

Ingram and Salmon (1955) said that the species was,'a common and widespread summer visitor, most numerous on the hills where it parasitises chiefly Meadow Pipits.' Nearly 60 years later the only change needed is from 'common' to 'uncommon'. This decline was due firstly to the huge loss of heather moorland and other losses of good upland habitat for Meadow Pipits in Radnorshire during the 1960s. National Atlas work since 1968 has shown a gradual decline across much of the British Isles which became very noticeable in Radnorshire from the early 1990s.

A number of the commons in Radnorshire have also lost their attractiveness to the species since the 1970s and 1980s due to a combination of overgrazing and spring burning of heather, gorse and semi-improved grassland.

This national decline has triggered a lot of research into the reasons since 2009; whether due to climatic change in the British Isles causing loss of insect food (particularly certain species of moth caterpillars), problems on migration or in the African wintering areas. Just as this work started there was a very noticeable and sudden widespread increase in numbers in the uplands of Radnorshire of about 25%-30% in 2010. This increase was also noticed elsewhere in mid-Wales. There were further noticeable increases in 2011 and 2013 for no obvious reason, but the species is still far from common in the county, and is a long way from the numbers of the 1980s and before. Since 2005 the species has been recorded in all 21 of the 10km squares wholly or partly in Radnorshire but the population in 2012 was probably only in the region of 70-100 calling males.

Based on 33 years records the average first date in spring is the 18th April with the earliest being 2nd April 2002 near Glasbury and 4th April 1971 at Penybont. The adults leave very early, often in June, whilst the juveniles of the year usually depart in August and there are records each year of dispersing birds throughout the month. The latest record is of one at Glasbury on 8th September 1984. Gatherings are unusual but there were eight birds, including males and females, excitedly chasing each other and calling at Rhosgoch Bog on 20th May 2000. Brown-phase adults have been seen in the Elan Valley on 10th May 1991 and at Rhosgoch Bog on 22nd May 2002.

Ingram and Salmon mention Blackbird and Grey Wagtail as unusual host species being used in the county. Meadow Pipits are certainly the commonest species parasitised but others found in the county have been Dunnock, Wren, Willow Warbler, Garden Warbler, Stonechat, Whinchat, Tree Pipit, Robin, Pied Wagtail and Reed Bunting.

Barn Owl *Tyto alba*

Uncommon resident breeding bird.

A

Breeds in central and southen Europe, the Canaries, Madeira and Cape Verde Islands, most of Africa, India, south-east Asia, Australia and many Pacific islands, USA, Central and South America. Mostly resident.

In the 18th and 19th centuries the Barn Owl was the commonest owl but in the middle of the 19th century there was the start of a big decline which it was said was due to increased persecution and the shooting and trapping of specimens for taxidermy.

The National Barn Owl Enquiry of 1932 came up with a figure of 48 pairs for Radnorshire but the high figures from this study are treated with caution as the survey was based on a questionnaire rather than fieldwork. Although a conspicuous, large and pale, bird reports of Barn Owls are often owls in a barn which turn out to be Tawny Owls on investigation. Also, they are considered one of the three most difficult species in Britain to survey accurately.

The very hard winter of 1946/7 undoubtedly had a major effect on numbers and Ingram and Salmon in 1955 said that the species was, 'a scarce resident ... and there are very few pairs in the county.' This situation probably persisted for most of the 1960s due to the continued use of organochlorine seed dressings, increased disturbance, increased grazing levels leading to lower numbers of Short-tailed Voles, loss of many old-style stone barns, agricultural land improvements and some very severe winters, especially those of 1961/2 and 1962/3.

However, there were obviously some increases later in the decade or in the early 1970s as the Atlas of 1968-72 found the species in 12 of the 21 10-km squares wholly or partially in Radnorshire. There were many more reports than usual in 1971 and 1972 with a comment from Nantmel of 'more than ever before'. A survey in 1978 found only five occupied territories and nine former sites unoccupied. However, 1978 was a low point after three poor breeding seasons following the big vole year of 1975.

Cold winters in the early 1980s, and probably the use of second-generation rodenticides, kept numbers down to about six to15 pairs in the decade. In 1990 there were at least 21 pairs after two mild winters and 1990 being a big year for Short-tailed Voles. However cold weather in February 1991 and a crash in vole numbers resulted in only six nesting pairs being found. Most of the winters in the 1990s were comparitively mild and in 1999 there were 22-25 occupied sites found and 24-27 in 2003. Although 2006 was an extremely poor year for young raised, 26 pairs were found in 2007.

From 2000 there was a noticeable spread into the uplands with breeding in the Elan Valley and birds present at the north end of Claerwen Reservoir, on Radnor Forest and elsewhere on and around the mid-county moorlands. Birds have been seen hunting regularly between 450 and 500 metres a.s.l. and over the same areas of upland grasslands as Short-eared Owl. The highest nest site found in the county was on the upstairs floor of a long-unoccupied house at 430 metres (1,400 feet) and a close second was one in a stone hay-barn at 380 metres (1,235 feet).

Several birds were found dead or dying during the very cold weather of February 2009 but 26 occupied sites were found in the summer. The cold weather, and particularly the snow-cover, of the winters of 2009/10 and 2010/11 had a much greater impact with only 16 occupied sites found in 2010, just six to eight in 2011 (even though it was a big vole year) but a recovery to at least 13 in 2012. The exceptionally cold March of 2013 resulted in many losses and several traditional sites were not occupied. Since 2005 the species has been recorded in all 21 of the 10-km squares wholly or partly in the county at some time of the year.

In years with high vole numbers, pairs are sometimes double-brooded and young have been found in the nest in Radnorshire in every month from April to November. Up to eight young have been recorded but the average brood raised is three. Most known nest sites in Radnorshire are in buildings and nest-boxes with about 40% in holes and cavities in trees especially Ash and oak, but also occasionally Sycamore and Beech.

There is definitely some competition for nest-sites with Tawny Owls, Grey Squirrels and Jackdaws. Kestrels and Stock Doves have also been found nesting in boxes put up for Barn Owls, as well as Goosander on two occasions. Barn Owls have been recorded as prey of Goshawk with kills seen at dusk near Newbridge in November 1993 and near New Radnor in March 2002. Road kills are reported every year as wide roadside grass verges beside faster stretches of road are often good hunting areas. Released birds of unknown origin carrying non-B.T.O. rings have been found as road casualties in the county in recent years, including one of the continental race.

There have been 13 ringing recoveries to and from Powys with the only movement of more than 100 km being to the coast of Gwent. Birds found in the Powys (9) have come from Clwyd, Dyfed (4), Gwynedd (2) and Shropshire (2) whilst those ringed in Powys (4) and found elsewhere have gone to Gwent, Hereford & Worcester (2) and Shropshire. A nestling ringed at Rhandirmwyn, near Llandovery, in July 1970 was killed by a car near Newbridge, 30 km north-east, in February 1971.

Little Owl *Athene noctua* C1

Rare resident breeder.

Breeds from western Europe, the Baltic countries and north-west Africa east across Europe and Asia to Mongolia, Tibet, China and Korea and south to the Sahara, north-east Africa and the Arabian Peninsula. Mostly resident throughout its range. Introduced to the British Isles and New Zealand.

The species was introduced into Kent in 1879 and was reported as 'known to have bred' in Radnorshire by Lewis Davies in 1912. However, the first definite record was of a pair in Knighton in 1914 and the first confirmed breeding was made there on 28th April 1918. The Little Owl Enquiry in 1936/7 had just one report for the county, at Llanbister. Ingram and Salmon (1955) stated that the species became widespread and quite numerous after 1920 but that the hard winter of 1946/7 almost exterminated it. After this they described it as still quite scarce although a few pairs had reappeared.

However, there were only three records published for the 1950s; at the soon to be completed Claerwen Dam on 10th May 1952 (still the only record from the Elan and Claerwen Valleys), at Rhayader in 'spring' 1955 and at Hindwell on 1st December 1959. In the 1960s the Hindwell bird was seen again in early 1960, one was near Rhosgoch in January 1962 and others were seen at Bailey Einon and north of Crossgates in 1966, at Pwll Patti in1967, Knighton in 1968 and Hindwell and nearby Evancoyd in 1969.

Although the species was in decline nationally between 1965 and 1975, six pairs were reported nesting in the Pwll Patti area in 1973. There were no reports from 1975 to 1977 but birds were seen at Llowes, Llandrindod and Kinnerton in 1978. The national increase of 1975 to 1985 was noticeable in the county with records from three sites each year in the 1980s and a description of 'abundant' for the New Radnor/Kinnerton area. In the 1990s records came from across the county including at Glasbury, Gladestry, Llowes, Rhosgoch, Howey, Knighton, Newchurch, Walton, Penybont, Bettws, New Radnor, Evenjobb, Newbridge, Llanelwedd and Builth Road. Breeding took place at Gilwern Common (340 metres, 1,105 feet) in 1991 and at Llwynpentre Bank (300m, 975 feet) in 1996, where the nest site was down a rabbit hole.

Since 2000 the species has undoubtedly become much scarcer with just single pairs found in 2002 and 2005. Repeated visits to all prevously occupied areas found birds at four sites in 2006, 2011 and 2012; at three in 2007 and 2010; seven in 2009 and eight in 2008. Since 2000 records have come from Presteigne, Glasbury, Old Radnor, New Radnor, Huntington, Burfa, Cregrina, Clyro, Llowes, Doldowlodd, Knighton, Pwll Patti, Llanelwedd, Llanbister, Rhayader, Boughrood, Franksbridge, Llandrindod, Nant Glas and Evenjobb. However, positive breeding reports have been few.

A full-grown bird ringed near Oswestry on 31st December 1981 was reported on 4th August 1982 as found freshly dead at Pant y Dwr (60 km SSW).

Tawny Owl *Strix aluco*

A

Common resident breeder.

Breeds from western Europe north to Scandinavia and north-west Africa east across Europe and Asia to China and south to the Atlas Mountains, Iran and the Himalayas. Resident.

Ingram and Salmon said in 1955 that the species was,'A common, widespread resident breeding species. It is probably the most numerous predator, exceeding even the Buzzard. It is found in the hills up to above 1,500 feet.' There is no change in 2012 and it is found in all of the Radnorshire 10-km squares.

The broadleaved woodlands of the county support the highest density of breeding Tawny Owls but birds also nest in coniferous woodlands, lightly wooded farmland and in and around most towns and villages, as well as larger gardens and churchyards where mature trees of some kind are present. The only areas where the species is rare are those largely treeless moorland areas of the north, west and central hills. The population of the county is likely to be between 250 and 400 pairs but many pairs do not breed every year and there are also a large number of non-breeding birds.

Nest sites are typically in holes or cavities in mature broadleaved trees, especially Oak and Ash, and chimney-style owl nest-boxes are quickly occupied. Although there is often conflict with Grey Squirrels over nest holes, at Evancoyd in 1965 an entrance hole was shared with the Tawny Owl having two eggs and the squirrel lodging further inside. Nests have also been found in old nests of Magpie and Carrion Crow as well as on ledges and old hay bales in dark, quiet, stone barns. In Radnorshire, two to four (very rarely five) eggs are typically laid from the last week of March but sometimes as early as the first week in the river valleys in advanced springs.

Young are rarely found in the nest after the end of May and usually only one or two are finally produced. Birds form a major proportion of the diet in all parts of the county, even at sites where mice and voles are abundant. On the edges of hills and commons it is not unusual for the remains of birds such as Wheatear and Meadow Pipit to be found at nest sites. Many small mammals are taken especially voles, mice and shrews with others found uneaten at nest-sites including young Rabbit, Mole, bat sp. and Weasel.

Roosts of thrushes and Starlings are frequently targetted in the winter months and in the spring amphibians can form a very high proportion of food items. Pellets collected at a roost near the Aberithon Turbary (Lower Bog) at Newbridge on Wye in the spring of 1984 contained nothing but frog or toad bones and skin. Earthworms are also a major source of food and to a lesser extent, slugs. On wet nights, worms are taken off road surfaces which results in many of the road casualties reported each year in the county. Locally the larger species of dung beetles and cockchafers are taken in high numbers at certain times of the year.

Despite the ringing of many nestlings there have only been three recoveries of more than 10km and none of more than 100km - which are extremely rare nationally. One ringed in the Elan Valley on 14th May 1992 was killed by a car at Llangurig on 26th April 1995, a distance of 15 km to the north.

Long-eared Owl *Asio otus*

A

Rare breeding bird and winter visitor.

Breeds from the Canary Islands, western Europe, parts of north-east and north-west Africa east across Scandinavia, Russia, Turkestan and Siberia to China and Japan; also much of Canada and the northern USA. Northern populations are partly migratory as far south as North Africa, northern India, southern China, Korea, southern Japan, southern USA and Mexico.

Ingram and Salmon (1955) said that the species was formerly fairly widely distributed and could be found breeding in several areas until the timber (coniferous woodland) was felled. They went on to say that it still bred, 'in several areas chiefly in the north of the county, but is a scarce bird.' This last sentence is still the case today.

Although there are no references to, or records of, the species in the county before 1951 it was present in all the neighbouring counties earlier and it is likely that it also bred in Radnorshire. Numbers across Wales declined between 1900 and 1950 due to persecution and egg collectors, and probably interaction with Tawny Owls which had increased over the same period.

Due mostly to a huge amount of fieldwork by the late G.M.Ireson many positive breeding records were made in the 1950s and 1960s. Nests were found in the Radnor Forest area in 1951 (sitting bird), 1952 (three eggs), 1953 (two young), 1954 (three eggs), 1955 (old Magpie's nest in larch), 1956 (in larch, four eggs laid and three young reared) and 1957 (old Magpie's nest). Also in the 1950s breeding took place in the Red Lion Hill area; three young raised in 1956, in an old Magpie's nest in 1957 and with four eggs in 1958. In 1957 successful breeding was also found at Bwlch y Sarnau, Pant y Dwr, St Harmon 'and other places in the area'. Other records in the 1950s were at St Harmon on 10th August 1952, Rhiw Pool on 20th May 1956 and at the Vron, a single on 7th and pair on 27th April 1958.

In the 1960s breeding season records came from the Vron Valley, the Radnor Forest area, Cilfaesty Hill (three eggs in an old Magpie's nest on 16th April 1967) and Rhosgoch in 1969. A pair bred near Erwood in 1971 but there was no fieldwork in the north during the 1970s. In the 1980s breeding was proved in most years in the northern conifer forests especially in the Abbeycwmhir, Bwlch y Sarnau and Radnor Forest areas. One was seen between Llangunllo and Llanbister on 15th November 1982 and one was found dead at Old Penywrlodd, near Clyro, in November 1987. Breeding was proved at three sites in 1989.

In the 1990s breeding was annual in the Llaithddu area until the plantations were clearfelled in September 1997, after which a single bird was seen in some remaining Sitka Spruce in March 1998. Breeding continued throughout the decade in the Radnor Forest, Abbeycwmhir and Bwlch y Sarnau plantations and took place just north-west of Rhayader in 1993 in an area of open mixed woodland and parkland. Breeding was proved at five sites in the north of the county in 1999. The only other records away from the usual areas were of presumed winter visitors; one in a garden in Llandrindod Wells on 15th November 1996 and one to three roosting in willow carr at Rhosgoch Bog from 10th October 1991 to at least 10th January 1992.

Since 2000 breeding records have continued from the northern conifer woodlands with one to six positive breeding records each year and birds found at eight sites in 2010. Winter records from Rhosgoch Bog came in January 2000, November 2008 and late October 2011 and breeding took place there in 2002 and 2004 in old Magpie's nests in dense willow carr a long way from any conifer plantations. Breeding may well have taken place there before and since. A pair bred near Knighton in 2010 raising at least one young and records came from the same area in 2011 and 2012. A nest was found in a Grey Squirrel's drey in 2008 and a single bird was seen at Burfa Camp on 20th January 2012.

A nestling ringed near Red Lion Hill on 5th June 1956 was found alive but injured at Bleddfa on 6th August 1957, a distance of 16km to the south-east.

Short-eared Owl *Asio flammeus* A

Rare breeding bird, passage migrant and winter visitor.

Breeds from Iceland and the British Isles east across northern Europe and Asia to Kolyma and Kamchatka and south to northern China and Transcaspia; also North America from northern Canada to California; also in parts of the Caribbean, South America, the Galapagos Islands, Hawaii and the Falkland Islands. Northern breeders migrate south as far as sub-Saharan Africa, India and Sri Lanka, Japan, southern China and Central America.

Ingram and Salmon (1955) said that this day-flying owl was not infrequently seen in winter and occasionally in spring, usually on the high moors between 1,000 and 1,800 feet. They went on to say that although breeding had been suspected in the past there were no definite records until forestry workers found a nest in 1954 in the Waun Marteg area with three young and three eggs. This large area of newly planted upland conifers on *Molinia* and heather moorland had large numbers of Short-tailed Voles and also held one to two pairs in 1955 and 1956 and five pairs in 1957. Six adults were counted on 29th March 1958 and one to three were seen on several dates between January and June with a single also on 14th April 1959. Other records in the 1950s included one in the Elan Valley on 5th January 1954, three near Llanfihangel nant Melan were put up by the hunt on 16th March 1959 as was a single at Colva on 23rd March.

Breeding continued to the north of Bwlch y Sarnau into the 1960s with a nest and three eggs found at Brondre Hill on 1st May 1960. Birds were seen annually in the spring/summer in the Waun Marteg area between 1960 and 1963 when a nest with two eggs was found and three adults seen on 16th April and five birds seen on 23rd June. Three young were found at Waun Marteg in 1966 but this was the last record of breeding there as the growing conifers made the area unsuitable. Birds were seen in the upper Elan Valley in May of 1964 and 1965 and breeding was considered to have probably taken place there betwen 1968 and 1976. Other records in the 1960s included singles in the Llanwefr Pool area from 22nd November to 6th December 1964, on Rhulen Moor on 16th August 1965, at Blue Lins on 13th October 1968 and at Fowler's Armchair on 13th November 1969.

In 1971 one to three birds were seen in the upper Elan Valley between May and August and also in April 1972. One was on Penybont Common on 15th April 1977 and one on Beacon Hill on 10th June 1979. Also in the 1970s singles were at Painscastle on 26th and 28th February 1972, at Penlanfawr on 12th August 1972, at Felindre on 12th March 1974 and on Maelinydd in 1977. The nationwide invasion from the continent in 1978/9 was noticed in the Llyn Heilyn area with one on Gwaunceste Hill on 28th October, two at Llyn Heilyn on 9th December, three at Beili Bedw on 17th and four around Llyn Heilyn itself on 18th.

In the 1980s there were records from Radnor Forest on 22nd March 1981, Gwaunceste Hill on 1st December 1982, Beacon Hill - two on 7th January 1984, one to two in the upper Elan Valley in January 1986, two on Penybont Common on 26th December 1987 as well as one to four breeding records from 1983 onwards from the Elan Valley, Radnor Forest and Gwaunceste Hill.

There was a big increase in records during the 1990s with up to five pairs present in four areas of the Elan uplands and one or two at least annually. There was also breeding again in the Radnor Forest and Gwaunceste Hill areas. Records also came from Nant Glas on 29th March 1991, Litton Hill on 9th November 1991, the Vron on 10th January 1994 and 20th March 1995 and on Little Hill on 4th May 1995. In 1996 there were records in late October and November from Elan Valley, Llandrindod Golf

Course, Rhiw Bottom and Penybont Common and in 1999 there were three at Radnor Forest on 19th November and singles at Tynbryniau Hill on 12th February and at Penybont Common on 16th December.

Since 2000 there have been one to four pairs annually in the upper Elan and Claerwen Valleys area and breeding also in new areas of clearfell and young plantation in the Radnor Forest and Bwlch y Sarnau areas as well as on Beacon Hill and Gwaunceste Hill. An extra effort in 2003 found at least eight pairs at six sites. Records from other areas between 2000 and 2010 came from Ireland Moor, Moelfre, Nant Glas, Penybont Common (five records), Rhosgoch Bog, Bronydd, Llandrindod Golf Course, near the observatory at Knighton, Nantmel and Gilwern Hill.

There was another noticeable invasion in the winter of 2011/12 with records of one to two birds between 22nd October and 14th January from Penybont Common, Black Mixen, Bleddfa, The Begwyns, Gwaunceste Hill, Elan Valley (up to seven in December), New Radnor, Ireland Moor, Aberedw Hill, Rhosgoch Bog (from 28th October, three on 6th December), Rhiw Bottom, Llandegley Rhos, Perthi Common, a road casualty near Builth Road in late October which was rehabiliated at Kington, Llanbadarn Fynydd, Great Rhos, Gors Lydan, Beacon Hill, Llandeilo Hill and Newchurch Hill.

The breeding birds are usually different from those seen in the winter months, even in the same areas. Breeding birds arrive in March and April and have usually departed or dispersed by mid-August. Winter birds usually arrive from late October and have gone by February. Although most breeding attempts are in years with high vole numbers, breeding birds are not all totally dependant on vole numbers with some taking a lot of other species of small mammals and birds including Brown Rats and young Rabbits, mice and shrews, as well as many Meadow Pipits and Skylarks. One pair was double-brooded in the upper Elan Valley in 1997 and this has been suspected in two other years.

Hunting, especially if vole numbers are low, is often undertaken over bracken clad hillsides, heathlands and grasslands a long way from the nesting sites. These are invariably in much denser vegetation with very low or no grazing pressures, such as deep heather, rank *Molinia* and young plantation with a deep ground layer of grass, rushes, willow-herb or brambles. Up to nine eggs have been found in the county and broods of five young, although three to five eggs laid and one to three young raised is usual. Predation is high (especially by Fox) of young which have recently left the nest and either cannot yet fly or are poor flyers.

Nightjar *Caprimulgus europaeus*

A

Rare breeding summer visitor.

Breeds from north-west Africa, Iberia, the British Isles and southern Scandinavia east across Russia to Lake Baikal and south to Turkestan and north-west India. Winters in sub-Saharan Africa.

Ingram and Salmon (1955) said that the species was formerly a fairly common and widespread summer visitor but had been getting scarcer for some years and was now quite rare. Walpole-Bond writing in 1903 said that they were already becoming less plentiful in mid-Wales. Five birds in the Maesllwch collection were shot in the south of the county in the late 19th century.

The only records in the 1950s were one in the Presteigne area in 1952, a male at Evancoyd on 29th May 1958 and one at the Vron on 21st July 1959. A pair were at Rhydspence in May 1962 and there were at least two there on 20th July. Churring was heard at Cwmgerwyn on 23rd June 1963 and birds were present at Boultibrooke, near Presteigne, in 1964. A pair at Stanage Park on 12th June 1971 was the only record in the 1970s. It is estimated that the population in the British Isles halved between 1972 and 1981.

No birds were found in the county in the national census of 1981 when 57 males were found at 36 sites in Wales. A single bird was seen on the road at Rhulen on 26th May 1988 and in the national census of 1992 there were 11-12 calling males at four sites (Radnor Forest, The Begwyns, Ffynnon Gynydd and Stanage Park) and a more than threefold increase over Wales as a whole. Doubtless significant was that, at the time, May 1992 was the hottest May of the century and June was the second hottest June. At least four males were found at Radnor Forest, Bwlch y Sarnau and Burfa in 1993, 1994, 1998 and 1999.

From the end of the 1990s and into the 2000s there was a great increase in the clearfelling of large areas of matured coniferous forestry and this resulted in a large increase in the numbers of Nightjars found in some years. These have varied hugely from year to year depending largely it seems on the weather in May and June. Eight churring males were found at six sites in 2000, five were found at five clearfell sites in 2002, 17 churring males at seven sites in 2003 and c. 20 at 13 sites in 2004 and 2005. If continuous-cover forestry management is widely undertaken rather than clearfelling then it seems very likely that Nightjars will decline considerably as a breeding bird in the county.

An all-Wales survey in 2004 found 244 churring males, a 30% increase on 1992 and a four-fold increase on 1981. Despite the summer of 2006 being often hot only six males could be found in Radnorshire. Nine were located in 2008, 14 in 2009, a record 33+ at 14 sites in 2010 and 19 at 9 sites in 2013. Records away from the breeding areas are rare: single birds were at Llandrindod Hall Farm on 3rd and 4th July 2000, at Penybont Hall on 5th September 2004, at Nantmel on 15th September 2009 (the latest county record) and in a garden at Llandegley on 5th September 2011. The earliest records have been in the Elan Valley on 14th May 2005, Radnor Forest on 17th May 2002 and New Radnor on 20th May 2004, but most birds seem to arrive in early June.

Swift *Apus apus* A

Widespread but declining breeder and a spring and autumn passage migrant.

Breeds from north-west Africa to the British Isles and Scandinavia east across Europe and Asia to Lake Baikal and China, north to northern Finland and south to Turkey, Israel, Iran and the Himalayas. Winters in sub-Saharan Africa.

Ingram and Salmon said that the species was, 'A quite numerous summer visitor, breeding regularly in towns and many villages.' This holds true today, although there has been a noticeable decline in some places over the last 50 years due, at least in part, to fewer breeding places in modern buildings and as a result of widespread repairs to many older ones. There are still populations in all the major towns in the county and in many villages and hamlets, as well as at some isolated farms and older houses. The population in 2011 was probably between 200 and 260 pairs.

Screaming flocks around towns are a feature of the late spring and early summer with 10-40 birds frequently counted and up to 70 occasionally. Non-breeders arrive later in June and July and these can swell numbers noticeably. Feeding birds are seen in summer all across the county, from the lowest river valleys to the highest hills. The earliest breeding birds arrive at the very end of April and early May and continue to arrive throughout the month. Flocks of over 100 are rare; 100 were at Llanelwedd on 29th August 1985, 100 over Llandrindod Lake on 14th June 2008, 150 at Llanelwedd on 19th July 1983 and 200 over the Elan Valley on 22nd June 1997.

Most birds usually leave abruptly at the end of July and early August but if the breeding season has been delayed by poor weather, such as in 2008 and 2012, young may still be in the nest until mid-month. The earliest records for the county have been on 20th April at Newbridge in 2011 and at Builth Road in 2003. There have been just four records in September, up to the 17th, and the latest county record is of one over Rhayader on 5th October 1983.

Alpine Swift *Apus melba*

A

Very rare visitor.

Breeds from north-west Africa and Iberia east across southern Europe and southern Asia to Turkestan, India and Sri Lanka; also eastern and southern Africa and Madagascar. Mostly resident in India and Africa, other populations winter in sub-Saharan Africa.

There has been just one record: One was watched at close range being mobbed by House Martins at Clyro on the afternoon of the 14th August 1959 before heading off southwards.

Kingfisher *Alcedo atthis*

A

Widespread, mostly resident, breeder.

Breeds from north-west Africa, Iberia and the British Isles east across central and southern Europe and much of Asia east to Sakhalin, China and Japan and south to Indonesia and New Guinea, Iran, India and Sri Lanka. Central continental and northern birds migrate south to winter as far as North Africa and south-east Asia.

Ingram and Salmon (1955) described it as,'A not numerous resident breeding species'. Despite crashes after some cold winters (there was only a single record in 1963) the species has been remarkably stable in Radnorshire with the same stretches of river usually occupied every year. The cold winters of 2009/10 and 2010/11 seemed surprisingly to have less effect than the severe ones of the past and, by having two to three broods annually, recovery was rapid.

Pairs are found breeding along all the major rivers and many smaller rivers and streams where there are suitable banks for nest holes. Young birds of the year especially, and some adults, are regularly seen at lakes and ponds from early autumn and throughout the winter. Most birds are seen along the River Wye which usually has 18-25 pairs between Cabalva in the south-east and the Nant Dernol confluence in the north. The Ithon (plus its tributaries the Aran, Dulas Brook, Clywedog Brook etc.) the Lugg and the Teme each have several pairs, as does the Edw upstream as far as Bettws. The Hindwell Brook, and even the often mostly dry Summergil Brook, usually have pairs as does the Marteg, Elan, Bach Howey, the Arrow upstream as far as Newchurch and the Gladestry Brook as far as Gladestry.

Birds are also often seen along very small brooks and streams and one nest site in the Wye Valley below Glasbury was in a bank 400 metres from the river. Birds are recorded at a wide variety of still waters including (usually briefly) at garden ponds often a long way from flowing water. Up to four birds have been seen at Llandrindod Lake, coming up from the nearby River Ithon, and also one or two most autumns at Llanbwchllyn. Records have also come from Pentrosfa Mire, Hindwell Pool, the Evenjobb ponds, ponds at the former Nantmel refuse tip, Llyn Heilyn (but only one ever), Penybont Lake, Glan Llyn, Llyn Gwyn, and even the pools at Maelinydd a few times. The latter were probably going across country between catchments, as was a bird seen at Beacon Hill.

A fairly thorough survey over three seasons between 2000 and 2002 found 48-60 pairs in the county with the highest along the Marteg at 290 metres (940 feet) a.s.l. A walk along parts of the Wye Valley Walk between Boughrood and Hay can sometimes produce 10-15 birds, especially in the autumn. Minnows are by far the most important prey species as well as Chub fry along the larger rivers.

A nestling ringed at Theale Gravel Pit, near Reading, in August 1989 was found dead in Powys just three weeks later and a young bird of the year ringed in Powys on 25th August 1974 was found dead in Calvados, France, on 27th October – a distance of 430 km south-east and one of only three Kingfishers ever ringed in Britain and recovered in France.

Bee-eater *Merops apiaster* A

Very rare visitor.

Breeds from north-west Africa and Iberia east to Israel, central Russia and Lake Balkhash and south to southern Iran; also breeds in parts of South Africa. Winters in western and south-east Africa.

The only record was of one on the 3rd and 4th August 1949 at Moelfryn above the Wye Valley about three miles north of Rhayader (not at the Moelfryn in the Elan Valley as stated in Ingram and Salmon and elsewhere). The bird was seen by Davina Stewart-Peter and her mother and was the third record for Wales. (*British Birds* vol.43 p.156).

Roller *Coracias garrulus*

Very rare visitor.

A

Breeds from north-west Africa, Iberia and southern France north to the eastern Baltic east to central Russia and south to Israel, Iran, Pakistan and northern India. Winters in western and south-east Africa.

The only record is of one seen by R.H.Baillie as it flew out of a Rowan tree at a few yards range on the west side of Penygarreg Reservoir on 12th July 1962. It was the fourth record for Wales.

Hoopoe *Upupa epops*

Rare spring and summer visitor.

A

Breeds over much of Africa including Madagascar, southern and central Europe and Asia from Iberia and France to the eastern Baltic east to north-east China and south to the Malay Peninsula, Iran, the Arabian Peninsula, India and Sri Lanka. Northerly populations are migratory to the western Mediterranean, sub-Saharan Africa, India and south-east Asia.

There were four undated records between 1901 and 1920: One was shot near Knighton about 1901, one was near Boughrood in 1903, one near Glasbury in 1904 and one near Llanbister about 1920. Since then there have been a further 20 records:

1953:	At Brilley Mountain, 'right on the border with Herefordshire' on 19th June.
1955:	In a field between Llowes and Clyro on 25th April.
1956:	One by the road at Pont ar Elan on 13th April and nearby beside Craig Goch Reservoir from 15th April 'for several days'.
1956:	Two by the Caban Coch Dam 'in the 2nd half of April' may have included the above.
1957:	In the Vron Valley on 2nd June.

1966:	Llan-ar-Ithon Farm, west of Howey, 'about the end of March'.
1966:	Doldowlodd from 10th to 13th April.
1966:	Gigrin Farm, near Rhayader, in July.
1968:	Glasbury from 12th to 15th April.
1995:	In the upper Dernol Valley, north of Rhayader, from 1st May to 4th June.
1997:	Near Bleddfa on 24th April.
1997:	Rhayader on 7th July.
1999:	About half way along the track beside the Claerwen Reservoir on 7th May.
1999:	New Radnor on 15th March.
2002:	Near Shaky Bridge on 11th April.
2007:	Near Knighton on 20th April.
2009:	At Buzzards Beat, Dolau, on 10th April.
2011:	In a garden at Whitton on 16th June.
2012:	In a garden by Llandrindod Golf Course on 4th May.
2013:	Near Yardro on 22nd and 23rd May and possibly the same bird two miles east at Dolyhir on the 26th.

Wryneck *Jynx torquilla* A

Rare visitor.

Breeds from north-west Africa, Iberia, France and Scandinavia east across Europe and central Asia to northern Japan and northern China. Winters in sub-Saharan Africa and from India to southern China and Japan.

H.E.Forrest writing in 1907 said that the species, '...ascends the Wye above Builth but rarely passes the hilly barrier' and Lewis Davies in 1912 said, 'known to have bred.' J.Williams-Vaughan mentioned two having been killed at The Skreen, without any detail or dates, but which presumably were in the late 19th century. One was seen near Builth Road about August 1908 and one at Llandrindod in August 1946.

There have been six records since then:

1988:	In a garden on Hundred House Common on 19th August.
1991:	Around Cefnllys Church, near Shaky Bridge, from 10th to 12th May.
1992:	Crossgates on 31st August.
2001:	In a garden near Cefn Llech, north-west of Pant y Dwr, from 1st to 16th July when it flew into a window and died.
2004:	At the edge of Penybont Common by the council depot on 12th May.
2010:	Hundred House Common on 21st September.

Green Woodpecker *Picus viridis*

A

Widespread resident breeder.

Breeds from north-west Africa, Iberia, the British Isles and southern Scandinavia east across most of Europe and western Asia east to the Caspian Sea and south to Iran. Mostly resident.

Although for the British Isles as a whole this species has approximately doubled in numbers since about 1990, in Wales there has been a decline of about 20% mainly as a result of a general contraction in distribution from the north-west. This level of decline is also about right for Radnorshire.

There were undoubtedly many more pairs in the west of the county in the 1980s and somewhat more over the rest of the county. This seems likely to be due to changes in the population levels of ants rather than any loss of habitat and this could account for the decline from the five to six breeding pairs around the Elan reservoirs at the end of the 1980s to its being just an occasional visitor after 1995.

Since 2005 the species has been recorded from over 30% of the 350 2-km squares (tetrads) wholly or partly in Radnorshire and in all except two of the 21 10-km squares (hectads). The population was estimated at 80-150 pairs in 2001 and as of 2005-2009 the population could perhaps be more precisely put at c.120-150 pairs. In the late 1980s the population was probably nearer 180 pairs.

The species is found breeding across the county apart from the treeless parts of the far west and north and the central hills, although it is often found much further away from any trees in the autumn and winter and up to 500 metres (1,625 feet) a.s.l. Generally the species avoids coniferous woodland preferring open broadleaved country rather than large blocks of woodland as well as parkland, commons, large gardens, hedgerows with scattered mature trees, copses, riverside and roadside trees. There is a great deal of such habitat in Radnorshire and most farms have the necessary pastures and grasslands essential for feeding although there are many fewer unploughed fields with anthills today than there were even thirty years ago.

As a ground feeder, the species suffers in hard and snowy winters and numbers were noticeably lower in Radnorshire after the winters of 1946/7, 1961/2, 1962/3, 1981/2, 1984/5, 2009/10 and 2010/11. Recovery in numbers is slow as the species is single-brooded and in Radnorshire rarely seems to successfully raise more than three or four young which are vulnerable to predators in some areas as they feed in open areas and have an often conspicuous and slow, undulating, flight. Birds have been seen taken by Goshawk and a Sparrowhawk attacked one unsuccessfully at Newbridge.

Great Spotted Woodpecker *Dendrocopus major* A

Common and widespread resident breeder.

Breeds from north-west Africa, Iberia, France and the British Isles across Europe and Asia to Kamchatka, north to northern Finland and Russia and south to Iran, Lake Balkhash and southern China. Resident but with occasional irruptions from northern coniferous forests.

The entry in Ingram and Salmon for this species in the mid-1950s was, 'Resident and breeds regularly. Possibly not more numerous than the Green Woodpecker.' It is a much commoner bird today and at least four times commoner in Radnorshire than its larger relative.

It has been increasing in range and numbers across the British Isles since the 19th century and there was a noticeable increase in Wales during the first half of the 20th century. There was a rapid increase in the 1970s and another big increase in Radnorshire, and nationwide, has taken place since the mid-1990s. Maturing coniferous woodlands in Radnorshire and increased use of garden feeding stations has undoubtedly aided the increase here but there has also been a 40%-50% increase over much of continental Europe since about 1980. The population in Radnorshire in 2012 was probably between 450 and 550 pairs.

The species has been found in every 10-km square in Radnorshire since at least the late 1960s and although it is mostly a bird of broadleaved woodlands it also breeds, at lower densities, in mature coniferous plantations, parks and gardens, in riverside woodlands and in well-treed towns and villages. In those woodlands in Radnorshire around the Elan reservoirs 14 pairs were located in 2004 of which four were in mature mixed-conifer woodlands and the remainder in Sessile Oak dominated broadleaved woodlands. As it finds its food mostly in fallen and standing dead wood, in general it is not found in such open wooded habitats as the Green Woodpecker. Family parties often visit garden feeding stations and in the garden of The Grove, Nant Glas, 11 different birds were trapped for ringing in 2002.

Lesser Spotted Woodpecker *Dendrocopus minor* A

Rare resident breeder.

Breeds from Iberia, Algeria, France, the southern British Isles and Fennoscandia east across Europe and Central Asia to Kamchatka, northern Japan and China, south to Italy, Greece, Turkey and the Caspian Sea. Resident but northern and eastern populations are occasionally irruptive.

This sparrow-sized, secretive and easily overlooked, woodpecker was formerly much commoner in the county than it is today. In 1955 Ingram and Salmon said that it was, 'found in suitable areas throughout the county' but 'comparitively scarce' - presumably in respect of the other two woodpeckers.

There was little sign of decline in the county until the early 1990s, or nationally until about 1980. The continuing decline across its range in England and Wales has been in the order of 80% up to 2010 whilst in Radnorshire it is probably at least 60%-70%. The Atlas of 1968-72 found the species in the breeding season in 12 of the 21 10-km squares wholly or partly in Radnorshire. The winter Atlas of 1981-84 found birds in seven squares whilst the next breeding season Atlas in 1988-91 found it in 10. Since 2006 it has been recorded in 11 squares but in no more than nine in any one year.

From the 1950s to the early 1990s it was reported from across the county; from Gladestry and Stanner in the east to the Elan Valley woodlands and Llanelwedd in the west and from Glasbury, Llowes and Kilkenny in the south to Knighton, Knucklas and Cefncennarth in the north. The decline began in the early 1990s in Radnorshire with the five or six pairs in the Elan Valley woodlands disappearing by 2002. Elsewhere there were losses from many higher areas, especially, and a general range contraction to the lower sites in the county, mostly in river valleys. In 2001 it was estimated that there were still 20-50 pairs in the county but by 2010 it was likely to be in the region of perhaps only 15-20. Birds were found at four to eight sites annually from 2003 to 2008 but then, without any special effort, from 15 sites in nine different 10-km squares in 2009, and then back to just five in 2010 and 2011. The general signs are, perhaps hopefully, that the species has undergone a decline but is now becoming stabilised at a lower level in Radnorshire.

It has been a very rare visitor to garden feeding stations in the county where it seems to prefer sunflower seeds to peanuts. A bird in a Presteigne garden in July 1957 was feeding on Raspberries and a bird at Llanbwchllyn in 1997 and 1998 spent long periods opening up the stems of *Phragmites* reeds presumably looking for insect larvae.

Woodlark *Lullula arborea*

Former resident breeder, now a very rare visitor.

A

Breeds from north-west Africa, Iberia, France and southern England east across Europe, including southern Fennoscandia, the Baltic countries and Russia east to the Urals and south to Italy, Greece, Turkey and western Iran. Migratory in the north and east of its range wintering within the south of the breeding range, the western Mediterranean and the Nile Delta.

The species has fluctuated in numbers nationally over the last 200 years due partly to the effects of cold winters but probably also to long-term climatic changes and landscape scale changes in land use. The Woodlark was a widespread breeding bird across much of England and Wales and even parts of Ireland in the early 19th century but went into a decline which reached its low point about 1880.

There was a period of increase from the 1920s to about 1950, despite the cold winters of the 1940s. Since then there was a major decline, particularly due to the 1962/3 winter, followed by an increase in the late 1960s and another decline around the mid-1970s. The population nationally more than doubled over the next five years but was halved again by the cold winter of 1981/2, which finally finished off any breeding birds in Radnorshire. Since then the species has increased ten-fold in England and is returning to many of its former haunts with about 20 pairs in Staffordshire being the nearest significant population to mid-Wales.

In Radnorshire the first reference to the species refers to the turn of the 19th/20th centuries when John Walpole-Bond, writing in 1922, said that he had found it in several districts of Radnorshire and that at one or two of them it was locally quite common. (*British Birds* vol.16 pp. 188-9). One of these was on the hills above Llanelwedd where he found it 'in fair numbers' in 1903. Several family parties were seen there in August 1907 and on 19th June 1910. O.R. Owen found a nest with an addled egg near Knighton in May 1920, another with three young on 8th May 1921 about three miles away and another pair midway between the two sites. He had been doing fieldwork in the area for 17 years and had not recorded the species before. (*British Birds* vol.15 p.154). Breeding was also recorded near Llandrindod Wells in the 1920s and it continued to increase in the Knighton area. It also bred above Aberedw until about 1945.

In 1950 a nest with four eggs was found at Crossgates and a pair was reported from there again on 17th October 1952. It was reported as 'numerous' on a farm near Rhayader in 1955 until heavy snow fell in May after which just one or two pairs were present until August. There were eight birds singing in the Ochre Cefn area near Rhayader on 22nd October 1956 and one was singing at Pencerrig on 14th February. Several were again present at the Rhayader site in the spring of 1957 but none in the autumn. In 1958 one was singing close to the Rhosgoch to Clyro hill road on 25th May and one was singing near the Grove Farm, between Huntington and Newchurch, on 14th June. One was seen flying around Llyn Heilyn on 7th October 1959.

In 1960 three birds were seen at Hendre Einon on 12th March and four were flushed off the road at Coxhead Bank on 11th September. Two were found singing at Cregrina and another nearby at Rhulen on 3rd April 1961. In 1962 one was in song at Old Radnor on 19th February, one at Llowes singing on 11th March, with another bird seen later about half a mile away and one by the River Edw at Hundred House on 25th April. Numbers were reported as 'reduced' by the severe winter of 1962/3 and there was just one record published for 1963 - a bird in song on Radnor Forest on 8th June, and one for 1964 - a single seen at Crossgates on 17th July.

There were no further records until 1968 when one was seen on the hillside above Llandrindod Lake woods on 28th April. The species was recorded in four 10-km squares between Rhayader and Builth Wells for the Atlas of 1968/72 and it seems likely that a small population may have continued along the hills between Llandrindod Wells and Llanelwedd over the coming decade as in April 1978 there was a record from above Llanelwedd Quarry. This was followed by a series of records from that area by Roger Lovegrove and Bob Haycock: a singing male on 10th May 1979 plus a female and another bird, and a singing bird again there on 17th May. A bird singing at the same place in 1980 was the last indication of breeding in Radnorshire, and anywhere in Wales until 2006.

There has been just a single record since 1980; one with a large flock of Skylarks in a field of stubble at Bronydd on 15th October 2009.

Skylark *Alauda arvensis* A

Common and widespread breeding bird and passage migrant.

Breeds from north-west Africa, Iberia, France and the British Isles east across Europe and Asia to Kamchatka, Japan, Korea and northern China, north to the North Cape of Norway, south to Italy, Turkey and northern Iran. Also introduced to New Zealand, south-east Australia, Vancouver Island and Hawaii. Mainly migratory, wintering within the breeding range and south to north-east Africa, the Arabian Peninsula, northern India and southern China.

The species is commonest as a breeding bird over the grass-dominated moorlands of the county but is also found in high numbers on short heather moorland and commons. Smaller numbers breed in most arable crops (except potatoes), especially those which are spring-sown, but tend to desert many such areas as the crop reaches maturity in late June and July.

From the late 1980s to at least 2005 there was a noticeable decline in numbers of up to 50% on test plots of 1-km and 2-km squares in the Elan uplands. However the decline seems to have stabilised and densities are still in the range of six to 12 singing males per square kilometre and post-breeding numbers in July may be as high as 70 birds per square kilometre. Breeding takes place from the highest ground of over 2,000 feet on the top of Radnor Forest down to fields beside the lower River Wye and in every 10-km and 5-km square in the county. The population in Radnorshire in 2012 was estimated to be between 4,300 and 6,000 pairs.

Birds arrive on the breeding grounds during February and March from the first fine spell of weather and most pairs are at least double-brooded, although young in the nest in August in Radnorshire are rare. Most birds leave the breeding grounds during August and September and are rarely seen on the hills in the late autumn and winter, other than when stopping off on passage. The only places where birds are seen all winter are in some fields of arable stubble and in autumn sown crops, especially of oil-seed rape.

Diurnal passage is very commonly seen and heard in fine weather with birds singly and in loose flocks flying north in February and March and, much more noticeably, flying south from September to November, calling as they go. At Llyn Heilyn on 20th October 1997 at least 180 birds flew south-west in two hours and at Penrhiw-wen, above Craig Goch Reservoir, 135 flew south-east in 75 minutes on 6th October 1992. They also migrate at night and are sometimes attracted to strong lights in towns and villages during sudden bad weather in late autumn. Birds passing through Radnorshire are most likely to be from further north in Britain although some from Scandinavia may also be involved

Large flocks are uncommon and are usually either in the early spring during spells of wintry weather or in the autumn/winter in arable fields. At Hindwell there were 150 on 19th December 1965; 250 were at Brynthomas, near Penybont, during heavy snow on 16th March 1979; 80 on stubble at Kinnerton on 22nd October 1999; flocks of 80 and 150 during wet snow in the Elan Valley on 12th March 2001; 170 in Elan Valley on 14th March 2002; 350 on stubble near Bronydd on 15th October 2009; 54 on Glog Hill on 9th October 2010 and 70 at Bronydd on 20th September 2010.

Sand Martin *Riparia riparia*

A

Widespread and in places a common breeding summer visitor and spring and autumn passage migrant.

Breeds from Iberia, France, the British Isles and Scandinavia to northern Norway east across Europe and Asia to Kolyma, Kamchatka, Sakhalin, northern Japan and China, south to Turkey and northern Iran, northern India and Pakistan. Also the lower Nile Valley and Delta, North America from Alaska south to California and Texas and east to the Atlantic coast as well as most of western and southern Canada. Winters in South America, sub-Saharan Africa and south-east Asia.

Unlike most parts of Britain the majority of Sand Martins nesting in Radnorshire do so in natural river banks rather than in man made banks at sand and gravel pits. In the mid-1950s Ingram and Salmon said that the species was,'Fairly numerous... a few moderate sized colonies on the Wye banks with smaller breeding groups up some of its tributaries.'

The crash in numbers during 1968/70 of 60%-80% due to the drought in the Sahel region of West Africa affected the whole of the British Isles and western Europe. In Radnorshire this was exacerbated by flooding in 1969 which claimed many first broods. However, the species was still found in all but one of the 21 10-km squares wholly or partly in Radnorshire for the Atlas of 1968-72. There were further drops in numbers in 1983/4 and again in the early 1990s either side of an almost total recovery between 1986 and1990.

Since 1995, and since 2005 especially, a noticeable surge in numbers has taken place in the county with the only limits seeming to be a lack of suitable nesting places and many birds present at colonies in recent years have been non-breeders. Birds wander widely over the countryside away from colonies during the spring and summer and records have came from every 5-km square in the county since 2005.

There have always been colonies in suitable banks of the River Wye between Boughrood and Cabalva with the number of occupied holes varying from c.40 in 1984 to 150 in 1989 (a 50%-70% increase on 1988), 190 in 2003, 210 in 2006 and 225 in 2010. There are also a few other small colonies on the upper Wye between Erwood and Newbridge usually totalling 60-70 pairs. On the other rivers in recent years there have been up to 180 pairs on the River Ithon and its tributaries upstream as far as Abbeycwmhir and Llanbadarn Fynydd in colonies of five to 40 pairs; 30-40 pairs on the Marteg upstream as far as St Harmon/Pant y Dwr; 110 on the River Teme as far up as Beguildy and 40 on the Lugg up to Monaughty. A few pairs started breeding at the top end of the Claerwen Reservoir and beside the River Elan upstream of the reservoirs in 1997 and have continued to do so with up to 15 occupied holes up as far as Bodtalog.

First brood young disperse widely from the end of June and can distort colony counts made later in the season. In fine years many pairs are double-brooded, particularly where new nest holes do not have to be excavated after winter bank erosion. Starling, Kingfisher and Tree Sparrow have been found taking over Sand Martin burrows in Radnorshre and Mink have been a major predator at colonies along the lower Wye since at least the early 1990s.

At man-made sites there was a colony at Llanelwedd Quarry in the 1980s with numbers varying from 11 pairs in 1985 to 200 in 1989. At a quarry near Moelfre and on the river adjacent there were c.100 pairs in 1996 and at a quarry at Doldowlodd there were 20 occupied holes in 1969. At Caerfagu builders merchants there were six to 13 pairs in a huge pile of compacted old river sand in the 1980s and 1990s and occasionally nests have been found in roadside drainage pipes above small streams.

Since 2008 the total population of the county has been in the region of 600-700 pairs having been down to probably fewer than 100 in some years in the 1970s and 80s. The terrible breeding season of 2012 saw most first nesting attempts flooded due to the wettest April ever followed by the wettest June to August since 1912. This resulted in the lowest numbers of fledged young for at least ten years. Many pairs along the lower Wye are double-brooded and in years with late springs and wet summers some young are still in the nest in the first half of September although in a fine summer colonies are usually birdless by the end of August.

The average first arrival date is the 16th March with the earliest at Glasbury on 7th March 1994. Migration of juveniles starts from early July with most birds leaving in August. September sightings are not uncommon and the latest record was at Glasbury on 30th September 1991. Visible diurnal passage is never as obvious as that of Swallows and House Martins but small numbers are seen flying north from mid-March to early May and south from early July to early September with gatherings often seen at lakes and ponds.

The highest counts have come from the lower Wye with 1,000-1,500 birds present in the Glasbury/Llowes area from 21st to 26th July 1963, 700 on 7th July 1981, 500 on 6th July 2000, 430 on 6th June 2007, 550 on 14th June 2008, 750 on 16th June 2009, 390 on 5th May 2010 and 350 on 7th July 2011. At Llandrindod Lake there are often feeding flocks in spring comprising birds from the colonies on the nearby River Ithon and passage birds. Counts are usually in the range of 20-100 but 200 were present on 22nd April 1995, 1st May 1996 and 17th April 2008.

In total there have been 124 ringed Sand Martins found in Powys from 30 different counties in England, Scotland and Wales and from France (9) and Spain. Most birds have come from Shropshire (33), Sussex (17) and Hereford & Worcester (10). Also 177 birds ringed in Powys have been found in 33 other counties and seven countries: birds have gone to Sussex (37), Gwent (15), Hereford & Worcester (14), Shropshire (13), Algeria, Belgium, France (12), Malta, Morocco, Senegal (7) and Spain (9).

Over 1,300 birds were ringed by James Cobb in the 1960s at Glasbury between June and August as part of the B.T.O's. Sand Martin Enquiry. Birds were exchanged with 18 other counties including birds controlled by other bird ringers in July, August and September in West Sussex (8), Kent (2), Norfolk, Cambridgeshire, Monmouthshire, Hampshire and Dorset. A young bird of the year ringed at Glasbury on 5th August 1965 was retrapped at Kings Lynn three days later (253km ENE), one ringed on 4th July was in Cambridgeshire on 14th and one ringed on 1st July was at Littlebourne, near Canterbury, on 23rd. All showing how the species starts migrating early and on a broad front.

Three birds ringed in Radnorshire have been reported from near Nantes in north-west France (c.540 km south): one was ringed at Glasbury on 30th July 1965 and recaught on 5th September, a young bird ringed at Penybont on 15th August 1929 was recovered on 16th September that year and a juvenile ringed on 12th July 2011 was recovered on 9th August. French ringed birds were caught below Glasbury in August 1968 and July 2011 and one from Spain in July 2013. Other already ringed birds caught there have included ones from West Sussex (3), Suffolk, Cheshire and Cumbria. A juvenile ringed at Rhosgoch on 4th August 1967 was recaught in Belgium on 27th (439 km ESE).

Swallow *Hirundo rustica*

A

Widespread and common breeding summer visitor and passage migrant.

Breeds in parts of North Africa and across most of Europe, Asia and North America. Winters in sub-Saharan Africa, Central and South America and south-east Asia from India to New Guinea.

Swallows breed across the county wherever there are buildings, barns, sheds and other outhouses with suitable ledges for nesting on. Most farms, villages and town edges have at least some Swallows and it is absent as a breeding bird only where there are no safe and suitable places to nest. However, it may be seen feeding anywhere in Radnorshire, from the lowest valleys to the highest hills.

Local declines are usually due to a loss of suitable nest sites such as the replacement of old barns with new, an increase in arable farming over livestock, resulting in less pasture and fewer flies, or a particularly heavy level of predation. Fixing canary nest-pans or simple wooden ledges to beams in outbuildings has been very successful in some parts of the county by creating suitable nest sites in otherwise poorly provided buildings. However, there has undoubtedly been a noticeable decline in overall breeding numbers in Radnorshire since at least 1990 and although the species is still found in every 10-km square the population in 2012 was probably down to between 1,600 and 2,200 pairs.

The first arrivals in the county are usually in late March, unless the weather is unusually cold with the wind in the north or east. The earliest ever record is of one at Glasbury on 14th March 1999 but the average first sighting is on 31st March. There has been a trend towards earlier first dates with the average pre-1995 being 3rd April but the 28th March post-1995. However, in Radnorshire the first main arrival of male birds (which usually precede the females by a week or more) is around the 10th-12th April and birds continue to arrive throughout the month with females often coming in well into May. Most pairs are double-brooded if the summer is reasonably fine and sometimes three broods are raised. At Penwyrlodd, near Clyro, in 2002 the last brood left the nest on 26th September.

Spring migration northwards carries on throughout April and all of May with visible passage, low over the hills, of single birds and small loose flocks a frequent sight. In springs which have been held up by unseasonably cold weather there can be a sudden huge rush of birds moving through when the weather improves with many hundreds counted. The worst year for such weather by far in recent years was 2012 when on 2nd May there was a gathering at Llyn Heilyn of at least 2,400 birds which slowly moved off northwards during the day.

Pre-migration autumn gatherings on telegraph wires are a feature of late August and September and counts of 50-100 birds, often mixed with House Martins, are widespread. There were 200 at Glasbury on 17th September 1994 and at Bronydd on 12th September 2007; 250 at Carregwiber Pool on 8th September 2010; 300 were at Newbridge on 15th September 1982 and 450 at Doldowlodd on 11th September 2010. At Glasbury on 15th September 1995 over 1,000 were counted flying west up the River Wye in 30 minutes and 1,000 were near Presteigne on 21st September 2010, with a similar number of House Martins. There are records to mid-October every year and usually a few in the last week. The latest record is of one at St Harmon on 7th November 2001.

There have been at least 12 ringing recoveries to Powys of birds ringed elsewhere coming from Cheshire (3), Channel Islands, Dyfed (3), Glamorgan, Hereford & Worcester, Yorkshire, France and South Africa. Twenty-five birds ringed in Powys have been recovered elsewhere going to Avon, Derbyshire, Dorset, Dyfed (3), Glamorgan (8), Gwent, Hampshire, Oxfordshire, Shropshire (2), France, Morocco (2), South Africa (2) and Spain. A nestling ringed in the Elan Valley on 7th July 1965 was found at Puertollano, in southern Spain, on 26th September.

House Martin *Delichon urbicum* A

Widespread and common breeding summer visitor and passage migrant.

Breeds from north-west Africa, Iberia, France, the British Isles and Scandinavia east to north-east Russia, China, Japan and northern India, south to Iran and Israel and north to northern Norway. Winters in sub-Saharan Africa and south-east Asia.

In the mid-1950s Ingram and Salmon said that House Martins bred, 'in perhaps slightly greater numbers than the Swallow.' This is undoubtedly still true today although both species have declined in numbers since then. The House Martin has been in decline across Europe since about 1980 and in Radnorshire there has been a noticeable decline since c.2000 with alarming reports of 50% fewer between 2010 and 2011 and further drops in 2012 and 2013. However censuses need to be done over large areas to take account of local changes in colony locations. Europe-wide the declines are thought to be due to a reduction in insect food because of changes in farming methods although unseasonal cold weather in Africa in our winter months can kill very large numbers.

Despite these declines they still breed the length and breadth of Radnorshire at farmhouses and in villages and towns. They prefer some buildings to others and may move en masse from one year to the next for no obvious reason whilst in some cases remaining faithful to one property for decades.

Damage to nests and predation of young by Great Spotted Woodpeckers is undoubtedly increasing in Radnorshire and can have a significant effect locally, as can nests being taken over by House Sparrows. Nests are usually under the eaves of houses but sometimes on single-storey dwellings and may be as low as two metres from the ground. Some still nest on the viaduct at Knucklas, where there were 150 nests in 1966, and occasional nests have been built in the past on the Elan and Claerwen dams, on various bridges and in quarries at Llanelwedd and Old Radnor. Up to six pairs nested on the cliffs above the Elan Valley centre from 1984-1990 but this is the only natural site recorded in Radnorshire. Birds are still found in every 10-km square in the county and the population in 2012 was probably between 2,200 and 2,400 pairs.

The average first arrival date is 13th April with the earliest records being in Llandrindod on 4th April 1990 and in the Elan Valley on 5th April 2009. Many birds often arrive in the last week of April but the main arrival is usually in the first fortnight of May with females still arriving until early June. Similarly migrants pass through the county from mid-April, throughout May, and into June, although never as numerous or obvious as daytime Swallow passage. Most pairs attempt two broods and in fine summers three may be raised. Young have still been in the nest as late as the 5th October. Migration takes place throughout August and September and often well into October. Records in the last week of October occur most years and the latest record is of four over Rhayader on 9th November 1965.

Autumn counts of 50-100 birds are widespread from mid-August to early October with the highest counts being 400 near Rhayader on 10th September 1989 and at Cwmbach on 22nd September 2007, 550 at Glasbury on 20th September 2010 and 500 still present there on 2nd October, 850 near Glasbury on 10th September 1989 and 1,000+, with a similar number of Swallows, near Presteigne on 21st September 2010.

Little is known about the House Martin in its wintering areas in Africa and it is thought that they spend day and night on the wing, unlike Swallows which roost in huge numbers in reed beds in South Africa and so facilitating ringing and recapture study. An adult ringed at Little Marlow sewage works in Buckinghamshire on 30th May 1993 was found freshly dead near Builth on 3rd May 1994 and a young bird of the year ringed at Newbridge on 10th September 1989 was reported found at Arcola, northern Italy, about 10th May 1991 (1,336 km SE). Another bird ringed in Powys was found in France and three birds ringed at St Alban's Head in Dorset have been found dead in Powys, as was a bird ringed at Sandwich Bay Bird Observatory in Kent.

Tree Pipit *Anthus trivialis*

A

Widespread, and not uncommon, breeding summer visitor and passage migrant.

Breeds from northern Iberia, France, the British Isles and Scandinavia east across most of Europe and Russia to the Lena River, south to Crete, northern Iran and the north-west Himalayas. Winters in sub-Saharan Africa and India.

Ingram and Salmon (1955) gave the status as, 'A quite numerous summer visitor' and this is still true today although there have been alarming declines to the east over most of England. These declines have been ongoing in many parts of England since at least 1970 and in the south-east since the 1950s and 60s, but since the late 1990s there has been a further major decline of some 80%. There has been no such noticeable decline in Radnorshire; in fact since c.2000 there has been a very noticeable increase, especially in the west of the county, where there is much more suitable habitat than in the east.

The average first arrival date is 8th April with the only March record being one in song beside Garreg Ddu Reservoir on 26th March 1995. Migrants heading northwards are seen and heard, usually singly, throughout April and into early May. An extremely unusual record was made by the late Jack Fox on 26th April 1959 when he found over 100 sheltering from a gale in the Vron Valley. Southward movement takes place from early August to the third week of September with the peak in late August . Most are seen in ones and twos; four were by Llyn Heilyn on 6th September 1987 and 12 in a loose flock flying south down the Elan Valley on 21st August 2011 being exceptional. The latest record was at Bettws on 4th October 1995.

The main breeding habitat in Radnorshire is ffridd, the bracken clad hillsides with scattered hawthorn and rowan and areas of rough acid grassland, where it can be the commonest bird. Recent areas of clearfell, young coniferous and broadleaved woodlands and commons with scattered trees can also support high densities and many also breed in and around more open broadleaved woodlands with clearings and wide rides. Trees for singing from are essential, even if it is just one or two in a territory. Newly cleared plantation compartments and newly created broadleaved woodlands are quickly occupied, usually in the first season after felling or planting, provided that song perches are present.

In the Radnorshire part of the Elan and Claerwen Valleys 38 singng males were found in May 2010, all between 300 and 450 metres (975-1,460 feet) a.s.l. In c.200 hectares of clearfelled conifers with young broadleaves and conifers north of Bwlch y Sarnau, 18 were found singing in late April 2006 - again all were at 300-450 metres. It was also described as 'common' in the same area when it was last suitable in the mid-1960s. Singing birds have been found up to 580 metres (1,900 feet) at Radnor Forest. In the Vron Valley, 13 singing males were found at the end of May 1958. Atlases have found the species in every 10-km square in Radnorshire and since 2002 it has been recorded in the breeding season in nearly every 5-km square. The breeding population in 2012 was thought to be between 1,200 and 1,500 pairs.

Meadow Pipit *Anthus pratensis* A

Very common breeding summer visitor, passage migrant and winter visitor.

Breeds from western Greenland, Iceland, the Faeroes, the British Isles, Scandinavia and northern France east across northern Europe to central Russia, south to northern Italy and northern Ukraine. Mainly migratory wintering from the south-west of the breeding zone south to northernmost Africa and southern Europe east to northern Iran and the Arabian Peninsula.

The Meadow Pipit is the commonest breeding bird in Radnorshire being very common or even abundant over most of the uplands as well as on some lower commons, rough areas of semi-natural grassland and clearfelled and young coniferous plantations.

The species is among the first to arrive on territory in early spring with singing birds often widespread in fine weather by the end of March, even in the uplands. Spring passage northwards is very noticeable with loose flocks of 30-100 birds often recorded in March and early April. Breeding densities may be up to 20 pairs per square kilometre although five to 10 is more common. On Maelinydd Common there were over 100 pairs in 1984. As the breeding season progresses numbers may reach 100 per square kilometre. However, there are some signs of decline with sample 1-km squares in the Elan uplands showing a 20% decline between 1992 and 2005 and undoubtedly habitat has been lost in the county over the last 50 years due to the increase in improved pastures and loss of moorland and rough grassland. Atlas surveys have found the species in 19-20 of the county's 21 hectads at all seasons. The county population in 2010 was calculated to be in the range of 10,500 to 12,500 pairs.

The species is usually double-brooded and young have been found in the nest near the Black Mixen at 2,000 feet (615 metres) as late as the last week of August. Autumn flocks begin to form in late July and early August and migration south starts from mid-month, with flocks of up to100 being frequent. This passage continues throughout September and the first half of October and may still be noticeable in some years as late as early November. In the upper Elan and Claerwen Valleys most years see counts of 1,000+ in late August and September, often closely accompanied by Merlin and sometimes Kestrel and Sparrowhawk. These passage birds come mostly from northern Britain but are also likely to include birds from the Faeroes, Iceland and Scandinavia as well as local breeders and their young of the year.

In the winter months of December to February comparitively few birds remain and although flocks of 30-100 birds are sometimes encountered they are notable and mostly occur away from the higher upland areas. However, small numbers are very widespread in winter including on areas of improved farmland where the species does not breed.

There is no evidence that continental birds winter here and those present are likely to be local breeders, or at least British. A nestling ringed at Penybont on 16th May 1925 was trapped and killed at Armamar, northern Portugal (1,285 km SSW) on 23rd January 1926 and one ringed by the River Wye below Glasbury on 21st September 1962 was recovered about the 1st January 1963 near Coimbre, central Portugal (1,373 km SSW). Most British Meadow Pipits winter in Iberia and Morocco.

Rock Pipit *Anthus petrosus* A

Very rare visitor.

Breeds on the coasts of north-west France, the British Isles and Scandinavia, Finland and north-west Russia. French and British birds (A.p.petrosus) are resident whilst those from Fennoscandia and Russia (A.s.littoralis) winter south from north-west Europe to Iberia and the Mediterranean.

The record from 1902 of a pair breeding on Aberedw Hill is probably best put down as an error. A very unusual record was the finding on the 16th June 1962 of the leg and some flight feathers, not necessarily fresh, at a Merlin's roosting place in the upper Vron Valley. They were identified as belonging to a Rock Pipit by the British Museum. At the same place, a month before, a dark pipit with dark legs was seen along a stream.

There have been four more recent records:

1973:	One in the Claerwen Valley on 17th April.
1999:	One of the 'British' race beside the River Wye upstream of Glasbury on 11th October.
2006:	One of the 'Scandinavian' race along the River Wye at Glasbury from 4th to 7th April.
2012:	One at Glasbury on 12th October.

Water Pipit *Anthus spinoletta*

Very rare winter visitor.

A

Breeds in the mountains of Spain, France, Italy, Corsica and Sardinia, east to parts of central Europe, Turkey and Iran. Descends to lower altitudes in winter with some dispersing as far as southern Britain.

From 1991 to 1999 one to three birds were seen each winter in the Glasbury area, usually at Pwll Patti but occasionally elsewhere. Undoubtedly the same bird(s) returned each winter for at least a few years judging by their habits.

The first record, and the latest, was at Glasbury on 21st April 1991, otherwise the latest was 24th March 1996 and the earliest on the 5th November 1999. In November 1996 there were two at Pwll Patti on 25th, two on the showground at Llanelwedd on 18th and one at Penybont on 20th. The only other records have been at Llyn Heilyn on 5th November 1995 and at Llanelwedd on 7th and 8th March 2009.

Yellow Wagtail *Motacilla flava*

Rare summer visiting breeder and passage migrant.

A

Breeds from northernmost Africa, Iberia, France, the British Isles and Scandinavia east across Europe and northern Asia to north-east Russia and western Alaska, south to the lower Nile Valley, Iran, central China and Kashmir. Winters in sub-Saharan Africa and south-east Asia from India east to New Guinea and the Philippines.

Ingram and Salmon said that the species was a rare summer visitor which had been recorded as having bred 30 or more years ago (pre 1925) near Llandrindod Wells, near Knighton, at Llanbwchllyn, near Builth Wells and near Rhayader in 1903, but that there had been no recent breeding records. However, it had been breeding along the Wye Valley from the Herefordshire border upriver as far as Boughrood Bridge since before 1954 and has done so ever since.

In 1964 it was described as a very common breeding bird between Glasbury and Hay Bridge with up to 20 pairs present and in 1965 there were roosts in August below Glasbury of over 100 birds. Many were caught for ringing by James Cobb including some blue-headed birds. Since then the species has had its ups and downs in the area depending on the crops grown and the grazing animals present. Mixed farming with arable, sheep and cattle has been best for the species. It seems that numbers were low in the 1970s but there were 15 pairs between Llowes and Boughrood in 1987 and about 20 pairs in the 10 miles or so of the Wye Valley between Glasbury and Cabalva in 1988.

In 1992 the number of pairs between Boughrood and Cabalva was at least 22 and there was a roost below Glasbury of about 120 birds on 28th/29th August, although these were probably a mix of local birds and migrants. Fifty males were counted along the lower Wye on 3rd May 1996 but this total undoubtedly included many migrants. In 2000 a thorough search of suitable areas from Boughrood down river to the Herefordshire border at Cabalva found 12-14 pairs. In 2005, 12 pairs were found between Glasbury and the border and 16 pairs found the next year with oil-seed rape fields favoured, especially ones with large muck piles nearby awaiting autumn spreading. Only 11 pairs were found down river from Boughrood in 2007 and 10 in 2008 and 2010. There was a very noticeable upsurge in numbers in 2013 with at least 15 pairs located. Other high/roost counts in the area over the years have been; 40 on 14th July 1979, 80 on 25th August 1990, 53 on 12th August 1991, 45 on 10th August 2004, 30 on 28th August 2010 and 22 on 26th August 2011.

Elsewhere a record from Beguildy in the Teme Valley on 18th July 1966 suggested breeding in that area and one to three pairs were found in the Valley between Knighton and Beguildy from 1986 until at least 1996. However, the habitat became largely unsuitable after then. Pairs also bred successfully in the upper Elan Valley in 1982 and 1990. The site used in 1990 was at 360 metres (1,170 feet) beside the River Elan with semi-natural grassland, an adjoining ungrazed meadow and a large, fly-attracting, muckpile. Since at least 1995 breeding has taken place on the Walton Plain and in the Lugg/Hindwell Valley east of Presteigne. Numbers have slowly increased on the Walton Plain where there is still a good variety of mixed farming. In 2012 at least seven, and possibly ten, pairs were found on the Plain between New Radnor, Old Radnor and Evenjobb as well as one to two pairs east of Presteigne. A pair at Penybont Common on 26th April 1970 may have indicated breeding there.

Nesting sites have been mostly in and around cereal fields as well as in oil-seed rape, potatoes, on well vegetated shingle banks and in and around riparian grazed meadows. Young have been found still in the nest near Evenjobb and in the lower Wye Valley in early August and it seems that the majority of pairs in Radnorshire at least attempt two broods.

Migrants used to be much commoner in Radnorshire than they are today due to the huge declines nationally in recent decades, especially in north-west England. In the 1980s and 1990s the species was a regular autumn migrant in small numbers e.g. one to two on many days at Bettws, near Franksbridge, between 10th August and 14th September 1989 to 1995. Up to 10 were seen at Llyn Heilyn on many dates between 14th August and 12th October in the years 1985 to 1995 where one to two was usual with high counts of five on 4th September 1993, six on 28th August 1990 and 10 on 4th September 1995. Also in the Elan and Claerwen Valleys there were one to three records most autumns between 1987 and 1998. There have been no records at either site since.

Until 1990 there were one to four records of spring migrants away from the breeding areas most years during April and throughout May. At Llyn Heilyn on 19th May 1955 there were 20-30 present following a snow storm on 17th.

Since 2000 records away from the breeding areas have been very rare with two at Gladestry on 6th September 2003 and one at Llandrindod High School playing fields on 18th August 2010. The earliest records have been at Glasbury on 31st March 1992 and 1994 with the average first date being 7th April. The latest record was at Llyn Heilyn on 12th October 1991.

Blue-headed birds have been recorded in the Glasbury area, breeding and on passage, in 1963, 1965, 1980, 1988, 1997, 1998, 2005 and 2011.

An adult female ringed at a roost below Glasbury on 23rd July 1963 was shot in central Portugal on 10th September 1965. Other birds from Powys have been found in Lancashire, Yorkshire and Morocco.

Grey Wagtail *Motacilla cinerea* A

Common, mostly resident, breeding bird and passage migrant.

Breeds from north-west Africa, Iberia, France and the British Isles east across Europe from southern Scandinavia to Turkey, Iraq and Iran, also across Russia east to Kamchatka, Japan, China and northern India. Mostly resident in south-west Europe, other populations mainly migrate south to East Africa, the Arabian Peninsula, India and southern China south to New Guinea and the Philippines.

The Grey Wagtail is an attractive, lively and elegant bird characteristic of most rivers and streams in Radnorshire and seems always to have been so, albeit with temporary declines due to severe winters. Breeding occurs from the lower Wye to small upland streams above the tree line as high as 480 metres (1,560 feet) a.s.l. as well as around many lakes and reservoirs, although usually closely associated with their inflowing and outflowing streams. They are also frequent visitors at all times of year to good feeding areas sometimes hundreds of yards from a river or stream such as farmyards with livestock and lawns and fields which they often share with Pied Wagtails. Very rarely they also come to garden bird feeding stations. However, nest sites are mostly above, beside, or close to flowing water.

Surveys have found breeding densities of a pair every one to three kilometres with the medium sized tree-lined rivers and streams, such as most of the Edw, Marteg, Ithon, Teme and Lugg, holding the highest densities and the slower stretches of the lower Wye holding the lowest. However, pairs are easily missed as they often nest a short distance up a small tributary brook but feed mostly along the main river. In most years there are probably between 400 and 500 pairs in the county. Unsurprisingly all the breeding Atlas surveys have found birds in every one of Radnorshire's 10-km squares.

From late August and throughout September most birds leave the more upland streams and rivers and move to the lower valleys and further south in England and Wales. At the same time diurnal passage is noticeable with birds, almost invariably singly, often seen purposefully flying high to the south, calling as they go. However, especially in mild winters, some birds will stay on territory throughout the year along the more wooded rivers even up to 300 metres (975 feet). A sudden very cold winter spell will usually move these birds to lower levels.

The winter Atlas of 1981-84 found birds in 15 of the 21 10-km squares wholly or partly in Radnorshire with the gaps being the far north and west. Most of the fieldwork was after the cold winter of 1981/82 when numbers were reduced, as they were after the winters of 1946/7, 1961/62, 1962/63 (very severely), 1984/5, 2009/10 and 2010/11.

Those birds which move away for the winter return to the breeding areas from early March onwards although after cold winters, in late springs and at higher elevations, some territories are not occupied until the first half of April. Most pairs, even in the hills, are double-brooded and some that get an early start in March may raise three broods with young still in the nest in early August.

A young bird of the year ringed at Cregrina on 6th September 1986 was found dead at Downderry, on the south coast of eastern Cornwall, on 20th November (214 km SSW). A nestling ringed on 7th June 1992 at Llanbister was retrapped by ringers at Little Marlow Sewage Farm, Buckinghamshire, on 19th February 1994 (195 km SE). Other birds ringed as nestlings in Powys have been recovered in their first autumn/winter in Wiltshire, Sussex, Devon, Dorset, Dyfed, Gloucestershire, Gwent (2), Hampshire (2), Shropshire (2), Hereford & Worcester and Hertfordshire.

Pied Wagtail *Motacilla alba*

A

Common breeding bird and passage migrant.

Breeds from north-west Africa, Iberia, France, the British Isles, eastern Greenland and Iceland east across most of Europe and Asia to the Bering Straits and westernmost Alaska, Japan, China, south to Iran, Kashmir, Burma and northern Vietnam. Most birds are migratory to the south and west of the breeding range as well as to much of North Africa, the Arabian Peninsula and India east to the Philippines.

Although Pied Wagtails (*M.a.yarrellii*) breed along most of the major rivers in Radnorshire, often alongside Grey Wagtails, they are less tied to water. They usually breed in more open and treeless areas and occupy many sites without any significant wetland habitat and in close proximity to man on most mixed farms as well as in villages and towns where they often come to garden bird feeding stations.

In some parts of the county, especially in the lowlands of the south and east and in towns and villages, Pied Wagtails are present all year but in many parts, especially in upland areas such as the Elan Valley, it is mostly absent from November to February. Where it is a migrant it is often the earliest to return in sunny weather in February or early March with males announcing their arrival noisily on the tops of buildings and catching flies awakened by early year warmth.

Spring migration is often noticeable with many birds passing through during March and early April with the peak usually in mid-March. Off-passage roosts are frequent with up to 50 birds at Pencerrig Lake in March 1992 and 20-80 birds often roosting in well-grown oil-seed rape fields. Such a roost at Clyro on 29th March 2012 comprised 60 birds, all of which were males.

The females arrive on the breeding sites a week or so after the males and egg-laying often starts before the end of March in the lowlands. Nest sites are found in all kinds of recesses in stone walls, ruins and quarries, on ledges in outbuildings, in timber stacks, occasionally in open-fronted nestboxes and, in the uplands, sites amongst scree and under rocks, over which there is often early spring competition with Wheatears. Two broods are normal and three is quite common with dependent young still in late August. A very late brood left the nest in the Elan Valley on 5th September 2002. Numbers are reduced by severe winters and this was particularly so after the worst of these in 1962/3. The population in Radnorshire in 2012 was probably between 1,500 and 1,700 pairs.

Autumn migration begins from mid-August and continues throughout September and usually into early October. In the 1980s and 1990s there were often large gatherings around the Elan Valley dams and reservoirs feeding on abundant craneflies. Flock counts included 150 on 31st August 1987, 250 on 16th September 1990, 100 on 24th August 1991 and 200 on 19th September 1995. Since then hatches of craneflies in the early autumn have been much smaller and flocks of more than 30 are rare. A striking, all-white, bird was present at Llyn Heilyn on 1st September 1960 and was said to have been present there for some two months before then.

Autumn high counts elsewhere have included 140 at Llyn Heilyn on 4th September 1993 and 100 there on 5th September 1996. Later roost counts have included 160 at Llanelwedd on 10th October 1983 and 80 at Boughrood on 13th October 1996. Mid-winter roosts of 20-70 birds are sometimes found on the tops of buildings in towns, on supermarkets and on industrial estates especially ones that are warm throughout the night. Such roosts were regular in Llandrindod, Knighton and Presteigne in the 1980s and 1990s but have been many fewer since c.2000 due to the better insulation of buildings, energy saving and, in some places, the closure of factories.

A young bird of the year ringed at Glasbury on 13th August 1965 was shot just north of Lisbon, southern Portugal, on 2nd January 1966. Many British Pied Wagtails winter in Iberia. Another first-year bird ringed at Oldbury Power Station, by the Severn Estuary north of Bristol, on 23rd November 1980 was found dead at Presteigne on 14th April 1981. Two birds ringed in Powys have been recovered in France (August to March and September to October) and one ringed in July was found in Dorset in September. A first-year bird ringed on the south coast of Devon on 27th September 2005 was found dead in Powys the following June.

The **White Wagtail** (*M.a.alba*), which is the race that breeds in Iceland and in continental Europe and parts of western Asia, has been recorded passing through Radnorshire about 70 times since the first was identified at Llyn Heilyn on 30th March 1956 and probably occurs annually in both spring and autumn in small numbers.

Most records have come from the lower Wye, especially on the fields and shingle banks between Glasbury and Llowes, with nine from Llyn Heilyn, eight from the Elan Valley and others from Llanelwedd, Maelinydd, Bettws, Rhayader, Presteigne, Llandrindod, New Radnor and Gladestry. About 15 records have been in autumn when the subspecies is less easy to separate in the field. Most of these were in the late 1980s and the 1990s when flocks, mostly of Pied, were frequent in August and September. Five were seen at Llyn Heilyn on 31st August 1987, six were lined up on the Penygarreg Reservoir dam with about 30 Pieds on 10th September 1990 and at least 10 were with 80 Pieds at Bettws on 15th September 1995. Spring records have been between 26th March and 14th May with all but six being in April and a trend in recent years for birds to pass through earlier in the month.

Most records have been of one to two birds with three to four seen occasionally and six found at Glasbury on 30th April 1988, 14th April 2003 and 6th April 2009. Exceptional numbers were found on shingle banks beside the Wye near Llowes in April 2013 with a peak count of 12 together on 16th. Most if not all birds seen in Radnorshire are migrating to and from Iceland.

Waxwing *Bombycilla garrulus* A

Rare winter visitor.

Breeds from northern Fennoscandia east across northern Russia to Kamchatka, also in Alaska, western Canada and extreme north-west USA. Migrates, often irruptively, sometimes reaching as far south as northernmost Africa, northern Iran, China, Japan and the western USA.

Although said to have been recorded in Radnorshire early in the 20th century by O.R.Owen, there are no dates or details. The first definite record was of two birds feeding in a roadside hedge (presumably on Hawthorn berries) near Pilleth in February and March 1957. There were eight or nine at Knighton in early December 1965, three were feeding on rotten apples at Boughrood Brest on 20th November 1966 and two were at Llowes on 30th November 1970.

Invasions come mostly from Scandinavia in years when berry crops, especially of Rowan, are quickly exhausted after a bumper breeding season but ringing has shown that birds coming to the British Isles also originate from a lot further east, even well beyond the Urals in Russia to the north of Kazakhstan. Since the 1980s these invasions have been more frequent and have brought many more birds into Britain and to Radnorshire. Four were present in a tall Hawthorn hedge at Howey from late December 1988 to 8th February 1989 with six there from 14th January to 6th February. They fed on Hawthorn berries and flew up and down from the hedge top catching flies on sunny days. Two birds seen at Llanelwedd on 4th January may have been different.

One was at Argoed Mill on 13th December 1990 and four birds were in Llandrindod for all of January 1992 but the next influx came in early 1996. One was at Glasbury from 20th January to 18th February and 12 were at Howey on 31st January. In February, six were at Doldowlodd and one in Llandrindod on 1st, six at Presteigne from 3rd to 10th, one at Builth Road from 4th to 16th, one at Clyro on 20th and four at Rhayader all month. At Knighton there were four from 25th December 1996 to 30th January 1997 and two groups of three in Llandrindod from 20th November to 10th December and on 8th and 9th December 1999.

In 2004 there were eight at Newbridge on 21st November, three at Glasbury on 7th December and 50+ in Presteigne from 27th to 31st December. Early in 2005 there were 20+ in the Crossgates Primary School area on 14th January, 34 in Llandrindod on 17th and 10 at a different site in the town on 18th. Singles were at Clyro and in the Elan Valley on 24th January and at Cefnllys Primary School, Llandrindod, on 25th February. Six birds were feeding in a Hawthorn hedge opposite Llandrindod Fire Station on 18th March 2005 - the latest county record.

Between 6th November and 24th December 2008 there were five records of two to 11 birds in Llandrindod, Crossgates, Knighton and Whitton and in early 2009 there were a further three records in January and three in February from Llandrindod, Presteigne and Knighton including 12 in a Presteigne garden in February feeding on Cotoneaster berries and two in Llandrindod on rosehips.

There was a big invasion into Britain in the autumn of 2010 with the first bird in Radnorshire below the Claerwen Dam on 25th October - the earliest county record. In early November there were records of up to six in Knighton and Presteigne with numbers along the bypass around Presteigne, and the adjoining industrial estate, increasing steadily to 44 on 20th. There were 11 records in all in November with the largest flock near Knighton on 30th November when a county record 110+ were present for much of the day before flying off high to the south-east. There were 28 still at Presteigne on 6th

December but numbers were generally lower as the berry crops were consumed. At Crossgates there were 16 on 15th December and six at Nantmel. In total there were 25 records up to the end of December with one to four birds also reported from Norton, Newbridge, Rhayader, Llandrindod, Hundred House, New Radnor, Old Radnor, Gladestry, Clyro, Glasbury and Boughrood. In January and February there were a further 17 records of one to two birds with the last in Presteigne on 21st February. Records came from Llandrindod, Cwmbach, Newbridge, New Radnor, Presteigne, Rhayader, Knighton, Glasbury and Gladestry. In total there were at least 42 separate records during the whole winter period, mostly from private gardens but including amenity plantings around industrial estates, supermarkets, schools and public buildings as well as on untrimmed Hawthorn hedgerows.

Another very successful breeding season on the continent in 2012 resulted in yet another invasion into Britain. The first birds in Radnorshire were three in Knighton on 13th November followed by records in Presteigne and Llandrindod the following day. At Crossgates there were six on 17th with records there on and off until 7th January with a maximum count of 30 on 18th December. Numbers in Presteigne increased from 11 on 18th November to at least 55 in three flocks on 2nd December. A further eight birds were newly arrived on 11th January. The largest flock recorded was one of at least 70 in Llanyre on 20th November which later broke up and doubtless some moved to Llandrindod where there were at least 56 in three flocks from 23rd into early December gradually declining to 15 by the end of January and further records there throughout February and into March with the last bird seen on 13th.

In Knighton numbers reached at least 48 on 23rd November whilst a flock in the Llanfaredd and Llanelwedd area from at least the 16th to 26th peaked at 32. One to 12 birds were also seen in the month at New Radnor, Nantmel, Howey and Evenjobb. Up to 17 were in Rhayader gardens in early December and during the month there were new records from Cwmbach (1), Newbridge (up to eight), Painscastle (4), Rhosgoch (11) and Nantmel (7). Birds were reported from nine places in January, some lingering and some new arrivals, but there were only three records of more than 20; at Knighton, Llandrindod and Presteigne. Two birds were feeding on Mistletoe berries at Glasbury. There were only five records of one to five birds in February and just three in March with the last two birds at Glasbury on 16th.

A bird colour-ringed on Orkney between 4th and 14th November 2012 was seen in Knighton on 23rd and one ringed on Fair Isle on 4th was seen in Powys in December. Colour-ringed birds ringed in Powys during late November and December were seen widely later in the winter including in Devon, Sussex, London, Merseyside, Yorkshire, County Wicklow, Cardiff, Nottinghamshire and Switzerland.

Birds have been seen feeding on a wide variety of berries with those of Hawthorn and Rowan species the most frequently recorded. Waxwings in Radnorshire have mostly been seen feeding on the pale-berried (yellow, white and pink) varieties of Rowan as the red and orange-berried varieties of our native *Sorbus aucuparia* are usually all eaten earlier in the autumn by crows, Wood Pigeons and thrushes before any Waxwings arrive. These pale-berried types include *Sorbus* 'Joseph Rock', *S.aucuparia* 'Xanthocarpa', *S.x kewensis*, *S.* 'Winter Cheer' and *S.commixta* 'Jermyns'. Birds have also been seen feeding on apples (pulp and pips), rosehips, Pyracantha, Ivy, Holly, Blackthorn (sloes), Mistletoe, Cotoneaster and Ash seeds as well as carrying out fly and gnat catching acrobatics in sunny weather.

Dipper *Cinclus cinclus*

Widespread and common resident.

A

Breeds from north-west Africa, Iberia, France, the British Isles and Scandinavia discontinuously east across Europe and Asia east to Lake Baikal and Mongolia and south to western China, the Himalayas, Iran and Turkey. Mostly resident.

Dippers are found on all the major rivers and streams of Radnorshire as well as along many smaller tributaries including well into the hills above the tree line. With so much good habitat there is a higher density in Radnorshire than in any other county in the British Isles and it is very unusual to take a walk of any length along a riverbank without seeing one or more zoom past up or downstream.

They are amongst the earliest of breeding birds in the county with eggs often laid in early March along the lower rivers. Most nest sites used are man-made, either on girders under bridges or in nest boxes. Singing has been reported in every month from September to May and most pairs are double-brooded, even those nesting above 400 metres. Numbers are reduced by cold winters but many birds move to the Wye in very severe weather and return to the smaller rivers and streams when milder conditions return. Any losses to severe weather are quickly recovered. However, pollution undoubtedly has reduced occupation of some rivers e.g. breeding (2 pairs) took place for the first time in at least 20 years along the River Elan above the reservoirs in 2008 and some streams in the county remain unoccupied. Predation by feral Mink has had an effect locally but many rivers have one to two pairs per kilometre and the population in the county is probably between 250 and 300 pairs. Outside of the breeding season birds disperse widely and are seen around some still waters such as the Elan and Claerwen reservoirs.

Although most birds are resident, there have been 28 movements of ringed birds from Powys to other counties: Dyfed (2), Glamorgan, Gloucestershire (2), Gwent (4), Herefordshire (7) and Shropshire (12). Also 23 birds ringed elsewhere have been found in Powys with birds coming from Dyfed (3), Gwent (3), Herefordshire (8) and Shropshire (9).

Some of the longer movements have been: A nestling ringed in Rhayader in May 1987 was found in Brampton Bryan, Herefordshire, in October (38km E); a nestling from near Llandovery was retrapped near Rhayader in August four years later (30km NE); a young male ringed near Knighton in September 1991 was retrapped at Cregrina two years later (32km SW); a nestling ringed at Pontrilas, Herefordshire, in May 1990 was at Aberedw at the end of August (38 km NW); a nestling from Clywedog Brook, Montgomeryshire, was also retrapped at Aberedw (34km SSE); a nestling from Glasbury was retrapped breeding in the Forest of Dean two years later (49km SE) and another from the same area moved to Pitching Green, also Gloucestershire, (64km SE); a nestling from Craswall, Herefordshire, was in the middle of Knighton the following April (38km N) and the ring put on a nestling at Hergest Bridge, near Gladestry, in April 1995 was found in a Peregrine's pellet in Breconshire two years later.

Wren *Troglodytes troglodytes* A

Very common resident.

Breeds from northernmost Africa, Iberia, France, Iceland and the British Isles east across most of Fennoscandia, central and southern Europe and southern Asia east to Kamchatka, Japan, Korea and China; also from Alaska across much of Canada and parts of the north-west and north-east USA. Resident in many places but most northerly populations are migratory south to milder areas within the breeding range and further south in parts of central and eastern Asia and the eastern USA.

Wrens breed in a wider variety of habitats than any other bird in Radnorshire. It is one of the commonest breeding birds in the county and by far the most widespread. They are found in parks and gardens, coniferous and all types of broadleaved woodland, reed beds, riversides, ffridd, moorland, cliff and crag; from the lowest valleys to coniferous woodland at 630 metres a.s.l. (2,050 feet) near the highest points in the county on Radnor Forest.

Surveys in ungrazed broadleaved woodlands in the county have found an average of a pair every 1.3 acres (0.6 ha) with similar numbers in some young conifer plantations. Mature gardens can hold higher densities with eight pairs found in a garden of 2.1 hectares near Llandrindod in 1990. Territories can be as small as 500 square metres provided that there is plenty of medium height vegetation to support a range of insect species and somewhere to nest.

Wrens are a small resident, insectivorous, bird and so very susceptible to severe winter weather. Numbers in the county were much reduced after the very cold weather of early 1947 and after 1962/3 numbers were down by 90% and took several years to recover. The very cold spells in the winters of 1961/2, 1978/9, 1981/2 and 1985/6 also had very noticeable effects. The cold winter of 2009/10 reduced numbers by some 40% on average with Wrens totally absent from some places the following summer whilst some, mostly lower sites, were largely unaffected. Similarly after the 2010/11 winter, when numbers were down by as much as 80% on 2008 levels, the species was totally absent from many higher areas whilst in lower places, such as around Llanbwchllyn, numbers were normal. At Gilfach RWT Reserve there were 12 singing birds on 25th May 1989 but on the same date in 2011 only two were found.

There is no doubt that during spells of severe weather birds leave many areas presumably for lower and more sheltered places. In early 2011 they were totally absent from most parts of the Elan Valley after the reservoirs froze and none were recorded until the 12th March with several arriving on 13th and others throughout the remainder of the month. In the breeding season of 2011 it was noticeable how well those remaining birds bred with many raising two large broods resulting in the recolonisation of many places by 2012 when the county population was estimated to be between 5,500 and 7,000 pairs.

In winter many birds roost, often communally, in outbuildings and nestboxes. During very cold weather in December 2000 and January 2001 there was a communal roost in an old House Martin's nest at Doldowlodd with video footage showing 37 birds entering at dusk on the 29th December and at least 60 on 16th January.

A xanthistic (yellow) individual was seen near Clyro on 14th June 1995.

Dunnock *Prunella modularis*

A

Common resident breeding bird and occasional migrant.

Breeds Iberia, France and the British Isles east across Fennoscandia, much of central Europe and northern Russia, east to the Caucusus and northern Iran. Mostly resident in the west and south of Europe, other populations are largely migratory as far south as the Mediterranean and Iraq.

Dunnocks are one of the most widespread birds in Radnorshire breeding in gardens and parks, thick hedgerows, all types of woodland edge, ffridd and even some areas of rank heather moorland devoid of trees. In fact just about everywhere where there is sufficient low dense vegetation in which to nest and where there is a variety of small invertebrates. Birds are found up to 610 metres (1,980 feet) alongside rides and in clearings in conifer plantations on Radnor Forest. Slow declines in numbers in recent years have been noticed in some parts of the British Isles but none has been obvious in Radnorshire. It is found at all seasons in all of the 10-km squares in the county and the population is probably in the range of 2,000 to 2,200 pairs.

Although the species is largely sedentary it is less effected by severe winters than most other small, largely insectivorous, resident birds. There were no reports of any decline in numbers even after the most severe winter of 1962/3. Undoubtedly birds do move locally in the autumn and winter, especially from higher breeding areas down into the valleys and villages, but there have been no ringing recoveries showing movements of more than 10 kilometres. However, continental birds do migrate and sometimes reach as far west as Wales, and therefore probably Radnorshire. A bird ringed in Belgium in September

1986 was found in Swansea in February 1989 and a bird ringed on the Lincolnshire coast has been retrapped in mid-Wales.

Although the species does not usually form flocks, up to ten birds and more have often been counted in winter at garden feeding stations and in January 2005 there were at least 35 birds in a kale crop near New Radnor and at last 40 in an oil-seed rape field near Glasbury in February 2010. In both these fields the attraction was the abundant seeds of Fat-hen *Chenopodium album*. The seeds of Common Nettle *Urtica dioica* are also a very important winter food source in Radnorshire.

Robin *Erithacus rubecula*

A

Common, mostly resident, breeding bird and passage migrant.

Breeds from north-west Africa, the Azores and Canaries, Iberia, France and the British Isles east across most of Europe, Fennoscandia and Russia to western Siberia, south to Iran and Turkey. Resident in much of the west and south of the range but most birds from Scandinavia and central Europe eastwards migrate as far south as around the Mediterranean and Iraq.

Robins are found throughout the county in all but the wettest wooded habitats from riversides, gardens and town parks to the highest conifer woods on Radnor Forest at over 2,000 feet (615 metres) a.s.l. It is found in all the county's 10-km squares at all seasons and the breeding population is probably between 5,500 and 6,500 pairs.

It is susceptible to declines due to severe winter weather and this was very obvious after those of 1947, 1961/2, 1962/3, 1981/2, 1984/5, 1990/1, 2009/10 and 2010/11. Many birds were found dead or dying during the very cold weather of January and February 2010. At Gilfach RWT Reserve there were 12 pairs found on 25th May 1989 but just six on the same date in 2011.

However, by no means all Radnorshire Robins are resident. There are noticeable influxes every autumn from about mid-September to mid-October with some birds staying for the winter and others moving on quickly or as soon as any very cold weather arrives. The most noticeable arrivals in recent years took place on 20th September 1998 and 10th October 2006. These birds are all likely to come from further north in Britain rather than from the continent.

A nestling ringed in Grampian in May 1979 was found in Powys on 20th April 1980 and a young bird of the year ringed in Merseyside on 11th September 1982 was found in Powys on 16th December 1982. Although the vast majority of Radnorshire Robins spend their whole lives near to where they were born an unknown, but probably small, proportion migrate. A nestling ringed in Powys in May 1966 was shot in Spain in January 1967, another local bird ringed in August was found in Bedford during the winter and a young bird of the year ringed at Sandwich Bay, Kent, in August 1995 was reported from Powys in October 1997. A first-year bird ringed on 12th September 2009 in north-west France was found dead in Powys in December 2010 (534 km N). A young bird of the year ringed at Stover Country Park, Devon, on 5th October 2002 was killed by a cat at Old Radnor on 19th July 2004 (189 km N) where it was presumably breeding.

Other ringed birds have come from Cumbria, Glamorgan, Gwent, Gwynedd and Herefordshire. And others ringed in Powys have gone to Cheshire, Herefordshire and Gwent (2).

Both males and females hold territories in winter but these tend to break down during perods of very cold weather, especially in gardens where feeding takes place. Eleven birds were in a feeding area of just a few square yards at Bettws during very cold weather on 26th January 1996 and 44 different birds were caught for ringing in one garden in the period 1st October to 8th April.

Nightingale *Luscinia megarhynchos* A

Very rare visitor and former breeder.

Breeds from north-west Africa, Iberia, France, south and east England across central and southern Europe and parts of central Asia east to north-west China, Kazakhstan, northern Afghanistan and Iran. Winters in sub-Saharan West and East Africa.

The Reverend A. Jordan, writing in 1926, said that one was singing for about a fortnight in 1894 in the garden of The Rectory at Llanbadarn-fawr, south of Crossgates. Nesting was reported from Glasbury in 1903 and 1926 and near Llandrindod in 1912. The only recent records are of one singing in a young conifer wood near Presteigne on 1st and 2nd May 2009 and one singing in a thicket near Glyndwr's Way about a mile north of Bwlch y Sarnau on 7th May 2013.

Bluethroat *Luscinia svecica* A

Very rare visitor.

Breeds very locally in Spain and France and throughout most of Fennoscandia east across Russia and a few parts of western Alaska, south to northern China, Kashmir and Iran. Winters in a belt from sub-Saharan West Africa east across the Arabian Peninsula to northern India, Cambodia, Vietnam and southern China.

The only record is of a male of the red-spotted, nominate, race present in the garden of 3 Rocks Meadow, Presteigne, for at least six hours on the afternoon of 27th May 1989.

Black Redstart *Phoenicurus ochruros* A

Rare visitor which has bred.

The first record was 'a pair near Landrindod Wells' in September 1923. Since then there have been a further 24 records:

1949:	Male in song on the roof of The Elan Valley Hotel on 26th May.
1952:	Male near St. Harmon on 10th August.
1975:	Male in the Elan Valley on 28th October.
1978:	Male in the Claerwen Valley on 2nd April.
1979:	Elan Valley on 4th April.
1983:	Female at Pont ar Elan on 19th March.
1988:	Gladestry on 23rd October.
1988:	Female/1st year by Claerwen Reservoir 25th October to 13th November.
1992:	Llandrindod Wells on 23rd October.
1993:	Crossgates 'in May'.
1994:	Male in song in Caban Coch Quarry on 20th and 21st May.
1998:	Juvenile in Knighton from 22nd to 24th July.
2002:	Female/1st year by the Elan Valley Visitor Centre on 7th November.
2008:	Female at Gilfach, north of Rhayader, on 14th March.
2008:	Female in Llandrindod Wells on 6th April.
2008:	Female/1st year Elan Valley from 27th October to 4th November.
2008:	Female/1st year, County Hall, Llandrindod Wells, 28th October to 7th November.
2009:	Two female/1st autumn birds at Llanelwedd on 29th and 30th October.
2009:	Female/1st autumn near Rhayader on 3rd November.
2010:	Female/1st year by the Claerwen Dam and Reservoir from 13th to 15th October.
2010:	Female/1st year, Church Street, Presteigne, on19th November.
2011:	Male at Glasbury Bridge on 20th April.
2012:	Male at Llanelwedd from 19th March to 20th April.
2012:	Male at Abbeycwmhir on 14th June.

In addition, a pair bred successfully in the county in 2010 and 2011 and probably also attempted in 2012 but no birds were seen in 2013. The juvenile in the middle of Knighton in July 1998 was certainly of very local origin and may not have been fully independent, although no adult was definitely seen.

Redstart *Phoenicurus phoenicurus*

Common summer visiting breeder and passage migrant.

A

Breeds from north-west Africa, Iberia, the British Isles and Fennoscandia east across Russia to Lake Baikal, south to Iran, Iraq and Turkey. Winters across sub-Saharan Africa north of the equator.

Ingram and Salmon in 1955 described the Redstart as a species, 'which breeds regularly' and 'is fairly widespread throughout the county ... though numbers fluctuate from year to year.' The species has suffered these fluctuations due to some of the periods of prolonged drought in the Sahel region of sub-Saharan Africa. One such drought occurred in the late 1940s and it is likely that numbers were still recovering in Radnorshire, and elsewhere in Britain, in the early to mid-1950s. A similar drought occurred during the period 1915-20 when a decline was noticeable in many parts of Britain. The species was described as very common in Radnorshire in 1958, with nesting up to 1,250 feet (380 metres).

Since modern monitoring and surveying by the B.T.O. started in the 1960s there has been a more detailed record of the population levels of British birds. There was a peak in Redstart numbers across Britain about 1965 following the wettest weather in the Sahel for many years but from 1969 to 1973 there was a very severe drought and a 50% to 80% decline across Europe. Recovery from this low point was quick in some areas but in others, especially in the lowlands, it has never happened. In Radnorshire recovery took several years but by the mid 1980s it seemed to be back to the levels of the mid-1960s. Even by 1979 an RSPB survey found as many as 40 singing males per square kilometre near Rhayader – a not unusual density in good habitat today. However, for unknown reasons, the Sahel drought of the early 1980s seemed to have no effect on Redstart numbers in Britain whereas it did cause declines to some other trans-Saharan migrant species.

In Radnorshire numbers remained high throughout the 1980s and 90s but from about 1997 there was a very noticeable increase and this upward trend has continued in the county ever since with the species particularly widespread and common in 2010 when 48 pairs were found in 82 hectares of broadleaved woodland in the Radnorshire part of the Elan Woodlands SAC. At Gilfach RWT Reserve seven singing birds were found on 25th May 1989 whilst on the same date in 2011 there were 15. Today the species is found in just about every area of suitable habitat where a nesting place is available be it in a large-holed nest box, hole in a wall or tree, under rocks or scree or in a hole in a bank. A pair at Bettws in 1988 nested in the middle of a very dense, two metre high, ornamental conifer and in 1991 one nested in a Tawny Owl nestbox in the Elan Valley after the owls had left in mid-May. Probably the commonest natural site used in Radnorshire is an old nesting hole of a Great Spotted Woodpecker.

In some places it is the commonest breeding summer migrant and is found in most types of broadleaved woodland, in ffridd habitats - often with few trees, hedgerows with scattered mature trees, farmyards, parkland and rural and larger suburban gardens. All the breeding bird Atlases have found the species in all of the county's 10-km squares and since 2002 it has been recorded in ever 5-km square. The breeding population in 2012 was estimated to be in the range of 2,300 to 2,700 pairs.

From at least the early 1990s there has been a trend for Redstarts to arrive earlier in the spring in the county and, in some early and fine summers such as 1987, to have two broods. The earliest date was of one singing in the Elan Valley on 26th March 1990 but there have been records in March in only three other years. The average first date is 6th April and in six late springs since 1990 there have been no records until 11th to 14th April. The first main arrival of males is usually around mid-April and females are often still coming in during early May. Birds leave from early August but are still sometimes seen in the second half of September and there are October records in about one year in two with the latest being at Penbont House, in the Elan Valley, on 19th October 1991.

There have been 22 recoveries of ringed Redstarts to and from Powys. A nestling ringed at Presteigne on 25th June 1981 was shot in Casablanca, Morocco, on 6th September. Another nestling ringed at Bettws, near Franksbridge, on 28th May 1987 was trapped and killed in Albufeira, Portugal, on 26th September 1988 and one ringed around Garreg Ddu Reservoir on 21st June 1995 was killed by a cat at Buxted, East Sussex, on 30th August. There have been seven other birds ringed in Powys and recovered in Morocco as well as singles to Spain and France as well as to Avon, Clwyd, Dorset (3), Glamorgan, Gwent and Hereford & Worcester. Also birds ringed birds in the Channel Islands and Dorset have been found in Powys.

Whinchat *Saxicola rubetra*

Widespread and not uncommon, summer visiting, breeder and passage migrant.

A

Breeds from northern Iberia, France and the British Isles east across Fennoscandia to north of the Arctic Circle, southern and central Europe east to the Caspian Sea and central Russia. Winters in sub-Saharan Africa.

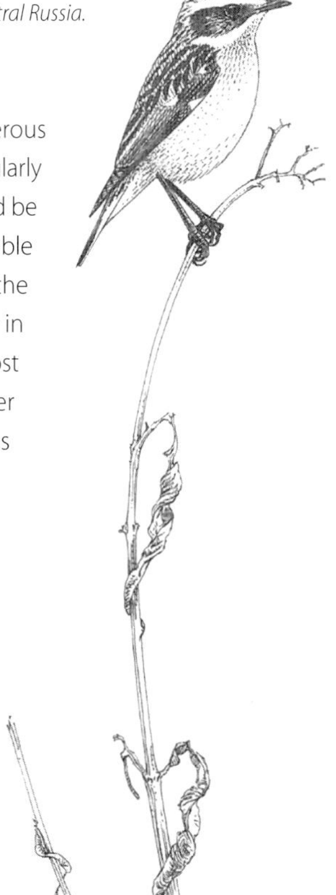

Ingram and Salmon said of the species that it was,'A fairly numerous regular summer visitor, breeding on most hill sides and tops, particularly in the bracken covered areas, up to over 1,500 feet.' The same could be said today some 60 years later although there has been a noticeable decline in numbers and distribution in the east and north of the county since the mid-1980s and, since the mid-1990s, a decline in numbers in the west, where the species is, and always has been, most numerous. Breeding has been recorded in newly planted conifer plantation bordering on moorland on Radnor Forest at 630 metres (2,050 feet) a.s.l.

The declines in the north and east could be down to the maturing of coniferous plantations as the species readily colonises clearfelled and newly planted areas. Many of these areas have been re-occupied in the years since 2000 following the clearfelling of huge areas of mature trees. However, the widespread declines in the west and south of the county are in areas where there has been no significant change in habitat.

A survey of some of the most suitable Radnorshire parts of the Elan and Claerwen catchments in 2008 found 36 pairs where there were 64 in 1995 and a comparison of two 5-km x 1-km areas of the best habitat found a decline of 50% between 1995 and 2006, but with stabilisation at around this lower level since then. However, across the county the slow decline in numbers was continuing in 2010 in all but optimal habitats (where numbers were stable or increasing) and in areas of clearfelled and very young woodlands.

There are still huge areas of Radnorshire suitable for breeding Whinchats particularly the ffridd habitats, areas of rank grassland, newly planted woodlands with widely spaced trees, and bracken clad commons and hillsides. It is a much more widespread species in the county than Stonechat and the two species breed side by side in many places.

Since 2005 Whinchats have been found breeding in every 10-km square except parts of the extreme south and east where there is little suitable habitat. The species is often double-brooded in the county, especially in the best habitat of south facing ffridd, and the population in 2012 was estimated to be in the range of 1,000 to1,300 pairs.

The earliest record was beside Garreg Ddu Reservoir on 18th April 1997 and the average first date is the 26th April. In late springs the first males do not arrive until the first few days of May and females continue to arrive until the month's end. Since about the mid-1990s there has been a definite trend for birds to arrive later and depart earlier. In autumn birds depart from the second half of August with many still leaving and passing through in September and into early October with the latest record being at Glasbury on 19th October 1998.

Small loose flocks sometimes occur on passage in autumn, usually attracted by a large hatch of craneflies, e.g. 10 were around Llyn Heilyn on 10th September 1989. Migrants in both spring and autumn turn up in a much wider variety of habitats than are used for breeding. Birds are often seen on and around all types of arable fields and grazing pastures at all elevations as well as around school playing fields, brownfield sites and golf courses with the only essential being hedgerows, fencelines, areas of scrub or some young trees on which to perch and look for food. There have been two birds ringed in Powys found in Spain and Portugal.

Stonechat *Saxicola torquata* A

Widespread, but uncommon, breeder which is partly resident.

Breeds across most of southern and western Europe east to north-east Siberia, northern Japan, Korea and central China, south to Burma, the Himalayas, northern India, Iran and the Arabian Peninsula; also in many parts of Africa including Madagascar. African populations are resident; western and southern European birds are resident or partly migratory; eastern European and Asian populations are migratory to North and East Africa, the Arabian Peninsula, India and south-east Asia.

In the 1950s Stonechats were described as scarce and local in Radnorshire and this held true until the late 1990s by which time the species had increased and spread considerably.The cold winters of 1947, 1961/62, 1962/3,1978/9,1980/81 and 1984/5 had all hit the species hard and there was little sign of any significant recovery until the 1990s following a series of mild winters.

In the Radnorshire parts of the Elan and Claerwen Valleys there were only two to three breeding pairs from 1987 to 1992 . Eight pairs were found in 1995, 13 in 1999 and 15 in 2000 and this scale of increase was also apparent across the county. Following further mild winters numbers rocketed to at least 50 pairs in the Elan and Claerwen in 2004 and the species could be found across the county in a much wider variety of habitats than just the gorse-clad areas of the past. Bracken dominated hillsides, pure rank heather moorland and rough grassland areas also became occupied, often alongside Whinchats.

The population of the county was undoubtedly at its highest ever level with probably 500-800 pairs and this was maintained until the cold winter periods of 2009/10 and 2010/11. In 2010 numbers were down by some 70% with the species totally absent from many sites. Although the 2010 breeding season was a good one with only the best areas occupied and two or three broods raised, the winter of 2010/11 reduced numbers again by 60%.

Undoubtedley many of the breeding birds in 2011 were birds which had migrated for the winter and the very cold weather had either driven all birds from the breeding areas or killed them. No birds could be found anywhere in the county in January and February 2011 but many returned in March and April. A big recovery in numbers was noticeable at the end of the 2011 nesting season and in 2012 sample surveys in May suggested a figure of 70% of the 2004 to 2009 peak, but with birds still absent from many places occupied in 2009.This rapid recovery in 2011 was doubtless due to the comparitively high previous population and that the species is often triple-brooded with young sometimes still in the nest in September e.g. the young of a late nest beside Garreg Ddu Reservoir left the nest on 11th September 2002 in a particularly fine and dry autumn.

Today birds breed on most of the commons in Radnorshire (especialy those with scattered gorse) heather moorland with fences and/or scattered bushes, very young conifer plantings and ffridd habitats. Nesting is regular on Radnor Forest up to 560 metres (1,820 feet) a.s.l. and since 2005 has been recorded in every 10-km square in the county.

A proportion of Stonechats migrate as far south as Iberia and North Africa, e.g. a nestling ringed in Powys in July was trapped in Algeria in early November. However, it is not known whether it is population pressure or genetics which causes a particular individual to migrate or stay the winter in or close to its natal area.

In mild winters many territories, especially those below 300 metres, are occupied throughout, usually by a pair. Returning migratory birds arrive on territory from early March and passage birds are recorded from late February, e.g. two at Pwll Patti on 27th February 1996, and continue throughout March and into early April with several birds sometimes seen in a loose group in a non-breeding area. In autumn, from late August to early November, dispersing and passage birds may be seen in a wide variety of habitats not used for breeding such as around arable fields and other farmed land, areas of rough grassland and along cultivated river valleys as long as there are low perches from which to look for food.

Wheatear *Oenanthe oenanthe* A

Common summer visiting breeder and passage migrant.

Breeds from north-west Africa, Iberia, France, the British Isles, the Faeroes and Iceland east across Europe and Asia to the Bering Straits, south to Iran, Afghanistan and northern China ; also much of Alaska, parts of the Yukon and north-east Canada and coastal Greenland to 80 degrees north. All populations winter in sub-Saharan Africa.

In the mid-1950s Wheatears were described as, 'still fairly common' but 'by no means as numerous as it used to be.' Today the species is still fairly common and widespread, particularly in the west of the county, and breeds in every 10-km square. However, there has been a noticeable decline since c.2003 in all areas, albeit from a very high level in the 1990s. Surveys indicate a present county population in the range of 1,100-1,400 pairs with 150-200 pairs in the Radnorshire parts of the Elan and Claerwen catchments. Surveys in the Elan uplands in 1976 and 1995 found Wheatears to be between 4.5 and 5.5 times commoner than Whinchats.

Past declines in Radnorshire have probably been due to upland habitat loss as a result of large-scale conifer planting, the ploughing of moorland and the loss of drystone and clawdd walls. High populations in the 1970s and 1980s were probably due to overgrazing in the uplands by sheep creating the very short sward that the species likes. Although the failure of the Sahel rains in Africa has caused some declines in the past the species seems largely immune from these droughts. In Radnorshire breeding birds are found in most rocky habitats with bare ground and/or short grassland including upland scree slopes, ffridd habitats, rocky outcrops, areas with drystone walls as well as beside upland minor roads and on many commons, moors and high pastures. Most birds nest under rocks or in stone walls but many also use rabbit holes and other holes in the ground or under dense vegetation. On passage in spring and autumn birds may also be seen stopping off on almost any bare arable field, school playing field, pasture or golf course.

Wheatears are some of the earliest and most conspicuous arrivals in spring with many birds, males especially, arriving in March. Arrivals, particularly of females and first-summer birds, continue to at least mid-April with passage birds heading for Iceland, Greenland, and even north-east Canada, dominating from mid-April to early May. The earliest record was of a male at Pont ar Elan on 28th February 1990 which appeared in front of a BBC wildlife cameraman. The average first date is 14th March although in late springs the first birds are not seen until well into the second half of the month with the latest first record being on 29th March 2007.

Pairs in Radnorshire are very rarely double-brooded at 500-600 metres on the highest ground of Radnor Forest but it is much more frequent on lower ground below 400 metres. Family parties and juveniles are very conspicuous from mid-May onwards. Autumn migration, particularly of juveniles, starts from mid-July and although most local breeding birds have gone by early September passage migrants from the far north continue to be seen occasionally throughout much of October with the latest county record being one beside the Claerwen Reservoir on 1st November 1990. Since the decline in breeding numbers in Radnorshire began around 2003 there has been a trend, similar to that for the Whinchat, of birds to arrive on average slightly later in spring and to leave earlier in autumn.

The race *leucorhoa* often called the 'Greenland Wheatear' breeds in Iceland, Greenland and eastern Canada. It probably occurs every spring and autumn in Radnorshire especially during westerly weather and in the later parts of the migration seasons, often staying for several days before moving on. It is on average larger than the race which breeds in the British Isles, Europe, Asia and Alaska (*oenanthe*) and the spring males are usually less blue above, richer, darker and more uniform below and with an often more upright stance. However, birds that breed on the Faeroe Islands are somewhat intermediate and the birds from north-east Canada and Greenland (those which have the furthest to fly to Africa) are the largest on average and with the longest wings.

The first record of *leucorhoa* was of one shot near Clyro by J. Vaughan Phillips on 28th September 1927 and identified by H.F. Witherby, presumably on its wing-length. A male road-casualty in the upper Elan Valley on 30th April 1994 had a wing-length of 112mm and a fresh weight of 42.2 grammes which are measurements at the very top end for the species and which was almost certainly a bird heading for Greenland or northeastern Canada. Similarly a female trapped for ringing in the same area on 2nd May 1988 had a wing-length of 101mm which is well into the range for *leucorhoa* but too big for female *oenanthe*. Other field records of the Greenland race reported over the years have been on The Begwyns on 4th May 1962 and 24th April 1977, Maelinydd on 19th April 1984, Caban Coch on 30th April 1990, Kinnerton on 4th May 1990, four in the upper Elan Valley on 7th May 2005 and by Penygarreg Reservoir on 29th April 2006.

During late April and early May 2012 cold and wet weather held up the northward migration of several species and races and there were many exceptional records in Radnorshire. From 21st to 30th April there were 10-18 male Wheatears showing the characteristics of *leucorhoa* on The Begwyns and smaller numbers were seen at 19 other places including Penybont Common, the Walton Plain, the upper Elan, Llandegley Rhos, Maelinydd, Llanelwedd and Hundred House between 18th April and 12th May. Many females were also present and were also doubtless 'Greenland' birds. It is likely that there were several hundred 'Greenland' Wheatears held up in Radnorshire at the time. The two races are similar plumage-wise in autumn but *leucorhoa* migrates south later than *oenanthe* and the vast majority of birds seen after mid-September are likely to be of the larger subspecies.

A nestling ringed in Powys on 10th June 1978 was on the Isle of Wight by the 19th July showing well the early departure of many birds. Three other nestlings have been recovered in Morocco, two were shot in September and November and the other reported in March.

Blue Rock Thrush *Monticola solitarius* A

Very rare visitor.

Breeds from north-west Africa and Iberia east across parts of southern Europe and Asia to China, Korea and Japan; also parts of Malaysia and Sumatra. Partly migratory to Africa north of the equator, the Arabian Peninsula east across India and most of south-east Asia.

A male was present on the scree and heather slope above the quarry at Caban Coch in the Elan Valley on the afternoon of the 11th April 2007. It was the second record for Wales and the fifth or sixth for Britain. It fed on bumblebees and a small lizard before disappearing as soon as the sun went off the area never to be refound.

Ring Ouzel *Turdus torquatus* A

Rare summer visiting breeder and uncommon passage migrant.

Breeds in one area of Algeria, parts of northern Spain, France and the British Isles, north and west Scandinavia and the Kola Peninsula; also some mountainous parts of southern Europe east to Turkey, northern Iran and Turkmenistan. Winters from north-west Africa and Iberia east to Iran.

The earliest reference to the species in Radnorshire was, 'probably breeds Radnor Forest' in the 1869 *Transactions* of the Woolhope Naturalists Field Club.

There seems little doubt that Ring Ouzels have been declining as a breeding bird in the county since at least 1945 and probably for a century before that with the lower altitude nesting sites being abandoned first. In 1955, although it was absent from a number of sites where found in 1954, it was still described as fairly common in suitable localities in the Rhayader area and was widely reported from most areas of heather moorland with steep slopes and rocky outcrops or crags throughout the 1960s and 1970s.

In the mid-1980s there were still at least 45 pairs in the county but by 1991 only 28-32 could be found. Another thorough search of all these sites in 1996 found 32 singing males but in 1997 only six were located. In the Elan and Claerwen Valleys there were 16 pairs in 1987, eight in 1996 but none in 1997, and none since. Thirteen singing males were found at eight sites in 1999 whilst in the Elan Valley there was just a single autumn record all year. Eight singing males were found at six sites in 2003 but just four pairs in 2004. Since then numbers have been fairly stable at a low level and at just a few sites. Counts have been six singing in 2006, seven in 2007, five in 2008, six in 2009, seven in 2010, five in 2011, six in 2012 and five in 2013. The breeding Atlas of 1968-72 found birds in 13 of the 21 10-km squares wholly or partly in Radnorshire but in just six in 1988-91. Since 2005 breeding has taken place in only five 10-km squares, all in the north and centre of the county. Most pairs in Radnorshire have always been double-brooded and even today those few left seem to raise good numbers of young, at least to the leaving-the-nest stage.

The reasons for the decline (which has also occurred in most parts of Britain and Ireland for a hundred years or more) are unknown although the species has often been recorded as Peregrine prey across Wales and certainly the pairs of Ring Ousel that persist in Radnorshire are mostly some distance from Peregrine sites. Cranefly larvae are a very important food source in Radnorshire during the spring and summer, as they are for other species that have declined in the county's uplands such as Golden Plover and Skylark, and there has undoubtedly been fewer of the huge autumn hatchings of craneflies (tipulids) since the mid-1990s. Competition with Blackbirds has also been cited in the past as a cause of the national decline and some Blackbirds do nest higher than Ring Ouzels in Radnorshire and have occupied some similar habitats in the past, although not the treeless areas, e.g. a pair near the source of the River Lugg on 15th April 1968 were decribed as 'high up on Ring Ousel ground'.

Another possible cause of decline being investigated is habitat change in the Atlas Mountains of Morocco where the winter is spent by many British birds and where a very important food for them is juniper berries. However, many Ring Ousels from mainland Europe also winter there and they are apparently not in decline. Other considerations are long term climate change and hunting pressures on the species spring migration through Spain and south-west France. The most likely cause of the recent rapid decline in Radnorshire was the increased predation levels of adults and recently fledged young on the breeding grounds.

Numbers on passage have also declined hugely over the years, especially in spring. Small flocks used to be recorded regularly; 10 were in Gilwern Dingle on 30th March 1964, in 1972 there were flocks of eight and 11 on Llanbedr Hill on 25th March and 10 were near Kesty on 16th April 1984. In autumn, post-breeding season birds often gathered on Bilberries and Rowan berries when the breeding population was higher; 18 were on Bilberries by Garreg Ddu Reservoir on 20th August 1987, there were three groups of 10-12 birds in the Elan Valley from 10th to 16th September 1988 and at least 30 on two Rowan trees below Craig Goch Dam in September 1992. Most locally bred birds have left by the end of September.

Autumn passage starts about mid-September but there are usually very few birds until mid-October with the peak in the last fortnight and a few still moving through in the first half of November. Small numbers are usually widespread, feeding on Rowan berries often with other thrushes, and remaining for some days before continuing south. Rarely are counts in double-figures but there has been an increase in autumn records generally in the county since 2002 for unknown reasons, although numbers do vary hugely from year to year.

Undoubtedly the biggest day of passage in Radnorshire was on 22nd October 2005. In the morning at least 32 birds had been counted dropping in to the area below the Caban Coch Dam from the north over the moorland and crags. Around the middle of the day at least a further 78 birds were counted coming in small flocks for an hour or more, many remaining to feed on Rowan berries, giving a total count of certainly 78 different birds and probably 110+ for the day. The only birds accompanying them were small numbers of Redwings and Fieldfares. In the days before and after at the same site, two were present on 18th, nine on 20th, 11 on 21st, 25 on 23rd, 18 on 27th, 11 on 4th November and the last on 7th. This movement was probably the largest ever recorded in Wales, certainly away from the islands, and almost certainly comprised Scandinavian rather than British birds.

Other double-figure counts from the Elan Valley have been 11 on 23rd and 17 on 24th October 2007, 14 on 23rd October 2009, 25 on 23rd September 2010 (suggesting a northern British rather than continental origin) and 13 on 4th November 2012. In 2010 there were records of 84 birds from 18 sites across the county between 16th September and 11th November.

The earliest spring arrival date was on 13th March in 1991 and 1993 by the same male in the Elan Valley. The average first date is 24th March with rarely no sightings at all until 2nd or 3rd April. In autumn the latest records in November have been in the Elan Valley on 15th in 2006, 16th in 2000 and 23rd in 2007. There have been three winter records; at Nant Glas on 26th January 1993, at Rhayader on 5th February 1996 and at Caban Coch on 14th January 2007.

Blackbird *Turdus merula*

A

Very common resident breeding bird, passage migrant and winter visitor.

Breeds from north-west Africa, Iberia and the British Isles east across Fennoscandia, central and southern Europe to Russia, Iran, the Himalayas, India and China. Introduced to southernmost Australia, Tasmania and New Zealand. Mainly resident but with most northern and continental birds migratory to western Europe, the Mediterranean, Iraq and Iran and parts of south-east Asia.

In the 19th century Song Thrushes outnumbered Blackbirds, but in Radnorshire, as elsewhere, Blackbirds increased hugely with the warmer climate of the 20th century and overtook its relation sometime in the 1940s. The peak was reached in the early 1950s, a level which it has maintained in the county since with some short-lived small declines caused by cold winters.

Today the species breeds in parks and gardens, on farmland with scattered trees and thick, tall hedges, in most types of woodland and scrub, in ffridd habitats and conifer plantations up to 620 metres (2,015 feet) a.s.l. It is found in every 10-km square throughout the year and the county population is probably about 4,500 to 5,500 pairs.

Nesting often starts in March in gardens where food is provided but often not until mid-April in the highest parts of the county. In 1989 a pair were feeding young in the nest at Hillcrest Rise, Llandrindod, on 18th January. Three broods are frequent in parks and gardens and four broods were raised and six nests built by a pair at Bettws, near Franksbridge, between March and August 1991.

Spring passage is hardly noticeable but autumn influxes occur from mid-October into November, although vary greatly in number from year to year. Early November is the typical peak time for passage and arrival of continental birds, although large flocks are rare. In the Elan Valley there was a roost of 100+ birds on 6th November 1989 following a large immigration over the previous two days. From late October to the 3rd week of November large numbers were present across the county with a big arrival, mainly of male birds, over the 2nd and 3rd November. By far the largest gathering was of at least 300 counted coming in and leaving a roost in the Gwaelod conifer plantation in the Elan Valley over the 2nd and 3rd November 2008. The number of birds on autumn passage and staying for the winter has been noticeably increasing in Radnorshire, and elsewhere, since at least 1990 as the species continues to expand its range northward in Fennoscandia.

During very cold winter weather gatherings are often recorded in gardens where birds are fed and in orchards with fallen apples: An orchard at Glasbury had up to 30 birds in early 1987; 17 were in a Rhayader garden in January 1997 and16 were on bird food at Penbont House, Elan Valley, on 13th

February 2007. At Great Vaynor, 50 were on bird food on 11th January 2010 and 43 on 22nd December. In a Llandrindod garden there were 30 on 25th January 2013, 20 were in a Huntington garden on 15th January 2010 and 17 on bird food at the Rock Park, Llandrindod, on 3rd February 2012. Many birds leave the county during late November and December, especially during spells of very cold weather with frozen ground, and move on as far south as France and Iberia.

However, many do stay throughout the winter and garden groups are doubtless a mixture of local birds and immigrants from the continent. A young male ringed in Belgium on 31st October 1987 was in a garden at Bettws from at least 22nd December 1990 to 21st February 1991. Other ringing recoveries have included: An adult ringed in Holland on 10th March 1960 was found dead at Walton in the very cold weather of February 1963; a female ringed at Holme Bird Observatory, on the Norfolk coast, on 14th October 1981 hit a window at Knighton on 21st February 1982 and another female ringed on Bardsey Island on 28th October 1963 was retrapped at Erwood on 13th July 1966 (where it was presumably breeding). A male ringed on Little Saltee Island, County Wexford, on 31st October 1956 was found dead at Rhayader on 26th March 1957. An adult female ringed in Norway on 15th April 1981 was reported from Rhayader in June 1986, although this was probably not the date on which the bird was found. A male ringed near Hundred House on 17th January 2006 was found dead having hit overhead wires near Trondheim, Norway, on 1st May 2007, a distance of 1,500 km NE. A bird ringed in Powys in January was in Finland in early April four years later and a nestling ringed in West Yorkshire was recovered near Hay two years later, although the month is uncertain.

In total there have been 24 Blackbirds ringed elsewhere and found in Powys and they have come from Cheshire, Devon, Dyfed, Gwent (2), Gwynedd, Hereford & Worcester (2), Kent, Norfolk, Shropshire (3), Warwickshire, Yorkshire, Co. Wexford, Belgium (2), Germany (2), Norway and the Netherlands (3). Eleven Powys ringed birds have gone to Dyfed, Gwent (3), Hereford & Worcester, Humberside (Spurn Bird Observatory), Shropshire, Finland, Germany (2) and Norway.

Fieldfare *Turdus pilaris* A

Common passage migrant and winter visitor.

Breeds from central Europe and Fennoscandia east across Russia to Lake Baikal and Kolyma, also rarely in the British Isles and Iceland. Winters in western, central and southern Europe east and south to the Nile Delta, Iraq, Iran, Qatar and Kyrgyzstan.

Ingram and Salmon writing in 1955 said that flocks of considerable size are seen from September and often remaining until mid-May. They go on to mention 6-700 birds arriving from the north-east into the Elan Valley on 28th September 1952 and a flock of about 250-300 on the hills about a mile north of Aberedw (Aberedw Hill) on 13th May 1951. These are both extraordinary records with no similar records from elsewhere in Britain at the time and must be mistaken either in date (most likely), number and/or species.

Records in April are usually few, apart from in the very late spring of 2013, and there have been fewer than 10 records in May in Radnorshire with all records of just one to three birds apart from 20-30 at Glascwm on 2nd May 1965. The latest record was at Bleddfa on 18th May 2002, apart from the four 'summer' records below. There have only been four September records, all of single birds, with the earliest being near the Fforest Inn, Llanfihangel nant Melan, on the 17th in 1996 and the others at Bettws, near Franksbridge, on the 24th in 1988, in the Claerwen Valley on the 28th in 1990 and at Llyn Heilyn on the 28th in 1994.

The first arrivals usually come in October with the average first date being the 12th. Numbers and timing vary hugely from year to year and the main arrivals turn up when the weather turns cold from the north which is often not until early to mid-November. In some winters birds stay in the county for many weeks but most pass through quickly or as soon as the berries of Rowan and Hawthorn are exhausted. Flocks of 2-300 remain in some places throughout the winter usually feeding on worm-rich pastures and in orchards with remaining fallen apples.

The arrivals and migration in October and November can be spectacular and there has been a definite increase in numbers in recent years. On 3rd November 1986 at least 5,000 came into the Elan Valley from the east; 2,000 were between Boughrood and Glasbury on 22nd November 1987; on 24th October 2002 there were 5,000 in the Penygarreg Reservoir area; 1,400 flew over Radnor Forest on 28th October 2006 and 1,000 were in the Elan Valley on 1st November; also in the Elan Valley there were 1,000 on 26th October 2008, 2,500 on 17th October 2011 and 3,600 on 29th October 2012.

On 25th October 1990 there were 1,500 below the Craig Goch Dam and more than 11,000 birds were counted flying south down the Claerwen Valley in two hours. However, by far the biggest movement of birds took place in late October 2009 in what was probably the most extraordinary passage of migrant birds ever seen in Radnorshire. On 27th October some 8,000 were present in the Elan Valley with birds pouring in from the east and north during the day. On the 28th there was a minimum of 40,000 birds present for most of the day filling fields and woodlands throughout the Valley. The next day there were just 1,000 birds remaining which moved off south during the day. Also on 28th October 20,000 birds flew south over Radnor Forest in just an hour and on the 29th there were 6,000 at Glasbury and 2,000 flew east over Llandrindod. It seems likely that the number of birds arriving across Radnorshire on the 28th was probably well into six figures.

Although most birds move on before the end of December variable numbers stay on into the late winter with many in some years and virtually none in others. Daytime passage north from February onwards can also be noticeable. High counts in the early year have been: 700 at Stonewall Hill on 29th

March 1967, 500 at Bettws on 15th March 1996, 1,100 flew over Presteigne on 5th February 1996, 600 at Hindwell on 24th February 1973 and 600 at Llanyre on 10th February 1973. On 25th February 2005 snow in the north of Britain brought in 1,250 birds to Glasbury, 1,000 to Four Stones and many other flocks of 100-500 arrived and passed through the county.

There have been four summer records in Radnorshire but no proof of breeding. A bird giving anxiety calls was in the Elan Valley on 3rd June 1988 but could not be found subsequently. Another was in the Elan Valley on 10th July 1990, one was in the Claerwen Valley on 24th June 1999 and one at The Begwyns on 4th June 1989.

Song Thrush *Turdus philomelos* A

Very common, mainly resident, breeding bird, passage migrant and winter visitor.

Breeds from northern Iberia, France and the British Isles east across Fennoscandia, central and southern Europe, Russia east to Lake Baikal and south to northern Iran and Turkey. There are also introduced, resident, populations in the Melbourne area of Australia and in New Zealand. Resident over much of western and southern Europe, other populations winter south and west as far as north-west Africa, the Nile Delta, Yemen, Iraq and southern Iran.

The Song Thrush is a widespread breeding bird and there has been no noticeable ongoing decline in numbers in the county in recent decades as recorded in some other parts of the British Isles. It breeds in all types of wooded habitats from town parks and gardens to deciduous and coniferous woodland from the lowest valleys to the highest plantations on Radnor Forest at 2,000 feet. Numbers were badly affected by the cold winters of 1962/3, 1981/2, 1984/5, 2009/10 and 2010/11 but have quickly recovered.

Counts of singing birds in the Radnorshire parts of the Elan and Claerwen Valleys found 41 in 1998, 50 in 1999 and 62 in 2000; part of a long term increase in the area due to the exclusion of sheep from the majority of the broadleaved woodlands. Within a one kilometre radius of the centre of Llandrindod 23 singing birds were located in March 2010. The large scale planting of conifers in the county since the Second World War has hugely increased breeding numbers generally and today Song Thrushes breed in every 10-km square and the breeding population is estimated at between 2,200 and 2,400 pairs.

Most birds leave their breeding grounds for the winter months, especially those from higher than 250 metres (810 feet) a.s.l., returning from early February onwards. This is the majority of Radnorshire birds and it is assumed that they move to the nearest lower wooded river valleys for the period October to February. However, some birds are to be found in every 10-km square year round, except in the most severe cold spells.

Singing usually starts in February but has been recorded in mild winter weather in towns from December onwards. Nestbuilding has been recorded as early as the 21st February, even at 1,000 feet. Two or three broods are usual, even at higher elevations, and where there is no understorey in a woodland nesting may take place on the ground amongst heather, Bilberry or rank grass, or on a ledge on a rocky outcrop.

In the autumn there are usually two periods of immigration by Song Thrushes into Radnorshire. The first is noticeable around mid-September and sometimes a second wave with other winter thrushes in the second half of October. The first arrivals often coincide with an influx of Robins and it is assumed that all these birds come from further north in Britain whilst those that arrive later with Redwings and Fieldfares probably originate from the continent.

Flock counts are never on the scale of other thrush species but typical records have been: 25 feeding on Hawthorn berries on Llanbedr Hill on 25th October 1978, 50 in the Elan Valley on 6th November 1989, 20 below Caban Coch Dam on 23rd Sepember 1990, 30+ near Dol y Mynach Reservoir on 19th September 1998, 20 at Tynllidiart in the Elan Valley on 10th October 1999, 20 below Penygarreg Dam on 7th October 2002 and 30 at Penbont in the Elan Valley on 16th September 2010. Numbers vary hugely from year to year with passage being hardly noticeable in some autumns. The biggest arrivals have taken place on 19th to 20th September 1998, 1st to 9th October 1972, 7th to 23rd October 1984, 10th October 2006, 18th to 20th September 2009 and16th September 2010. Spring passage is rarely obvious but has included a flock of 15 near Dol y Mynach Reservoir on 19th March 1995.

Ringing recoveries to and from Powys have included a nestling ringed in June that was shot in the Gironde, France, on 13th October, a bird ringed in Holland in late September found in mid-Wales in early March and one ringed on the north Norfolk coast on 22nd October was hit by a car in early December. Other ringed birds found in Powys have come from Cumbria, Gwent, Merseyside, Norfolk and Nottinghamshire whilst Powys ringed birds have gone to Anglesey, Gwent and West Yorkshire.

Redwing *Turdus iliacus* A

Common passage migrant and winter visitor.

Breeds from Iceland, the Faeroes and Scotland (few) east across Fennoscandia, the Baltic countries and Russia east to Kolyma and south to Lake Baikal and northern Kazakhstan. Winters from north-west Africa, Iberia, Iceland and the British Isles across much of western and southern Europe east to the Nile Delta, Syria, Iraq and northern Iran.

As the arrival of the first Swallow is a sign of the start of spring so the first Redwings make it clear that autumn is well under way and that winter is waiting in the wings.

The first Redwings usually arrive in Radnorshire in the second half of September, although in some years when the berry crop in Scandinavia is very heavy and/or the weather is mild and the wind in the southerly half, then the first arrivals may not turn up until early October. Most birds come from Scandinavia but also some at least come to Wales from much further east into Russia and small numbers from the Faeroe Islands and Iceland.

The earliest ever record was in the Elan Valley on 14th September 2011, but after that there were no more in that year until 22nd. There were two on the 17th September in the Elan Valley in 2004 and 11 on the same date at Llyn Heilyn in 1996, accompanied by the county's earliest ever Fieldfare. There has never been an autumn in Radnorshire when the first Fieldfare has been recorded before the first Redwing, although the first dates have coincided in four years.

The main arrivals are usually in October but rarely may not be until early November. Large flocks are recorded either quickly flying through or stopping to rest or feed avidly on Hawthorn and Rowan berries. Huge numbers also pass through at night as their calls are very commonly heard flying overhead after dark. Overall numbers have undoubtedly increased markedly in Radnorshire since the 1980s, possibly a sign of climatic change affecting berry crops elsewhere.

Flocks of hundreds are common whilst four-figure counts are sometimes made: 1,000 flew south-west over Newbridge on 5th October 1984, 1,000 came into the Elan Valley from the east on 3rd November 1986, 3,000 flew south down the Elan and Claerwen Valleys in two hours on 25th October 1990, 3,000 were at Nantmel on 21st October 1995, 1,000 at Newbridge on 10th October 2004, 3,000 at Radnor Forest on 4th November 2008, 2,500 at Radnor Forest on 13th October 2011, 2,000 flew south and east over Llyn Heilyn on 14th October 2011, 1,200 were in the Elan Valley on 17th October 2011 and 1,100 on 29th October 2012.

There have been three very large arrivals of Redwings into Radnorshire. On the night of the 1st to 2nd November 1992 probably many tens of thousands were grounded across the county. Alongside the A44 in the Llandegley/Penybont area there were at least 20-30,000 birds on pastures and in Hawthorn hedges on the early morning of the 2nd and flocks of 300-1,200 were present across the length and breadth of the county. There were still many thousands present for the next two weeks or so but nearly all had moved on by the 21st November by when just about every Rowan, Hawthorn and Holly berry in the county seemed to have been eaten.

Another major arrival took place on 28th October 2006 on which date there were 5,000 at Glasbury, 3,500 at Llanyre, 2,500 in the Elan Valley, 1,000 at Nant Glas and 7,500 flying south-west over Radnor Forest. In October 2009 a roost at the Gwaelod plantation in the Elan Valley held at least 6,650 birds on 15th and 2,000 were counted flying south there on 19th. With the huge numbers of Fieldfares recorded in the Valley on 28th October there were a minimum of 6,000 Redwings and 3,400 still present the following day.

From January to March there are many fewer birds present with berry crops usually exhausted. Those remaining feed mainly in pastures and orchards and any three-figure count is notable. In some years the species can be very scarce in the second half of the winter such as in the early months of 2000 when the highest count was just 10 at Walton in February followed by a count of 15 at Pantydwr in early April, which were probably birds passing through on return passage to the north and east. Severe winter weather usually moves any remaining birds on to the south or, if the freezing weather or snow is just elsewhere in Britain, then it can bring a late influx. On 25th February 2005 such conditions brought 450 to Glasbury, 300 to Four Stones and many other flocks of 50-250 across the county.

Most of any remaining winter visitors depart in late February or March with April records being unusual, and usually of migrants. However, the very cold March of 2013 resulted in many counts of 30-200 throughout the first three weeks of April as most birds were in no condition to migrate earlier. There have been five May records of single birds of which four have been in the Elan Valley: on the 2nd in 1988, on the 3rd in 2004, the 4th in 2008 and on the 20th in 1992. The other record being of one at Gilfach, north of Rhayader, on 20th May 2006.

The vast majority of Redwings seen in Radnorshire are of the continental race with birds showing the characteristics of the Icelandic race *T.i.coburni* seen in some Octobers and occasionally on spring passage. All the May records in the Elan Valley, and several late April birds seen in the county, were considered to be of this race which is much more heavily streaked underneath than the continental subspecies.

Mistle Thrush *Turdus viscivorus*

A

Common resident breeding bird and possible passage migrant.

Breeds from north-west Africa, Iberia, France and the British Isles east across most of Europe and western Asia to Lake Baikal south to the far west of China, Afghanistan and northern Iran. Mostly sedentary in western and southern Europe, other populations are migratory south throughout the breeding range and to Syria and Iraq.

Although much less common than the Song Thrush or Blackbird, Mistle Thrushes, being tree nesters, do not require low shrubs, hedgerows or scrub in which to nest and so are able to breed in grazed woodlands and open habitats with scattered trees and no understorey. Prior to 1800 the species was an uncommon bird in southern England and a bird of montane areas in Europe. By 1850 the species had spread rapidly to most parts of Britain and Ireland and to other habitats and countries in Europe. The reasons for this rapid Collared Dove-style expansion are unknown. The colonisation of Radnorshire and most of Wales seems to have taken place early in the 19th century.

In 1955 Ingram and Salmon gave its status as, '...by no means numerous. Small flocks may be met with in autumn and winter.' The extensive plantings of coniferous woodlands since 1950 has greatly increased the population in Radnorshire and today the species is found in every 10-km square in the county year round in all types of woodland edge, parkland and mixed farmland. The species has a large territory compared to other thrushes and wanders widely for feeding. Short grassland of some type is very important for feeding so areas in the south and east of the county that are mostly arable support fewer pairs than those used for stock rearing.

In the woodlands of the Elan and Claerwen Valleys, both coniferous and broadleaved, which are surrounded by sheep pastures and hillside acid grasslands, 12 singing birds were found in 2000 where there were 62 singing Song Thrushes. A survey in March 2010 within a 1-km radius of the middle of Llandrindod found six singing birds where there were 23 singing Song Thrushes. The species is an early nester, often nest-building in early March, and is double-brooded. As first nests are often built in a fork of a broadleaved tree before the leaves are out they are vulnerable and Mistle Thrushes are very aggressive towards potential predators such as Magpies, Jays, Carrion Crows and Grey Squirrels which come too close. Undoubtedly first attempts in coniferous trees are much more successful. Nests are built mostly of small twigs, wool, mud, grass and moss but also often include man-made materials with coloured plastic baler twine especially popular in rural Radnorshire.

At the end of the breeding season from mid-July onwards into October small groups are often found on fields, commons, moorland hillsides and ffridd habitats feeding on invertebrates (especially worms, slugs and grasshoppers) and Bilberries followed by ripening Rowan berries. These groups are comprised of one or more family parties and often number 10-20 birds which in September are often mistaken for early Fieldfares as they noisily feed on Rowan berries before their continental cousins arrive.

The largest flock counts have been: 30 above Penygarreg Reservoir on 15th October 2000, 35 at Penglaneinon, Elan Valley, on 9th October 1997, 40 on Rowans at Clyro on 2nd September 1968, 41 in a field at Penybont on 1st November 1969 and 45 to roost at Nant Glas on 25th September 2004. On 20th October 1968 near the bridge over the River Ithon south of Crossgates a flock of about 100 thrushes 'were mostly Mistles'.

In November these small groups and flocks break down and territories are established with berried trees of Rowan, Holly and, especially, Hawthorn defended against all-comers for as long as possible through the winter months. Trees with Mistletoe berries, particularly in orchards, are sometimes defended late in the winter but they are not a common food source. A summary of submitted records of wild fruit eaten by thrushes in Hampshire, South Wales and Berkshire/Oxfordshire between 1947 and 1953 published by the Edward Grey Institute (*British Birds* 1954 vol.47 pp 97-107) failed to find a single instance of Mistle Thrushes eating Mistletoe berries. Although the specific name *viscivorus* means 'mistletoe–eating', and there are British 18th century references to such, it is very likely that the species was in fact named from its common habit of eating the berries of the Red-berried Mistletoe *Viscum cruciatum* which is found on Olive trees and Hawthorns in the Mediterranean area.

The movements of British Mistle Thrushes has attracted varying opinions over the years with northern birds being said to be mostly migratory by some authorities. However, ringing recoveries show the species to be highly sedentary with very few long-distance movements of British bred birds. Some continental birds, most of which are highly migratory, do reach eastern Britain regularly but whether any of these come as far west as Radnorshire is unknown.

There are occasionally some signs of migration of birds through the county in September, which may be of northern British birds, but these are difficult to tell from local groups flying high and purposefuly from one feeding area to another. Certainly it is very rare to see Mistle Thrushes acting as part of a flock of Fieldfare and/or Redwing in Radnorshire which might indicate immigration. British Mistle Thrushes are best described as partially migratory but to an unknown extent. Another familiar bird about which we know comparatively little.

Cetti's Warbler *Cettia cetti*

A

Very rare visitor.

Breeds from north-west Africa, Iberia, France, Belgium, the Netherlands and the southern British Isles south-east across Europe to Turkey and the eastern Mediterranean, east to Kazakhstan and south to Iran. Western European race and south-west Asian/Middle Eastern race both mainly resident, eastern race mostly migratory south to Iran, Afghanistan and Pakistan.

There have been three records of singing birds:

2003:	Near Glasbury Sewage Works 15th April, 6th and 9th May.
2008:	By the Gilwern Brook at Stanner from 18th-21st December.
2009:	Near Llowes on 18th and 28th October.

Grasshopper Warbler *Locustella naevia*

A

Uncommon summer visiting breeder and passage migrant.

Breeds from northern Spain, France and the British Isles east across southern Fennoscandia, central Europe to central Russia, western Mongolia and Kazakhstan, south to Georgia and Uzbekistan. Winters in sub-Saharan Africa and the Indian sub-continent but distribution is poorly known.

Ingram and Salmon described the species as a scarce summer visitor which may breed regularly but was very local. They gave breeding records, 'on low ground under Llandeilo Hill' in 1907 (which was almost certainly around Llanbwchllyn) and near Llandrindod, near Knighton and at Rhosgoch Bog.

Throughout the 1950s and 1960s breeding took place at Rhosgoch Bog, the Pant y Dwr/Waun Marteg area and Red Lion Hill with one to three pairs at each site and including breeding in young coniferous plantations. Five birds were at Red Lion Hill on 21st May 1955 and the species was described as 'fairly common' at Waun Marteg in 1958.

There were still reports of breeding in the early 1970s, including four singing at Stanage Park on 12th June 1971, but the nationwide decline between 1972 and 1974 caused by the Sahel droughts resulted in fewer records throughout much of the decade. 'Several' were at Rhosgoch on 31st May 1975 and singing birds were reported from Hundred House in 1979 and from the Glasbury area. In the 1980s breeding season records came from Llanwefr Pool, Rhosgoch, Presteigne and Llanbwchllyn. A passage bird was at Llyn Heilyn on 2nd August 1982 and others turned up in mist-nets set for ringing in July and August in 1983, 1988 and 1989 at Newbridge and Bettws, near Franksbridge.

The species remained scarce throughout the 1990s with the only multiple records being three singing at Rhosgoch Bog on 16th May 1990, at Llanbwchllyn on 2nd May 1991 and at the disused refuse tip at Nantmel on 12th May 1999. However, there was a noticeable increase beginning in 2002, becoming more widespread in 2004 and continuing until at least 2012 with many birds occupying recently clearfelled and young coniferous plantations as in the 1950s. Six were singing in recent clearfell on Radnor Forest on 30th April 2005 and breeding also took place at Pentrosfa and Colwyn Brook Marshes. There were four singing at Nantmel tip in 2006 with a further seven at a young plantation at nearby Nantglas and four on an adjoining area of rank grassland. A total of 27 singing birds were found in suitable breeding habitat in the county in 2006 of which 18 were in clearfelled and young forestry.

In 2009 birds were found singing at 32 sites of which 22 were at clearfell and young plantations at Abbeycwmhir, Bwlch y Sarnau, Radnor Forest, Nant Glas and New Radnor. Others were in several areas of rank *Molinia* grassland in the Elan Valley, grassland and scrub at Nantmel tip, at Llanwefr Pool, Rhiw

Bottom, Moelfre, Rhosgoch Bog, Colwyn Brook Marshes, beside the River Wye below Glasbury (including in oil-seed rape) and on The Begwyns and Gilwern Common. Most pairs seem to be double-brooded with young very recently out of the nest found in the Elan Valley, Radnor Forest and at Llanbwchllyn in late July and early August. The 1968-72 Atlas found birds in 13 of the 21 10-km squares wholly or partly in the county whereas the 1988-91 Atlas had reports from just five. Since 2005 singing birds in suitable breeding habitat have been recorded in 16 of the squares and today probably 50-100 pairs breed annually in Radnorshire.

The earliest records have been on 10th April at Penbont in the Elan Valley in 2010 and at St. Harmon in 2011. Birds are sometimes heard singing on spring passage for a day or so in gardens with dense cover, in thick hedgerows and scrubby corners and on heather moorland up to 550 metres (1,800 feet) a.s.l. When not in song Grasshopper Warblers are usually very inconspicuous, skulking in low, dense, vegetation and often behaving in an almost mouse-like way. Hence autumn records are relatively few with birds rarely seen but sometimes turning up in mist-nets set for bird ringing indicating that passage is probably quite widespread in low numbers. The latest record was at Llanbwchllyn on 14th September 1994.

Sedge Warbler *Acrocephalus schoenobaenus* A

Uncommon summer visiting breeder and passage migrant.

Breeds from France and the British Isles east across most of central and northern Europe and Russia to the Yenesei River and northern Kazakhstan, north to the North Cape of Norway and south to central Turkey. Winters over most of sub-Saharan Africa.

Ingram and Salmon described the status of the Sedge Warbler as, 'A scarce summer visitor, breeding regularly in a very few localities.' Today it is not quite as rare and breeds annually in a number of wetland and marshy areas across the county.

In the 1950s there were up to six pairs at Rhosgoch Bog, three around Llyn Gwyn and four at Llanbwchllyn. Breeding also probably took place around Pencerrig Lake. In the 1960s Rhosgoch Bog was a lot more open than it is today with much less willow growth. Eleven pairs were found there in 1961, 10 in 1962 and eight in 1963. Five nests were found on 12th June 1965 and 18 singing birds were counted on 7th May 1966. Two pairs bred on marshy ground around Llandrindod Lake from 1966 to 1969, five pairs were located at Colwyn Brook Marshes on 7th July 1968 and two were around Llanwefr Pool in 1969. Breeding also took place by the River Ithon at Penybont in 1967 and probably in 1964.

In the1970s and 1980s breeding season records came from Llanwefr, Pentrosfa Mire, Llanbwchllyn, Pencerrig, Llyn Heilyn, Glan Llyn, Colwyn Brook Marshes, Penybont Lake, the lower bog (Aberithon) at

Newbridge, below Cefncennarth, around Llandrindod Lake and at a few places beside the River Ithon. There were at least six pairs at Rhosgoch in 1977 when 10-15 singing birds were found along the River Wye between Glasbury and Llowes. Three pairs were at Llanwefr in 1981 and two or three at Pentrosfa in 1986. Ten birds were in song at Rhosgoch on 2nd May 1988 and eight on 16th May 1990.

Since 1995 birds have been found most years singing in very young conifer plantations, especially in wetter areas with plenty of growth of rushes, brambles and willow-herb. In 1995, which was the hottest summer since 1976, singing birds were particularly widespread and found in plantation areas at Bwlch y Sarnau, Radnor Forest and Abbeycwmhir as well as at the usual wetland sites and several new places, including around Dol y Mynach Reservoir and near Howey. In 1999 a pair bred successfully at the north-west end of the Claewen Reservoir at 380 metres (1,235feet) a.s.l. Since 1999 the old refuse tip at Nantmel has attracted birds with six singing there in early May 2010 and eight on 27th April 2011. Doubtless some of these move on after a few days with one to three pairs staying to breed annually.

In 2005 there were10 birds in song along the Wye between Glasbury and Cabalva on 30th April (including two in oil-seed rape crops), four at Colwyn Brook Marshes on 1st May and others at Bwlch y Fedwen ponds, Pentrosfa, and in the Lugg, Elan and Claerwen Valleys. Eight were singing in oil-seed rape fields in the lower Wye Valley in 2006 and six in 2010 out of a total of 15 alongside the river. Breeding took place around Llyn Heilyn (370 metres, 1,214 feet) in 2000, 2001, 2002 and 2010 and in the new marginal vegetation around Llandrindod Lake in 2012 and 2013. The 1968-72 Atlas found birds in 10 of the 21 10-km squares falling wholly or partly in Radnorshire and in eight during the Atlas of 1988-91. Since 2005 birds have been found singing in suitable breeding habitat in 16 of the hectads and the population today is likely to be at least 40-60 pairs.

The earliest spring record was by the River Wye at Bronydd on 16th April 2008 and breeding birds arrive until mid-May. Birds singing off-passage in gardens, hedgerows and small areas of scrub and marsh are frequent with birds arriving and singing for a day or two from late April well into June. At least some of the pairs breeding in the lower Wye Valley are double-brooded and juvenile dispersion and southward passage starts from mid-July with most local birds gone by mid-August. Records in September are rare in the county and the latest was below Glasbury on 15th September 1992. Passage birds have been recorded around mawn pools on Beacon Hill on 25th June 2000 and at Pool Hill on 30th August 1983.

Marsh Warbler *Acrocephalus palustris* A

Very rare visitor.

Breeds from eastern France, extreme south-east England, Belgium and the Netherlands east across southern Fennoscandia and much of central Europe to Russia and northern Kazakhstan south to Turkey and northern Iran. Winters in south-east Africa.

There has been only one record: A male in song between Glasbury and Llowes from 22nd June to 22nd July 1984. It mimicked a wide range of European and African species including Swallow, House Sparrow, Yellow Wagtail, Oystercatcher, Wood Sandpiper, Nightingale, Didric Cuckoo and Streaky Seed-eater.

Reed Warbler *Acrocephalus scirpaceus* A

Rare breeding summer visitor and passage migrant.

Breeds from north-west Africa, Iberia, France and the south of the British Isles east across southern Fennoscandia and much of Europe to central Russia and Kazakhstan and south to Israel, the Nile Delta and Iran. Winters in sub-Saharan Africa.

Reed Warblers seem to have bred on and off around Llanbwchllyn since the early years of the 20th century. Breeding there has been annual since at least 1983 with usually three or four pairs present and a count of six in song on 5th July 2004. Breeding was recorded at Rhosgoch Bog from 1942 to 1963 after which the area with *Phragmites* became mostly succeeded by willows. Since 1987 breeding has been recorded annually along the River Wye between Glasbury and Hay in small areas of bankside reeds and once in oil-seed rape. There are usually two to three pairs present but at least five were found in 2004. Occasional breeding has also taken place at Colwyn Brook Marshes since at least 1971.

Following the planting of small areas of *Phragmites* around Llandrindod Lake in 2009, at least two Reed Warblers were seen on passage in late August 2010. Up to three birds were singing there in May and June 2011, when breeding may have been attempted, and in 2012 and 2013 successful breeding took place. The best years in the county were in 2004, 2006 and 2010 with eight to twelve pairs found at three to five sites. The lack of *Phragmites* reedbeds in the county at present restricts any significant increases.

Single singing birds, but with no sign of breeding, have been recorded beside the Wye at Builth in 1979 and 2002, the lower bog at Newbridge on 25th May 1986, at Pentrosfa Mire in June 1987 and around Glan Llyn and Llyn Heilyn in July 2010. Migrants have been seen at Hundred House on 19th June 1972 and at Llyn Heilyn on 3rd September 1989.

The earliest spring records have been at Llanbwchllyn on 16th April in 2011 and 2012 and most males have arrived at the breeding sites by the first week of May. Pairs are usually double-brooded and although most young from first broods depart in late July and August, newly fledged young from second broods are often seen in early and even mid- August. The latest record was at Llanbwchllyn on 20th September 2001.

Blackcap *Sylvia atricapilla*

Common breeding summer visitor and passage migrant; rare winter visitor.

A

Breeds from north-west Africa, Iberia, France and the British Isles east across Fennoscandia and most of Europe to central Russia and northern Kazakhstan, south to northern Iran. Winters in parts of western and southern Europe, north-west and sub-Saharan West and East Africa.

Ingram and Salmon described the species as,'A quite scarce summer visitor distributed very thinly over the county.' Since the mid-1950s numbers have greatly increased in Radnorshire, as elsewhere in the British Isles and parts of mainland Europe, and this increase continues year on year.

Today it is a characteristic bird of woodlands in the county which have a good shrub layer, especially of brambles, in which to nest. Sadly very many broadleaved woodlands in the county are heavily grazed making them unsuitable for Blackcaps, as well as many other species. They also breed in many conifer and mixed plantations, epecially older stands with clearings and wide rides, which permit shrub growth, and this habitat supports large numbers in Radnorshire.

Areas of broadleaved woodlands which are fenced to exclude livestock are soon colonised. The best example of this in the county is in the broadleaved and coniferous woodlands of the Elan and Claerwen Valleys where in the 1980s the species was very rare with just three to five pairs in the Radnorshire parts. Since the 1990s, following stock exclusion, numbers increased steadily to 28-32 singing males by 2010. Ten were singing at Gilfach RWT Reserve on 25th May 2011 (where there was just one on the same date in 1989) and 11 in the woodlands around Llandrindod Lake on 6th May 2012. Breeding takes place in all of the county's 10-km squares and has done so since at least the first Atlas of 1968-72. The county population in 2012 was probably between 650 and 800 pairs but there was a huge increase in numbers returning to breed in 2013 and doubtless the total is now in excess of 1,000 pairs.

Most male Blackcaps arrive in Radnorshire during early April with usually a few recorded each year in late March and the earliest on 18th March 2012 at Boughrood. There has been a definite trend for birds to return earlier since about 1990 with large arrivals in Radnorshire often now in the first week of April and nests with eggs before the month's end. Two broods are usual and most birds leave during August and September although October records are common and some passage birds are seen annually in the first half of November.

An adult male ringed at Glasbury on 17th August 1966 was trapped and killed in Morocco on 25th October, a distance of 2,234 km south. Ringed birds from Northern Ireland, Kent and the Channel Islands have been found in Powys and two birds have been recovered in Spain and one in Morocco.

The number of birds from central Europe wintering in the British Isles has increased over the last 40-50 years as the breeding population on the continent has increased. In 2010 it was estimated that at least 10,000 now spend the winter months here and a few are seen each year in Radnorshire. Orchards with mistletoe and fallen apples on which to feed are often favoured with up to four birds present at Glasbury from December to February in most winters since 1970. Gardens, especially with feeding stations, are also attractive and one or two birds have been recorded in the winter months in recent years in Knighton, Llandrindod, Llowes, Presteigne, Newbridge, Penybont, Nant Glas, Rhayader, Crossgates and Old Radnor.

Garden Warbler *Sylvia borin* A

Common breeding summer visitor and passage migrant.

Breeds from Iberia, France and the British Isles east across Fennoscandia, most of Europe and Russia to the Yenisei River, north to northern Norway and south to northern Turkey and Armenia. Winters in sub-Saharan Africa.

Lewis Davies in 1912 said that the species was a rarity in the county but the *Zoologist* of 1891 gave it as a numerous summer visitor. Ingram and Salmon said in 1955 that it was far more numerous than the Blackcap and found breeding up to 1,200 feet. Along with some other trans-Saharan migrants, numbers were much reduced by the Sahel drought of the early 1970s but since then numbers have recovered to their highest ever levels. Today it is certainly commoner than its close relative by a factor across the county as a whole of about 3:2. It is found not only alongside Blackcaps in some mature woodland types but also in more open, scrubby habitats, mature hedgerows, ffridd, commons, parks and larger gardens and up to 1,800 feet a.s.l. in young plantations on Radnor Forest.

As with the Blackcap the presence of low shrubs such as bramble in which to nest is essential and so stock-grazed woodlands are largely unsuitable. Like the Blackcap, it has also responded accordingly in the Elan Valley with the number of singing males in all the wooded habitats in the Radnorshire parts rising from just three in 1987 to 37-40 in 2010, although in areas of mature woodland Blackcaps are the more numerous. The predominantly mature oak woodlands of the Llandrindod Lake LNR held four singing Garden Warblers where there were 11 Blackcaps on 6th May 2012 whilst a part survey of the woodlands at Gilfach RWT reserve found a ratio of 2:10 on 25th May 2011.

The earliest record is of one at Crossgates on 17th April 1995 with the average first date being 22nd April and a definite trend towards earlier arrivals since about 1990. The first major arrivals are usually in the first week of May although in 1995 there were many singing across the county by 20th April. Birds were recorded in all but one of the county's 10-km squares for the Atlas of 1968-72 and in every one since the Atlas of 1988-91. The population in 2012 was estimated to be between 1,300 and 1,500 pairs. Local birds mostly depart in August with passage continuing throughout September and into early October in small numbers. The latest record was of one feeding on garden berries at Penybont on 3rd November 1992.

An adult bird ringed at Sturminster Newton, Dorset, on 26th April 1987 was hit by a car in Llandrindod the following day. A young bird of the year ringed at Icklesham, Sussex, on 10th August 1990 was killed by a cat at Knighton on 23rd June 1992 and another young bird ringed at Bettws, near Franksbridge, on 13th August 1998 was retrapped at Walton-in-Gordano, on the north Somerset coast, on the 27th.

Lesser Whitethroat *Sylvia curruca*

A

Uncommon to rare breeding summer visitor and passage migrant.

Breeds from the east of France, England, Wales and southern Fennoscandia east across the Central Siberian Plateau to the Lena River and south to central China, Iran and Israel. Winters in sub-Saharan north-east Africa and the Arabian Peninsula east to Bangladesh.

Walpole-Bond found a nest at Llanelwedd on 6th June 1902 and also in the first decade of the 20th century breeding was recorded from the upper Teme Valley, north-west of Knighton, and near Rhayader. One was seen at Glasbury in 1904 and one was singing by the road between Llanelwedd and Hundred House on 17th June 1908. John Williams-Vaughan writing in 1909 said that a pair nested every year in the garden of the Rectory at Llanelwedd (Woolhope Society *Transactions* 1909 p.85). In the 1920s breeding was reported from Maesllwch Park, at Llanelwedd, near Llandrindod and near Knighton. One was singing near Erwood Railway Station in 1937.

The species is at the western extremity of its range here in mid-Wales and has always been an uncommon bird since its spread to Wales which probably started in the mid-19th century. Numbers vary hugely from year to year with the number of singing birds found ranging from just two to over 30, although with many not attracting a mate. Records come mostly from the south and east of the county, particularly the Wye Valley below Boughrood and the Walton Plain.

The species is rare in the west and although breeding has been recorded around Rhayader Quarry for many years there has only been a single record of a male singing on one day from the Elan and Claerwen Valleys. In the 1950s and 1960s records came from Rhayader Quarry, Presteigne, Knighton, Michaelchurch, Rhosgoch, Glasbury and Penybont. Additional sites in the 1970s and 1980s included Walton, Felindre, Crowther's Pool, Dolycannau, Llanelwedd Quarry, Four Stones, Llandrindod, Pwll Patti, Llowes, Penybont, Gladestry, Maesllwch, Bettws and Gaufron. Singing birds were found at 13 sites in 1983,11 in 1984 and 23 in 1987.

During the hot May and June of 1992 singing birds were particularly widespread and a record total of 32 singing birds were found of which 14 were in hedgerows and scrubby areas in the lower Wye Valley and 11 in the New Radnor, Old Radnor and Presteigne area. Atlas work found birds in nine of 21 hectads in 1968-72 and 11 in 1988-91 and singing birds were recorded in 14 of the 10-km squares between 2005 and 2012. Lesser Whitethroats have a short song period and are much more difficult to census than its commoner, and more conspicuous, cousin. It is likely that on average 20-40 pairs breed each year in Radnorshire.

Tall and thick hedges are the favoured habitat in the county with areas of ungrazed dense scrub around quarries and along railway lines also popular. Areas adjoining Llandrindod High School have held singing birds in 1986, 1987, 1990, 1991, 2002, 2008, 2010, 2012 and 2013 and the scrub above and around Llanelwedd Quarry has possibly held breeding birds since Walpole-Bond's find in 1902. Although mostly a lowland bird, one was singing at Llanfihangel nant Melan at 310 metres a.s.l.(1,010 feet) on 27th May 1991.

The earliest record is of one at New Radnor on 19th April 2013 and the average first date is 27th April. Most birds arrive in the first half of May, although singing birds can turn up throughout May and June. Most birds leave in August and migrants were trapped for ringing in a garden at Bettws, near Franksbridge, on 30th August 1994 and 11th August 1996. Some double-brooded pairs are still in their breeding areas in late August and even early September and the latest county record was at Glasbury on 20th September 1991.

Whitethroat *Sylvia communis* A

Uncommon breeding summer visitor and passage migrant.

Breeds from north-west Africa, Iberia, France and the British Isles across most of Europe north to the Arctic Circle in Norway, east to Lake Baikal in Russia and south to Kazakhstan, northern Iran, Turkey and Israel. Winters in sub-Saharan Africa.

Ingram and Salmon gave the species' status as, 'A quite common summer visitor.' And this was the situation until 1969 when numbers across the British Isles, and most of Europe, crashed by some 70% due to drought in the Sahel region of sub-Saharan North Africa. Further declines continued until 1974 and the Whitethroat suffered more than any other species from the drought period as it not only fattens up in the Sahel prior to the spring crossing of the Sahara but European birds also largely winter there.

The species was scarce in Radnorshire throughout the 1970s and for much of the 1980s until 1987/1989 when increases were very noticeable. Numbers in the Walton Plain in 1989 were 30% up on 1988 for example. A slow increase in numbers and range has continued in the county since then but numbers are still nowhere near what they were before the crash.

Today Whitethroats are mainly found in tall, thick, hedgerows mostly in the arable areas of the south and east of Radnorshire. They are also found on gorsey commons and moorland edge, railway embankments, bushy ffridd habitats, ungrazed scrubby woodland around quarries and wasteland, and in newly clearfelled and planted conifer plantations and woodlands, where breeding has taken place up to 1,900 feet (580 m) on Radnor Forest. In recent years some pairs have been found nesting in oil-seed rape crops, especially where they are surrounded by tall and thick hedgerows.

The species has always been found across most of the county except parts of the wet extreme west and north. The Atlas of 1968-72 found birds in 20 of the 21 10-km squares wholly or partly in the county and in 16 during the repeat undertaken in 1988-91. Since 2005 singing birds have been found in 19 of the hectads and 55 of the county's 67 5-km squares with the first sign of breeding in the Elan Valley recorded in 2011, an area where there had only been three previous recent records. Some sites have lost their attractiveness to the species over the years due to natural succession to woodland e.g. Rhosgoch Bog NNR and Llanbwchllyn; both held several pairs in the late 1970s and the1980s but just one or none in recent years.

The earliest spring record is of one at Crossgates on 4th April 2011 with the next earliest birds being on 17th April 2008. The average first date is 22nd April with the majority of birds arriving in early May. There has been a very noticeable tendancy for birds to arrive earlier since about 1993. Birds continue to arrive, and be seen on passage, throughout May and even into early June. On the Walton Plain and in the lower Wye Valley pairs are usually double-brooded and in hot summers, such as in 2006, they do so even at high elevations. Migration starts from late July and continues throughout August and into early September with birds turning up in a variety of habitats including gardens with good cover. e.g. birds were trapped for ringing at a garden in Bettws, near Franksbridge, on 10th September 1991, 6th September 1993 and 11th August 1996. The latest record was at Cwmbach on 16th September 2009.

Dartford Warbler *Sylvia undata* A

Very rare visitor.

Breeds in extreme north-west Africa, Iberia, parts of south and west France, southern England and locally in South Wales, also southern Italy, Corsica and Sardinia. Mostly sedentary but many migrants winter in Sicily, Algeria and Morocco.

The only record is of one to two birds near Painscastle from October to December 2008. A first-winter bird was found on 24th October and on 5th November two first-winter birds were present, about 300 metres apart, remaining until at least 10th December.

Yellow-browed Warbler *Phylloscopus inornatus* A

Very rare visitor.

Breeds across Siberia from the Pechora River east to Kolyma, south to parts of China and the north-western Himalayas. Winters from the eastern Arabian Peninsula east to southern China and Taiwan.

The only records are of one around the farmhouse at the north-west end of the Claerwen Reservoir on 17th October 1992 and one at The Warden, Presteigne, on 30th November and 3rd December 2003.

Western Bonelli's Warbler *Phylloscopus bonelli* A

Very rare visitor.

Breeds in the extreme north-west of Africa, Iberia and France east to Austria and Italy. Winters in sub-Saharan, north-west, Africa.

The only record is of one in song near the top of Dyffryn Wood, south of Rhayader, on 17th and 18th May 2006.

Wood Warbler *Phylloscopus sibilatrix*

A

Common breeding summer visitor and scarce passage migrant.

Breeds from France, Italy, the British Isles and Fennoscandia east across Europe to central Russia and northern Kazakhstan, north to the Arctic Circle in Norway and south to southern Italy and Bulgaria. Winters in Central Africa.

Ingram and Salmon (1955) said that the Wood Warbler was, 'A quite numerous summer visitor, confined to the deciduous woodlands where it breeds regularly at all altitudes.' The only difference today is that breeding is also frequent in coniferous and mixed woodlands. The Sessile Oak dominated woodlands of the west of the county support the highest densities of breeding birds although ones that are heavily grazed by livestock have few if any pairs, as do woods with a dense understorey, but these are generally not closed-canopy and on richer soils than the nutrient-poor hanging oak woods of the cwms. All types of closed-canopy, broadleaved woodland (other than willow carr) are usually occupied and stands do not need to be mature with new woodlands of only 10-15 years and stunted hillside woods of scrub-oak also attracting some birds.

Larch woodlands are not the only coniferous type chosen with singing birds also often found in mature stands of Douglas Fir, Norway Spruce and Sitka Spruce, especially after the second thinning phase. However, coniferous and young broadleaved woods are sub-prime habitats for the species and males that sing in these areas, which are usually first-summer birds, often remain unmated.

The first males usually arrive in mid-April with the earliest records being at New Radnor on 10th April 2011, in the Elan Valley on 11th April 1995 and near Rhayader on 12th April 1991. The average first date is 19th April and in late springs the first birds may not arrive until the 27th to 30th. Females arrive a week or more later than the males and both sexes, especially first-summers, continue to come in throughout May. One brood is raised although, like its classic companions in the broadleaved woodlands of Radnorshire, the Redstart and Pied Flycatcher, some males are polygynous.

During the national census of the species in 1984/5 there were 14 singing birds in 15 hectares of Garth Wood, near Painscastle, and 56 in the 10-km square SO06 between Llandrindod and Rhayader. In 2012 there were 14 singing birds in 110 ha of mixed woodlands south and west of Presteigne and seven were singing in the Bachowey Gorge on 2nd May 2004. At Gilfach RWT Reserve there were five in song on 25th May 2011 compared with seven on the same date in 1989. In 95 hectares of suitable coniferous and broadleaved woodlands in the Radnorshire parts of the Elan and Claerwen Valleys, 39 singing males were found in 1991 but this had fallen to 30 by 2000 and to 24-26 by 2010. A similar level of decline has taken place in most other parts of the county, and elsewhere in Wales and the British Isles, although the level of decline in the east of the county is possibly higher. The reasons for this decline are unknown. Birds were recorded in every 10-km square during the 1968-72 Atlas, all but one in the far north in 1988-91 and in every one since 2005. The population today in Radnorshire is probably in the range of 600-800 territorial males.

Birds leave from late July and records after the third week of August are rare. Passage Wood Warblers are very infrequently met with anywhere in the British Isles compared with other warblers and the only ones trapped for ringing in a garden at Bettws, near Franksbridge, between 1987 and 1998 were on 9th September 1992 (the latest county record), 22nd August 1993, 12th August 1994 and 31st August 1995.

The species usually migrates south-east out of the British Isles on a route which takes it over the central part of the Sahara Desert to Central Africa. A nestling ringed near Glasbury on 17th June 1930 was shot at Avellino, southern Italy, on 2nd October 1930 (1,853 km SE).

Chiffchaff *Phylloscopus collybita* A

Common breeding summer visitor, passage migrant and rare winter resident.

Breeds from France and the British Isles east across Europe and Russia east to Kolyma, south to Turkey and northern Iran. Winters in south-west Europe, around the Mediterranean and North Africa east across southern Asia to Bangladesh.

The entry in Ingram and Salmon gave the status of the Chiffchaff in Radnorshire in the mid-1950s as, 'A relatively scarce summer visitor which breeds regularly in small numbers in the river valleys.' Undoubtedly the main factor limiting the species' abundance has always been that it nests in low shrub ground cover (especially brambles) in woodlands and for the most part overgrazing by livestock has limited this habitat.

There was some increase in numbers during the 1960s but then a decline due to the sub-Saharan Sahel droughts between 1969 and 1975. However, this decline was greatly tempered by the many Chiffchaffs which winter north of the Sahara. Numbers in the 1970s and 1980s seemed to be back to about the same as in the 1950s but since about 1990 onwards there has been a steady increase which continues today, not only in Radnorshire but nationwide.

In Radnorshire a major factor in the population increase has been the huge amount of increased favourable habitat created in stock-free coniferous and mixed forestry plantations over the last twenty years or so. Also some significant areas of broadleaved woodlands have been fenced to exclude livestock under various agri-environment schemes and SSSI and woodland management plans. In the Elan Valley woodlands there were no breeding Chiffchaffs in 1987 but fencing in the early 1990s resulted in a steady increase so that by 2011 there were at least 14 singing birds in mid-May in both broadleaved and coniferous areas.

Today, conifer dominated plantations, especially alongside wide rides and around clearings, hold by far the densest populations and there are many places where it is now commoner than the Willow Warbler. High counts of singing birds in late March and early April often include many birds stopping off on passage north e.g. eight singing in Kilkenny (Cilcenni) Dingle on 23rd March 1991 and unusually many across the county on 2nd April 1988. At Burfa Camp there were 12 singing on 18th April 2002 and no Willow Warblers. At Caerhyddwen plantation, near Nant Glas, there were 14 singing Chiffchaffs and 10 singing Willow Warblers on 16th April 2006 and in the same tetrad on 3rd May 2009 counts were 15 Chiffchaff and 22 Willow Warbler. At Gilfach RWT Reserve on 25th May 2011 counts of singing birds included three Chiffchaff and seven Willow Warbler whilst on the same date in 1989 there were no Chiffchaffs and 12 Willow Warblers. On 6th May 2012 the woodlands around Llandrindod Lake held four singing Willow Warblers and eight Chiffchaffs in song. The Atlases of 1968-72 and 1988-91 found birds in 20 of the 21 10-km squares wholly or partly in the county and since 2005 singing birds have been found in all of them. Sample surveys suggest that the current county population would seem to be in the range of 1,000 to 1,300 pairs.

Like some other summer migrants arrival dates have been getting earlier over the last 20 years or so and it is now usual for singing birds to be widespread across the county before the end of March. The earliest records were on 10th March 1997 around Llandrindod Lake and by Dol y Mynach Reservoir. The average first date is 15th March and in late springs the first birds may not arrive until 22nd-23rd. The main arrival of males usually occurs in the first few days of April and females and late males continue to come in throughout April and even into early May.

Most pairs are double-brooded and autumn passage is usually noticeable from the last third of August with numbers peaking in the second half of September when calling and singing birds may be found widely in many wooded habitats including gardens, parks and hedgerows. Records continue throughout the first half of October with late October and early November birds probably being mostly immigrants from the continent coming to stay in Britain for the winter. Records between 28th November and 13th February have come from Glasbury (4), Llanbwchllyn (2), Llandrindod Wells (3), Boughrood and Presteigne and have occurred in 10 years since the first in 1982; 7 of these were between 2002 and 2012.

A full-grown bird ringed at Glascwm on 3rd August 2005 was recaught by a ringer at Castlemorton Common, Worcestershire, on 22nd September 2009 (61 km ESE). One ringed at the Calf of Man Bird Observatory in April 1988 was retrapped in Powys the following January.

Willow Warbler *Phylloscopus trochilus*

A

Very common breeding summer visitor and passage migrant.

Breeds from France and the British Isles east across northern Europe and Russia east to north-east Siberia. Winters in sub-Saharan Africa.

The entry in Ingram and Salmon (1955) was, 'An abundant summer visitor with a widespread distribution ... from the river valleys up to hill-dingles at over 1,500 feet.' The species has undoubtedly undergone a noticeable decline, especially in the east of the county, since about 2000 and is no longer abundant anywhere in Radnorshire, although still the commonest summer visitor. Percentage declines range from 20%-50% in the west of the county to 60%-80% in parts of the east and south.

Today the species breeds in most types of broadleaved woodland, in young coniferous woodland and around clearings and along wide rides of more mature stands, scrubby ffridd, commons and moorland edge, tall, untrimmed, hedgerows, large wooded gardens, railway embankments, parks and churchyards – in fact just about anywhere with dense ground cover in which to nest and trees or bushes to sing on the top of and feed in, from the lowest river valleys to 2,000 feet (610 m) on Radnor Forest.

Young conifer and mixed plantations hold the highest densities with up to 44 singing birds found in a single 1-km square. However, counts of singing birds in April, and even early May, may include migrants stopping off before heading further north and the average number of pairs per 1-km square from sample surveys suggests a current population in the county of between 2,500 and 3,000 pairs. Successive Atlases have found singing birds in every 10-km square in Radnorshire.

The first spring arrivals are usually heard singing in the last week of March with the average first date being the 31st and the earliest at Clyro on 18th March 1967. Although the earliest record since 1971 was on the 26th March 2009, the species is one of those summer migrants generally arriving earlier than in the past although in late springs the first birds are still not heard until well into the first week of April. However, the first main arrival of males does usually occur between 2nd and 9th April, with most females turning up some days after.

Birds continue to arrive on territory throughout April and into May and young fledge from the end of that month to mid-July, although raising two broods is rare. Migration south starts in late July and peaks in the second week of August with most birds gone by the month's end. Records are rare after mid-September and the latest were of birds caught for ringing at Bettws on 25th September 1995 and at Glasbury on 1st October 1992.

The following series of ringing recoveries illustrate well the migration periods. A bird ringed at Portland Bird Observatory in Dorset on 10th May 1961 was found dead in Llandrindod on 5th July 1963. A nestling ringed at Glascwm on 12th June 1981 was retrapped at Titchfield Haven, Hampshire, on 5th August 1981. A young bird of the year ringed at Sandwich Bay Bird Observatory on 17th August 1992 was killed by a cat at Gwystre, near Crossgates, on 8th June 1993 and an adult bird ringed on the Isla de l'Aire, off the southern end of Menorca in the western Mediterranean, on 3rd April 1998 was found freshly dead hit by a car in Llandrindod on 4th May 1999 - a distance of 1,501 km NNW and only the 9th Willow Warbler to be ringed in Spain and recovered in Britain.

In total six birds ringed elsewhere and found in Powys have come from Dorset (2), Kent (2), Dyfed and Shropshire. Twelve birds ringed in Powys have been found in Avon, Devon, Dorset, Gloucestershire, Gwent (3), Hampshire, Suffolk and Sussex (3).

Goldcrest *Regulus regulus* A

Very common partly resident breeding bird, passage migrant and winter visitor.

Breeds on the Canary Islands and the Azores and from the far north of Tunisia, northern Iberia, France and the British Isles east across Fennoscandia and most of central and southern Europe and parts of Asia to Sakhalin and Japan, south to Turkey, north-west China and the Himalayas and north of the Arctic Circle to northern Norway. Mostly resident; northern populations move south to winter within the breeding zone and beyond as far as southern China, northern Iran, southern Russia and around the northern Mediterranean.

In the mid-1950s Ingram and Salmon said that the Goldcrest was,'...a somewhat locally distributed species, found breeding in scattered pairs here and there throughout most of the county.' However, they went on to mention that the huge conifer plantations on Radnor Forest, which were then about 25 years old, held very large numbers.

The species was unknown in many parts of the British Isles before the extensive planting of conifers in the 19th century and would have been rare in Radnorshire. Today the species is abundant in most middle-aged and mature conifer plantations in the county (especially those of Norway Spruce, Sitka

Spruce and Douglas Fir) and this habitat probably holds 99% of the county's population. However, some birds do breed in mature broadleaved woodlands (where nests are most often built in climbing ivy) as well as in ornamental conifers in parks, churchyards and gardens, and in even the smallest clump of spruce planted as a windbreak.

Most pairs are double-brooded with young often still in the nest in the first half of August. Atlases in both summer and winter have found Goldcrests in every 10-km square and sample surveys in the conifer plantations of Radnor Forest in 1993 and 1998 found breeding up to 2,050 feet (625 m) and densities of 195-270 pairs per square kilometre in the most favourable stands suggesting a county population of 8,000 -11,000 pairs after mild winters.

Although many birds are resident in the county, a high percentage, especially of the young of the year, leave the breeding areas in the autumn and winter for lowland areas locally, and elsewhere in England and Wales. Migration is very noticeable in both spring and autumn when birds may be found very widely, even in areas of gorse and low scrub, in gardens and along hedgerows. Most of these birds originate in northern Britain and Ireland and are passing through en route to and from southern England and Wales whilst others will stay the winter in the county and some are likely to be birds of continental origin.

Spring passage is most noticeable from early March to mid-April with a peak usually in the second fortnight of March. However, the biggest spring fall in the county was undoubtedly on 13th March 1993 when birds were very widespread and in large numbers, especially in the Elan Valley. Autumn passage is noticeable from late August to early November with often two peaks; one in the second half of September and another in the second half of October, perhaps indicating movements of British birds followed by immigrants from the continent. Autumn passage is much more noticeable than in spring, especially after good breeding seasons and a succession of mild winters, with loose groups of five to 20 birds often found in association with mixed tit flocks. Major arrivals and periods of passage in recent years have included October 1988, October 1992, September and October 1993, 25th-30th September 2007, 16th October 2009 and 13th October 2011.

The species suffers badly in cold winters, especially ones with prolonged very cold spells and/or severe ice-glazing and riming of trees. However, recovery can occur within two or three years given favourable breeding seasons and mild winters. The worst winters for Goldcrests in Radnorshire were 1962/3, 1975/6, 1978/9, 1985/6 and 2009/10.

A bird ringed on the Isle of May, off the east coast of Scotland, on 12th October 1950 was found dead at Doldowlodd on 20th December. A first-year bird ringed in Powys in early September was in Suffolk in mid-October and one ringed in Gloucestershire at the end of September was retrapped by ringers in Powys on 22nd October.

Firecrest *Regulus ignicapillus*

Very rare summer visiting breeder and passage migrant.

A

Breeds form north-west Africa, the Azores, the Canaries, Madeira, Iberia, France and parts of southern Britain east across Europe to western Russia and parts of northern Turkey. Mainly resident, apart from eastern European birds which migrate south and west to within the breeding zone.

The first record was of a bird watched at close range in a garden in Llandrindod on 14th November 1971. One was at Llandrindod Lake woods on 22nd April 1986 and singing males were at Penbont, Elan Valley, on April 12th 1990 and at Water-break-its-neck, near New Radnor, on 16th June 1994.

In 2001 there were two singing males in the Presteigne area in June and a bird at Penbont from 13th November to 3rd December. Three singing males were found near Presteigne in 2003 and there were records at Penbont on 24th April 2003 and 1st October 2007. Four pairs were proved to breed between Evenjobb and Presteigne in 2008 and seven singing birds were found at four sites in 2009 with young fledged by at least three pairs. Four were found singing in the Presteigne area in 2010, none in 2011, one in June 2012 but none in 2013.

The habitat occupied by the breeding birds comprised well-spaced, tall, conifers of a variety of species with a well developed understorey of young deciduous trees, particularly Elder, willow and Hazel, adjacent to open glades or wide rides between 660 and 990 feet a.s.l. In the breeding areas, the earliest record was near Presteigne on 4th April 2009 and the latest at Evenjobb on 2nd September 2008.

Spotted Flycatcher *Muscicapa striata*

Common summer visiting breeder and frequent passage migrant.

A

Breeds from north-west Africa, Iberia, the British Isles and Fennoscandia east across Europe and Russia east to northern Mongolia, north to beyond the Arctic Circle in northern Norway and south to northern Iran. Winters in sub-Saharan Africa mostly south of the Equator.

The species was described by Ingram and Salmon as, 'A fairly widespread summer visitor... Numbers vary considerably from year to year. It was very numerous in 1951... but quite scarce in 1954'. It is still common and widespread today but has undoubtedly undergone a decline in some parts of the county since about 2001, particularly in the east, whilst in other areas numbers have been remarkably stable, or even increasing, in recent years.

In Radnorshire the species breeds in and around mature coniferous and broadleaved woodlands, especially on the woodland edge and alongside rides and clearings, and up to 1,650 feet (503 m) in Radnor Forest. It is also found in parks and gardens with mature trees and around quarries and farmyards. Nests are often in climbing ivy or other creeper and sometimes in open-fronted nextboxes, the fork of a tree (especially where camouflaged by mosses and lichens), on ledges and in crevices in walls and trees. Nests have even been built in the past on the face of the Elan Valley dams, especially at Craig Goch (1,050 feet, 320 m).

The first spring arrivals are usually in the first week of May with the earliest records being on 18th April 1970 at Penybont, 20th April 1993 at Gladestry and on 23rd April 1987 at Franksbridge. The average first date is 3rd May and the first major arrivals are usually in mid-May, with females continuing to arrive into early June. Some pairs, regardless of altitude, seem to raise one brood and finish whilst others at least attempt to raise two or sometimes even three broods in long, hot summers. The third brood of a pair left the nest in a Llanbister garden on 13th September 2002 and just fledged young were seen at Llowes on the same date in 1959.

Breeding Atlases found birds in every 10-km square in the county in 1968-72 and in all but one (in the far north) in 1988-91. Since 2005 birds have been found in the breeding season in every square. Surveys in 2010 found 11 pairs within half a kilometre of the middle of Rhayader, 11 in a similar area of Llandrindod Wells, seven in and around Newbridge, 14 within a kilometre of the middle of Presteigne, nine in a similar area of Knighton and 15 in the Radnorshire parts of the Elan and Claerwen Valleys.

Although not the easiest woodland bird to census, being rather quiet and inobtrusive in many habitats, it is likely that the population in the county today is between 350 and 500 pairs.

Birds start to leave in early August and passage continues well into September. Records in the last week of September are rare and there have been two October records, both at Glasbury on the 3rd in 1995 and on the 12th in 1991.

Like many summer visitors, Spotted Flycatchers often return in the spring to their natal areas. A nestling ringed at Newbridge in 1984 returned to breed in the same farm building where it was born in 1985 and 1986. A nestling ringed at Penybont in July 1926 was found in Llandrindod Wells in June 1932.

Pied Flycatcher *Ficedula hypoleuca* A

Common summer visiting breeder and frequent passage migrant.

Breeds from north-west Africa, Iberia, France and the British Isles east across much of central and northern Europe and Russia to the Yenisei River, north to the far north of Norway and south to Romania. Winters in sub-Saharan West Africa.

The Woolhope Naturalists Field Club *Transactions* for 1896 described the Pied Flycatcher as common in the Elan Valley. And in the mid-1950s, Ingram and Salmon said that it was, 'still a widespread and quite numerous summer visitor... confined to the river valleys and adjacent woodlands.' In early May 1945 they found 25 singing males in one small wood near Aberedw but noted that numbers reduce as they pass on northwards.

There was a range expansion in Britain during the 1880s and 1890s which included a spread to southern Scotland and expansion from the west of mid-Wales to east Radnorshire, Herefordshire and Shropshire. There was another period of increase in the 1940s and early 1950s followed by a decline. Since the 1960s the widespread provision of nest boxes has somewhat confused any 'natural' population changes although numbers were definitely at their highest in Radnorshire, and many other counties, in the early to mid-1980s. Since then there has been a slow decline with noticeable, sudden, slumps in numbers in Radnorshire in 1995, 2001 and 2010. There was also a short-lived increase in 1992 and 1993 after the exceptional breeding season of 1991.

The present population in Radnorshire, based on sample surveys in 2010, is about 1,000 to 1,200 pairs which is about 40% of what it was during 1983-86, when the county population peaked at some 2,500 to 3,000 pairs. Probably a third of pairs in Radnorshire today breed in nest boxes. Numbers in many of the Sessile Oak dominated woodlands have experienced the highest declines and those in mixed deciduous and Alder woodlands alongside the county's major rivers, the least. It seems likely that there is a long term cycle of population levels linked to temperatures in the winter quarters and perhaps also, and not unrelated, the weather patterns in North Africa and south-west Europe during the spring migration period.

In Radnorshire the species is found in most types of mature, deciduous, woodlands, either with natural nesting holes or nest boxes. Birds may also be found in low densities in open, mature, coniferous woodlands, especially where nest boxes have been put up. Nesting sites also include holes in banks, walls and stone-buildings, provided that there is some wooded habitat close by. In the west of the county breeding takes place regularly in broadleaved woodlands up to 1,450 feet (442 m) a.s.l. Successive breeding bird Atlases have found birds in all of the county's 10-km squares.

The males arrive in numbers usually in the second half of April and early May with the average first date being the 11th April and the earliest records on 1st April 2012 and 2nd April 1989. The females arrive on average a week after the males from mid-April (earliest on 6th) to the middle of May. The majority of birds have been arriving noticeably earlier year on year since at least the late 1990s and the nesting season has been ending earlier as a result. Eggs are usually laid in the middle fortnight of May and young leave the nest from about the 10th June, with late broods found to the third week of July. Males are frequently bigamous and females promiscuous. The only two definite instances of females double-brooding in the county both occurred in 1987 and both were paired with different males for each brood.

Southward migration starts at the end of July and nearly all birds have left by the middle of August. The majority of later records are likely to be of continental birds on passage; September sightings are rare and there have been just four in October, with the latest on the 12th in 1994 in the Elan Valley.

More Pied Flycatchers have been ringed in Radnorshire than any other species and there have been more than 800 ringing recoveries to and from the county, although none as yet from the wintering areas south of the Sahara. Although most birds come up through Iberia and France in spring, ringing has shown that some come up through Italy, Austria and Switzerland to mid-Wales.

The ease with which adult birds are caught at nest boxes is the reason for the very high number of ringing exchanges between British counties. In total there have been 356 birds ringed elsewhere and found in Powys with birds coming from 15 counties including Dyfed (110), Gwent (63), Hereford & Worcester (49) and Shropshire (109). A total of 459 birds ringed in Powys have been found in 27 other counties with the main recipients being Clwyd (21), Devon (15), Dyfed (49), Gwent (60), Gwynedd (12), Hereford & Worcester (75) and Shropshire (165). Birds ringed in Italy and Spain have been found in Powys and birds ringed in Powys have gone to Algeria (3), Channel Islands (2), France (12), Morocco (40), Portugal (6), Spain (18), Switzerland, the Netherlands and Tunisia.

Most birds are faithfull to their natal site but nestlings ringed in Radnorshire have been found breeding as far away as Devon and Yorkshire. An early nestling ringed near Presteigne on 27th May 2011 was found freshly dead near Bath on 24th July, illustrating the early autumn departure time for the species. A nestling ringed in the Elan Valley on 6th June 1997 was caught at Landguard Point Bird Observatory, Suffolk, on 12th May 1998 and another ringed in the Ean Valley on 12th June 1996 was in Algeria on 22nd

April 1997 having probably just crossed the Sahara from the wintering quarters to the south. Another nestling from the Elan Valley oak woodlands ringed on 13th June 1993 was killed flying into wires in Portugal on 5th September and one ringed near Llanbister Road on 11th June 2006 was retrapped on Lundy Island on 8th May 2008. A nestling ringed at Llananno on 7th June 2009 was retrapped (and sexed male) at Portland Bird Observatory, Dorset, on 21st April 2010 and a female caught there on 3rd May 2012 had been ringed as a nestling near Rhos y Meirch, Knighton, on 6th June 2011. An adult female ringed near Cadiz, in the very south of Spain, on 13th April 1983 was found breeding at Newbridge on 24th May. Nestlings ringed at St Harmon and Penybont in mid-June 1985 were retrapped by ringers in Sark and Guernsey on 17th and 18th August. There have been several birds in Radnorshire known to be eight years old from ringing studies and one female still breeding as a nine-year old.

Bearded Tit *Panurus biarmicus* A

Very rare visitor.

Breeds locally across much of Europe as far north as Estonia and south to Turkey and Greece; much more widespread across Central Asia from the Caspian Sea east to northern China. Mostly resident but also dispersive and occasionally irruptive.

The only record is of a male at Pentrosfa Mire on 31st October 2004.

Long-tailed Tit *Aegithalos caudatus* A

Common resident breeder.

Breeds from Iberia, France, the British Isles and Scandinavia east across Europe and Russia to Okhotsk as well as Japan, Korea and north-west China, north to northern Norway and south to north-west Iran. Mostly resident but some Russian populations are migratory and others are sometimes irruptive southwards e.g. from the north-west of Russia and Fennoscandia.

The entry in Ingram and Salmon for the species was, 'A few pairs are resident and breed regularly in the more sheltered valleys'. Although numbers may have still been recovering from the severe winter weather of early 1947, it is difficult to imagine that it was so uncommon a bird in the early to mid-1950s.

Today it is a widespread and reasonably common bird in a variety of woodland types up to 1,500 feet (457 m) as well as along well-grown hedgerows and in areas of scrub and gorse. Numbers are reduced by very cold winters, especially those with ice-glazing and riming of branches. In recent decades those having the most noticeable effect have been 1962/3, 1978/9, 1981/2, 1984/5, 2009/10 and 2010/11, with the first four listed causing by far the biggest losses in Radnorshire.

Undoubtedly since the late 1980s the species has undergone a huge increase in numbers in the county and today it is probably three or four times as common as it was 25 years ago with a total probably in the range of c.750-850 pairs. Summer and winter Atlases have found birds in every 10-km square in Radnorshire, apart from the 1988-91 breeding Atlas which had records from 19 of the 21.

Long-tailed Tits are early breeders and often start the long process of nest-building during fine weather in mid-March. The single broods appear from mid-May and post-breeding season flocks of one to four family parties may be seen from June onwards and throughout the following autumn and winter, sometimes in the company of other tits, Treecreepers and Goldcrests. Flocks of 10-15 birds are common whilst groups of 20-25 are recorded annually and counts of 30 were made in the Elan Valley in November 1989, November 2000 and September 2004. The largest flock counted was 31 at Bettws, near Franksbridge, on 20th June 1987.

Since about 2000 records of birds coming to garden feeders have increased hugely. Peanuts attracted six to eight birds at Boughrood in January 2000 and at Cefn y Bettws, Clyro, in early March 2000. At a Huntington feeding station there were 15 regularly in December 2009 and 13 in a Painscastle garden in early April 2010.

A white-headed bird seen near Dol y Mynach Reservoir in early May 1993 was an aberrantly plumaged local bird rather than a very rare visit to the British Isles by one of the white-headed, continental, races.

British-ringed Long-tailed Tits are rarely recovered more than 10 kilometres from where they were ringed and when they do move further they invariably do so as a family group. One of several caught at Llanbwchllyn on 21st August 1994 was ringed at Chelmarsh Reservoir, Shropshire, on 3rd October 1993, a movement of 74 kilometres to the south-west.

Blue Tit *Cyanistes caeruleus* A

Very common and mainly resident breeder.

Breeds from north-west Africa, the Canary Islands, Iberia, France, the British Isles and Scandinavia east across most of Europe and in Russia west of the Urals, north to the Arctic Circle in Norway, south to north-west Iran, northern Iraq and Turkey.

Blue Tits seem to have always been a very common bird in Radnorshire with numbers reduced by some cold winters such as 1946/7 but not significantly by 1962/3. Recent cold winters have had little noticeable effect and since about 1990 numbers have noticeably increased steadily year on year so that in 2010 it was calculated that the county population was probably in the range of 7,000 to 9,000 pairs.

The highest breeding densities are in broadleaved woodland, especially those in the river valeys, with few in coniferous plantations unless nestboxes are erected. Farmland with scattered trees and copses, tall hedgerows, parks and gardens are also occupied and even town centres. Nestboxes are readily used but however many are put up a proportion of Blue Tits will always use natural sites such as holes in trees and banks as well as crevices in walls and buildings and a wide variety of other man-made nooks and crannies. They are the commonest occupier of nest-boxes in most parts of the county, except in the higher Sessile Oak woodlands where they are usually third to Great Tits and Pied Flycatchers.

Two broods are extremely rare in British Blue Tits and no instance has ever been recorded in Radnorshire. Broods of eight to11 are the norm and there have been several instances of 14 found in the county. Post-breeding season flocks, usually mixed with other tits, form from early autumn and continue throughout the winter. These are usually found in broadleaved woodlands but in early autumn Blue Tits are often found in ffridd habitats, reed beds and rank heather moorland as well as in stands of Bracken, where moulting adults find shelter and there is an abundance of the caterpillars of the Brown Silver-line moth.

An exceptionally large loose flock of over 240 mixed tits, Treecreepers and Nuthatches in the Penygarreg area of the Elan Valley in November 1989 included over 100 Blue Tits and nearby at a feeding station at Penbont House there were counts of 100 on 15th December 2005 and 102 on 10th December 2002. In 2001 a total of 315 different birds were caught for ringing in a Nant Glas garden over the year.

Large numbers also feed on the seeds of Downy Birch in autumn and winter and flock counts include 100 in the Elan Valley in November 1987 and 70 (with 50 Siskins) at Penbont on 15th December 2000. Garden feeders at Garnfawr Bungalow, near Franksbridge, attracted 84 at one time on 18th December 1996. Counts at garden feeders can be at least quadrupled to give a true picture of the number of birds actually using a site and up 100-120 different birds have been caught for ringing in one garden in a day on several occasions.

Most Blue Tits stay within 10 km of where they were ringed and the longest movement either to or from Powys was of 105 km to Warwickshire. An adult female ringed near Presteigne on 11th June 1983 was in Brecon (43 km WSW) on 14th January 1984. A nestling ringed at Crossgates on 6th June 1994 was caught by ringers at Llangorse (42 km S) on 5th November and a nestling ringed at Garnfawr Bungalow on 3rd June 1995 was caught by ringers at Nantyglo, Gwent, (47 km S) on 8th December whilst several of its siblings remained in the garden where they were born throughout the winter. In total 21 birds ringed elsewhere have been recovered in Powys and have come from Clwyd (2), Glamorgan, Gloucestershire (4), Gwent (3) and Shropshire (11). Also 12 birds ringed in Powys have been found in Clwyd, Dyfed (2), Glamorgan, Gwent (3), Hereford & Worcester (3), Shropshire and Warwickshire.

Two white-headed birds, presumably from one brood, were in a Pant y Dwr garden in January 1993. An unusually brightly plumaged adult male shot near Erwood on 29th October 1939 by J.G.Williams was said by H.F.Witherby to be of the continental, nominate, race and the specimen is now housed at the National Museum of Wales. On recent re-examination it is probably safer to say that it shows some of the characteristics of that sub-species.

Great Tit *Parus major*

Very common and mainly resident breeder.

A

Breeds from north-west Africa, Iberia, France and the British Isles across Europe and much of central and southern Asia east to Sakhalin, Japan, China and the Malay Archipelago, north as far as northern Norway, south to Sumatra and Timor, India, Sri Lanka, Iran and Jordan. Resident in Britain; northern populations are occasionally irruptive and some races are migratory.

The Great Tit is the most widespread species of the world's tits, has one of the greatest ranges of any Palearctic bird and comprises some 30 sub-species. In Radnorshire there seems to have been no major changes in its status for at least the last century, other than short-period fluctuations and a very noticeable, gradual, increase since about 1990. Prolonged, very cold, winter weather reduces numbers, particularly if there has been a poor crop of Beech mast, but this effect has been greatly mitigated in recent times due to the widespread provision of peanuts and sunflower seeds in gardens. Breeding and wintering Atlases have found the species in every hectad in Radnorshire and the county population in 2010 was calculated as being in the range of 5,500 to 6,500 pairs.

It is principally a bird of broadleaved woodland and in the hanging Sessile Oak woodlands it is often the commonest tit. Certain types of mature coniferous woodlands are occupied, especially those with at least some larch and a scattering of broadleaves. Pure stands of young to medium aged spruce are shunned, whether or not nest boxes are provided. Farmland with scattered trees and well-grown hedges, gardens and parks are also occupied, especially where nest boxes are erected. Natural holes in trees are the usual nest-site although holes in walls and buildings are also commonly used.

Singing males are often heard on sunny days from December onwards and nest-building usually begins in early April. Two broods are raised very rarely and in years with exceptional numbers of defoliating moth caterpillars, such as in 1987 and 1989 when at least three pairs did so in the Elan Valley oak woodlands. Family groups are noticeable from late-May onwards and often combine with other tits to form roaming feeding flocks in autumn and winter. As with the Blue Tit, many birds are found in areas of Bracken, especially on south-facing slopes, in July and August feeding on moth caterpillars. However, there are usually many fewer Great Tits than Blue Tits in these gatherings although the flock of 240+ birds in the Elan Valley in November 1989, after the exceptional breeding season, contained at least 100.

In 1971 there were c.40 near Dol y Mynach Reservoir on 12th December and 46 at nearby Penygarreg in the Elan Valley on 26th. At garden feeding stations 10-25 are sometimes counted at one time and at Garnfawr Bungalow there were 34 on 20th December 1996. A total of 126 birds were caught for ringing in a Nant Glas garden in 2001.

Most British Great Tits stay within one to two kilometres of where they were hatched and so the majority of recoveries are of under 10 km. There have been 22 ringed birds from elsewhere found in Powys and these have come from Dyfed, Shropshire (5), Gloucestershire (4), Gwent (5), Staffordshire, Warwickshire, Gwynedd, Hereford & Worcester, Lancashire, Merseyside and Nottinghamshire. Five birds ringed in Powys have been found in Dyfed, Glamorgan, Shropshire, Gwent and Gwynedd. A female ringed at Longhope, Gloucestershire, on 19th February 1989 was found breeding at Gilfach Nature Reserve on 10th June 1994 (88 km NNW). A nestling ringed at Llangorse on 30th May 2010 was found long-dead (drowned in a water butt) at Lloyney on 14th January 2011 (52 km NNE) and a juvenile ringed in Powys in July was found in south-west Pembrokeshire in October (114 km SSW). A nestling ringed near Rhos y Meirch, Knighton, on 5th June 2012 was retrapped at Little Sutton, near Ludlow, on 5th November (28 km ENE) and a ringed bird found dead at Howey in 2008 was at least eight years old.

Coal Tit *Periparus ater* A

Very common resident breeder.

Breeds from north-west Africa, Iberia, France and the British Isles east across Europe and much of Central Asia to Kamchatka, Japan, Korea, China and Taiwan, north to the Arctic Circle in Scandinavia, south to the Himalayas, Turkey and northern Iran. Mostly resident but some northerly populations are migratory or irruptive.

Being principally a species associated with coniferous woodlands, the Coal Tit underwent a huge increase in numbers in Radnorshire during the 20th century when many of the county's plantations were established. It does suffer some losses during very cold winter weather but usually only following years with a poor Beech mast crop which is a very important autumn and winter food source in many parts of the county. The only winter which resulted in major losses was 1962/3, although there were some losses in 1981/2, 1984/5 and 2009/10. The smallest of our true tits it is also a very agile bird able to feed underneath snow-covered branches where it finds one of its most important winter foods, the Green Spruce Aphid *Elatobium abietinum*. It also stores a significant proportion of its food including not only seeds of conifers and food from garden feeders but also, in times of plenty, 'packs' of aphis which it collects on the top of its beak and on its forehead and then hides, usually in a bark crevice.

Coal Tits are also found in small numbers in many of the broadleaved woodlands in the county but rarely far from conifers, even if only one or two isolated specimens. In autumn and winter birds are found more widely in parks and gardens and in small numbers in roaming flocks of mixed tits. It comes commonly to garden feeding stations for peanuts and sunflower seeds, especially so in years with low levels of natural food. However, the species is always commonest in conifers where year round it is often the second commonest bird to the Goldcrest in Radnorshire. Most plantations have breeding Coal Tits and they are found from the lowest valleys to the highest plantations of Radnor Forest at over 2,000 feet.

As with the Blue Tit and Great Tit, there has been a noticeable, steady, increase in numbers since c.1990 and the species has been found in every hectad in Radnorshire in all the breeding season and winter Atlases. In 2010 it was calculated that the county population was in the region of 4,000 to 4,500 pairs.

Coal Tits are the earliest nesters of the true tits and often start laying in early April in Radnorshire. Nest boxes are often used, especially if positioned low down, as well as natural holes in trees and holes in the ground, especially those of mice and voles. Broods are generally larger than those of other tits with 12-14 young quite often found in the county in fine and warm springs. Second broods have very rarely been found in the county and have comprised small broods of just 4-6 young.

Family parties are found from mid May onwards and small numbers mix with other tits, Goldcrests and Treecreepers. Gatherings in winter of more than ten birds are uncommon; 25 were with other tits at Penygarreg in the Elan Valley in November 1989, 20+ were regular at garden feeders at nearby Penbont House in January and February 2001 and 28 were counted there taking black sunflower seeds on 26th December 2002.

The species rarely wanders far from its natal area although a first-winter male ringed near Craven Arms, Shropshire, on 15th March 1990 was re-caught in the Elan Valley on 10th March 1994, a distance of 65 km WSW.

Willow Tit *Poecile montana* A

Uncommon resident breeder.

Breeds from the British Isles and north-east France and Scandinavia east across most of central Europe and Asia to north-east Russia, China and Japan, north to the far north of Norway and south to northern Greece and the far south of Japan. Resident, but northern populations are irruptive in some years.

Willow Tit and Marsh Tit were only described as separate species in 1897 and although Willow Tits were probably present in Radnorshire in the 19th century the eminent ornithologist John Walpole-Bond never mentioned it during his visits to the county in the early 1900s.

The first definite record for Radnorshire is of one shot at Llanbwchllyn by J.G.Williams on 22nd September 1934 followed by a series of positive breeding records leading to its distribution being described by Ingram & Salmon in 1955 as, 'not been worked out, though it appears to be fairly widespread in the southern part of the county.'

Distinguishing between the two very similar species has always been a problem and continued to be so through successive Atlases, and still is to the present day. However, there is no doubt that Willow Tits have always been much scarcer than Marsh Tits in the county, a gap which has widened hugely over recent years.

The 1968-72 breeding Atlas found birds in 17 of the county's 21 10-km squares (hectads). The winter Atlas of 1981-84 found it in all 21 and the breeding Atlas of 1988-91 found birds in 20. Since 2005 records have come from 20 of the 21 hectads, combining records from all seasons. However, these summaries hide the fact that the species has declined by at least 75% in Radnorshire since c.1990; a decline which seems to be continuing year on year in broadleaved habitats. In 2002 birds were found at only two sites of 20 where there were birds in 1988. They rarely come to garden bird feeding stations and usually only those very near to nesting areas. In 2010 it was likely that the population in the county was between 60 and 80 pairs with 16 pairs found in a survey of about 20% to 25% of previously occupied habitat.

It has disappeared from many of the broadleaved woodlands in and around the river valleys and increasingly also from the wetter Alder and willow woodlands. Today more than 90% of records come from conifer-dominated woodlands although it is absent from some major blocks, such as in the Elan Valley. Its strongholds are in the plantations north-east and south-east of Rhayader and those of Radnor Forest (up to 1,600 feet) with occasional records coming from the wet woodlands of Rhosgoch Bog, Llanbwchllyn and beside the lower Wye below Glasbury. This association with coniferous woodlands is very like Willow Tits on the continent and may be where the future lies for the species in Radnorshire, and perhaps some other counties.

The reasons for the decline in numbers associated with broadleaved woodlands in the county are unknown but are not due to any loss of habitat or potential nesting sites (the species excavates its own hole in a rotten tree stump) or competition with other tit species. The decline of Willow Tits (and Marsh Tits) in Radnorshire since c.1990 coincides with increases for Coal, Blue and Great Tits and it seems most likely that some subtle effects of recent climate/environmental change are the cause, perhaps influencing invertebrate food availabilty in certain woodland habitat types.

Marsh Tit *Poecile palustris*

Uncommon but widespread resident breeder.

A

Breeds from northern Iberia, France, England, Wales, southern Scotland and southern Scandinavia east across Europe to the Urals, south to northern Turkey, Greece and Italy; also in Asia from Central Russia east to Sakhalin, northern Japan, Korea, northern China and an isolated population in Burma. Resident and non-irruptive.

Although both Willow Tit and Marsh Tit sometimes visit the same garden bird feeding stations in autumn and winter, during the breeding season the former is usually accociated with coniferous woodlands in the county and the latter with mature deciduous woodlands, especially those with at least some Ash. However, there are still some places in the east of the county where both species breed in the same, mixed, woodlands.

Like the Willow Tit, the species has declined greatly since c.1990 in Radnorshire; a decline also obvious in recent decades throughout the British Isles and much of Europe. In particular in Radnorshire it has disappeared from most of the higher Sessile Oak dominated woodlands. Around the Elan Valley reservoirs there were eight to 10 pairs in the mid-1970s but this had declined to just three to four by the mid-1990s and there has been none since 2000. In recent years it has been a rare autumn and winter visitor with just a lone singing male in April 2004.

The breeding Atlas of 1968-72 recorded birds in all 21 hectads in the county, as did the winter Atlas of 1981-84. The breeding Atlas of 1988-91 had two hectads without records and since 2005 there have been breeding season records from 16 hectads and winter records in 20. Although these are similar distribution returns to those for Willow Tit, Marsh Tits are much the commoner, and more widespread, species in Radnorshire today as they were in the mid-1980s, and most likely to always have been given their preference for broadleaved woodland. In recent years Marsh Tits are have been found in four times as many tetrads as Willow Tit and is ten times more likely to come to a garden feeding site, although these are invariably very close to, or within, breeding territories. They are regular users of nest boxes in the county in very low numbers. They prefer a nest site less than a metre from the ground and some success has been achieved by placing boxes low down on trees.

Although still a fairly frequently met with species in the county, numbers have declined by at least 60% since c.1990; however, there is some indication that this decline has levelled out since about 2005. The population in 2010 was calculated to be in the range of 250-300 pairs.

The reasons for the decline are unknown but, as with the Willow Tit, are likely to be some climatic/environmental effect on invertebrate food. In Radnorshire, at least, it is definitely not due to the loss of understorey in mature broadleaved woodlands as has been suggested for some sites elsewhere.

Nuthatch *Sitta europaea*

Common resident breeder.

A

Breeds from north-west Africa, Iberia, the south of Britain and Scandinavia east across much of Europe and Asia east to Kamchatka and Japan, south to China, India, Thailand and Burma. Resident; northern populations are sometimes irruptive.

In the 19th century it seems that the Nuthatch was mostly a bird of east Radnorshire spreading to the rest of the county, and much of Wales, in the first three decades of the 20th century, particularly during the 1920s and 30s. Today it is a common bird of mature, mixed, deciduous woodland throughout the county from the lowest river valleys to 1,300 feet (396 m) at Cefncennarth and above Penygarreg Reservoir. It is also frequent in well-wooded farmland, parks and larger gardens as well as in mature, mixed broadleaved and coniferous woodlands, especially those with larch, Hazel and Beech.

In 1996 in those broadleaved woodlands within Radnorshire in the Elan and Claerwen Valleys there were 26-30 pairs in 180 acres (73 ha.) of broadleaved and mixed woodland. It has been found in every hectad in the county in all the Atlases since the first was carried out in 1968-72. Sample counts in 1995 and 1996 suggest a county population of 900 to 1,100 pairs.

The Nuthatch is a relatively early breeding bird in Radnorshire with eggs usually laid in the third week of April. Nesting sites are mostly in holes in trees, especially old nest holes of Great Spotted Woodpecker, as well as frequently in nest boxes and sometimes in holes in walls or buildings - all of which they usually reduce in size with mud. Nearly all nests are made purely of bark flakes of Scots Pine or larch and birds will fly several hundred yards from the nesting place to collect them.

Birds often wander widely in August and September but rarely more than a mile from where they were born and seldom across more than a few hundred yards of open country without trees. In some autumns birds are seen wandering further afield, presumably in poor years for Hazel and Beech nuts. By far the most noticeable year for this was 2012 with many sightings of birds in unusual places from late August to early October. Birds are occasionally found with roaming tit flocks in autumn and winter; four were with a mixed flock of about 240 tits in the Elan Valley in November 1989.

Ringed birds are rarely recovered more than 10 km from where they were ringed and most birds stay within 1 km. Of nearly 60,000 Nuthatches ringed in England and Wales fewer than 20 of the 450 recoveries have been found more than 20 km from the place of ringing and one of the longest movements was of a nestling ringed near Craven Arms, Shropshire, on 2nd June 1985 and found freshly dead in October at Nantmel, a distance of 40 km WSW.

An all white, leucistic, bird was seen near Dolafallen Bridge, south-west of Rhayader, on 14th November 2002.

Treecreeper *Certhia familiaris*

Common resident breeder.

A

Breeds from northern Iberia, France, the British Isles and Scandinavia east across much of Europe and central Asia east to Sakhalin and Japan, north to northern Norway, south to central China, the Himalayas, northern Iran and southern Greece. Mostly resident, some northern populations are partly migratory and sometimes irruptive.

There seems to have been little change in status of this species in Radnorshire over at least the last hundred years, other than decreases due to very cold winters. Severe winters with ice-glazing have had the most effect and by far the most severe was that of 1962/3 with 1961/2 and 1978/9 also causing significant declines. The severe and prolonged cold of 2009/10 reduced numbers by an average of 15% across six broadleaved woodlands in the county at various altitudes.

The species is often under-recorded in surveys because the best time to count singing birds is in late February and March and most breeding bird surveys do not start until at least April. However, Treecreepers were found in every 10-km square in Radnorshire in each of the breeding Atlases and in the winter Atlas of 1981-84. A survey of 180 acres (73 ha.) of broadleaved and mixed woodlands in the Radnorshire parts of the Elan and Claerwen Valleys found 44 singing birds in 1996 and from sample sites the county population in 1995/6 was calculated to be c.1,050 to 1,300 pairs.

Treecreepers are found in the breeding season in most areas of broadleaved woodland in Radnorshire from the lowest valleys to 1,300 feet (400 m) a.s.l. In the autumn and winter birds have been seen up to 1,800 feet (550 m) associating with tit flocks in the conifers of Radnor Forest. Small numbers also breed in mature, open, coniferous woodlands but usually only those with some broadleaves nearby or alongside the rides. In most years many pairs in Radnorshire are double-brooded and males often sing strongly again between the broods in late May and early June.

Birds do wander widely outside of the breeding season and can be found along overgrown hedgerows, in gardens, in sparsely wooded habitats and areas of scrub, often with tits and Goldcrests. There were at least 13 with a large mixed tit flock in the Elan Valley in November 1989, but this was exceptional and one to four is the more usual number recorded. One was in Sycamores at the remote Claerwen Farm, at the north-west corner of the Claerwen Reservoir, on 17th October 1992 - at least two miles from the next tree. A bird ringed at Newbridge in January 2008 was retrapped by a ringer near Hundred House in March, 12 km ESE - a very long movement for a Treecreeper.

Wherever the Coast Redwood, *Sequoia sempervirens*, or the Wellingtonia, *Sequoiadendron giganteum*, occur and Treecreepers are present they excavate recesses in the well-insulating bark in which to roost. In January 1998 there were at least 11 birds roosting in the trees around Llandrindod Wells Museum in the centre of town.

Golden Oriole *Oriolus oriolus* A

Very rare visitor.

Breeds from north-west Africa, Iberia, France and southern Scandinavia east across Europe to central Asia, north to southern Finland and south to the Himalayas. Winters in the Indian sub-continent and southern Africa.

The only record is of an adult male seen along the disused railway line north of Erwood Craft Centre on 7th April 1990.

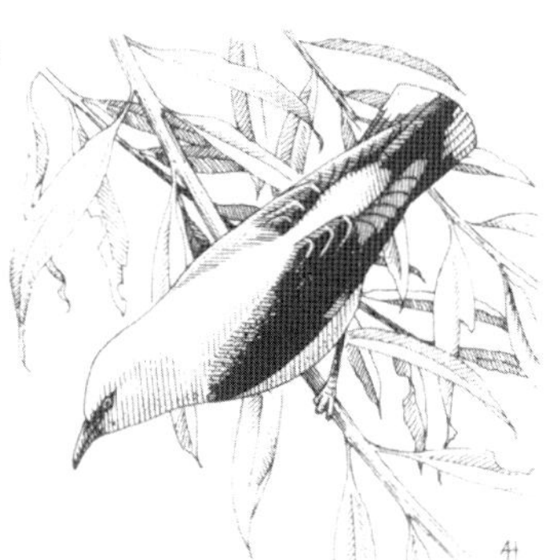

Red-backed Shrike *Lanius collurio* A

Former summer visiting breeder now a very rare visitor.

Breeds from northern Iberia and France to southern Scandinavia and Finland east across much of Europe and Russia as far as the headwaters of the Yenisei River and northern Kazakhstan, south to northern Iran, Turkey and Crete, and north to just south of the Arctic Circle in Sweden and Finland. Winters in Africa south of the equator.

Although probably always an uncommon breeding bird in Radnorshire, and over much of Wales, the 'Butcher Bird' was a familiar species to many in the 19th century. However, starting in the late 19th century and continuing throughout the 20th century, the Red-backed Shrike declined across Britain until today it is all but extinct everywhere with only the occasional pair breeding. Long-term climatic change is thought to be the cause of this demise.

In the first decade of the 20th century the species was described as quite common in the Knighton area by O.R.Owen but began to decline soon afterwards. It was also still quite common on the Radnorshire/Herefordshire border between 1901 and 1912, but quite rare by 1925. In the 1920s there were still several pairs in the area from Llandrindod south to Llanelwedd, where Woodlarks also used to be found.

Also in the 1920s, pairs nested in the Elan Valley and near Aberedw in 1925, whilst in the 1930s there were pairs found again in the Elan Valley in 1930, near Builth Road in 1932 and at Painscastle in 1933. The last breeding record in the county was in 1944, probably in the Llanelwedd to Llandrindod area.

Since then there have been just two records: one was singing at Llandrindod on 20th August 1947 and a young bird of the year was at The Begwyns on 20th and 21st August 1995.

Great Grey Shrike *Lanius excubitor* A

Rare winter visitor and passage migrant.

Breeds from France to Fennoscandia east across northern Europe and Asia to north-east Siberia, Sakhalin, Mongolia and northern China. Winters within the breeding areas and over much of western and southern Europe and central Asia.

The first record was of a male shot in Radnorshire near Builth Wells on 10th March 1865 (*The Field*, April 7th 1866 p.295). There have been about another 57 records since. One was seen near Clyro on the 24th October 1913 and another near Builth, in Radnorshire, on 14th February 1915. Both were reported in *The Field*. A male was seen in the winter of 1925 near Llandrindod and another reported between Llandrindod and Penybont on the extraordinarily early date of 2nd September 1947 (*British Birds* vol.51 p.357). The only record in the 1950s was of one seen in the Elan Valley on 18th October 1951.

Between 1962 and 1969 there were a further 12 records between 23rd October and 23rd April. They came from Whitewall Sewage Farm (Presteigne), Llandrindod Lake Common, Llandrindod Hall Farm, near Beguildy, Llyn Heilyn, Shaky Bridge (2), by the Blue Lins Brook, Llanbister Road, between Hindwell and Evenjobb, Llandegley and at Penybont Common.

There were six records in the 1970s between 1970 and 1977: at Dolberthog Common on 5th November 1970, by the A483 north of Llanbadarn Fynydd on 29th November 1970, at Aberedw from the 9th-15th November 1971, Llanbister on 25th April 1973 (the latest county record), Aberedw on 16th April 1976 and Cwmbach on 9th April 1977. The five records in the 1980s came from Gladestry on 22nd November 1982, Llanbadarn Fynydd on 4th December 1982, Doldowlodd from 1st to 4th April 1983 and Llandeilo Hill from 3rd-16th April 1983. A record at second hand of one at Stonewall Hill on about 26th August 1984 quoted elsewhere was probably erroneous.

The seven records in the 1990s included a singing male near Abbeycwmhir on 22nd April 1994 and sightings near Llanwrthwl, at Glasbury, Pont ar Elan, Nant Glas (2) and one at Radnor Forest which stayed from 8th November 1999 to at least 22nd February 2000.

Since 2000 there have been records in every year except 2003, although there has been a special effort to visit all likely places at least twice during the winter period. In all there were about 27 records between 2000 and 2013, including birds returning to the same area in successive winters at Whitton (early 2000 and 2001/2), in the Elan Valley (early 2005 and 2005/6) and Radnor Forest (2007/8 and 2008/9). Other records have come from Bwlch y Sarnau (2), Abbeycwmhir (2), Radnor Forest (4), Elan Valley (2, including the earliest recent record on 5th October 2008), New Radnor, Cwmbach, Heartsease, Llandegley, Monaughty, near Rhayader (2), The Begwyns (2), Penybont Common and at Pant y Dwr. All records have fallen between 5th October and 12th April with many presumed over-wintering birds seen over protracted periods of weeks or months.

Most records have come from gorsey and or scrubby commons, ffridd and young and clearfelled coniferous plantations. However there have also been sightings along hedgerows, on roadside wires and even attacking birds at garden feeders. Checks on a larder of a bird in the Elan Valley showed that it had killed at least 14 Wrens, six Blue Tits and four Short-tailed Voles during its three month stay in early 2005.

Jay *Garrulus glandarius*

A

Common resident breeder.

Breeds from north-west Africa, Iberia, France, the British Isles and Fennoscandia east across Europe and Asia to Sakhalin, Japan, Korea and China, south to Burma, the Himalayas and Israel. Mostly resident but occasionally irruptive in the north and east.

Ingram and Salmon said in 1955 that the species, 'has apparently decreased considerably from its former numbers. It is not a common species anywhere and in some quite large woodlands not even a single pair can be found.'

Jays were heavily persecuted by gamekeepers in the 19th and early 20th centuries but there has been a large increase in numbers in Radnorshire since the 1950s due to the demise of gamekeeping and the large-scale planting of conifer plantations. This increase continued into the 1980s but since then there has been a very noticeable decline in some areas due to predation by introduced Goshawks.

Today in the county Jays are found in all types of mature woodland as well as in and around towns and villages with extensive tree cover. It is found in every 10-km square in the county but is commonest in the well-wooded river valleys. It is by far the most difficult corvid to census accurately due to its shyness but the county population is probably in the range of 350-450 pairs. Local birds are very sedentary and the few results from ringing have shown no movements of more than seven kilometres. However, an adult ringed in June in Gwynedd was shot in Powys in April two years later for an exceptionally long movement for a Jay of 55 km.

Broadleaved woodlands are the favoured feeding areas throughout the year. In particular Sessile Oak woods are much frequented, especially in autumn, depending on the acorn crop. Each bird may bury up to 5,000 seeds in the season, in hundreds of different caches, carrying several at a time in the gullet, as well as usually one in the beak. They are often to be seen flying a kilometre or more to bury the acorns, often in open hillsides, in ffridd habitats and commons as well as around the woodland edge. One bird was seen to repeatedly fly over 2.5 km each way to bury acorns on The Begwyns in November 2010.

Although they remember where many are buried right through to the following spring, a large percentage are not retrieved and undoubtedly Jays are by far the species most responsible for the spread of oak trees in Radnorshire, as they are over many parts of their range. They have also been seen in Radnorshire collecting and burying Beech nuts, as well as peanuts, sunflower seeds and other bird food from garden feeding stations. Up to 15 birds were at a site near Gladestry in the winter of 2012/13 feeding on the fallen seeds of Scots Pine, including digging through up to six inches of snow.

Most nests in Radnorshire are today built in conifer woodlands, especially in unthinned stands if available where they are least vulnerable to predation. Other nests have been found in dense birch woodland, Holly and Blackthorn thickets.

Although usually seen singly or in pairs, like most other species of corvid, Jays sometimes gather into social groups in the late winter and early spring. Groups of Jays rarely reach double figures however, and usually comprise one or two females and several males getting together for just 10-20 minutes early on fine mornings: 10 were near the Penygarreg Dam on 16th February 1997 and 11 were there on 7th March 2008. Very rarely groups may be seen in May and are thought to be groups of failed or non breeders: eight of a group of 11 flew high to the west from the Claerwen Valley on 6th May 2006.

Although the main food of the Jay in autumn and winter is usually mainly acorns, in the summer months large quantities of invertebrates are eaten as well as the eggs and nestlings of small birds. Recently fledged woodland birds such as tits, Redstarts and Pied Flycatchers are undoubtedly heavily predated by Jays in many woodlands in Radnorshire where nest boxes are provided and birds can be seen from late May to early July systematically going through the canopy of broadleaved woodland searching for very young fledglings. One in the Elan Valley was seen to catch, kill and swallow four young Pied Flyatchers which had just left the nest within a few minutes. Eggs and young are also taken from nest boxes with large enough holes and adult birds have been seen being repeatedly attacked as they come and go to boxes in some places in the county.

Autumn irruptions of Jays from the continent combined with large numbers of British birds have been recorded in most decades since the early 19th century and are thought to be the result of acorn crop failure and very successful breeding seasons. However, these irruptions have rarely been noticeable as far west as Radnorshire. The large irruption of 1957 was noticed as far west as Herefordshire but the huge one of 1983 reached many parts of Wales, including Radnorshire.

The movement was noted from late September and throughout much of October and to give some idea of the scale of the event records included: 896 flying south-west at St Margaret's, Kent, on 2nd October, 700 flying west at Bridport, Dorset, in 3.5 hours on 6th October, 2,000 on The Lizard, Cornwall, on 15th October included 800 in a single field, 3,000 in small groups headed west over Plymouth on 17th October when 1,800 flew west in an hour at Kenidjack, Cornwall, included 1,000 in just ten minutes. (*British Birds* vol.78 pp.611-637).

After this mass movement westwards many birds were seen heading north and north-west from west Cornwall (not a single bird reached the Scilly Isles) and doubtless many dispersed into western Britain and Wales. In Radnorshire small groups were obvious from the end of October into January 1984. There were many counts of five to 10 birds, usually engaged in collecting and burying Sessile Oak acorns, with the largest concentrations being along the well-wooded parts of the river valleys especially the Wye, Edw and Ithon. Twelve were near Rhayader on 12th November, 16 near Builth Road on 22nd December, 15 near Aberedw on 30th October and 18 near Hundred House on 6th November. On a drive down the A470 between Rhayader and Builth (14 miles) on 10th November a total of 67 birds were counted flying both ways over the road in groups of 1-6. There were probably several hundred 'extra' Jays in Radnorshire for much of November and December 1983.

Magpie *Pica pica*

A

Common resident breeder.

Breeds from north-west Africa, Iberia, France and the British Isles east across much of Europe and Asia to north-east Siberia and China, north to the North Cape of Norway and south to Iran and Hainan; also North America from Alaska south across much of west and central Canada and USA. Resident; some northern populations are very rarely irruptive.

Numbers of Magpies in Radnorshire, as elsewhere, increased throughout most of the 20th century due to the reduction in gamekeeping, the gradual decline in the use of poison baits set for birds of prey and corvids and the huge increase in improved pasture for livestock rearing. Ingram and Salmon described it as 'numerous and widespread' in the mid-1950s and the county population seems to have reached its peak in the 1980s. Roost counts at Rhosgoch Bog of 75 and c.100 birds were made in November and December 1980 and reached a high of 150 in February 1982. At St Michael's Pool there was a roost of 54 birds on 20th November 1982 and one of 45 at Abbeycwmhir on 8th December.

Since the end of the 1980s there has been a very noticeable decline in numbers in most parts of the county due to introduced Goshawks and the spread of Red Kites east of the A470. Young Magpies are commonly taken from the nest by Red Kites and Buzzards and full-grown birds are the frequent prey of Goshawks. Sample counts in 2008 suggested a population of between 1,100 and 1,400 pairs, approximately 70% of what it was at its peak 20 years earlier.

However, the species is still common and found in every 10-km square in Radnorshire; occupying most woodland types, towns, villages, farmland with tall hedgerows, woods and shelter belts, and larger gardens. Counts of more than 15 birds together have been rare in recent years: 17 were near Dolafallen Bridge, Elan Valley, on 10th December 2000, 27 were at Discoed on 2nd January 2007 and 25 near Oleuddu Isaf on 14th February 2012.

Chough *Pyrrhocorax pyrrhocorax* A

Very rare visitor.

Breeds locally in north-west Africa, the Canary Islands, Iberia, France, the west coast of Britain, Italy and parts of south-east Europe east to China, Mongolia and the Himalayas. Resident.

The first record was of one collected in the Rhayader area in September 1914, the prepared skin of which was sold to the Oxford University Museum by the taxidermists J.Betteridge & Sons of Birmingham in March 1934. Since then two were seen near the Fforest Inn in February 1954 and possibly the same birds were near Cascob on 15th October 1955.

Two were on Maelinydd Common feeding on tipulid larvae with a large flock of Jackdaws, Rooks and Carrion Crows from at least 4th-11th August 1994 and one was on Craig Dyfnant, above the Claerwen Reservoir, on 23rd March 1995 and on crags near Maen Serth on 7th May. At least the 1994 and 1995 birds are likely to have been wanderers from the then inland breeding sites at Cwmystwyth, in Ceredigion, and near Staylittle in Montgomeryshire.

Jackdaw *Corvus monedula* A

Common resident breeder.

Breeds from north-west Africa, Iberia, France and the British Isles east across southern Fennoscandia and most of Europe and western Asia east to the Yenisei River and Kazakhstan, south to northern Iran and Turkey. Mostly resident but migrates more than other British corvids and many continental populations are partly or wholly migratory and sometimes irruptive.

Ingram and Salmon gave the species' status in 1955 as, '...very numerous and widespread...with some quite large colonies amongst crags in the hills.' It is still a very numerous bird but crag colonies are now very rare, if not extinct, due to the resurgence of the Peregrine population and in general it is much more of a lowland bird in all seasons today than it used to be in the late 1980s and is scarce in the far west and north.

Jackdaws are familiar birds in all the towns of the county feeding in gardens and refuse areas as well as in surrounding fields. Large flocks often gather to roost at dusk, especially in the winter months. At Knighton there is a regular flock of 100-150; 300 were at Llandrindod in February 2012; 500 gathered to roost at Presteigne from January to March 2002 and up to 250 are regular in Rhayader. The chimneys of the many Victorian and Edwardian houses are favourite nesting places but many more pairs breed in the Radnorshire countryside in holes in trees, especially Ash and oak, and in barns and outbuildings.

There used to be several colonies of 10-30 pairs on crags in the Elan Valley but these gradually moved into Rhayader from the mid-1980s until the last ones bred above Dol y Mynach in 1990. The old, disused, buildings at Cwm Elan mines also held a small colony of two to six pairs in many years between at least 1972 and 2008.

Overall, numbers have increased in Radnorshire since at least the early 1970s and today, judging by the numbers of non-breeding birds, the major limiting factor is the availability of suitable nesting places. It is recorded in every hectad (10-km square) in the county in all seasons and the population in 2008 was thought to be between 1,400 and 1,600 pairs.

Large post-breeding flocks form in the early autumn with other corvids and are often to be found feeding with them on tipulid larvae on hillsides and commons, although with the large decline in the tipulid populations on the hills in recent years this is not on such a large scale as it was in the 1980s and 1990s. At Maelinydd Common there were 1,550 on 2nd July 1991 and 2,500 on 9th August 1995 and at Glasbury there were 1,500 on 19th July 1998. Smaller flocks are more usual; 420 were at Evenjobb on 12th July 2011, 350 at Glasbury on 9th July 2013 and 160 near Painscastle on 23rd August 1997.

On fine autumn days town flocks sometimes make high flights to the west, presumably looking for new breeding areas, and often travel several miles before returning home. A noisy flock of 170 birds left Rhayader for tours of the Elan and Claerwen Valleys on 14th and 17th October 2009 and smaller flocks have been seen behaving similarly out of Knighton, Presteigne and Llandrindod.

Late autumn and winter flocks and roosts are widespread: at Llanfihangel nant Melan there were 1,500 to roost in January and February 1994 and 800 in February 2011, at Glasbury there were 1,000 on 1st January 1981, 440 went to roost at Glan Llyn woods on 14th October 1979, 450 were at Llowes on 15th December 1999, 500 at Rhosgoch on 31st December 1980, 250 at St Michael's Pool roost on 20th November 1982 and 450 at Old Radnor on 24th September 2010.

Rook *Corvus frugilegus*

Common resident breeder.

A

Breeds from France, northern Spain and the British Isles east across most of Europe and central Asia to Amurland and Manchuria, north to southern Finland and south to central China, Kazakhstan and Turkey. Introduced to New Zealand. Mostly resident in western Europe, elsewhere partly or wholly migratory to within the breeding range and south to Iberia, southern China, northern India, Iran, Israel and the Nile Delta.

Although primarily a bird which feeds on worms, beetles and other invertebrates, Rooks have long been persecuted by farmers and gamekeepers as a member of the crow family whose colonies are an easy target. The population level in Radnorshire, as in many places, is largely determined by current farming practises and the increase in improved pastures (and therefore the numbers of worms supported) especially over the last 50 years has undoubtedly favoured the species.

Prior to the 1960s there was much more mixed farming in the county and, as Rooks will also eat grain and follow the arable cultivator for invertebrates, they have always been a fairly common bird in Radnorshire despite the localised persecution. However, they undoubtedly prefer pasture to arable as a feeding ground.

The national survey of Rooks undertaken during 1944-46 was not very detailed and no figure for Radnorshire can be determined. However, there was almost certainly a decline in the county between then and the next survey carried out in 1975/6, but that decline seems to have actually taken place in the late 1960s and early 1970s.

The survey of 1975-77 (usually referred to as the '1975 survey') found c.39,000 nests in Wales of which 2,117 were in Radnorshire. A total of 70 rookeries were located in 15 of the 21 hectads wholly or partly in the county with only parts of the (mostly treeless) far west and north (not surprisingly) having no colonies. The size of the rookeries ranged between two and 87 nests with 35 holding 25 and under, 23 with 26-50 and 51-87 nests in the other 12. Altitude varied from 100 metres a.s.l. (325 feet) to 315 metres (1,025 feet) although a small rookery was found at Bryngwyn in 1980 at an altitude of 347 metres (1,128 feet), the highest recorded in Wales.

Of the rookeries found in Radnorshire in 1975/6 there were 30 with nests only in oak and another 15 with nests in oak and other species. Ash was an important nesting tree at 19 sites and nests were found in a total of at least 10 other tree species: Beech/Copper Beech, Birch/Silver Birch, Hawthorn, Sycamore, Lime, Wych Elm, European Larch, Scots Pine, Alder and Californian Nutmeg.

The national survey in 1996 was based on 2,000 randomly selected tetrads of which eight were in Radnorshire. A total of 163 nests was found in four of the 2kmx2km squares with the other four having none. All this survey revealed was that there were either some new rookeries since 1975/6, or some had been missed, and that there had been an increase of about 25% over the 20 years. Counts of a small number of sample rookeries showed an increase of c.40% between 1985 and 2008 when it was estimated that the number of rookeries in Radnorshire was probably between 90 and 100 and the number of nests in the range of 2,800 to 3,000.

However, since then the severe winter weather of 2009/10 and 2010/11 has undoubtedly had a serious effect on the species in the county and at least some colonies have been much reduced. Similarly prolonged summer droughts, such as in 2006, result in poor breeding seasons for some rookeries and locally predation by Goshawk of adults and young, and of young in the nest by Tawny Owl, has been significant.

After the breeding season feeding flocks form, often with Jackdaws and Carrion Crows. The bare hillsides in the upper Elan Valley hold varying numbers every year feeding on tipulid larvae, ground and dung beetles: 350 were counted there on 7th June 1999 and 17th June 2003 and 500 on 20th June 2009. At Maelinydd Common there were 1,000 on 9th August 1995 and 650 near Glasbury in December 1996. Much commoner are flocks of 100-200, which probably comprise all the birds of a colony or group of colonies.

Although British bred Rooks rarely move more than a few miles from their birthplace throughout their lives, immigration along the east coast from the more migratory continental populations has frequently been recorded, although not so often in the last 30 years or so. However, no ringed birds from the continent have been found in Radnorshire although a Polish ringed nestling has been found in neighbouring Herefordshire in winter and a bird ringed on the east coast at Spurn Point Bird Observatory and found in the West Midlands was possibly an immigrant.

Carrion Crow *Corvus corone* A

Common resident breeder.

Breeds in Iberia, France and parts of the British Isles east to western Germany and northern Italy; also in north-east and central Asia from the the West Siberian Plain east to the Bering Sea, Kamchatka and Japan and south to north-west China, Kazakhstan and the Himalayas. Western European birds are essentially resident; some Asian populations are mostly migratory.

Although Carrion Crows seem always to have been a common species in Radnorshire there is no doubt that numbers have considerably increased since the decline of gamekeeping in the county, the (almost) total decline of poisoning and the increased prosperity of less-favoured-area sheep farming resulting in the much reduced shooting of the species. However, large numbers are still shot and trapped and Carrion Crows remain a major concern of the farmer lambing outdoors.

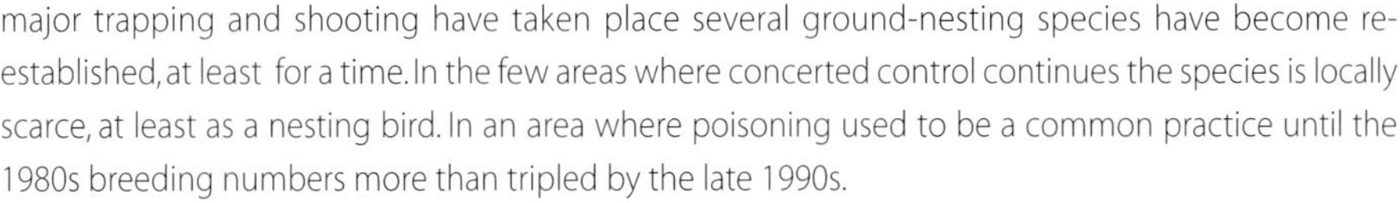

Tests with dummy eggs showed that they have also been a major cause of the rapid decline in the numbers of Lapwing since the 1980s and in areas where periods of major trapping and shooting have taken place several ground-nesting species have become re-established, at least for a time. In the few areas where concerted control continues the species is locally scarce, at least as a nesting bird. In an area where poisoning used to be a common practice until the 1980s breeding numbers more than tripled by the late 1990s.

As well as the increase in breeding numbers there is also a huge number of non-breeding birds in the county which often form year-round flocks of 30-50. In most parts of the county the limiting factor on the numbers breeding is simply the availability of trees. Today the density of nesting pairs is on average six per square kilometre on well-treed farmland with nests spaced about every 300 metres. Up to 12 active nests have been found in a single kilometre square. A study by the RSPB around Newbridge in 1981 found 117 nests in 24 square kilometres of farmland. In 1999 a nest was found on the ground amongst the rush, *Juncus effusus*, in a treeless part of the upper Elan Valley; eggs were laid but the attempt failed.

The species is found in every 10-km square and the breeding population in Radnorshire today is probably in the range of 4,000 to 4,500 pairs with a similar number of non-breeders.

Post-breeding season flocks are common with the breeding adults and their young often combining with the non-breeders of the local area. At Penybont there were 300 on 16th September 1978 and on the Claerwen NNR over 200 were present on 24th July 1998. At Maelinydd Common there were 320 on 2nd July 1991 and 800 on 9th August 1995. A flock of 500 near Pont ar Elan on 18th June 1997 were feeding on tipulid larvae with Rooks. At Glasbury there was a flock of 400 on 6th October 2000 and 400 were also counted near St. Harmon on 31st July 2011.

British Carrion Crows are highly sedentary and the average of a thousand recoveries of ringed birds has been about 3km with fewer than 30 moving more than 20km. A juvenile ringed on Newchurch Hill on 7th June 1954 was found dead near Erwood on 11th March 1955 a distance (as the crow flies) of 16km to the south-west.

Hooded Crow *Corvus cornix*

A

Very rare visitor.

Breeds in northern Scotland, the Isle of Man, Ireland, Italy, Germany and Fennoscandia east across Russia to Lake Balkhash and the West Siberian Plain south to the Nile Valley and Iran. British birds are resident, northern continental populations are wholly or partially migrant to the south within the breeding range.

Ingram and Salmon mention, without a date, 'one, seen many years ago, near Craig Pwll-du' (3km east of Erwood) either by, or reported to, J.Williams-Vaughan. They also mention, 'Four said to have occurred at different times, but none dated', with the name of Mr.R.P.Bufton attached as either observer or reporter.

The only recent record is of one flying steadily north over the hills east of the Claerwen Reservoir on 8th May 1983.

Raven *Corvus corax*

A

Common resident breeder.

Breeds in north-west Africa and throughout much of Europe, Asia, North and Central America. Mostly sedentary.

Ravens have been persecuted for hundreds of years and the intensity of shooting, trapping, poisoning and the destruction of nests during the 19th century resulted in it becoming a very rare breeding bird by the 1880s. There were still pairs in the Elan Valley at the ancient nesting place on Craig Gigfran (Raven's Rock) near Caban Coch, and at Stanner Rocks until at least the 1860s. The Elan Valley birds moved up the valley to Craig Dolfaenog whilst the dams were being built in the 1890s but were rarely allowed to raise young. It is likely that there were also a few other pairs nesting in the remoter parts of the county at the end of the 19th century.

Although still persecuted throughout the 20th century, by about 1925 there were probably a dozen pairs in the county, all nesting on cliffs and crags. Between then and the mid 1950s numbers had increased to about 30 pairs, with most by then nesting in trees. The estimated number of pairs in Radnorshire in the early 1990s was 50-75 pairs, but this figure was probably on the low side. Breeding numbers in the Elan uplands tripled between the mid 1970s and the late 1990s when there was also a non-breeding population there of some 40-50 birds.

Breeding numbers also continued to increase throughout the county, particularly in the east and south, throughout the 1980s and 1990s and in recent years the only restriction in many areas is the lack of suitable nesting places. Most nests today are in mature trees, especially conifers, but are also to be found in a few steep hillside Rowans and Hawthorns just a few metres tall. Nesting still takes place on suitable crags, often in competition with Peregrines, and on derelict upland farm buildings. Breeding takes place in every hectad in the county and since 2005 the population seems to be in the range of 170-200 pairs with probably at least 350 non-breeding birds.

Flocks of 10-40 are often seen at all times of the year. The former refuse tips at Clyro, Rhayader and Nantmel regularly attracted 30-60 birds and the Red Kite feeding station at Gigrin Farm, near Rhayader, has also produced counts of 50-100 birds. At Llanbwchllyn a flock of about 75 was seen in 1971 and one of 55 was seen in the Elan Valley on 6th February 1991. A chicken waste dump on the border with Herefordshire, near Knill, regularly attracted over 100 birds in the 1990s, with the flock loafing and roosting in the adjacent forestry at Burfa Camp. The highest count there was 162 on 10th February 1996 with 100-150 regularly counted in 1998, at least 120 on 4th January 1999 and 95 on 14th April 2000.

Ravens rarely wander far from there natal area and of the 40 ringing recoveries to and from Powys none have been of more than 100km. A nestling ringed at Kington on 19th April 1959 was found dead at Knighton on 1st April 1966 (17km N) and another ringed at Cwmystwyth in Ceredigion on 1st May 1982 was recovered north of Rhayader on 21st May 1989 (10km E).

'Dick', a pet Raven kept at Maesllwch Castle in the 19th century, died on 21st February 1855 aged 22 years.

Starling *Sturnus vulgaris* A

Uncommon breeding bird; very common winter visitor and passage migrant.

Breeds in the Azores, Canary Islands, France, the British Isles and the Faeroe Islands east across most of Europe, western and central Russia east to the Central Siberian Plateau and Manchuria, north to the North Cape of Norway, south to the far north of India, northern Iran and Turkey. Winters within the breeding range and south to north-west Africa, the Mediterranean, the Himalayas, Afghanistan and the Arabian Peninsula. Introduced in South Africa, North America, southern Australia and New Zealand.

The history of the Starling in Radnorshire is one of ups and downs as it has been over much of Britain, especially in the west and north. In the 18th century the species went into widespread decline and was unknown as a breeding bird over most of Wales, although still a common passage migrant and winter visitor from the continent. However, a resurgence started around 1830 and continued until the end of the 19th century with the recolonisation of Radnorshire probably occurring between 1860 and 1870 with numbers continuing to increase well into the 20th century. A noticeable decline started in the 1960s with another more pronounced downward trend, which was very noticeable in Radnorshire, starting in the early to mid 1980s. Breeding numbers have declined rapidly since then and continue to do so. Similar reductions, and even regional extinctions, since about 1980 have also taken place over much of northern Europe.

Today it is a rare breeding bird in the county away from the towns with most pairs in the countryside closely associated with rough and heavily grazed commons and some mixed farms. It is absent now as a breeding bird from the Elan and Claerwen Valleys, although there were a few pairs around some of the farms and also nesting in cliff crevices until the early 1990s. It is also now absent as a nester from the far north of the county but is found in small numbers locally throughout the rest of the county, especially the lower parts of the south and east, and has been recorded as breeding in all but two of the county's 21 hectads (10-km squares) since 2004. Such is the scarcity of the species in the spring and summer that every breeding record, and post-breeding flock seen in July and August, is now noteworthy in Radnorshire.

Overall breeding numbers in the county have declined by over 80% since 1980 and this is reflected in the size of the late summer flocks that gather on the hills and commons. These flock sizes in recent years are mostly in the low tens rather than in the low hundreds. On 30th July 1975 there were some 3,000 feeding on tipulid larvae on the hillsides above Pont ar Elan and the last triple-figure count in the area was 200 beside Craig Goch Reservoir on 25th August 2001. Since then it has been rare to see more than 50 anywhere in the area at that time of year and in most years there are none. Similarly there were 2,000 around Llyn Heilyn on 12th August 1979 - unheard of numbers today until October. Judging from sample surveys and counts in July and August, the breeding population of Radnorshire in 2012 was probably fewer than 300 pairs.

It seems likely that these peaks and troughs over the last few hundred years are due to climatic fluctuations affecting the availability of summer food, particularly tipulid larvae, and therefore the survival of the season's juveniles.

British bred Starlings are very sedentary with 80% of the 11,000 ringing recoveries being found under 20km away from the place of ringing and the mean distance being only 1km. Birds from the continent start to arrive in September, especially from the low countries. However, the main influxes come in late October and November, usually at the same time as Wood Pigeons, Fieldfares and Woodcock arrive in numbers in the county. Arrivals continue throughout November and even into December, especially when there is cold weather to the north and east. Groups of birds may be seen by day flying west and south anywhere in the county and many tens of thousands of birds sometimes arrive and pass through in just a few days.

The following are typical examples of such movements: At the end of October 2006 there were 8,000 near Craig Goch Reservor on 27th and 11,000 flew south-west over Radnor Forest on 28th when 2,000 were at Glasbury. In 2009 there were 3,500 newly arrived near Llyn Heilyn on 23rd October and 4,000 were in the upper Elan Valley on 28th. Three thousand flew south and east down the Edw Valley on 14th October 2011 and on 29th October 2012 a total of 4,500 flew west up the Wye Valley at Glasbury and 3,300 flew west at New Radnor.

Many tens of thousands of birds stay in Radnorshire throughout the winter provided that the ground does not become frozen and snow cover does not last for any length of time. Noisy flocks of several hundreds systematically probing grasslands is a common sight in the county, as are groups of 10-50 ridding garden lawns of leatherjackets and aerating the soil in the process. At Garnfawr, near Franksbridge, there were 3,000 in the fields throughout the winter of 1987/8 and 5,000 near Llandrindod Wells on 15th February 1974. Large feeding flocks are often present in the Elan and Claerwen Valleys in winter, depending on the tipulid populations. There were 7-8,000 present in the Pont ar Elan area from January to March 2007 and 4,000 at Claerwen Farm on 13th March 1999.

The main roosting area in Radnorshire is in the conifer plantations of the Llanfihangel nant Melan/Llandegly Rhos area which has been used since at least the late 1970s. The plantation by Llandegley Rhos held 20,000 birds on 16th January 1978 and 29th November 1983 and had 10-50,000 occasionally between November and March in most winters between 1986 and 2000. Plantations in the nearby Fforest Inn area used to hold most of the birds with a small wood at Llanfihangel having a roost of 10-60,000 birds for most of the time during the winters between 1984 and 2002. However, shooting of the roost took place at times in an effort to persuade the birds to go elsewhere, which they have done for the most part ever since.

Since 2003 the roost has largely moved to Llandegley Rhos and steadily increased in numbers with counts at dawn and dusk producing average figures of between 135,000 and180,000 birds. It is likely that even more birds use the roost on occasion especially in early November and late February/early March - soon after the main arrivals from the continent and prior to emigration. The highest counts are made during periods of fine, calm, weather and the fewest during very windy, wet and stormy, conditions when birds presumably find somewhere closer to their daytime feeding areas to spend the night. The current age and planting density of the plantation seems to be ideal for roosting Starlings and although predators such as Hen Harrier, Merlin, Sparrowhawk, Goshawk and Short-eared Owl are in attendance most evenings, the site is undoubtedly safer than ones used in the area in the past.

At least 65% to 75% of the birds now come from areas to the east of the roosting area and this seems to account for most of the increase in numbers as many fewer did so prior to 2001. Birds not only come from all parts of Radnorshire but also from well into Herefordshire with flight lines traced at least as far east as Shobdon. In general birds come in from a radius of c.25km.

Another roost in conifers by Perthi Common (on lower ground about five miles to the south-west of Llandegley Rhos) also held a large roost in some winters between 1987 and 2009 when the site was clearfelled. The site was used mainly as an alternative to the Llanfihangel/Llandegley area during periods of very cold and windy weather. There were at least 70,000 there on 25th November 1988 and 50-75,000 during January and February 1993 and January 1999.

A roost in *Phragmites* and willows at Aberithon Turbary held 50,000 birds during the first half of January 1995, declining to 1,000 by the end of the month, and there were 50,000+ at a roost at Stonewall Hill on 20th February 1971.

Roosts are usually occupied from October to March but many thousands of birds continued to use Llandegley well into April during the exceptionally cold late-winter/early spring of 2013.

There have been 16 birds ringed elsewhere in England and Wales and recovered in Powys coming from Gloucestershire, Dyfed (3), Glamorgan, Gwent, Gwynedd, Hereford & Worcester, Lancashire, Yorkshire (2), Shropshire (2), Staffordshire, Suffolk and the West Midlands. Also 11 birds ringed in Powys have been recovered in Dyfed, Glamorgan (4), Gwent (2), Hereford & Worcester, Oxfordshire (2) and Warwickshire. In addition to these there have been birds from Belgium, Denmark (2), Estonia, Latvia, Lithuania (4), Poland, Russia, Sweden (2) and the Netherlands (3). And birds ringed in Powys have been found in Germany (3), the Netherlands (2) and Sweden.

Birds ringed and retrapped at Garnfawr, near Franksbridge, in the 1990s provided an interesting series of recoveries. A breeding female ringed at Norg, Netherlands, on 29th May 1996 was caught there on 22nd December and a nestling ringed at Bladers Hage, Sweden, on 28th May 1994 was caught on 28th December 1995. An adult ringed at Garnfawr on 24th January 1996 was killed hitting a window at Friesland, Netherlands, about the 25th March 1996 and one ringed on 27th December 1995 fell down a chimney and then hit a window at Sawbridge, near Rugby, on 3rd July 1997. Two birds ringed on 21st and 24th December 1996 were both recovered in Germany in April and July of the following year just 20km apart. A young male ringed on 31st December 1996 was killed by a cat at Pembridge, Herefordshire, on 2nd August 1997, where it was doubtless breeding. It seems that the flocks found in Radnorshire in winter are a mixture of birds which breed 'locally' in England and Wales as well as from various parts of the continent.

Other ringing recoveries have included an adult male ringed at Duinberg, Belgium, on 3rd November 1978 and reported dead from Howey on 21st January 1980. A first-year female ringed at Bardsey Island Bird Observatory on 16th October 1988 was found dead at Llanyre on 20th March 1989 and a first-year male ringed in North Yorkshire on 26th September 1954 was shot at Presteigne on 16th June 1955. A first-year female ringed at Howey on 19th January 1997 was caught at Heligoland Island Bird Observatory, off the coast of northern Germany, on 21st November 2001.

Rose-coloured Starling *Pastor roseus* A

Very rare visitor.

Breeds from the Balkans and southern Ukraine east across south-west Russia, Kazakhstan, Uzbekistan and Turkmenistan to north-west China, south to northern Iran and Afghanistan. Winters mainly in India, Sri Lanka and Pakistan, with some in the south-east of the Arabian Peninsula; occasionally irruptive to western Europe.

The only record is of an immature bird in the garden of Bell House, Cwmdauddwr, from 21st to 28th September 1994. It defended the bird-table there vigorously against other birds and fed voraciously on lumps of cooked fat.

In early May 1994 flocks of thousands were seen flying in off the Black Sea into Bulgaria and large numbers were subsequently seen in Hungary, Romania and Slovakia. At least 5-600 pairs bred in Hungary, including a colony of some 200 pairs at a pig farm. This was the first breeding in the country since 1961. In July and August small flocks of dispersing juveniles were reported widely from Greece to the U.A.E. and five adults turned up in Britain. These were followed in September by at least two more adults and six juveniles, including birds at the bird observatories on Fair Isle, Portland and Cape Clear.

House Sparrow *Passer domesticus*

Very common resident breeder.

Breeds in north-west Africa, most of Europe north to the North Cape of Norway, and west, central and southern Asia east to Manchuria and Burma. Introduced to North and South America, South Africa, New Zealand and eastern Australia. Resident.

House Sparrow colonies are found in every hamlet, village and town in Radnorshire as well as on most lowland and many upland farms where suitable buildings are present for nesting. However, it is a very sedentary species and many upland farms have no House Sparrows despite being within just a mile or two of ones that do, whilst at some farms the birds leave for the worst of the winter months. It is a rare species at any distance from human habitaton and at more remote houses, even with bird-feeding stations. At Penbont House in the Elan Valley there were just three very brief visits by single birds between 1998 and 2011.

The species was probably much more widespread and commoner prior to the 1960s, after which government policies caused the decline of mixed farming in favour of more intensive sheep production. However, since the turn of the century arable crops have had a resurgence, at least in the east and south of the county, and numbers of House Sparrows have very noticeably increased although still absent from some parts of the far west and north. Late and difficult harvesting of cereal crops due to poor weather, such as in 2008 and 2012, have been hugely beneficial to House Sparrows in Radnorshire with large quantities of grain available late into the autumn and many stubble fields left unploughed throughout the winter.

Unlike in England where numbers are still in many places down by more than 50% on what they were in the mid 1970s, the population across Wales has recovered any losses and has in fact more than doubled in numbers between 1994 and 2011 and this is near to the level of increase which has taken place in Radnorshire.

It has been found in every 10-km square in the county in all Atlases and other surveys, except for the winter atlas of 1988-91 when there were no records in the two squares in the far north-west. Nearly all nests are located in buildings, with some in nestboxes, disused or taken-over House Martin nests and holes in trees. Near Franksbridge, where removal of crows and Magpies over a 1-km square took place in the 1990s, many free-standing nests were built in a colony in overgrown Hawthorn hedges in the 'natural' way of this very close relative of the weaver birds. In favourable areas with abundant food supplies three or four broods may be raised between March/April and August/September. The population in Radnorshire today is probably between 4,000 and 5,000 pairs.

Autumn and winter flocks of 40-60 are common with several counts of over 100 in recent years. Counts at garden feeding stations have included 82 at Garnfawr, near Franksbridge, on 26th August 1996, and 50-60 at Nant Glas from July to September 2004. At Y Bryn, St Harmon, there were 60 on 16th July and 91 on 27th August 2011. In a garden at Nant Glas 76 birds were caught for ringing in 2001 and 59 in 2002. At Llowes there were 120 on 3rd September 2006; in Presteigne there was a flock of 100+ on 20th August 2010 and one of 150+ near Burfa on 13th August 2008.

There have been two instances of hybridization with Tree Sparrows, both of male Tree Sparrows with female House Sparrows. One pair raised two broods in the gable end of a house adjoining the Red Lion Inn at Llanfihangel nant Melan in June and July 1993 and another fledged a brood from a nest in a hole in the wall of the tower of Bettws Church, near Franksbridge, in June 1995.

Tree Sparrow *Passer montanus*

A

Uncommon, mainly resident, breeder.

Breeds from Iberia, France, the British Isles and southern Fennoscandia east across much of Europe and Asia to the Sea of Okhotsk, China and Japan, north to the Arctic Ocean in Russia and south to Java, Pakistan, northern Iran and Turkey. Mainly sedentary but more northerly Russian populations are mostly migratory; occasionally irruptive to the south and west. Introduced to central USA, south-east Australia and the Philippines.

Ingram and Salmon gave the Tree Sparrow's status in the mid 1950s as, 'A scarce, local and irregularly distributed species which has bred', going on to list breeding season records from Glasbury, Knighton and between Builth and Aberedw as well as winter sightings from Llandrindod Wells and near Old Radnor.

The species is known for its population fluctuations: There were high levels in Britain at the turn of the 19th/20th century followed by a decline and range contraction so that by about 1930 it had disappeared from much of Wales. An increase began in the late 1950s or early 1960s with a gradual return to some northern and western areas. This increase peaked in the late 1970s and for the following 20 years there was a rapid decline over much of Britain reducing numbers by 90-95%. There has been a European-wide decline since about 1980.

In Radnorshire there was undoubtedly an increase during the 1970s, if not earlier, which had probably peaked by the mid to late 1980s. There was a decline in numbers and range from the mid 1990s to about 2005 since when there has been a very noticeable increase and spread in some parts of the county, but not in others, seemingly due to an increase in the growing of cereals. The county population in 2012 was probably in the range of 180-220 pairs which is about a third of what it was in the1980s but at least 50% higher than the in the decade 1995-2005.

Despite being a species which is easily overlooked, the breeding Atlases of 1968-72 and 1988-91 and the winter Atlas of 1981/2 to 1983/4 found Tree Sparrows in 19 or 20 of the 21 hectads (10-km squares) wholly or partly in the county with the only blank areas being in the far north-west. Since 2005 birds have been found in the breeding season in 17 hectads, with the only gaps in the west and north, and in 20 hectads in the winter months. The species is very rare at all seasons in many parts of the county especially in the north and north-west; it bred at St. Harmon between 1984 and 1990 but there have been no records in the Elan Valley above Caban Coch Dam since at least 1987.

Although these ups and downs, both locally and nationally, may be due to agricultural changes the reasons are not definitely known with colonies disappearing suddenly for no apparent reason and with no obvious change in local land management. The starts of periods of increase in the British Isles have coincided with greater passage noticed on the continent and this possible immigration has been suggested as an explanation for the initiation of the upsurges in numbers.

The strongholds for Tree Sparrows have always been in the more arable south and east of the county and those colonies in Radnorshire that flourish today do so because of a variety of cereal crops and good numbers of scattered mature trees, especially oak and Ash, in which to nest. Colonies are mostly of three to 15 pairs with two broods the norm. Nests are most frequently built in holes in trees but crevices in walls are often used and one to three pairs occupied Sand Martin holes near Crossgates and Llanbister in the early 1990s and near Llowes in 2002. A lack of suitable nest sites is undoubtedly a restricting factor in several parts of the county and nest boxes can increase numbers locally. In the 1980s there were several small to medium sized colonies of two to eight pairs not associated with arable land but these are very rare today. Records of hybridization with House Sparrows appear under that species.

Autumn and winter flocks, which often persist well into April, are usually found around cereal crops, stubble fields, weedy fields with fat-hen etc., chicken pens and, increasingly, at garden bird feeding stations e.g. up to 20 birds were counted at 16 sites in 2008.

Most flocks comprise fewer than 25 birds but high counts over the years have been: 50-100 in the St. Michael's Pool and Painscastle areas in December 1961, 50 at Four Stones in early March 1968, 50 at Evenjobb in November and December 1969, 50+ at Newchurch on 17th December 1971, 80 at Llandrindod Wells on 9th March 1974, c. 60 at Llanbister on 3rd November 1977, c.70 at Glasbury on 20th January 1983, c.60 at Kinnerton on 31st March 1984, c. 80 at Glasbury on 22nd September 1984, 100+ in a root field by Pwll Patti on 7th December 1985, 60 at Glasbury Farm on 14th August 1987, c.80 at Llanbwchllyn in a stubble field on 20th October 1987, 70 at Llyn Heilyn on 5th September 1990, 50 on Llandrindod Golf Course on 15th November 1991, 60 in a stubble field near Boughrood in January 1994, 60 at Burfa on 25th January and near Rhayader in October and November 1995, 95 in three flocks near Glasbury on 15th December 2000 and 70-85 near New Radnor in September and October 2011.

Most Tree Sparrows in Radnorshire stay close to their natal area year round and the only notable recovery of a ringed bird was of a female ringed south of Knighton on 1st June 1999 which was hit by a car on 18th September 2003 at Stapleton, near Presteigne, a distance of 6 km to the south-east.

Chaffinch *Fringilla coelebs*

A

Very common breeder, migrant and winter visitor.

Breeds from north-west Africa, the Canary Islands, Madeira, the Azores, Iberia, France, the British Isles and Fennoscandia east across Europe, Russia and northern Kazakhstan to the Yenisei, north to northern Norway and south to northern Iran, Turkmeniya and Lebanon. Mostly resident in western and southern areas, most northern European and central Asian populations are wholly migratory to within the breeding range and south as far as Iraq and the Nile Delta. Introduced to South Africa and New Zealand.

The Chaffinch is one of the three commonest breeding birds in Radnorshire being found in all woodland types especially in mature broadleaved stands but also in parks, gardens, hedgerows, scrub and ffridd habitats and in coniferous plantations up to 2,000 feet (610 m) in Radnor Forest. There seems to have been little noticeable long-term change in the population other than a steady increase since at least the mid 1980s, amounting to about 15%, and some small percentage declines due to very cold winters and small local losses in recent years caused by trichomonosis. The species has been recorded in every 5-km square in the county in all seasons and the breeding population in 2010 was probably in the range of 9-11,000 pairs.

Most pairs in Radnorshire breed in May and June and raise a single brood on a diet of caterpillars and a wide variety of other insects. Post-breeding season flocks of 20-50 begin to form in late July after which flocks of 100-200 become widespread throughout the autumn and winter months. Birds from northern Britain and the continent arrive from late September onwards with the main arrivals in the second half of October and early November. Many Radnorshire birds undoubtedly leave the breeding areas during mid to late September (especially those from the uplands and conifer forests)and return in March and early April but ringing shows that most are resident and remain close to their natal site throughout their lives.

Flocks of over 300 are uncommon and high counts have been 500 at Newchurch on 17th December 1971, 2,500 at Llyn Heilyn in December 1978, 1,200 in a single 5-km square near Painscastle in November 1981, 350 near Rhayader on 11th November 1983, 350 near Rhayader on 12th December 1989, 500 on Beech mast at Glannau (Elan Valley) in October 1990, 550 in a stubble field at Glanwye in January 1994, 500 at Boughrood on 4th November 1995, 350 in a weedy field near Rhayader on 7th December 1998, 350 near Nantmel on 22nd October 2006 and 500 in stubble near New Radnor on 3rd November 2010. The species is also common at garden feeding stations with peaks of 105-150 (30th August 2004) at Penbont House, Elan Valley, every autumn between 1998 and 2010 during late August and early September with 40-60 remaining through the winter. In a garden at Nant Glas 148 birds were caught for ringing in 2001.

There have been nine birds ringed elsewhere and recovered in Powys. These have come from Cornwall (2), Dyfed (2), Gwent, Gwynedd, Merseyside and the Netherlands (2). An adult female ringed at Castricum in the Netherlands on 16th October 1996 flew into the window of the blacksmith's at Penybont on 13th February 1997 (537 km W). The ring from an adult male ringed at Dam 6, Middelburg, in the Netherlands on 11th October 1991 was found at a bird of prey roost/nesting site between Painscastle and Erwood in September 2004 (570 km WSW).

Eight birds ringed in Powys have been found elsewhere with single birds to Clwyd, Cornwall, Dyfed, Kent, Lancashire, Belgium, Norway and Sweden. A juvenile female ringed at Gilfach, near Rhayader, on 8th July 1994 was found dead at Launceston, Cornwall, on 9th January 2000 and a first-year female ringed at Nant Glas on 1st October 2004 was found freshly dead at Colne, Lancashire, on 18th June 2005.

Brambling *Fringilla montifringilla* A

Passage migrant and winter visitor.

Breeds from Fennoscandia east across Russia to Kamchatka, northern Kazakhstan and northern Mongolia. Winters from southern Sweden and coastal Norway to the British Isles, France and Iberia east across much of central and southern Europe, Iraq, northern Iran, north-west India to southern Kazakhstan, eastern China and Japan.

Ingram and Salmon (1955) said that the species was, 'A regular winter visitor. Numbers are usually small, but occasionally quite considerable'. The same is true today.

Bramblings are often found in the county with other finches, especially Chaffinches, in weedy fields and root crops with fat-hen, in cereal stubble fields and game crops, under Beech trees feeding on mast, on Rowan berries and, increasingly, at garden bird feeding stations. The first migrants usually arrive for the winter, or pass through, in the second half of October and early November. Records in late September are very rare and the earliest was of one in the Elan Valley on 26th September 2002.

In some autumns and winters numbers are very low in Radnorshire with just a handful of counts in double figures and every sighting notable. In 1991/2 the only counts were in single figures. In other years birds are widespread with many counts of 20-50 and some into three figures. High numbers invariably coincide with a heavy crop of Beech mast. The most recent winters with high numbers have been 2007/8, 1995/6, 1994/5, 1986/7, 1983/4, 1971/2 and 1966/7. Flock counts have included 300 at Cascob on 12th March 1967, 200 at Newchurch on 17th December 1971, 300 near Rhayader on 2nd January 1984, 250 at Howey from November 1986 to March 1987, 1,500 in a weedy failed swede crop near Rhayader on 7th December 1994, 400 in the Elan Valley, 200 at Newbridge and 350 at Boughrood in October and November 1995 and 300 near Newbridge on 16th January 2008. In some autumns, such as 1992, there have been many records of 10-50 birds recorded on passage in late October and early November but with few staying to overwinter in the county. It is recorded in the majority of 10-km squares each year, albeit in some just as a fly-over migrant. Since 2005 it has been reported from all the 21 hectads (10-km squares) in Radnorshire.

There is a noticeable passage north through Radnorshire most years in late March and April and this is when there is the peak number of records from garden feeding stations, usually of one to 10 birds. Since 2000 there has been a considerable increase in visits to garden feeders throughout the winter months with birds feeding on peanuts, sunflower seed and various seed mixes. They are usually in the company of Chaffinches and most records are of one to five birds.

The majority of overwintering birds leave Radnorshire during March and early April, although in most years there are at least a few records of birds remaining into the last week. The latest records were in the Elan Valley on 2nd May 1988, at Dolau on 4th May 1997 and at Glasbury on 5th May 2013. Singing males have been recorded at Garnfawr, near Franksbridge, from 26th March to 10th April 1990, at Llanbadarn Fynydd on 23rd April 1997 and at Penbont House, Elan Valley, on 26th April 2005.

Ringed birds from northern and southern Norway and the Netherlands have been recovered in Powys and one ringed in Powys was found in Denmark.

Greenfinch *Carduelis chloris* A

Common, mostly resident, breeder and uncommon passage migrant and winter visitor.

Breeds from north-west Africa, the Canary Islands, Madeira, Iberia, France, the British Isles and Fennoscandia east across most of Europe and Russia to southern Kazakhstan and Uzbekistan, north to inside the Arctic Circle in Norway and south to northern Iran, Israel and Jordan. Mostly resident but northern populations are wholly migratory to within the breeding range and south as far as Iraq, southern Iran and the Nile Delta. Introduced in the Azores, Uruguay, south-east Australia and New Zealand.

Greenfinches increased markedly during the first half of the 20th century over much of the British Isles and on the continent, where range expansion continues in Fennoscandia. It has also become much more a bird of gardens, towns and villages as well as farmland and the wider countryside throughout much of its range. It has probably long been a common bird in Radnorshire in areas of arable farming which were much more widespread prior to the 1960s when most farms grew at least some cereal and root crops.

Away from areas of arable farming and human habitation in Radnorshire it is often a scarce or even rare bird. For example in the Elan Valley above the bottom dam at Caban Coch (a large area where there is no arable) it is a very rare visitor with just a few records of passage birds each year and only two breeding records in the last 25 years - both associated with well-stocked garden feeding stations in 2004. However, nearby between the Valley and Rhayader it is quite common with flocks of 20-40 birds regularly seen in arable fields and in gardens. It is commonest in the main arable areas of the south and east of the county especially in and around the towns and villages where it is often common at garden feeders on peanuts and sunflower seeds.

Nesting usually begins in early May and the species is often double-brooded in Radnorshire. In some fine years, especially with late harvests, three broods have been recorded. Most nests are built in tall and thick hedgerows, ornamental conifers and dense shrubs and scrub.

Flocks start to form usually in late August and early September and continue throughout the winter months, finally breaking up in late February and March. At Glasbury there were 150 on 2nd September 1989 but the largest flocks are usually seen between late October and the end of February. On 1st November 1953 about 500 were on an abandoned field of oats at 1,400 feet (427 m) at David's Well and 200 were near Rhayader in October and November 1995. At Kinnerton 300 were counted in root crops on 7th February 1967 and on 7th December 1971. Over 500 were at Newchurch in a root crop with abundant fat-hen on 17th December 1971 and 250 were still present on 19th January 1972. At Howey there were 300 in November and December 1986.

Cold winters have reduced numbers in some years and in the early 1960s there was a nationwide decline due to the use of seed dressings containing dieldrin and organochlorines. Since 2005 there have been large and widespread declines in numbers due to trichomonosis with few places escaping the disease. In 2007 flock sizes and numbers visiting garden feeders in the county were on average down by 50% on 2005. Numbers were further reduced in 2008 and again another noticeable drop took place in 2010 by when the species was no longer recorded at all in some places whilst in others it had become rare where once common.

However, the species is still widespread, if in reduced numbers, across Radnorshire and has been found in all but one or two of the county's 21 hectads in every Atlas, with the only gaps being in the far west and north. The population in 2011 was probably within the range of 1,100 to 1,400 pairs, a half to a third of what it was in the 1990s.

The largest flock recorded anywhere in Radnorshire in 2010 was one of 55 and the last triple-figure count was of 110 at Clyro in November 2004. However, in some gardens numbers have been much less affected than in others; there were 32 at a garden feeding station at Discoed in October 2007, 30 at one in Huntington in January 2006, 20 there in February 2010 and 50 at a feeding station at Nant Glas on 9th September 2006.

There is a small but noticeable passage through the county in October and November most years and a less noticeable spring movement in April. Migrants have been recorded in the Elan Valley on 11th, 23rd and 24th October and on 9th November, 10th, 17th and 19th April.

There have been 31 ringed birds from other counties found in Powys which have come from: Cambridgeshire, Cheshire (2), Clwyd (2), Dyfed (3), Glamorgan (2), Gloucestershire, Gwent (5), Gwynedd (2), Hereford & Worcester, Isle of Man, Kent, Lancashire, Oxfordshire, Shropshire (7) and the West Midlands. Also nine birds ringed in Powys have been found elsewhere with birds to Gloucestershire, Greater Manchester, Hereford & Worcester (2), Lincolnshire, Northamptonshire, Shropshire (2) and Surrey.

A first-winter male ringed at Dolau on 30th January 1996 was found freshly dead in Greater Manchester on 30th June 1996 so was likely to have been breeding there. Similarly a first-winter female ringed at Nant Glas on 29th January 2005 was found sick (probably with trichomonosis) at Desborough, Northants, on 24th June 2006. A first-winter female ringed at Old Weston, Cambridgeshire, on 4th February 2005 was found freshly dead at Whitton, near Presteigne, on 15th April.

Goldfinch *Carduelis carduelis* A

Common, mostly summer visiting, breeding bird and passage migrant.

Breeds from north-west Africa, the Canary Islands, Madeira, the Azores, Iberia, France and the British Isles east across southern and central Europe and Russia to the Altai and north-west Mongolia, south to the Himalayas, southern Iran and the lower Nile. Partly migratory wintering within the breeding range. Introduced in Uruguay, Bermuda, south-east and south-west Australia and New Zealand.

Ingram and Salmon (1955) said that the Goldfinch was, '... rather sparsely distributed over most of the county . It is resident and breeds regularly. Flocks are to be seen in winter.' The species was trapped for the cage-bird industry in huge numbers in England and Wales during the 19th century but increased steadily throughout much of the 20th century with a surge in numbers in Radnorshire, and elsewhere, since the 1980s which continues year on year to the present.

It is found in every 10-km square in the county during the breeding season but is rare on the higher ground in the north and north-west, although several pairs breed most years in the Elan Valley. The population in Radnorshire in 2012 was probably in the range of 1,100 to 1,300 pairs, perhaps three times what it was until the early 1980s. Although still a widespread species in small numbers in the winter months, about 80% of birds (especially females and first-year birds) emigrate to Iberia, western France and Belgium.

In Radnorshire today Goldfinches are found mostly in small, loose, colonies in parks, gardens and orchards as well as in areas with scrub and scattered trees, especially Hawthorn and Blackthorn. They are predominantly a lowland bird in the county and although rarely found breeding above 1,200 feet (365 m) small flocks have been seen in autumn and winter up to 1,700 feet (518 m) a.s.l.

Most breeding birds return in April and there is sometimes a noticeable passage through the county around the third week of the month. Most pairs raise two or even three broods between May and September and it is common to see recently fledged juveniles well into September, and even into early October, especially in fine and dry autumns.

The seeds of composites such as thistles, knapweeds, Groundsel, ragworts and Teasel are the main food throughout the year, although some insects and caterpillars are fed to the young together with regurgitated seeds. The seeds of Dandelion are a very important food source early in the breeding season and road-side verges and waste lands in the county are valuable areas in this respect. In winter, birds will also feed on the seeds of birch, Alder, larch and ornamental conifers as well as on any remaining in Teasel and thistle heads.

Post-breeding flocks form from late July and increase throughout August and September when most emigrants leave. Flocks of 10-40 birds are frequent but counts of over 100 are rare. At Franksbridge there were 120 on thistles on 12th September 1989 and at Glasbury there were 100 on 21st September 2002, 140 on 3rd September 1995 and 12th September 2001, and at least 200 on 7th September 1990. At Penglaneinon, Elan Valley, a flock of 180 birds were feeding on the seed heads of Black Knapweed on 6th September 2004 and a flock of 100 was seen on Llandrindod Golf Course on 14th September 2005.

Winter flocks are usually much smaller and rarely of more than 30 birds. At 1,600 feet (488 m) on Radnor Forest a flock of 160 was seen on 21st November 1971 and there were 150 in a wildlife cover crop at Tyncoed, near Newbridge, on 31st December 2002. In the Elan Valley a flock of 45 (with 40 Siskins) fed on birch seeds, in situ, throughout much of the 1996/7 winter and in 2011/12 a huge crop of larch seed attracted flocks of 40-60 birds to cones at Burfa and Radnor Forest. At Llanbwchllyn on 29th November 2012 a flock of 40 were feeding on Alder seed from the cones.

Goldfinches were unknown at garden feeding stations until the 1980s and the first record of such behaviour in Radnorshire was of one to three feeding on mixed small bird seed from 10th-30th April 1988 in a Gladestry garden. Since the 1990s there have been many reports of birds on peanut dispensers whilst in recent years the availability of niger (Nyjer) seed, *Guizotia abyssinica*, has proved to be very attractive to the species being a small composite seed of a yellow-flowered member of the Asteraceae family native to Ethiopia. Counts have soared as a result with 50 in a Discoed garden in December 2007 and January 2008 and 52 on niger feeders there on 2nd March 2010. There were 42 at a Nant Glas feeding station on 8th January 2010 and 40 at Howey in November 2012.

There have been ringing recoveries from Powys to Dorset, Kent, Warwickshire, France (3), Spain (2) and Portugal and birds ringed in Hampshire and Shropshire have been found in Powys. An adult male ringed at Llangorse, Brecon, on 7th February 2008 was caught and released by another bird ringer at Nantmel on 24th March 2010.

Siskin *Carduelis spinus*

Common breeding bird, passage migrant and winter visitor.

A

Breeds locally in Iberia and France and over much of the British Isles and Fennoscandia east across parts of central Europe and Asia to Sakhalin Island and north-east China. Mostly migratory, wintering south within the breeding range and to southern China and Japan, northern Iran, the Nile Delta and north-west Africa.

Until the middle of the 19th century Siskins were found breeding in the British Isles only in the remnant Caledonian pine forests of Scotland but due to the increased planting of conifer plantations, ornamental and amenity conifers, the species has spread south to many parts of England and to most of Wales over the last 150 years.

These colonisers are likely to have been winter visitors from Scotland, and possibly the continent, deciding to stay. Siskins had long been known as a winter visitor and passage migrant and small flocks were often seen in the county: 'a large movement' was noted near Erwood on 29th October 1939, 50-60 were between Colva and Gladestry on 19th April 1962, 55 between Llowes and Glasbury on 27th January 1963 and 31 near Erwood Station on 5th December 1965.

The first sign of possible breeding was a sighting of a single bird seen in a fir spinney between Doldowlodd and Llanyre on 9th June 1965. The first positive breeding record came from the Elan Valley in 1967 when a pair with a recently fledged juvenile was seen in Caban Lakeside Woodland, on the western shore of Caban Coch Reservoir, on 28th May. A pair with three recently fledged young were seen feeding in birch trees below the Craig Goch Dam in July 1971, two pairs bred at Beguildy in 1972 and 1974 and a nest with four young was found at Llangunllo on 13th July 1975. For the 1968-72 Atlas there was confirmed breeding in two 10-km squares (hectads) and possible breeding in two others. Birds were found in 20 of the 21 hectads for the winter Atlas of 1981-84 and in 12 during the breeding season survey of 1988-91. The increase in breeding numbers and range continued in the county throughout the 1990s and into the new millennium. Since 2005 the species has been found in every 10-km square in the breeding season and during the winter months.

The population in the county in 2010 was probably within the range of 1,800 to 2,600 pairs. The majority breed in the large coniferous dominated areas of the west and north of the county but many are found in town parks and gardens with mature ornamental conifers such as *Cupressus* species, e.g. up to 30 pairs have bred in some years in Llandrindod Wells.

Numbers do vary hugely from year to year depending largely on the ripening cycle of larch and spruce cones in the county. In the Elan Valley since 2000 numbers have varied from 15-20 to over 100 pairs and such fluctuations have been found in many parts of the county. In years with abundant seed breeding starts early; at the Gwaelod plantation in the Elan Valley in 2003 many pairs were nestbuilding and egg-laying from mid March and fledged broods appeared at garden feeders at Penbont House from 20th April. In other years breeding does not start until May and fledging of second, or perhaps third, broods has been noted as late as 14th August. In spring in Radnorshire many birds feed on oak catkins and the abundant aphis on larch and spruce. Defoliating caterpillars of oak are also fed to young as well as the regurgitated seeds of Dandelion, other composites and conifers.

The breeding birds in most of the major coniferous areas leave during the second half of August and early September and ringing recoveries suggest that many spend the winter in south-west England. From mid-September (sometimes August) to early November birds from the north of England, Scotland and the continent pass through the county and arrive for the winter. Numbers vary hugely from year to year essentially reflecting the two to three year cycle of ripening spruce and larch cones. In years with heavy crops of Norway Spruce on the continent, breeding success, and as a result immigration into the British Isles, is high. In other years numbers are low with no flocks of more than 50 seen in the county. Autumn/winter periods in recent years when many birds have been seen in Radnorshire generally follow this pattern and have been 1980/1, 1983/4, 1988/9, 1992/3, 1995/6, 1996/7, 2000/1, 2002/3, 2004/5, 2008/9 and 2011/12.

In autumn and winter the majority of flocks are seen feeding on birch and Alder seeds although the very large gatherings are most often on particularly heavy crops of mature larch cones. High flock counts have been: In 1983, 230 near Builth Wells on 22nd December and 300 at Doldowlodd in November and December; 200 in the Claerwen Valley in January and February 1990 were all females or immatures and fed on fallen birch seed; flocks of 400 were in Radnor Forest and in the Elan Valley in November 1992 (the biggest autumn ever for the species in Radnorshire); 400 were in Radnor Forest in February 2003, 230 at Boughrood on 15th November 2004, 450 in Radnor Forest on 19th November 2008 and 250 there on 15th October 2011 and 320 at Glasbury on 19th March 2013. In a garden at Nant Glas a total of 120 different birds were caught for ringing during 2001.

Siskins were first recorded coming to garden peanut dispensers in the British Isles in Guildford, Surrey, in March 1963 but there seems to have been no records of such behaviour in Wales until the 1970s. It was widespread in Radnorshire by the mid 1980s. Niger seed is also proving very attractive to the species as are other small seed mixes. Numbers visiting vary greatly from year to year depending on the extent of 'wild' seed, and inclement weather brings more birds to the easy food. The highest counts have come from a garden in Evenjobb where there were 60+ at the end of February 2013 and at Caenbrook Meadow, Presteigne, where up to 51 were on peanuts during the period January to March 2002 and up to 53 in the same period the following year. The peak month for Siskins visiting garden feeders in Radnorshire is March and birds have been recorded in every month.

A total of 31 birds ringed elsewhere in the British Isles have been found or retrapped in Powys with birds coming from Clwyd, Cumbria, Devon (3), Dumfries & Galloway, Dyfed, Glamorgan (3), Gloucestershire (2), Gwent, Hereford & Worcester (2), Highland (4), Norfolk, North Yorkshire, Nottinghamshire, Shropshire (4), Somerset (2) and Surrey (3). Also 10 birds ringed in Powys have been found elsewhere with birds to Clwyd, Devon, Glamorgan, Grampian, Highland (3), Lincolnshire, Northumberland and Strathclyde. There have been single birds to Norway and Germany and one from Belgium.

An adult male ringed at Nantmel on 17th March 2008 flew into a window at Haverasen, southern Norway, on 27th April 2009. An adult male ringed in southern Norway in July 2012 was retrapped in Powys in November. A male ringed at Hockai in eastern Belgium on 11th March 2012 flew into a window in Llandrindod on 6th February 2013 (683 km W). A one-year old male ringed at Gilfach on 8th July 1994 was retrapped at Wonford, near Exeter, on 10th February 1995 (180 km S). A female ringed at Nant Glas on 14th March 2001 was retrapped by a ringer at Reay, Highland, on 26th May 2003 (699 km N). A first-winter male ringed at Weybourne, Surrey, on 12th February 2011 flew into a window at Llangunllo on 22nd June 2011. A first-year bird ringed at Pett Level, Sussex, on 19th October 2011 was retrapped near Bwlch y Sarnau on 21st April 2012 (325 km WNW). An adult male and female ringed at the same time near Axminster, Devon, on 3rd May 2009 were retrapped together near Rhayader on 9th May showing how late northward passage can be and also how pairs of some species migrate together.

Linnet *Carduelis cannabina* A

Common, mainly summer visiting, breeding bird and passage migrant.

Breeds from north-west Africa, the Canary Islands, Iberia, France and the British Isles east across southern Fennoscandia, most of Europe and Russia east to the Yenisei, south to Kazakhstan, northern Afghanistan, northern Iran and northern Israel. Partially migratory south to within the breeding range and to northern Egypt, Iraq and Kashmir.

Unlike the Siskin, the Linnet is a cardueline finch in decline. It was trapped for the cage-bird industry in the 19th century and due to agricultural intensification and loss of habitat it has been in steep decline as a breeding bird for the past fifty years at least. In Radnorshire large areas of moorland, scrubby hillsides and gorse-clad commons have been lost and hedgerows grubbed-up. Intensive sheep-rearing has largely taken over from mixed farming and the use of herbicides has escalated. Linnets feed almost entirely on seeds, especially those of arable weeds and ruderals, and feed them regurgitated to their young. Much of our countryside today is too manicured for Linnets and although it is still a widespread species in Radnorshire its numbers are probably only 25% of what they were in the 1960s.

The only increases in numbers in recent years have been local and associated with temporary areas of fallow set-aside and the growing of oil-seed rape, which has been much more significant and continuing, albeit on a relatively small scale in the south-east of the county. Linnets are rarely recorded in gardens in Radnorshire and very rarely at garden feeders but are often seen around business parks and waste ground on the outskirts of towns and taking grit from old roadside salt piles.

Most Linnets return to their breeding areas in the county in April and usually raise two broods in loose colonies of three to 30 pairs. They are still to be found in the breeding season in all the county's 10-km squares, although it is a rare breeding bird in the upper Elan Valley and in many improved upland areas. However, some nest in very young upland conifer plantations, up to 1,900 feet (580 m) in Radnor Forest. The population in the county in 2011 was probably in the range of 950 to 1,150 pairs.

The species is at its commonest and most widespread in the months of August and September when local birds plus migrants from the north flock to feed on weedy fields, seeding meadows and stubble fields of cereals and oil-seed rape. Most birds leave for the south-west of France and Iberia between August and October and the species is generally uncommon during the winter months of November to March although widespread in small numbers and recorded in the majority of 10-km squares. Wintering numbers vary hugely from year to year and some large flocks will remain in the lower parts of the county throughout the winter if there is a good food source and the weather does not turn too cold or snowy. Return, diurnal, passage northwards is often noticeable from late March to the end of April with flocks of 10-50 sometimes seen flying through or stopping over to feed.

Flocks of 100-250 are seen in every autumn/winter but counts of over 300 birds are rare: there were 500 at The Begwyns on 30th July 2000, 500 at Glasbury on 3rd August 1997, 350 at Clyro on 6th September 2004, 300 at Nantmel on 10th September 2006, 1,000 at Llangunllo on 26th September 1965, 400 near Knighton on 8th October 2010, 300 near Evenjobb in October and November 1986, 300 at Boughrood on 4th November 1995, 350 at Glanwye on 17th November 1993, 300 at Hindwell in November 1978, 300 at Newchurch on 28th December 1971, 3-400 between Newbridge and Disserth on 31st December 2002, 400 at New Radnor on 8th January 1967 an 400 at Newchurch on 22nd January 1973.

A nearly all-white bird was seen amongst a flock of 200 near Llandeilo Graban on 6th November 1988.

Twite *Carduelis flavirostris* A

Very rare visitor.

Breeds in parts of northern England, Scotland and western Ireland, Norway to the North Cape and the far north of the Kola Peninsula; also discontinuously from eastern Turkey east to north-west China, south to Tibet and north to northern Mongolia and Kazakhstan.

There have been just four records: John Walpole-Bond saw one at Builth Road on 14th March 1902, four to six were at Waun Marteg on 6th April 1977 and four were with Linnets near Glasbury from at least 30th December 1995 to 8th January 1996. An intriguing record was of a pair in good looking breeding habitat in the Elan Valley on 16th June 2002. However, subsequent searches failed to relocate the birds.

Common Redpoll *Carduelis flammea* A

Very rare visitor.

Breeds Iceland, Greenland, Svalbard and Fennoscandia east across northern Europe and Asia to the Bering Sea, Alaska and northern Canada. Partly migratory, winters within the breeding range and south to the Mediterranean, Kazakhstan, Japan, northern China and northern USA.

Until 2000 this species was treated as conspecific with Lesser Redpoll but has now been separated. However, since then, DNA testing has found no genetic differentiation between the three species of redpoll (Common, Lesser and Arctic) and so there is no genetic support for the separation. It seems that a return to a single species of redpoll is likely.

In Radnorshire there have been only four records of birds clearly showing the characteristics of 'Common Redpoll'. All have been of the continental, nominate, race:

At least six, of a flock of eight redpoll, by the River Edw at Bettws, Franksbridge, from 20th November 1987 to 2nd January 1988. Five in birches beside Garreg Ddu Reservoir on 3rd February 1988 and singles in the Penygarreg and Penbont areas of the Elan Valley from 13th December 2001 to 26th January 2002 and from 5th-19th April 2002.

There have been several other sightings of birds showing at least some characters of 'Common Redpoll' but without conclusive detail. These include three at Newbridge on 2nd December 1993 and singles at Glasbury at the end of March 1999, by Penygarreg Reservoir on 10th April 1996 and near Penybont on 16th April 1996.

Lesser Redpoll *Carduelis cabaret* A

Common breeding bird, passage migrant and winter visitor.

Breeds British Isles, eastern France, the Netherlands, Denmark, southern Sweden and Norway and much of central Europe south to Italy and east to the Czech Republic. Partly resident; many British birds move south and south-east for the winter to southern Britain, the Netherlands, Belgium and north-west France.

Redpolls underwent a nationwide increase in the first decade of the 20th century and the first records of the species in Radnorshire were made by John Walpole-Bond near Builth Wells and at Hundred House in 1903. There were further records from Knighton, Llandrindod Wells, Newbridge, Rhosgoch and Womaston before Ingram and Salmon said in 1955 that the species was, 'Locally distributed only and quite uncommon as a resident breeding species. Flocks are seen in winter.'

There was a huge increase during the 1960s and early 1970s amounting to a four-fold increase nationally. A decline began to be noticeable in Radnorshire from about the mid 1980s reaching a low point in the late 1990s. A very noticeable, ongoing, increase has taken place since and the species is probably commoner in the county today, in all seasons, than it has been since the early 1980s. Lesser Redpolls have become very scarce as breeding birds over much of England in recent years, declining by some 80-90%. The possible failure of the birch-seed crop has been suggested as a reason.

The breeding Atlas of 1968-72 found the species in 19 of the 21 10-km squares wholly or partly in Radnorshire; the winter Atlas of 1981-84 found it in 17 and the breeding Atlas of 1988-91 also in 17. Since 2005 it has been recorded in the breeding season and in the winter months in every square. The population in 2011 was probably in the range of 600-800 pairs.

Redpolls have a very strong association with birch which in Radnorshire includes both Downy Birch and Silver Birch and their hybrids. They are rarely found in the breeding season where birch is absent and its seed is by far its most important food for much of the year. They also feed on the seeds of larch, willowherb, nettle, Meadow Sweet, Chickweed and a wide variety of composites. Regurgitated seeds and many invertebrates are fed to the young. Coniferous plantations with birch scrub and scattered mature trees are particularly favoured and there are large areas of such habitat in Radnorshire. Wet woodlands with a mixture of willows, Alder and birch, such as at Rhosgoch Bog, also support colonies.

The species is usually double-brooded in the county with recently fledged young often seen well into August.

Flocks of local birds form in August and immigrants from the north of Britain pass through and arrive for the winter from late September to early November. In the winter months, the species is very often found feeding on Alder seeds, either from the cones in situ or on the ground where they often form mixed flocks with Siskins and sometimes Goldfinches. In recent years it has come to bird tables for niger seed and up to 20-40 birds have been counted at some favoured feeding stations in the winter months.

Most winter flocks are of 10-40 birds and are very often mixed with Siskins in varying proportions. Flocks of more than 60 are unusual and have mostly been seen in recent years: 80 were at New Radnor on 10th November 2004 and beside Penygarreg Reservoir in December 2005, 90 were seen at Boughrood on 21st September 2009, 110 at Rhosgoch Bog in December 2011 and in Radnor Forest on 28th March 2011, 120 at Llowes on 15th February 2013 and 145 near Glasbury on 15th November 2004. Flocks break up in late March and April but any spring passage through the county is very rarely noticeable.

Ringed birds from Fife, Yorkshire, Cleveland and Shropshire have been found in Powys and birds ringed in Powys have been recovered in Hampshire and Worcestershire. A first-year female ringed at Seal Sands, Cleveland, on 9th October 2007 was retrapped at Nantmel on 17th March 2008 (298 km SSW). A first-winter male ringed at Nantmel on 30th March 2009 was retrapped at Blashford Lakes, Hampshire, on 6th February 2010 (194 km SE) and another first-year male ringed at Nant Glas on 28th September 2011 was retrapped at Castlemorton Common, Worcester, on 18th November 2011 (85 km ESE). A first-year female ringed as either Common or Lesser Redpoll at the Isle of May Bird Observatory, Fife, on 1st November 1991 was recovered in Powys as a ring found on a leg at a Peregrine nest site on 24th May 1993 (487 km S).

Two-barred Crossbill *Loxia leucoptera* A

Very rare visitor.

Breeds from north-west Russia east to the Sea of Okhotsk, north to the Kola Peninsula and south to Lake Baikal, also Alaska and Canada. Resident, occasionally irruptive to the south of the breeding range.

The first record for Wales was of a male 'picked up dead in a pine-wood' near Llandrindod Wells in November 1912.

There has been just one record in Wales since (near Denbigh in March 1991) out of a total of over 200 for the British Isles of which more than half have been in Orkney and Shetland.

Common Crossbill *Loxia curvirostra*

A

Uncommon breeding bird, autumn and winter passage migrant and visitor.

Breeds from north-west Africa, Iberia, France, the British Isles and Fennosandia east to the Sea of Okhotsk, north to northern Finland and south to Greece, Armenia, north-west China and the Himalayas; also southern Canada and the western USA. Mostly resident, frequently irruptive.

In the first half of the 20th century the Common Crossbill was known only as an intermittent visitor and breeding bird in the British Isles being dependant on irruptions from the continent due to the cycle there of maturing conifer cones. The only places where there were regular populations were in the coniferous woodlands of Breckland and the New Forest.

Ingram and Salmon gave the species' status in Radnorshire in the mid 1950s as, 'A rather rare visitor, which, it is thought, may have bred.' This statement was followed by several records: seven seen by John Walpole-Bond at Llanfaredd on 15th January 1903; several records near Knighton in January and the autumn - but with no further detail or years; one shot at Stanage Park in January 1913 and a small party seen near Knighton in August 1927. The first breeding record was of a pair and three recently fledged young seen in a small plantation south-west of Aberithon Bog, south of Newbridge, by Charles Venables-Llewelyn c.10th May 1910 and later that month by the Reverend Edmondes Owen (who saw six to seven birds including a red male) and several other naturalists. (Woolhope Society *Transactions* 1911 pp 232-4). There had been irruptions into the British Isles in both 1908 and 1909 and some stayed on to breed.

There was a record of two in Presteigne on 1st December 1956 and c.19 were near Felindre on 10th March and two near the Black Mixen on 19th April 1957. Five were seen at Water-break-its-neck on 2nd May 1959 and later in 1959, although not an irruption year, there were many records, mostly of birds flying north, by one observer in the county on most days in the second half of July. The maximum was 15 seen north of Llanelwedd on 20th July and the last three reported were beside Penygarreg Reservoir on 7th August. These were the only published records for the 1950s and the only ones for the 1960s were in 1962, 1966 and 1967 – all were single figure groups apart from 18 in Scots Pine in Llandrindod from 3rd to 6th September 1966.

There were only eight records for the 1970s, most of which came from the Radnor Forest area with the largest flock being 30 near Rhiw Pool on 30th October 1972 (an irruption year) and 22 near Kinnerton on 10th October 1976. The species was very probably under-recorded throughout the 1950s, 60s and 70s as observations in the 1980s found the species to be regular throughout the year, including many instances of breeding, in the major forested areas of Abbeycwmhir, Waun Marteg, Radnor Forest and the Elan Valley. Undoubtedly the maturing plantations planted post-war with their huge crops of cones, especially Sitka Spruce, were becoming increasingly attractive.

Irruptions of Common Crossbill into the British Isles have been known since 1251 and since 1800 there have been at least 80 of varying intensities with interludes of up to 11 years and sometimes taking place in two or three successive years. The origin of most of these birds is thought to be Russia west of the Urals. By far the largest of these inluxes, at least in recent times, took place in 1990 resulting in at least half a million (possibly 1 to 5 million) birds in Scotland and 40,000 in the 34,000 acres of Kielder Forest in Northumberland by the early winter and birds reported throughut western Europe as far south as Gibraltar.

The first arrivals in Radnorshire were seen in the Gwaelod Plantation in the Elan Valley on 30th June where numbers had risen to at least 200 by 29th July and to 600+ by October forming spectacular flocks, including many red males, as they frequently came down to drink along the shore of the adjoining Penygarreg Reservoir. A flock of at least 250 was in the Abbeycwmhir plantations from August onwards and several flocks of 100-200 were in the extensive plantations of the Radnor Forest by October. Throughout the period July to October there were also many records of small flocks of 5-30 birds flying westwards over the hills.

By December 1990 there were at least 50 singing males in the Gwaelod plantation with nest building noted from mid-month and at least 200 birds still present in February 1991. At least 60 pairs are thought to have bred in the Elan Valley between January and April and many post-breeding flocks of 20-50 birds, comprising adults and young, were seen during May and June in the Elan Valley, Waun Marteg, Red Lion Hill, Abbeycwmhir, Radnor Forest, Nantmel, Stanner, Nant Glas, Burfa and Llanstephan. Successful breeding also took place at Llanelwedd and Clyro. There was a rapid departure during May and June and very few birds remained in July and August.

In 1993 there was a small invasion in the summer followed by an unusually large arrival in October with flocks of 30-50 in the Elan plantations and at Abbeycwmhir and 200+ in the Radnor Forest. The few that stayed to breed in 1994 included two pairs feeding recently fledged young in the Elan Valley on 12th April and three pairs at Ednol Hill, Radnor Forest. Nest building was recorded in Radnor Forest on 30th December 1995 and at least a few pairs bred in the Elan Valley in 1996, where there were family parties seen at three places in May and June. A flock of 50+ was seen at Abbeycwmhir on 30th October.

The next major influx took place in 1997 with the first birds seen near Warren Wood on 25th May followed by a major arrival in the first week of June when flocks of 20-70 were widespread. In July there were at least 300 at Abbeycwmhir and at Radnor Forest. In 1998 at least four pairs bred in March at Llanerchi plantation, Elan Valley, feeding on larch seeds.

Few birds were seen in 1999 and a handful of flocks of 10-20 were seen in 2000. A flock of c.30 birds comprising six family parties was seen at Abbeycwmhir on 7th April 2001 and there were several family parties in the Elan Valley and Radnor Forest on 25th May. The highest counts in 2002 were of 120+ at the Gwaelod plantation on 26th September and 30 at Burfa Camp mid-month. A flock of 80 was present in the Radnor Forest on 20th March 2003, one of 95 in the Elan Valley on 10th Ocober 2004 and 50 at Nant Glas on 14th November. The largest flocks seen in 2005 were 55 in the Radnor Forest on 12th May, 45 at Abbeycwmhir on 17th May and 30 at the Gwaelod plantation from mid-May to mid-July. In 2008 there were 150 in Radnor Forest on 26th January and 75 at Abbeycwmhir on 15th May.

Breeding took place very widely in early 2009 and another major invasion took place in July followed by a further big arrival at the end of October. There were 200+ at the eastern end of the Radnor Forest on 27th October, including many singing males, and 50 at the Gwaelod plantation on 15th were newly arrived.

There were 30-110 birds in the Radnor Forest throughout 2010 and of 40 birds in the Gwaelod plantation on 26th September there were many singing birds and juveniles. Numbers remained high in 2011 with 250+ in Radnor Forest, 100 at Abbeycwmhir in January and three to four family parties at Gwaelod on 10th April.

Breeding numbers in recent decades have varied from none to at least 200 pairs in 1991. The breeding Atlas of 1968-72 found no birds in Radnorshire, the winter Atlas of 1981-84 found birds in five of the 21 hectads (10-km squares) and since 2008 birds have been particularly widespread and have been found in 20 of the 21 in both summer and winter.

In summary, there have been Common Crossbills in Radnorshire, in variable numbers, in all months and in most years since 1990. Breeding takes place between December and April; invasions take place mostly from late May to July with sometimes a second wave in the autumn, usually in late October, and some birds stay for the winter, depending on the cone crop. By far the commonest food in Radnorshire is the seeds of Sitka Spruce followed by those of larch - European, Japanese and their hybrids. Some Douglas Fir and Norway Spruce seeds are taken and the seeds of Scots Pine are taken from ripe, open, cones.

As well as the seeds of these conifers, birds have also been seen feeding on Alder cones, Ash seeds, Beech mast, Apple pips, Heather seeds and Sessile Oak catkins. Aphids are eaten from larch and spruce shoots in the spring and, especially, from Sycamore for much of the spring and summer. Birds have also been seen eating oak defoliating caterpillars and taking in grit from roadside salt piles. Single birds have also been recorded a few times, briefly, at peanut dispensers in gardens near the plantations in the Elan Valley.

Parrot Crossbill *Loxia pytyopsittacus* A

Very rare visitor and breeding bird.

Breeds from Fennoscandia east across Russia to the Ural Mountains. Mostly resident, occasionally irruptive.

The Parrot Crossbill is the largest of the crossbill species-group and is monotypic, as is the Scottish Crossbill *L.scotica* which may be a subspecies of the Common Crossbill which has some 20 or so sub-species recognised around much of the northern hemisphere. Some or all of these sub-species may warrant specific status in their own right whilst others, particularly from southern Europe and northern Africa, are probably best aligned with Parrot Crossbills.

It may well happen that Parrot Crossbill, Scottish Crossbill and Common (Red) Crossbill are all lumped as one species in the future as DNA analysis has found no significant differences in the DNA of the three 'species'.

There is undoubtedly a great deal of taxonomic work to be done on this very closely related group which are specialist feeders, often on a single species of conifer, and which have evolved differing bill shapes to extract the seeds from the cones.

The only records of Parrot Crossbill in Radnorshire came from the crossbill invasion of 1990, when there were an unprecedented 200+ records of Parrot Crossbills in the British Isles, followed by a few instances of breeding in 1991.

The first two birds were seen on the edge of the Gwaelod plantation, in the Elan Valley, on 29th November remaining into 1991. In January and February up to ten birds were found in searches of all the areas of Scots Pine in the coupes around the edges of, and adjacent to, the Gwaelod plantation. At least two males were singing on several dates between 2nd and 17th January but, although nestbuilding was suspected in late January and early February, no birds could be found after the 25th February.

All the birds fed exclusively on Scots Pine seeds, quite separately from the many hundreds of Common Crossbills present in the plantation, and had the characteristic much larger bill, head and overall body size. Those watched calling gave very noticeably deeper calls than the Common Crossbills present and the song of the two singing males was also noticeably deeper and slower. Side by side comparisons with Common Crossbills were made on several occasions, including in flight and when coming down to drink.

Common Rosefinch *Carpodacus erythrinus* A

Very rare visitor.

Breeds from Fennoscandia, parts of central Europe and northern Turkey east across Russia to Kamchatka and across parts of central Asia to Mongolia and eastern China. Winters from Pakistan and India east across Burma to southern and eastern China.

There have been five records:

The first record for Wales, and the third for the British Isles, was 'a male in full plumage' shot by the gamekeeper of the Maesllwch Estate, John Sharp, probably in the spring c.30 years before 1904, and 'about a mile beyond Glascombe' (Glascwm). It was stuffed and seen in the Maesllwch collection by Professor John Salter (Professor of Botany at the University College of Wales, Aberystwyth) in May 1904.

What was probably an adult female, rather than an immature of either sex, was in the garden of a bungalow beside the River Elan by Dolafallen Bridge, near Rhayader, from 1st to 5th June 1994 where it was watched through windows at very close range by several local birdwatchers as it fed on the seeds of Shepherd's Purse.

A female or first summer male was at Penbont House, Elan Valley, on 11th June 2001 where it fed avidly for two spells of about 20 minutes each, morning and afternoon, on black sunflower seeds spread on a lawn and on a bird table where it was very aggressive towards the other feeding birds. A red-headed male fed from a peanut dispenser in the garden of 5 Cwm-yr-Gerwyn, Bleddfa, on the 6th June 2003 and another red-headed male fed from a niger seed dispenser in the garden of The Old Vicarage, Llangunllo, on 23rd and 24th May 2013.

Bullfinch *Pyrrhula pyrrhula* A

Common, mostly resident, breeder.

Breeds from nothern Iberia, France and the British Isles east across much of Europe and northern Asia east to Kamchatka and Japan, south to Armenia and Kazakhstan and north to northern Norway. Mostly resident but northern populations are migratory to within the breeding range and south to the Mediterranean, Afghanistan and northern China.

Ingram and Salmon gave the status of the Bullfinch in Radnorshire in the mid-1950s as, 'A resident breeding species, very thinly distributed.' From that date the species underwent a nationwide increase

until about the mid 1970s which coincided with the huge decline in the Sparrowhawk population due to pesticide poisoning. During that time Bullfinches became much commoner in farmland hedgerows, gardens and parkland. However, since then there has been a nationwide decline, which lasted until about 2000, followed by a slow but steady increase which continues to the present day.

Any declines since the early 1980s have not been noticeable in Radnorshire and today the species is probably commoner than it has been in at least the last hundred years. This is undoubtedly due largely to the huge increase in conifer planting and restocking which is very attractive to Bullfinches for nesting in, especially when the trees are between two and ten metres in height and there are at least some broadleaves, brambles and scrub present.

Most of the broadleaved woodlands in Radnorshire are unsuitable for the species as they are heavily grazed and so lacking any understorey to nest in. Also, many Hawthorn and Blackthorn dominated hedgerows in the county have lost there wildlife interest in recent decades due to so-called 'restoration' schemes and many have been totally removed during developments and field-size increase work on many farms.

Today the species is to be found in ungrazed woodlands, overgrown as well as tall and thick hedgerows, areas of scrub, larger gardens and parkland. The often conspicuous nest is usually built between five and fifteen feet up and two broods are commonly raised in Radnorshire between May and early September.

Until the early 1990s the species was absent from parts of the far west and north of the county but improved woodland management, by way of excluding sheep grazing, around the Elan Valley reservoirs has resulted in a population of six to ten pairs there and clearfelling and restocking in the far north has increased the area of suitable habitat. Today the species is found in every 10-km square in the county in all seasons, from the river valleys up to 1,800 feet (548 m) in Radnor Forest. Although it is difficult to census accurately due to its quietness and lack of territoriality, the population in 2012 was calculated to be of the order of 750 to 1,100 pairs.

Undoubtedly the most important foods for Bullfinches in Radnorshire are the buds of Blackthorn and Hawthorn, Ash seeds, Blackberries (including the dried and shrivelled berries through the winter), Rowan berries, nettle seeds, the seeds, buds and shoots of Downy and Silver Birch, seeds of *Polyganum*, Meadowsweet and those of a wide variety of crucifers and composites. Also, where woodlands adjoin heather moorland, the seeds of Heather are sometimes an important food source in the autumn and winter months. Many small invertebrates are also taken, especially when the young are being fed in the nest.

Increasingly in recent years Bullfinches have been attracted to bird-feeding stations where a wide variety of seeds are eaten including niger (nyjer) and sunflower. Up to 20 birds have been counted at garden feeders but usually just two to four birds are seen at any one time. Weedy fields and strips planted for finches and buntings can be attractive to Bullfinches and 10-14 were regular near Newbridge in the winter of 2005/6. Also flocks on Ash trees can reach double-figures; there were at least 13 on one tree at Penbont, Elan Valley, throughout much of November and December 2004.

Although birds are more conspicuous in the county during the winter months, there is no evidence of immigration or emigration and claims of sightings of the larger, northern, continental race have so far proved to be mistaken or unproven.

Hawfinch *Coccothraustes coccothraustes* A

Rare breeding bird and probable winter visitor.

Breeds from north-west Africa, Iberia, France and the British Isles east across southern Fennoscandia and much of Europe and central Asia east to Sakhalin and Kamchatka and south to northern Iran. British birds are largely resident whilst continental birds are partly or wholly migratory south as far as the Mediterranean, Turkey, the Nile Delta, Japan and north-east China.

Ingram and Salmon (1955) gave the species status as, 'A very scarce and local species which has been found breeding from time to time in the Wye valley and near Knighton'. Little has changed since then – it is a very difficult bird to find in the county at any time of year and seemingly confined to a few larger areas of quiet, ungrazed, mixed broadleaved woodlands, mostly in the larger river valleys.

The species was confined to the south-east of England until the second half of the 19th century during which there was a major expansion in range. It was recorded from the Elan Valley in 1887, and once again there before 1896, and near Llanfaredd in 1902. A party of four above Llanelwedd on 19th June 1910 was probably a family group and singles were seen near Builth Wells in 1914 and undated near Glasbury, Llandrindod Wells and Rhayader. A pair was reported 'always nesting' in the Newbridge district by Sir Charles Venables-Llewelyn who also said that one was killed there in July 1927. Several pairs were reported as nesting at Stanage Park in April 1927 and a pair nested near Doldowlod in 1932. A pair with juveniles were seen near Llandrindod Wells in early August 1952.

The next records were for the breeding season Atlas of 1968-72 when birds were found in three 10-km squares in the far south of the county and in the one around Rhayader. Even for such a shy and elusive bird it is very surprising that there were no further records until the 1980s when records came from Glasbury in 1981, the Elan Valley annually from 1982, Llanbwchllyn in 1985, Bailey Einon and Penybont from 1987, near Llanbadarn Fynydd in 1987, near Knighton in 1988/9 and at several places along the Wye Valley between Llanwrthwl and Llanstephan from 1986.

Sightings came in all months and included at least ten positive breeding records mostly of adults with very recently fledged young in the Elan Valley area where there were probably 3-5 pairs in the woodlands around the reservoirs until 1993 when a family party of five was seen west of Garreg Ddu Reservoir on 20th August.

Although no breeding records have come from around the reservoirs in recent years there have been many records from the Elan Valley below Caban Coch Dam to the Elan/Wye confluence and it seems that at least 2-3 pairs probably breed annually with family parties seen feeding, especially on wild and ornamental cherries, in July and early August.

Since 1990 other records have come from the Knighton, Presteigne and Penybont areas, the southern dingles e.g. Cilcenni Dingle, the Glasbury/Cwmbach area and elsewhere in the Wye Valley, especially in the Newbridge/Llanwrthwl and Aberedw to Llanstephan areas. There seems to be a strong association in the breeding season with areas of Beech, Sycamore and Ash although the only nests found have been in Western Hemlock, Sessile Oak, Hawthorn and Downy Birch (Elan Valley), Crab Apple, amongst dense ivy growing up young oaks and once up a thickly covered roadside telegraph pole. In 2004 a pair bred successfully in a tall *Leylandii* hedge at Clyro. In recent years there were records from six places in 2007 including three family parties, from seven sites with three confirmed breeding in 2008, from nine (5) in 2009, 12 (2) in 2010, seven (0) in 2011and five (1) in 2012. The 1981-4 winter Atlas found birds in one place in the south of the county whilst the breeding Atlas of 1988-91 had records in two 10-km squares in the north-west. Between 2006 and 2013 records came from 11 of the county's 21 hectads in both summer and winter combined and it seems likely that a minimum of 10-15 pairs breed in Radnorshire today with signs of an increase in some places but also apparent disappearances in others.

In recent years there have been several records from garden feeding stations in the Elan Valley and at Presteigne, Glasbury and Knighton with the only food noted being sunflower seeds, both husked and unhusked. Natural food recorded has included the seeds of cherry (including from Blackbird pellets), Beech, Yew, Hornbeam, Sycamore, Field Maple, apple pips and defoliating moth caterpillars on Sessile Oak.

No large flocks have ever been recorded and the highest counts have been eight near Knighton on 8th December 2001 and seven near Newbridge from 8th to 20th January 1995. Although most British birds are resident and rarely move more than a few kilometres, little detail is known about the species movements although some continental birds undoubtedly winter here and may well come as far west as Radnorshire. A first-year female colour-ringed near Dolgellau on 28th March 2011 was seen at Doldowlodd on 18th June 2012 (62 km SSE) where it was probably breeding.

Lapland Bunting *Calcarius lapponicus* A

Very rare visitor.

Breeds from central and northern Scandinavia and northern Finland east across northern Russia to the Bering Sea, north to 81 degrees and south to northern Kamchatka, also Alaska and much of Arctic Canada and coastal Greenland. Winters in parts of western and central Europe and Asia east to northern China and in southern Canada and the northern USA.

There has been one record: At least one, and probably three birds, with Skylarks in a stubble field near Clyro on 29th September 2010.

Snow Bunting *Plectrophenax nivalis* A

Very rare visitor.

Breeds from Iceland, western and northern Scandinavia and Svalbard east across Arctic Russia to the Bering Sea and south to Kamchatka, also Alaska, Arctic Canada and coastal Greenland north to 83 degrees. Winters from northern Britain, southern Scandinavia and central Europe east across central Asia to Sakhalin Island, also southern Canada and the northern USA.

The first record was of two males and 11 females on the south-west side of Great Rhos (Rhos Fawr), Radnor Forest, during a spell of very cold weather on 15th March 1958.

There have been a further nine records since:

1995/6:	Eight near the Black Mixen from 28th December to 11th January.
1996:	Male at Pont ar Elan on 12th November.
1996:	Nine near the Black Mixen from 12th to 16th December.
1998:	One near Crugyn Ci on 28th December.
1999:	One beside the track alongside the Claerwen Reservoir on 30th October.
2011:	One at Bache Hill on 6th November.
2011:	Two at Whinyard Rocks on 17th December (possibly including the above).
2011:	Two near the Black Mixen on 17th December.
2012:	Six near Great Rhos on 6th January.

Yellowhammer *Emberiza citrinella* A

Locally common resident breeder.

Breeds from northern Iberia, France and the British Isles east across Fennoscandia, much of central and south-east Europe and across Russia to Lake Baikal and the Lena River, north to the North Cape of Norway and south to Georgia, Greece and southern Italy. Mainly resident, northern populations are wholly migratory to within the breeding range and south to Uzbekistan, north-west Iran, Iraq, Jordan, Israel, Turkey, the Mediterranean and sometimes north-west Africa. Introduced to New Zealand.

Ingram and Salmon writing in 1955 said that the Yellowhammer was,'A widespread and quite common resident breeding species which nests up to near the 1,500 feet contour in the hills. Flocks, often considerable, seen in winter.' Today this could still be said - although it is not so common, apart from in some arable parts of the east of the county, and winter flocks are nothing like the size they once were.

The last flocks of three figures were in the 1960s and 70s when there were counts of c.100 on stubble at Four Stones on 8th January 1967, near Llandrindod Wells in the first half of February 1967 and at Glasbury on 18th February 1979. Flocks of 30-50 birds were also frequently seen. In the 1980s the largest flock was 85 in the Four Stones/Kinnerton area on 8th January 1983 and there were only a few counts of 50 in the decade. The 1990s were undoubtedly the low point for the species in Radnorshire and the only count of 50 was on winter stubble at Penywrlodd, Clyro, on 25th November 1998.

Since 2000 there have been counts of 35 at feeders at Gigrin Farm in January 2000, 55 in a weedy stubble field near Bronydd in January 2004, 27 in a wild bird crop at Gilfach RWT reserve on 4th December 2006, 25 at Discoed on 18th March and 26 at Clyro on 16th September 2007. Thirty singing males were found on the Walton Plain in early June 2008 and a total of 85 in several small flocks there on 15th September 2009. Fifty were in a wild bird crop near Newbridge in January 2009 and 40 were at a garden feeding station near Knighton on 4th March 2010. Birds are increasingly being recorded at garden feeding stations with 5-10 birds often counted and occasionally 20-25.

There has been a very noticeable increase in numbers and distribution since 2006 recouping most of the losses of the 1990s and coinciding with a large increase in the acreage of cereals, especially in the east and south. However, numbers are still nowhere near those of the days of mixed farming prior to the 1960s and much good habitat has been lost in recent years. The gorse-clad commons, e.g. The Begwyns, Maelinydd, Penybont and Hundred House, have lost much of their attractiveness to the species in the last 10-20 years due to illegal burning, overgrazing and mowing. Many hedgerows have also been grubbed-up or made useless for nesting Yellowhammers (and other wildlife) by government subsidies, so-called restoration schemes and, most recently, the Hedgerow Regulations.

The Atlas surveys found birds in all of the county's 21 hectads (10-km squares) in the summers of 1968-72, in 19 for the winter Atlas of 1981-4 and in 20 for the summer Atlas of 1988-91. Birds have been recorded in 19 hectads in all seasons since 2005. The only total losses have been in the far north-west of the county in line with the widespread declines across most of the west of the British Isles during the 1970s and 80s. Yellowhammers are very rare today in the Elan and Claerwen Valleys above Caban Coch Dam with just a single instance of breeding since 1990 (in 1997) and two, very brief, visits to a garden feeding station at Penbont House in 2002 and 2006.

The population in Radnorshire in 2012 was estimated to be between 650 and 800 pairs with breeding found from the lowest parts of the Wye Valley up to 500 metres (1,625 feet) in gorse, heath and bracken on the south-facing slopes of Radnor Forest.

Cirl Bunting *Emberiza cirlus*

A

Very rare visitor and former breeder.

Breeds from north-west Africa, Iberia, France and south-west England south-east to western and northern Turkey. Resident.

There have been two records of breeding: The egg-collector John Walpole-Bond found a nest in Radnorshire near Builth Wells (probably in the Llanelwedd Rocks area) in 1902 and Captain H.A.Gilbert found a pair nesting near Clyro in June 1928.

A pair were seen near Michaelchurch on 2nd June 1960 by Miss W. Lindsey-Scott of Upper Bridge Court, Brilley, at close range from her chauffeur-driven parked car.

Ortolan Bunting *Emberiza hortulana* A

Very rare visitor.

Breeds from Iberia and parts of France north-east to the Arctic Circle in Sweden and Finland and east across much of central and southern Europe and parts of central Russia to northern Mongolia and Kazakhstan, south to Turkmeniya, northern Iran and Crete. Winters in sub-Saharan Africa, mostly in the north-east and north of 5 degrees N.

The only record is of one, probably a juvenile, watched for several minutes on 4th September 1993 on the edge of a stubble field on the Middle Gro, north of Glasbury, before flying north over the River Wye.

Reed Bunting *Emberiza schoeniclus* A

Common, mostly resident, breeding bird; passage migrant and winter visitor.

Breeds locally in Morocco and Iberia, also France, the British Isles and Fennoscandia east across much of central Europe and Asia east to Kamchatka and northern Japan, south to north-west China, Afghanistan, Armenia and locally in Turkey. Resident in parts of the south and west of the range, other populations are migratory to within the range and south to around the Mediterranean, Iran, north-west India, southern Japan and south-east China.

Ingram and Salmon writing in 1955 gave, 'A resident breeding species with a very local and irregular distribution. A pair or two may be found here and there....' It is a much commoner bird today and has increased very noticeably since the late 1980s and is still occupying new places. In particular the species has been increasingly found breeding in dry habitats such as ffridd, very young conifer plantations, heather moorland and commons, especially areas with Bracken. This breeding in dry areas was first noted in Hertfordshire in the 1930s and elsewhere in England in the 1960s. It is thought that this has been due to high population levels and the reduction in competition from the declining Yellowhammer.

Having said that, some wetland sites in Radnorshire have become less attractive to Reed Buntings over the years. Fifteen pairs were found at Rhosgoch Bog on 8th/9th June 1963 and 18 males located on 12th June 1965. Nine pairs were found in 1973, at least 5 in 1981, six to seven singing males on 4th July 1987, eight singing males on 30th May 2000 and six on 3rd June 2011.

The 1968-72 breeding Atlas found birds in all 21 hectads, the winter Atlas of 1981-84 had records in 11 and the breeding season Atlas of 1988-91 in 16. Since 2006 the species has been recorded in every hectad in both spring/summer and late autumn/winter. Nearly all of the county's well-vegetated wetland sites (lakes, rivers, marshes, mires and bogs) have breeding birds and at most of these birds are present year round. The larger commons all have at least one or two pairs whilst there are usually at least eight to 10 in the Beacon Hill area, four to six at Maelinydd and six to eight on The Begwyns. The Elan uplands have at least 20 pairs with concentrations in the upper Elan Valley. The Wye Valley between Boughrood and Rhydspence has had up to 15 singing males in recent years with an increasing tendancy for birds to sing and nest in crops, especially oil-seed rape but also occasionally in cereals. The population in the county in 2012 was estimated to be between 300 and 370 pairs.

Most birds leave the upland areas, especially above 300 metres, for the winter months of November to March (unless the weather is very mild) and return in late March and April. At least some of the overwintering birds in the Elan uplands feed largely on the seeds of Purple Moor-grass *Molinia caerulea.*

Passage is rarely noticeable although birds sometimes turn up in unusual places especially in late September and October. A group of five birds dropped into the Sycamore trees by the farmhouse at the north-west end of the Claerwen Reservoir on 15th November 1990 and then flew off high to the west.

Small groups are often encountered on farmland in autumn and winter sometimes with finches, Tree Sparrows and Yellowhammers, but rarely number more than ten. There were 50 in a root field at Evenjobb on 13th December 1969, 30 at Llowes on 20th September 2004, 18 at Clyro on 15th November 2004 and 17 on Llandrindod Wells Golf Course on 26th February 1972. Roost counts have included 55 near Glasbury on 18th December 2011, 25 at Newbridge Bog (Aberithon) on 22nd January 1981 and 15 at Llandrindod Lake on 12th March 2012. Increasingly, birds are visiting bird feeding stations, especially in the winter months. Just one or two birds are usual but at sites near to good nesting habitat counts of ten and more are regular; up to 22 were present at a Nant Glas feeding station between 1st March and 19th June 2004.

Black-headed Bunting *Emberiza melanocephala* A

Very rare visitor.

Breeds from southern Italy east to Iran and north to Georgia and the extreme south of Russia and Ukraine between the Caspian and Black Seas and south to Israel. Winters in north-west India.

The only record was of a male around the bungalows and cemetery on the north-east edge of Rhayader from 3rd to 12th June 1994. It arrived very tired but recovered during its stay when it fed on seed put out in gardens and with House Sparrows and Yellowhammers.

Another record of a male seen at a bird table at Llandeilo Graban on 25th May 2013 was still being considered by the *British Birds* Rarities Committee at the time of printing.

Corn Bunting *Emberiza calandra* A

Very rare visitor.

Breeds from the Canary Islands, north-west Africa, Iberia, France and parts of the British Isles east across much of central and southern Europe and to Iran and southern Kazakhstan. Mostly resident but migratory populations winter as far south as the Nile Delta, Iraq, Oman and the UAE.

Ingram and Salmon (1955) said that the species had been recorded once near Llandrindod Wells but without a date or any details. The only definite record is of two birds seen at the Gladestry end of Hergest Ridge on 3rd May1984.

Unconfirmed records of species otherwise unrecorded in the county which have appeared in earlier publications.

Purple Heron *Ardea purpurea*
A mounted specimen, which was still in the collection at Maesllwch Castle until at least the 1950s, was likely to have been shot in Radnorshire at the end of the 19th century or early in the 20th along the lower Wye between Boughrood and Llowes, or possibly at Llanbwchllyn or Rhosgoch Bog. However, no details are known.

White-tailed Eagle *Haliaeetus albicilla*
The *Hereford Journal* of the 2nd December 1835 reported, 'A noble eagle shot at Beguildy', and the Rev. D.E.Owen writing to Professor J.H.Salter (Prof. of Botany at Aberystwyth University) in February 1920 said, 'I reported a visit of the White-tailed Eagle to Radnorshire some eight years ago'. Both records lack any supporting details unfortunately.

Great Snipe *Gallinago media*
The Woolhope Society Field Club *Transactions* for 1895-7 included some notes on the flora and fauna of the Elan Valley (including parts of Ceredigion, Breconshire and Radnorshire) from the then owner, R.Lewis-Lloyd. These were received in early 1896 and included the statement, 'Of rarer birds I have killed two Solitary Snipe...'. However, there were no details and no mention has been found of any being shot in any of the estate game books examined. The species was mostly known as the Solitary or Double Snipe in the 19th century and, although very rare, was undoubtedly a commoner vagrant to Britain in the 19th century than it is today. Its range in Europe has greatly reduced over the last 200 years or so.

Collared Pratincole *Glareola pratincola*
One was watched 'for some time' by at least two members of the Baskerville family of Clyro Court 'on the Wye near Clyro...some time before 1899' (E. Cambridge-Philips *Victoria History of the County of Herefordshire* volume 1. London 1908). Although the observers were said to be 'well acquainted with the species' in *The Illustrated Manual of British Birds* (Saunders, 1899), the record lacked any date or detail and was square-bracketed and tagged 'supposed seen' in volume four of *The Handbook of British Birds*, Witherby, 1940.

Snowy Owl *Bubo scandiacus*
Two birds, possibly of this species, were seen by Dr C.D.Edwards in the Newchurch Hill/Bryngwyn area about 1936 after strong northeasterly winds. There have only been eight Welsh records. *Herefordshire Birds* (Walker and Smith, 1975) also includes a record of the species from Dr. Edwards; flushed from wet moorland near Huntington 'on a winter afternoon in the 1920s' when he was impressed by the bird's 'great size, white plumage and powerful flight'. Huntington is on the border of Herefordshire and

Radnorshire and some three miles or so north-east of Newchuch Hill. Whether both reports refer to the same sighting(s) is not known and without sufficient detail any record for Radnorshire remains unconfirmed.

Escapes and exotics – Mostly species in Category D and E, neither of which are included in the British List.

Category D species are those where there is reasonable doubt that they have ever occurred in a natural state and those in Category E are species recorded as introductions, human-assisted transportees or escapees from captivity, and whose breeding populations (if any) are thought not to be self-sustaining.

Black Swan *Cygnus atratus* E
All records have come from the lower Wye Valley: in the Glasbury area in July 1982, the Bronydd to Clyro area in January 1995 (which had been ringed as a first-winter bird on the River Severn at Worcester), at Cabalva in April 2002 and, intermittently, in the the Bronydd and Clyro area from November 2012 to January 2013.

Snow Goose *Anser caerulescens* (AC)E
One at Pwl Patti on 10th October 1999 was most likely of captive/feral origin.

Taverner's Cackling (Canada) Goose *Branta hutchinsii taverneri* E
A bird showing the characters of this very small version of the 'Greater' Canada Goose *Branta canadensis* was seen in the lower Wye Valley between Glasbury and Cabalva on many dates between 28th October 2009 and 20th March 2012. This subspecies/form breeds in Alaska and winters in north-west USA.

South African Shelduck *Tadorna cana* E
Two to four birds were seen in the Glasbury and Clyro area on several dates between January 2010 and March 2012.

Wood Duck *Aix sponsa* E
A pair were on the River Wye at Doldowlodd on 13th June 1999 and a female there on 8th August. A drake was on the River Elan, near Rhayader, on 13th October 2007.

Flamingo sp. *Phoenicopterus sp.* E
One at Llyn Heilyn on 8th July 1968 was probably a Chilean Flamingo *P.chilensis.*

Striated (Green) Heron *Butorides (virescens) striata*
One was seen along the River Wye below Glasbury between 22nd and 29th January 1991. It carried a greyish (probably old and discoloured) leg-ring and was then assignable to one of the grey-necked

African or Australian races of Green Heron. These races have since been split by most authorities from the now wholly North American Green Heron (which is 'A' listed on the British list) and renamed Striated Heron.

Sacred Ibis *Threskiornis aethiopicus* E

One was in the Glasbury area from end of July 1972 to the end of January 1973. Escapes from free-flying groups kept in zoological gardens have occurred since the 19th century.

Great White Pelican *Pelecanus onocrotalus* DE

An adult flew north from the River Wye at Bronydd on 24th October 2001.

Hooded Vulture *Necrosyrtes monachus*

One was present in the Kinnerton and Cascob area from about the 13th to 15th August 2000. It had escaped from a collection in North Devon and was also seen in many other places in Wales.

Cinereous Vulture *Aegypius monachus* E

Without doubt the most controversial and talked about bird ever to turn up in Radnorshire. An unringed adult was present, mainly in the Edw Valley, between the end of October 1977 and 8th February 1978. It first attracted attention when it was reported to a local birdwatcher by a farmer at Rhulen on 29th November. However, it had been seen by farmers further up the Valley in the Hundred House and Llandegley Rhos area for at least a month before then.

The bird spent several weeks in the Rhulen area, wandering occasionally south towards Glasbury, The Begwyns and other hills around Painscastle, before moving back to the Llyn Heilyn and Llandegley Rhos area in January. After leaving there on the 8th February it was refound in Carmarthenshire where it stayed until 20th February – disappearing mysteriously just before lambing started.

There was a long debate by the two British records committees as to whether it could have been a wild bird from eastern or southern Europe or an escape. Eventually it was put into Category D in 1992 and transferred to Category E in 2008.

The species is on average the largest true bird of prey in the world being up to four feet in length, with a ten-foot wingspan and weighing up to 13kg (28lbs) – ten times the weight of a fat female Buzzard and twice that of a Golden Eagle.
(*British Birds* 87:613-622. *British Ornithologist's Union*:37th Report of the Records Committee, 2009.)

Golden Eagle *Aquila chrysaetos* E

An escaped immature bird which was first seen in Breconshire in 2009 later settled in Ceredigion, mostly in the Tregaron Bog (Cors Caron) area, where it remained for most of the time until at least 2013. In early

March 2010 it wandered into Montgomeryshire and Meirionnydd and also into Radnorshire where it was photographed as it flew over Craig Fawr, south-east of the Claerwen Reservoir. It was seen several times subsequently later in the year and in 2011 and 2012 visiting from the Cors Caron/Pontrhydfendigaid area with sightings coming from around the Claerwen Reservoir and over the Claerwen National Nature Reserve.

Eagle Owl *Bubo bubo*

One was present in the Presteigne area from January 2008 until at least early September 2009. Prey items included a domestic/feral cat and a Tawny Owl but were mostly Carrion Crows, Rabbits and Brown Rats.

Gazetteer - place names mentoned in the text with Ordnance Survey grid references. Numbers beginning 8 or 9 are prefixed by SN, others are within the SO 100-km square.

Abbeycwmhir	0571
Aberedw Hill	0850
Aberedw	0847
Aberithon Bog (Turbary)	0157
Bache Hill	2163
Bachowey Gorge	1143
Bailey Einon	0861
Bailey Hill	2472
Beacon Hill	1776
Beguildy	1979
Begwyns	1544
Bettws	1156
Black Mixen	1964
Black Pool	1270
Bleddfa	2068
Blue Lins	0582
Bodtalog	8675
Boughrood	1339
Boultibrooke	3165
Brilley	2651
Brondre Hill	0478
Bronydd	2245
Bryngwyn	1849
Bryn Tytli	9375
Brynderllwyn Bog	0259
Bryndraenog Wood	2078
Brynthomas	1062
Brynwern Bridge	0156
Builth Road	0253
Burfa Wood(Camp)	2861
Burl Hill	2057
Burlingjobb	2558
Bwlch y Sarnau (Bwlchysarnau)	0374
Bwlchyfedwen	0959
Bwlchyllyn	1282
Cabalva	2446
Caban Coch Reservoir	9163
Caban Lakeside Woodland	9163
Caergynon Pool	1370
Carneddau	0654
Carregwiber Pool	0859
Cascob	2366
Cefncoed Pool	9862
Cilcenni Dingle	1741
Cilfaesty Hill	1284
Claerwen Dam	8763
Claerwen Reservoir	8565
Claerwen Valley	8862
Clyro (Court)	2143
Colva	2053
Cors y Llyn	0155
Coxhead Bank	1571
Craig Goch Reservoir	8969
Cregrina	1252
Crossgates	0864
Crowther's Pool	2148
Crugyn Ci	9268
Crugyn Llwyd	0279
Cwm Byddog	2144
Cwm Coel	8963
Cwm Kesty	1754
Cwmbach Llechrhyd	0354
Cwmbach	1639
Cwmcynydd	0572
Cwmdeuddwr	9667
Cwmmaerdy	1458
David's Well	0578
Discoed	2764
Disgwylfa Hill	2251
Doctor's Pool	1550
Dol y Mynach Reservoir	9061
Dolafallen Bridge	9566
Dolau	1467
Dolberthog	0460
Doldowlodd	9962
Dolycannau	1949

Downton	2360
Dutlas	2077
Ednol Hill	2264
Edw River	1154
Elan River	9566
Elan Valley	9067
Erwood	0943
Evancoyd	2663
Evenjobb	2662
Felindre	1681
Ffordd Fawr Oxbow	1840
Ffynnon Gynydd	1641
Four Stones	2460
Fowler's Armchair	0479
Franksbridge	1156
Garnfawr	1157
Garreg Ddu Reservoir	9165
Gaufron	0068
Gigrin Farm	9767
Gilfach	9671
Gilwern Common (Hill)	0958
Gilwern Dingle	2456
Gladestry	2355
Glan Llyn	9469
Glanwye	1538
Glasbury	1739
Glascwm Hill	1652
Glascwm	1553
Glog Hill	2269
Gors Lydan	1276
Goytre Pool	0054
Great Rhos	1863
Great Vaynor	0269
Gwaelod Plantation	9167
Gwaunceste Hill	1555
Gwyn Llyn (Gwynllyn)	9469
Hanover Pool	1757
Harley Valley	1961
Hawthorn Hill	2867
Hay (on Wye)	2242
Heartsease (Llanddewi)	1369
Heartsease (Knighton)	3472
Hendre Einon	0653
Hendregenny Pool	2569
Henllyn	1046
Hergest Ridge	2556
Hindwell Pool	2560
Howey	0558
Hundred House	1154
Huntington	2453
Ireland Moor	1548
Ithon River	0764
Kesty	1754
Kinnerton	2463
Knighton Racecourse	2673
Knucklas	2574
Little Hill (west)	1453
Littlehill Common	1473
Little Hill (east)	1753
Little Hill (Llandrindod)	0760
Llangunllo	2171
Llaithddu	0679
Llan y Felin	2454
Llananno	0974
Llanbadarn Fynydd	0977
Llanbedr Hill	1348
Llanbister (Road)	1073
Llanbwchllyn	1146
Llandegley Rhos	1360
Llandegley	1362
Llandeilo Hill	0946
Llandewi	1068
Llandrindod Hall Farm	0660
Llandrindod Lake	0660
Llanelwedd Quarry	0552
Llanelwedd	0451
Llanerchi	9063
Llanfaredd	0650
Llanfihangel nant Melan	1858
Llanstephan	1141
Llanwefr Pool	1359
Llanwrthwl	9763
Llanyre	0462
Llowes	1941

Lloyney	2475
Llwynpentre Bank	1171
Llyn Cerrigllwydion Isaf	8469
Llyn Gwyn	0164
Llyn Heilyn	1658
Maelinydd	1371
Maesllwch	1740
Marteg Valley	9872
Michaelchurch (on Arrow)	2450
Middle Gro Oxbow	1840
Milo Brook	0949
Milton Hill	2450
Moelfre (Turbary)	0074
Nant Glas	9965
Nantgwyllt	9162
Nantmel	0266
New Radnor	2160
Newbridge (on Wye)	0158
Newbridge Bog	0157
Newchurch HIl	2050
Newchurch	2150
Norton	3067
Ochre Cefn	9568
Old Radnor	2559
Oleuddu Isaf	9579
Painscastle	1646
Pant y Dwr	9874
Park Farm	1571
Penbont (House)	9167
Pencerrig Lake	0454
Penlanfawr	8974
Penrhiw-wen	9270
Pentrosfa Mire	0559
Penywrlodd	2146
Penybont Common	1265
Penybont	1164
Penyclawdd Pool	1870
Penygarreg Reservoir	9067
Penyfforest	1943
Perthi Common	0954
Pilleth	2568
Pont ar Elan	9071
Pont ar Ithon	0157
Presteigne	3164
Pwll Patti	1639
Radnor Forest	2065
Red Lion Hill	0577
Rock Park	0560
Rhiw Bottom	1458
Rhiw Pool	1866
Rhodoldog	9467
Rhogo Pool	0757
Rhosgoch Bog	1948
Rhos Hirnant	8970
Rhos y Meirch	2769
Rhosfallog	1274
Rhulen Hill (Mawn Pool)	1348
Rhulen	1349
Rhydspence	2447
Skreen	0943
St Harmon	9972
St Michael's Pool	1869
Stanage Park	3371
Stannage	0161
Stanner (Rocks)	2658
Stonewall Hill	3168
Summergil Brook	2460
The Begwyns	1544
The Skreen	0943
The Whimble	2062
Tynbriniau Hill	1277
Vron Valley	1861
Walton	2559
Water-break-its-neck	1860
Waun Marteg	0176
Wern Fawr	0457
Whimble	2062
Whinyard Rocks	2062
Whitton	2767
Womaston	2660
Yr Wylorn	9572

Non-avian species mentioned in the text

Plants

Alder	*Alnus glutinosa*
Apple	*Malus domestica*
Ash	*Fraxinus excelsior*
Beech	*Fagus sylvatica*
Bilberry	*Vaccinium myrtillus*
Black Knapweed	*Centaurea nigra*
Blackberry	*Rubus fruticosus* agg.
Blackthorn	*Prunus spinosa*
Californian Nutmeg	*Torreya californica*
Copper Beech	*Fagus sylvatica* 'Purpurea' gp.
Cotoneaster	*Cotoneaster* spp.
Crab Apple	*Malus sylvestris*
Cherry	*Prunus avium*
Chickweed	*Stellaria media*
Dandelion	*Taraxacum* agg.
Douglas Fir	*Pseudotsuga menziesii*
Downy Birch	*Betula pubescens*
European Larch	*Larix decidua*
Field Maple	*Acer campestre*
Groundsel	*Senecio vulgaris*
Hawthorn	*Crataegus monogyna*
Heather	*Calluna vulgaris*
Holly	*Ilex aquifolium*
Hornbeam	*Carpinus betulus*
Ivy	*Hedera helix*
Japanese Larch	*Larix kaempferi*
Juniper	*Juniperus communis* var.
Knapweed	*Centaurea nigra*
Larch	*Larix* sp.
Lime	*Tilia x europaea*
Meadowsweet	*Filipendula ulmaria*
Mistletoe	*Viscum album*
Nettle	*Urtica dioica*
Norway Spruce	*Picea abies*
Nyjer('niger')	*Guizotia abyssinica*

Pond Water-crowfoot	*Ranunculus peltatus*
Purple Moor-grass	*Molinia caerulea*
Pyracantha	*Pyracantha* spp.
Ragwort	*Jacobaea* spp.
Reed	*Phragmites australis*
Rowan	*Sorbus aucuparia*
Scots Pine	*Pinus sylvestris*
Sessile Oak	*Quercus petraea*
Shepherd's Purse	*Capsella bursa-pastoris*
Silver Birch	*Betula pendula*
Sitka Spruce	*Picea sitchensis*
Sunflower	*Helianthus annuus*
Sweet Chestnut	*Castanea sativa*
Sycamore	*Acer pseudoplatanus*
Teasel	*Dipsacus fullonum*
Thistles	*Cirsium* spp.
Western Hemlock	*Tsuga heterophylla*
Willowherb	*Epilobium* spp.
Wych Elm	*Ulmus glabra*
Yew	*Taxus baccata*

Mammals

Brown Long-eared Bat	*Plecotus auritus*
Brown Rat	*Rattus norvegicus*
Daubenton's Bat	*Myotis daubentonii*
Fox	*Vulpes vulpes*
Grey Squirrel	*Sciurus carolinensis*
Hare	*Lepus europaeus*
Mink	*Mustela vison*
Mole	*Talpa europaea*
Pipistrelle	*Pipistrellus* spp.
Rabbit	*Oryctolagus cuniculus*
Short-tailed (Field) Vole	*Microtus agrestis*
Weasel	*Mustela nivalis*
Wood Mouse	*Apodemus sylvaticus*

Fish

Brown Trout	*Salmo trutta*
Carp	*Cyprinus carpio*
Chub	*Squalius cephalus*
Goldfish	*Carrasius auratus*
Pike	*Esox lucius*
Rudd	*Scardnius erythrophthalmus*
Salmon	*Salmo salar*

Amphibians

Common Frog	*Rana temporaria*
Common Toad	*Bufo bufo*

Reptiles

Common Lizard	*Zootoca vivipara*

Invertebrates

Emperor Moth	*Saturnia pavonia*

Bibliography

Cramp, S. *et al* (1977-1994) *Handbook of the Birds of Europe, the Middle East and North Africa – The Birds of the Western Palearctic.* Oxford.

Davies, L. (1912) *Radnorshire.* Cambridge County Geographies, Cambridge.

Dementiev, G.P. & Gladkov, N.A. (1951-1954). *The Birds of The Soviet Union.* vol 1- 3. Jerusalem.

Etchécopar, R-D. & Hüe, F. (1967). *The Birds of North Africa.* Edinburgh.

Etchécopar, R-D. & Hüe, F. (1978/1983). *Les Oiseaux de Chine, de Mongolie et de Corée: passereaux/non-passereaux.* vols 1/2. Pape'ete/Paris.

Gibbons, D.W., Reid, J.B. & Chapman, R.A. (1993) *The New Atlas of Breeding Birds in Britain and Ireland: 1988-1991.* Poyser, London.

Glutz von Blotzheim, U.N. & Bauer, K.M. (1966-1997). *Handbuch der Vögel Mitteleuropas.* vol 1-14. Frankfurt am Main.

Green, J. (2002) *Birds in Wales 1992-2000.* Welsh Ornithological Society, Cardigan.

Hagemeijer, W.J.M. & Blair, M.J. (eds). (1997). *The EBBC Atlas of European Breeding Birds: their distribution and abundance.* Poyser.

Herefordshire Ornithological Club *Annual Reports* 1951-1987.

Howse, W.H. (1949) *Radnorshire.* Hereford.

Ingram, G.C.S. & Salmon, H.M. (1955) *The Birds of Radnorshire.*

Jennings, P.P. (1987-2013) *Radnorshire Bird Reports.* Radnorshire Wildlife Trust Newsletters.

Lack, P.C. (1986) *The Atlas of Wintering Birds in Britain and Ireland.* Poyser.

Lovegrove, R., Williams, G. & Williams, I. (1994) *Birds in Wales.* Poyser.

Marchant, J.H., Hudson, R., Carter, S.P. & Whittington, P. (1990). *Population Trends in British Breeding Birds.* British Trust for Ornithology.

Mead, C. (2000) *The State of the Nations' Birds.* Whittet Books, Stowmarket.

Moreau, R.E. (1972). *The Palearctic-African Bird Migration Systems.* Academic Press, London.

Page, W. (ed.) (1908) . *Victoria History of the County of Hereford,* vol.1. London.

Parslow, J.L.F. (1973). *Breeding Birds of Britain and Ireland – an historical survey.* Poyser.

Riddiford, N. & Findley, P. (1981). *Seasonal Movements of Summer Migrants.* B.T.O. Guide 18. British Trust for Ornithology.

Sharrock, J.T.R. (1976) *The Atlas of Breeding Birds in Britain and Ireland.* Poyser.

Snow, D.W. (1971) *The Status of Birds in Britain and Ireland.* B.O.U., Blackwell.

Walpole-Bond, J.A. (1903) *Bird Life in Wild Wales.* London.

Welsh Ornithological Society. *Welsh Bird Reports.* 1978-2012.

Wernham, C.V., Toms, M.P., Marchant, J.H., Clark, J.A., Siriwardena, G.M. & Baillie, S.R. (eds). 2002. *The Migration Atlas: movements of the birds of Britain and Ireland.* Poyser.

Witherby, H.F., Jourdain, F.C.R., Ticehurst, N.F. & Tucker, B.W. (1938-1941) *The Handbook of British Birds* . vols.1-5. Witherby, London.

Woolhope Naturalists' Field Club *Transactions* 1852-1953.

Zink, G. & Bairlain, F. (1985-1995). *Der Zug europäischer Singvögel – ein atlas der wiederfunde beringter vögel.* vol 1-3. Wiesbaden.

Index

Index of Bird Species in the Systematic List:

NOTES

NOTES

NOTES